Leading Cases in Administrative Law

Anna Shavers, Christopher J. Walker, Matthew Lee Wiener
EDITORS

AMERICAN BAR ASSOCIATION
Administrative Law and
Regulatory Practice Section

Cover design by Sara Wadford/ABA Design

Printed in the United States of America.

30 29 28 27 26   5 4 3 2 1

ISBN 978-1-63905-730-6

For Anna Shavers
colleague and friend
(1946–2022)

Professor Anna Shavers with Justice Antonin Scalia—both former chairs of the American Bar Association's Section of Administrative Law and Regulatory Practice—at the Supreme Court in 2014. Credit: Archives of the Administrative Conference of the United States.

Contents

Acknowledgments

We have accumulated many debts in editing this book. We thank, first and foremost, the 36 contributors (listed on pages xxiii–xxvi) for their excellent work and for bearing with us during what has been a long and challenging process. We also thank the 19 members of the Case Selection Committee (listed on pages xxvii–xxix), many of them also contributors, for their collegiality and thoughtfulness in selecting the cases included in this book.

Two contributors and former chairs of the American Bar Association's (ABA's) Section of Administrative and Regulatory Law (Section)—Ronald Levin and Michael Herz—deserve special recognition and thanks. They helped us, among other things, identify potential contributors and prepare our drafting guidelines. They also played important roles in the deliberations of the Case Selection Committee.

Another former Section chair, Jeffrey Rosen, the author of the book's Foreword, also deserves special thanks. Not only did he launch this book while serving as Section chair, but he also helped assemble the Case Selection Committee. And throughout the book's production, he offered welcome encouragement, even when much more important matters occupied his time.

We also thank Jeffrey Litwak, the chair of the Section's Publications Committee, for guiding us through the publishing process; our editor at ABA Book Publishing, Carlie Wall, for helping move this book to publication; and Anne Kiefer, the Section's director, for helping on sundry administrative matters. We are also indebted to Kate Britt, reference librarian at the University of Michigan Law School, for reviewing and copyediting the manuscript before it went through the editorial review process at ABA Publishing.

Finally, we thank the following students at The Ohio State University Moritz College of Law and the University of Michigan Law School for their excellent work checking citations, suggesting edits, and proofreading drafts: Tess Hancock, Alfred Kalantar, Sam Lioi, Neena Menon, and Rebecca Turnbull.

One of your editors (Matt Wiener) thanks the other (Chris Walker) for joining him as an editor after his original co-editor, Anna Shavers, passed away unexpectedly. Professor Walker's willingness to assume this responsibility, despite his many other commitments, reflects the steadfast dedication to the Section for which he is known.

Christopher J. Walker
Matthew Lee Wiener

Foreword

Jeffrey A. Rosen

This book fills a unique need, focused as it is especially on non-specialist practitioners who need familiarity with a few leading cases about the law governing how administrative agencies can operate, as well as others who need the focused review this book provides. There are many excellent books about administrative law—treatises, handbooks, and the ABA Section of Administrative Law and Regulatory Practice's own core publications on rulemaking,[1] adjudication,[2] judicial review,[3] and blackletter principles,[4] as well as its *Sourcebook of Administrative Procedure*.[5] But none provides what this book does: succinct summaries and analyses of the foundational cases in administrative law, as identified by leading experts. And this book is especially timely in an era when the U.S. Supreme Court is so focused on administrative law.

This book was conceived in 2016, while I was serving as the chair of the Section. Then, as before, I would receive periodic requests from practicing lawyers asking me to identify the "leading case" dealing with a particular topic on which they were working. Others had told me of similar experiences at their law firms, companies, and agencies. A few years earlier, the Section had published a revised edition of its *Blackletter Statement of Federal Administrative Law*,[6] which was relatively short and helpful. But

1. A Guide to Federal Agency Rulemaking (Jeffrey S. Lubbers ed., 6th ed. 2018).
2. A Guide to Federal Agency Adjudication (Jeremy S. Graboyes ed., 3d ed. 2023).
3. A Guide to Judicial and Political Review of Federal Agencies (Michael E. Herz et al. eds., 2d ed. 2015).
4. Section of Admin. L. & Regul. Prac., Am. Bar Ass'n, A Blackletter Statement of Federal Administrative Law (2d ed. 2013).
5. Admin. Conf. of the U.S. & Section of Admin. L. & Regul. Prac., Am. Bar Ass'n, Federal Administrative Procedure Sourcebook (n.d.), https://sourcebook.acus.gov/wiki/Federal_Administrative_Procedure_Sourcebook/view. This online, continuously edited publication is a joint initiative of the Section and the Administrative Conference of the United States.
6. Section of Admin. L. & Regul. Prac., *supra* note 4.

that was not what they were looking for, and I knew of no book that even came close to responding to these inquiries. The only thing I could suggest, perhaps unhelpfully, was thumbing through administrative law casebooks.

Several of my Section colleagues and I perceived a need for a book that would offer lawyers—whether counseling agencies or litigating with or against them—a brief reminder of (and in some cases an introduction to) the leading administrative law cases and their significance, without regard to the organic statutes and regulations of any one particular agency. After many discussions with members of the Section's governing council and several of its committee chairs, the idea was validated, and we decided to pursue it.

The vital first step was to gather a number of the Section's experts from both academia and law practice to develop a consensus as to what cases should be included if an arbitrary limit of 25 to 30 cases were to be adopted. (The limit was to make the book short and convenient, not a long reference work or treatise.) As explained more fully in the Preface, around 20 experts came together as the Case Selection Committee to develop as close a consensus as possible. (They are identified at pages xxvii–xxix and deserve our thanks and gratitude. They certainly have mine.) From my vantage point, the Committee's discussion of what cases to include was itself a very interesting exercise. Readers may have their own views of what cases were included or omitted from the "all-star ballot," but whatever lively discussions may result about where the lines were drawn, there is little doubt that the cases included are vitally important to this area of the law.

The project was most fortunate that Matt Wiener and then Anna Shavers stepped forward to lead it as editors. Unfortunately, during the life of the project, Professor Shavers—a universally well-liked and respected former Section chair—was not able to see the project to completion due to her untimely passing. But another former Section chair, Christopher Walker, jumped in commendably and ably to work closely with Matt, the multi-talented former acting chair, vice chair, and executive director of the Administrative Conference of the United States. All three editors are widely respected scholars of administrative law, with practical experience as well, so the project was in outstanding hands.

Among the many tasks they undertook, the book's editors recruited stellar authors—many of them affiliated with the Section—to write chapters about each of the lead cases. The Section was uniquely positioned to offer so many contributors. Indeed, it is probably one of less than a handful of organizations that could do so. Which actually underscores again why there is such a need for this book.

Do the cases included in this book answer every question about administrative law? Of course not. That is not the goal. There are other books and resources to help with that. But, like the Section's *Blackletter Statement of Federal Administrative Law*, this short book offers important help in getting started. As noted, the vision behind the book is to provide succinct and "practitioner-helpful" summaries and incisive analyses of the cases it covers. I suspect the book will also prove helpful to more experienced practitioners, as well as scholars, judges, law students, and others, as a result of the keen analytical and practical insights the contributors have brought to bear on each case.

Apart from serving its core purpose, this short book also contributes to a continuing conversation about administrative law, about the appropriate limits of government agency actions, about how to make government work better, and about how to ensure the essential balance between the needs of effective government and the protection of private liberty in a free society.

For nearly a decade now, I have had in mind writing an essay about four "wrong turns" in administrative law in the years after the passage of the Administrative Procedure Act—about cases in which the Supreme Court seemed to me to produce detrimental outcomes. I am happy to report that all four of those cases are included in this book. (Perhaps I can wish that developments before a future edition might result in some of them no longer belonging!) I don't know if or when I will get that essay completed, but I am very appreciative and admiring of Matt Wiener, Anna Shavers, and Chris Walker—and all the case selectors and chapter authors—for contributing to this terrific book. Their perseverance and tenacity in completing it is both a testament to them individually and a tribute to what the Section offers. The excellence of what they collectively have produced will be evident.

With this book, in the words of playwright Robert Bolt in *A Man for All Seasons*, "in the thickets of the law, oh, there I'm a forester." I hope this book will be well received by readers of all types and prove as helpful as all of us envisioned at its conception.

Preface

This book has been a long time in the making. As former Acting Attorney General Jeffrey Rosen explains in the Foreword, the Council of the American Bar Association's Section of Administrative Law and Regulatory Practice, then under his leadership, commissioned this book nearly seven years ago. One reason we delayed its publication until now is that in the years since the Section first commissioned the book, the Supreme Court has given more attention to administrative law than it has done during any comparable period in its history.

Whereas the Court might once be said to have "abjure[d] judicial responsibility for the development of administrative [law],"[1] today's Court has taken an especially active, and no doubt contested, role in developing its doctrines in just the past few years—most notably those concerning the allocation of power between the federal courts and federal agencies in interpreting statutes and regulations. The Court's recent engagement with administrative law has resulted in the addition of several new "leading cases" to the book since it was initially commissioned and significant revisions to several chapters prepared early in the drafting process. The coverage of the Court's cases brings the book current through the Court's 2023–2024 term—perhaps the most consequential of the Court's recent terms as far as administrative law is concerned. It may be some time before a new edition of the book needs to be considered, and even then, the cases covered here will almost certainly remain "leading."

This book's purpose, as the Section conceived it, is mainly to offer newcomers to administrative law concise summaries and analyses, each written by a leading expert, of several dozen "leading cases" in the field (all but two a Supreme Court case). Learning about the leading cases covered

1. Antonin Scalia, *Vermont Yankee: The APA, the D.C. Circuit, and the Supreme Court*, 1978 SUP. CT. REV. 345, 345.

in this book will equip newcomers to the field with an understanding of many, if not most, of the foundational (and still) governing doctrines and principles of administrative law—much more so, we think, than learning about three dozen or so cases would in many other areas of law (including even constitutional law).

Most of these doctrines and principles find their origin or most sustained articulation in a single "leading case"—many decades-old, some very recent. Even so foundational a matter as the two categories of agency action around which the Administrative Procedure Act (APA) is organized (i.e., rulemaking and adjudication[2]) can be traced, as Michael Herz notes in Chapter 1, to two cases that predated by several decades the APA's enactment in 1946. Some cases addressed in this book have even given their names to foundational doctrines or principles of administrative law, among them the "*Chenery I* principle" or "*Chenery* doctrine" (providing that courts may uphold agency action based only on the reasons offered by the agency when it acted, not post hoc agency rationalizations offered in court),[3] the recently overturned but still important "*Chevron* doctrine" (providing that courts must defer to a reasonable agency interpretation of an ambiguous statute that the agency administers),[4] and the "*Vermont Yankee* principle" (providing that courts may not add to the procedural requirements of the APA).[5] Administrative lawyers cannot speak knowledgeably about these and other doctrines without knowing something about the cases after which they are named.

By reading the concise summaries and analyses of the leading cases covered in this book, newcomers to administrative law can learn much (though certainly not all) of what they need to know about the judicially developed doctrines and principles, both statutory and constitutional, on which administrative law is built.[6] The approach taken here of introducing

2. *See* 5 U.S.C. § 551(4)–(7).
3. SEC v. Chenery (*Chenery I*), 318 U.S. 80 (1943). The case is the subject of Chapter 22.
4. Chevron U.S.A., Inc. v. Nat. Res. Def. Council, 467 U.S. 837 (1984). The case is the subject of Chapter 16.
5. Vermont Yankee Nuclear Power Corp. v. Nat. Res. Def. Council, 435 U.S. 519 (1978). The case is the subject of Chapter 25.
6. The qualifier "judicially developed" is important. Much administrative law "happens" at agencies without the involvement of the federal courts, in part because agency action often "evades" judicial review for one reason or another. Christopher J. Walker, *Administrative Law Without Courts*, 65 UCLA L. Rev. 1620, 1624 (2018); *see also, e.g.*, Gillian E. Metzger & Kevin M. Stack, *Internal Administrative Law*, 115 Mich. L. Rev. 1239 (2017).

those doctrines and principles through the particular cases from which they developed may also help ground them contextually in a way that makes them easier to grasp, not to mention make them more interesting. Readers seeking a concise doctrinal overview of administrative law as a companion to this book are encouraged to read the Section's *Blackletter Statement of Administrative Law*, which is cited throughout this book.[7]

Although this book is mainly focused on newcomers to administrative law, practitioners, academics, and judges already familiar with the subject—and even those with expertise in it—will find much here to compel their attention. The chapters, though short, offer incisive and original analyses. They also identify the leading secondary sources for readers interested in more in-depth study.

The cases are grouped along lines common in many administrative law casebooks. The first group of cases (Part I) concerns the increasingly contested position of the administrative agency in the constitutional structure. These cases address, among other issues, the constitutionality of congressional delegations of regulatory authority to agencies, congressional mechanisms to control the exercise of authority once delegated, and especially congressional limitations on presidential control of agencies by conferring tenure protections on high-level agency officials. The second group of cases (Part II) concerns the two main forms of agency actions with which the APA is concerned—adjudication and rulemaking—and when and how they are constrained by constitutional due process. The third, fourth, and fifth groups of cases address judicial review of federal agency action: the third (Part III) prudential and constitutional prerequisites to judicial review (such as standing), the fourth (Part IV) the allocation of authority between courts and agencies to interpret statutes and regulations, and the fifth (Part V) judicial review of the merits of agency action (including arbitrary-and-capricious

---

7. *See* SECTION OF ADMIN. L. & REGUL. PRAC., AM. BAR ASS'N, A BLACKLETTER STATEMENT OF FEDERAL ADMINISTRATIVE LAW (2d ed. 2013). A much more in-depth overview of these doctrines can be found in KRISTIN E. HICKMAN & RICHARD J. PIERCE, JR., ADMINISTRATIVE LAW TREATISE (7th ed. 2024), the leading administrative law treatise. Several excellent Section books address particular aspects of administrative law. They include A GUIDE TO FEDERAL AGENCY RULEMAKING (Jeffrey S. Lubbers ed., 6th ed. 2018); A GUIDE TO FEDERAL AGENCY ADJUDICATION (Jeremy S. Graboyes ed., 3d ed. 2023); and A GUIDE TO JUDICIAL AND POLITICAL REVIEW OF FEDERAL AGENCIES (Michael E. Herz et al. eds., 2d ed. 2015).

review). Of course, all the cases covered in this book can be said to address judicial review of agency action in some sense.

Each chapter addresses a single case—or, in a few instances, two often commonly paired cases—and follows the same basic structure. A chapter begins by identifying the issue addressed by the case and situates that issue in its doctrinal context; then succinctly summarizes the case's facts and the court's holding and analysis; and concludes by identifying the case's significance and important issues left unresolved and, in some instances, addressed in later cases. A bibliography of the leading secondary sources (mostly law review articles) appears at the end of each chapter.

Readers will note that, at our request, footnotes have been kept to a minimum, at least by the standard of legal writing. Each chapter provides a single citation (if available, to the *United States Reports*) of the case it addresses right under its title. No additional (page-specific) citations of the case are provided. Footnotes cite only other cases and secondary sources. Textual footnotes and law review-style parentheticals following citations are used sparingly.

A book with the title "leading cases" raises an obvious question: What makes a case leading or leading enough to justify its inclusion in this book? More to the point: How were the three dozen cases included here selected for inclusion among potentially hundreds of cases?

Unlike some books in the leading-cases genre, this book's case selections were not based on the editors' own judgments as to what cases are most significant, let alone what cases interest them the most.[8] They are based, rather, on the collective wisdom of a 19-member Case Selection Committee established to recommend the cases for inclusion in this book. (The Committee's members are listed on pages xxvii–xxix.) The Committee's members were chosen by the Section and one of us. They included agency officials, private lawyers, and legal academics.

The process was simple: Committee members were asked to identify 25 or so "foundational" or "canonical cases" in administrative law. No additional criteria were provided.

8. *Cf.*, *e.g.*, MICHAEL C. DORF, CONSTITUTIONAL LAW STORIES 1 (2d ed. 2009) (noting that the book's case-selection decisions reflect the editor's "*own* idiosyncratic" preferences).

Despite this deliberately vague charge, Committee members reached near consensus. One of us resolved the relatively small differences among Committee members—in most cases by expanding the number of cases for inclusion—and made the final selection decisions. Any case recommended for inclusion as a leading case but not included here is discussed somewhere in this book. Readers will find that the leading-cases selections reflected here largely align with those in most doctrinally focused casebooks.

After the Committee completed its work, the Supreme Court decided a number of important administrative-law cases. The editors, without further consultation with the Committee, selected four of them for inclusion here.[9] They are obvious choices. We are confident that the Committee members would agree with our decisions.

* * *

Professor Anna Shavers, for many years the Cline Williams Professor of Citizenship Law at the University of Nebraska College of Law, as well as a former Section chair, joined as the second editor of the book soon after the Selection Committee completed its work. She worked with the authors of nearly half the chapters in this book (mostly those on judicial review in Parts III–V). Sadly, Professor Shavers passed away before the book was completed. One of us, Christopher Walker, another former Section chair, joined as a third editor to bring the book to completion.

We dedicate this book to Professor Shavers—an exceptional colleague and still better friend—with our profound sorrow that she did not live long enough to see it in print. We know she would have been pleased with the result.

Christopher J. Walker
Matthew Lee Wiener

9. *See* Loper Bright Enters. v. Raimondo, 603 U.S. 369 (2024) (Chapter 21); West Virginia v. EPA, 597 U.S. 697 (2022) (Chapter 20); United States v. Arthrex, Inc., 594 U.S. 1 (2021) (Chapter 35); Kisor v. Wilkie, 588 U.S. 558 (2019) (Chapter 19).

Contributors

Michael Asimow
Professor of Law Emeritus
UCLA School of Law

Aditya Bamzai
Martha Lubin Karsh and Bruce A. Karsh Bicentennial Professor of Law
University of Virginia School of Law

Kent Barnett
Dean and J. Gilbert Reese Chair in Contract Law
Moritz College of Law, The Ohio State University

Jack M. Beermann
Philip S. Beck Professor of Law and Harry Elwood Warren Scholar
Boston University School of Law

Emily Bremer
Professor of Law
Notre Dame Law School

Reeve T. Bull
Director
Office of Regulatory Management
Commonwealth of Virginia

Ronald A. Cass
Dean Emeritus
Boston University School of Law

Cary Coglianese
Edward B. Shils Professor of Law and Professor of Political Science
University of Pennsylvania Carey Law School

Rebecca S. Eisenberg
Robert and Barbara Luciano Professor of Law
University of Michigan Law School

Blake Emerson
Professor of Law
UCLA School of Law

William Funk
Lewis & Clark Distinguished Professor of Law Emeritus
Lewis & Clark Law School

Jeremy S. Graboyes
Research Director
Administrative Conference of the United States

Michael Herz
Arthur Kaplan Professor of Law
Benjamin N. Cardozo School of Law, Yeshiva University

Kristin E. Hickman
McKnight Presidential Professor in Law, Distinguished McKnight University Professor, and Harlan Albert Rogers Professor in Law
University of Minnesota Law School

Linda D. Jellum
Professor of Law
University of Idaho College of Law

William S. Jordan III
Professor of Law Emeritus
The University of Akron School of Law

Kathryn E. Kovacs
Professor of Law
Rutgers Law School

Ronald Levin
William R. Orthwein Distinguished Professor of Law
Washington University School of Law

Jeffrey S. Lubbers
Professor of Practice in Administrative Law
American University, Washington College of Law

Jennifer Mascott
Associate Professor of Law
Columbus School of Law, The Catholic University of America

Nina A. Mendelson
Joseph L. Sax Collegiate Professor of Law
University of Michigan Law School

Gillian Metzger
Harlan Fiske Stone Professor of Constitutional Law
Columbia Law School

Richard Murphy
AT&T Professor of Law
Texas Tech University School of Law

Aaron L. Nielson
Charles I. Francis Professorship in Law
The University of Texas at Austin School of Law

Craig N. Oren
Professor Emeritus of Law
Rutgers Law School

Connor Raso
Deputy General Counsel
Public Company Accounting Oversight Board

Bijal Shah
Professor of Law and Provost Faculty Fellow
Boston College Law School

Peter M. Shane
Jacob E. Davis and Jacob E. Davis II Chair in Law, Emeritus
Moritz College of Law, The Ohio State University

Anna W. Shavers
Cline Williams Professor of Citizenship Law
University of Nebraska School of Law

Kate Shaw
Professor of Law
University of Pennsylvania Carey Law School

Kevin M. Stack
Lee S. and Charles A. Speir Chair in Law
Vanderbilt University Law School

Peter L. Strauss
Betts Professor Emeritus of Law
Columbia Law School

Christopher J. Walker
Professor of Law
University of Michigan Law School

Kathryn A. Watts
Formerly Jack R. MacDonald Endowed Chair
University of Washington School of Law

Adam J. White
Resident Scholar
American Enterprise Institute

Matthew Lee Wiener
Visiting Distinguished Lecturer of Administrative Law
University of Pennsylvania Carey Law School

Members of the Case Selection Committee

Michael Asimow
Professor of Law Emeritus
UCLA School of Law

Reeve T. Bull
Director
Office of Regulatory Management
Commonwealth of Virginia

Neil R. Eisner
Formerly Assistant General Counsel for Regulation and Enforcement
U.S. Department of Transportation

William Funk
Lewis & Clark Distinguished Professor of Law Emeritus
Lewis & Clark Law School

Michael Eric Herz
Arthur Kaplan Professor of Law
Benjamin N. Cardozo School of Law, Yeshiva University

Linda D. Jellum
Professor of Law
University of Idaho College of Law

William S. Jordan III
Professor of Law Emeritus
The University of Akron School of Law

Peter D. Keisler
Partner
Sidley Austin LLP

William Kelley
Associate Professor of Law
Notre Dame Law School

Renée M. Landers
Professor of Law
Suffolk University Law School

Ronald Levin
William R. Orthwein Distinguished Professor of Law
Washington University of Saint Louis School of Law

Jeffrey S. Lubbers
Professor of Practice in Administrative Law
American University, Washington College of Law

Richard Murphy
AT&T Professor of Law, 2009
Texas Tech University School of Law

Richard J. Pierce, Jr.
Lyle T. Alverson Professor of Law
The George Washington University Law School

Jeffrey A. Rosen
Of Counsel
Cravath, Swaine & Moore LLP

Paul R. Verkuil
Former Chairman
Administrative Conference of the United States

Christopher J. Walker
Professor of Law
University of Michigan Law School

Kathryn A. Watts
Formerly the Jack R. MacDonald Endowed Chair
University of Washington School of Law

Matthew Lee Wiener (Chair)
Lecturer in Law
University of Pennsylvania Carey Law School

PART I

Adjudication, Rulemaking, and Due Process

Chapter 1

Londoner v. City & County of Denver, 210 U.S. 373 (1908); *Bi-Metallic Investment Co. v. State Board of Equalization*, 239 U.S. 441 (1915)

Michael Herz

Side by side in every administrative law casebook, forever linked, sit the two oldest decisions in this book: the venerable cases of *Londoner v. City & County of Denver* and *Bi-Metallic Investment Co. v. State Board of Equalization*. The pairing is irresistible. The decisions come from the same state and the same era, they involve similar claims under the 14th Amendment's Due Process Clause, and they have different outcomes. Together, the two decisions established the fundamental constitutional distinction between legislation and adjudication. That distinction is now woven into the warp and woof of administrative and constitutional law, reflected in statutes, in judicial decisions, and, less visibly, in arguments not made and cases not brought.

Londoner

Londoner was a substantive and procedural challenge to the decision of the Denver City Council to pave a street and charge the owners of property fronting on the street for the work. Under the challenged regime, the paving process began when a majority of the property owners fronting on a particular street filed a petition with the Board of Public Works. The Board could then proceed, laying out a "paving district," determining specifications for the work, and making an estimate of costs and their allocation. Interested persons could submit written comments. The Board then presented a proposed ordinance embodying its recommendations to the City Council. If the City Council enacted the proposed ordinance, the work proceeded. When it was complete, the Board made a tentative allocation of costs, heard any objections in writing, and recommended another ordinance to the City Council, which, if enacted, made the final assessment.

Wolfe Londoner owned property on a stretch of Eighth Avenue in Denver that was paved pursuant to this process. He was unhappy with just about every aspect of the decision, objecting that a majority of property owners had not in fact signed the petition, the paving was no good, and the costs were misapportioned. When the Board issued its tentative apportionment of the costs, Londoner filed a written objection with eleven specific complaints. This was unavailing, and the City Council imposed the assessment. Londoner and others sued. Among their many arguments was that they had been denied due process. Ruling 7–2, with Chief Justice Fuller and Justice Holmes dissenting without opinion, the U.S. Supreme Court agreed. In an extraordinarily bare-bones, conclusory discussion, it held that, while a full trial-type hearing was not required, Londoner was due more than just the opportunity to submit objections in writing. He had "the right to support his allegations by argument, however brief: and, if need be, by proof, however informal."

Bi-Metallic Investment Co.

Bi-Metallic returns us to Denver, a few years later. Two state agencies ordered that the valuation of all taxable property in the city be increased by 40 percent. Bi-Metallic was a Denver property owner, predictably dismayed that its real estate taxes would rise. It challenged the new assessment, arguing that due process had been denied because the affected property owners were given no opportunity to be heard. In a very brief, unanimous opinion by Justice Holmes, the Court made quick work of this contention. "Where a rule of conduct applies to more than a few people," it held, the remedy for those with complaints is through the ballot box rather than the impractical mechanism of allowing them all to be heard.

Distinguishing *Londoner* and *Bi-Metallic*

The two decisions together add up to more than the sum of their parts. They are side by side in the casebooks, and together in this book, because each is best understood in light of the other. They look an awful lot alike. Both involve an agency determination regarding how much money to take from property owners. In each, the property owner wants an opportunity to be heard. Why did Londoner get one and Bi-Metallic did not? Justice Holmes distinguished *Londoner* by noting that in that case "[a] relatively small number of persons was concerned, who were exceptionally affected, in each case upon individual grounds." Consider these points in turn.

In noting the "relatively small number of persons" affected in *Londoner*, Justice Holmes was alert to considerations of administrative convenience; "[t]here must be a limit to individual argument in such matters if government is to go on." Administrative convenience surely counts,[1] but it can be a dangerous argument. After all, usually constitutional requirements are *not* determined by convenience. Indeed, just the opposite. Government can be relied on to do what is convenient and easy; an essential function of a constitution, especially when it comes to procedures, is to force the government to go the long way round.

A less obvious reason why sheer numbers may matter is that a larger group of affected people is a more effective political force (though as to agencies only an indirect one). Where large numbers are affected, those who do not like the rule (or law) have a meaningful political remedy; an adversely affected individual can exert no meaningful pressure on the legislating authority to change it. Justice Holmes did not make this point explicitly, but it was implicit in his observation that in cases like *Bi-Metallic* "rights are

1. *See* Minn. State Bd. for Cmty. Colls. v. Knight, 465 U.S. 271, 285 (1984) ("Government makes so many policy decisions affecting so many people that it would likely grind to a halt were policymaking constrained by constitutional requirements on whose voices must be heard.").

protected in the only way that they can be in a complex society, by [affected individuals'] power, immediate or remote, over those who make the rule."

The more important distinctions, however, lie in the nature of the governmental decisions in these two cases, not the number of people affected. Justice Holmes observed that *Londoner* involved "individual grounds"; the increase challenged in *Bi-Metallic* rested on a conclusion about the general state of assessments. Because the increase was across the board, "all are equally concerned"; the agency reached no conclusion about any individual property.

Justice Holmes did not explain *why* the presence or absence of individual circumstances matters. There seem to be at least three reasons, all of which go to the value of individual hearings. First, if the point of a hearing is to ensure an informed decision, and each affected party is in exactly the same boat, then individual hearings will provide rapidly diminishing returns.

Second, the distinction rests on the difference between what Kenneth Culp Davis labeled "adjudicative facts" and "legislative facts." (Indeed, Professor Davis invoked these two decisions in elaborating the distinction.[2]) The first are specific to an individual or case; the latter are facts about the world. For Professor Davis (and Justice Holmes), reliance on trial-type individual hearings to determine legislative facts—facts about the world—was "unnecessary and costly."[3] On the other hand, adjudicative facts—which are particular to the parties and their activities and uniquely known to the parties themselves—are best determined through an evidentiary hearing, including some opportunity for the affected individuals to rebut or explain.[4]

The third, and perhaps most important, point rests on the generality of legislative enactments. That generality is some protection against abuse of the most vulnerable. If *everyone's* property assessment goes up by 40 percent (including properties owned by those making the decision and their friends and family members), the decision is unlikely to be arbitrary, oppressive, or preferential. Thus, a hearing is less important because the abuses that the hearing will protect against are less likely to occur.

---

2. *See* Kenneth Culp Davis, *The Requirement of a Trial-Type Hearing*, 70 HARV. L. REV. 193, 199–201, 207 (1956).
3. KENNETH CULP DAVIS, ADMINISTRATIVE LAW TEXT § 7.05 (3d ed. 1972).
4. *Id.* § 7.03.

Rule

The hornbook rule that emerges from the cases is this: Where life, liberty, or property is deprived, the Constitution requires "due process" when an agency adjudicates but not when it makes rules. "The Constitution does not grant to members of the public generally a right to be heard by public bodies making decisions of policy."[5] The same principle distinguishes decisions made by courts from those made by legislatures. In the language of the American Bar Association (ABA) *A Blackletter Statement of Federal Administrative Law*: "An adjudicatory hearing is not required, as a matter of constitutional due process, when agency action is legislative in character rather than adjudicatory."[6] This is true even though the *impact* on an individual may be no different; thus, if the legislature eliminates welfare benefits for all, due process need not be provided, even though the Due Process Clause is triggered when an agency terminates a specific individual's benefits.[7] In brief, due process applies to adjudication; it does not apply to legislation and rulemaking.[8]

To apply this rule requires working definitions of "adjudication" and "legislation" (or "rulemaking"). Consistent with the core rationale for *Londoner* and *Bi-Metallic*, the courts have focused on standard characteristics: legislation is prospective, policy based, and, most importantly, general in its application; adjudication is retroactive, involves the application of law to facts, and is particular in its application.[9]

It is unclear whether the rule is that the Due Process Clause does not apply to legislation or that it applies but is satisfied by the legislative process. *Bi-Metallic* is opaque on that question. Some Supreme Court opinions seem

5. *Minn. State Bd. for Cmty. Colls.*, 465 U.S. at 283 (citing *Bi-Metallic*).
6. SECTION OF ADMIN. L. & REGUL. PRAC., ABA, A BLACKLETTER STATEMENT OF FEDERAL ADMINISTRATIVE LAW pt. 1, § I.E (2d ed. 2013).
7. *See, e.g.*, McMurtray v. Holladay, 11 F.3d 499 (5th Cir. 1993). *See generally* Goldberg v. Kelly, 397 U.S. 254 (1970) (subject of Chapter 4); Board of Regents v. Roth, 408 U.S. 564 (1972) (subject of Chapter 3); Perry v. Sindermann, 408 U.S. 593 (1972) (also subject of Chapter 3).
8. *See* Jeremy S. Graboyes, *What Is Federal Agency Adjudication?*, *in* A GUIDE TO FEDERAL AGENCY ADJUDICATION 3, 6–7 (Jeremy S. Graboyes ed., 2d ed. 2023).
9. For a useful discussion, see LC & S, Inc. v. Warren Cnty. Area Plan Comm'n, 244 F.3d 601, 602–05 (7th Cir. 2001).

to take the latter position,[10] but the former is frequently asserted.[11] This is a nice jurisprudential question but not of much practical importance, for under either approach the Constitution grants *no* opportunity to be heard in the legislative setting.

Significance

Paul Verkuil has written that these two decisions (along with one or two others) "introduced the modern era of administrative law."[12] What he means is that they marked a shift from a judicial preoccupation with the legitimacy of administrative decision-making to an acceptance of administrative power and a focus on procedure. More specifically, *Londoner* is arguably the first modern procedural due process case, the distant source of the *Goldberg-Roth-Sindermann* trilogy.

Still, these two decisions were not instant classics. Early citations were scant, and as Ronald Cass has pointed out, it was not until the 1940s that scholars started paying attention.[13] The decisions became important when administrative law came firmly to reflect what Cass labels the "bipolar model." Under that model, which is built into the very structure of the Administrative Procedure Act (APA), administrative action is either adjudication or rulemaking. It is possible that the APA's structure is the *result* of *Londoner* and *Bi-Metallic*, but that likely confuses correlation with causation. It is difficult to tell how much those decisions contributed to the APA structure and how much they and the APA both reflect the same influences. (After all, this distinction has roots in the Constitution's separation

10. *See, e.g.*, United States v. Locke, 471 U.S. 84, 108 (1985) ("In altering substantive rights through enactment of rules of general applicability, a legislature generally provides constitutionally adequate process simply by enacting the statute, publishing it, and [providing an opportunity to comply]."); Logan v. Zimmerman Brush Co., 455 U.S. 422, 433 (1982) (stating that a "legislative determination provides all the process that is due").

11. *See, e.g.*, Rogen v. Bensalem Twp., 616 F.2d 680, 693 (3d Cir. 1980) ("the protections of procedural due process do not extend to legislative actions").

12. Paul R. Verkuil, *The Emerging Concept of Administrative Procedure*, 78 Colum. L. Rev. 258, 264 (1978).

13. *See* Ronald A. Cass, *Models of Administrative Action*, 72 Va. L. Rev. 363, 368 (1986).

of powers.) What is clear is that the *Londoner/Bi-Metallic* adjudication/rulemaking dichotomy is embedded at the very heart of the APA.

In the century since *Bi-Metallic* was handed down, the distinction between general policymaking and individual adjudication has remained remarkably robust. Accordingly, there is no such thing in American constitutional law as "legislative due process." Courts consistently have rejected calls from litigants and some scholars[14] to extend due process protections to the legislative or rulemaking setting.[15]

The most important example of this steadfastness involves the question whether oral testimony (or even cross-examination or other trial-type procedures) must ever be provided in a rulemaking. *Londoner* and *Bi-Metallic* would suggest that the answer is a firm "no." When the U.S. Court of Appeals for the D.C. Circuit started ruling otherwise in the 1970s, the Supreme Court squashed that trend in the famous *Vermont Yankee* decision,[16] relying on *Bi-Metallic* explicitly. The Court left open the possibility that a particular proceeding, though technically a rulemaking, might have the characteristics of an adjudication and so trigger due process requirements.[17] Ratemaking would be an example, but otherwise that exception is more theoretical than real.[18]

This pair of decisions has also informed judicial application of nonconstitutional requirements. For example, the Supreme Court's decision in *United States v. Florida East Coast Railway Co.*,[19] which showed the Court quite reluctant to impose formal (i.e., trial-type) procedures in rulemakings pursuant to the APA, was very much informed by *Londoner* and *Bi-Metallic*, reflecting the same disinclination to require individualized hearings for essentially legislative decisions. Similarly, judicial development and enforcement

14. *See, e.g.*, Peter M. Shane, *Back to the Future of the American State: Overruling* Buckley v. Valeo, 57 U. PITT. L. REV. 443, 454–58 (1996).

15. A rare exception—one that truly does "prove the rule" in that it is a dissent—is found in *Fullilove v. Klutznick*, 448 U.S. 448, 548–49 (1980) (Stevens, J., dissenting) (arguing for closer judicial review of legislative procedures where statute draws a suspect classification).

16. Vermont Yankee Nuclear Power Corp. v. Nat. Res. Def. Council, Inc., 435 U.S. 519 (1978). The decision is the subject of Chapter 25.

17. *See id.* at 542.

18. *See* JEFFREY S. LUBBERS, A GUIDE TO FEDERAL AGENCY RULEMAKING 318 (6th ed. 2018).

19. 410 U.S. 224 (1973). The case is the subject of Chapter 5.

of rules regarding agency bias and ex parte contacts in the adjudicatory setting, with much milder or nonexistent counterparts in the rulemaking setting,[20] rests on the conceptualization reflected in these two decisions.

The robustness of the *Londoner/Bi-Metallic* distinction does not mean that the boundary between the two categories is never vague or porous. One setting of recurring uncertainty is zoning. For example, if a municipality rezones (townwide? in part? in just a small area?), the decision could plausibly be portrayed as either legislative or adjudicative. In general, courts have found that adoption of a comprehensive plan or general zoning code is legislative; more specific decisions have sometimes been held to be adjudicative.[21]

Bibliography

Ronald A. Cass, *Models of Administrative Action*, 72 VA. L. REV. 363 (1986).

Developments in the Law: Zoning, 91 HARV. L. REV. 1427 (1978).

CHARLES H. KOCH, JR. & RICHARD MURPHY, ADMINISTRATIVE LAW AND PRACTICE § 2.11 (3d ed. 2010–2018).

SECTION OF ADMIN. L. & REGUL. PRAC., ABA, A BLACKLETTER STATEMENT OF FEDERAL ADMINISTRATIVE LAW pt. 1, § 5.E (2d ed. 2013).

20. *Compare, e.g.*, Portland Audubon Soc'y v. Endangered Species Comm., 984 F.2d 1534, 1540 (9th Cir. 1993) (finding bar on ex parte communications applicable to committee whose determinations were "*quasi*-judicial"), *with* Sierra Club v. Costle, 657 F.2d 298, 406–07 (D.C. Cir. 1981) (noting that ex parte communications that "directly concern the outcome of adjudications or quasi-adjudicatory proceedings" are problematic, but accepting ex parte contacts in a rulemaking). *Sierra Club* is the subject of Chapter 9.

21. *See, e.g.*, Onyx Props. LLC v. Bd. of Cnty. Comm'rs, 838 F.3d 1039 (10th Cir. 2016) (citing cases); 75 Acres, LLC v. Miami-Dade Cnty., 338 F.3d 1288 (11th Cir. 2003) (finding imposition of building moratorium legislative and not subject to procedural due process requirements).

Chapter 2

SEC v. Chenery Corp. (Chenery II), 332 U.S. 194 (1947)

Ronald A. Cass and Matthew Lee Wiener

Statutes often require agencies to establish policy to implement general commands. For instance, an agency might have to give content to an undefined statutory term, as when the National Labor Relations Board (NLRB) decides who qualifies as an "employee" entitled to certain rights under federal labor law.[1]

Conventional administrative law identifies two main procedural mechanisms (or policymaking forms[2]) by which an agency might do this. First, the agency might promulgate a rule (or regulation), if Congress has given it substantive rulemaking authority. The regulation will govern decisions in subsequent agency adjudications—and sometimes in enforcement actions in federal court. Second, the agency might establish policy common-law style, through case-by-case adjudication. One or more decisions in particular cases may establish a decisional "rule," much as court decisions do. Although this is not a "rule" under the Administrative Procedure Act (APA), as it will have resulted from adjudication rather than rulemaking,[3] the agency's decisions often supply binding precedent for subsequent adjudications between different parties.

1. *See* Loper Bright Enters., Inc. v. Raimondo, 603 U.S. 369, 388–89 (2024) (discussing NLRB v. Hearst Publ'ns, Inc., 322 U.S. 111 (1944)).
2. *See* M. Elizabeth Magill, *Agency Choice of Policymaking Form*, 71 U. Chi. L. Rev. 1383 (2004).
3. *See* 5 U.S.C. §§ 551(4) (definition of "rule"), 551(6) (definition of "order"). *But see* Matthew C. Stephenson, *Embedded Rules*, 39 Yale J. on Regul. Bull. 59 (2021).

These two policymaking forms need not be mutually exclusive. They may be combined—and often are. An agency may promulgate a rule that, when applied in adjudication, must itself be given further content.

Some statutes require an agency to establish policy by rule,[4] but more commonly, statutes do not require rulemaking. This raises a recurring issue in administrative law: May an agency choose between rulemaking and adjudication to make policy and, if so, under what (if any) judicially enforceable limitations? The U.S. Supreme Court's 1947 decision in *SEC v. Chenery Corp.*—commonly known as *Chenery II*—remains the leading decision on these questions.

Policymaking by Adjudication in *Chenery*

Chenery II arose from adjudicative decisions of the Securities and Exchange Commission (SEC) refusing to approve, under the Public Utility Holding Company Act, a proposed corporate reorganization of the Federal Water Service Corporation. Officers, directors, and controlling stockholders of Federal Water asked the SEC to approve a plan allowing preferred stock they had purchased during the reorganization to be converted into common stock in a newly created holding company; the plan would "protect" their "interest in the new company." Instead, the SEC approved an amended plan, over the objection of the management shareholders, under which their preferred stock, but no other shareholders', would not be converted into common stock but instead would be surrendered at cost. The SEC concluded that the management's proposed treatment of their stock transactions was not "fair and equitable" under the act. Although the act conferred rulemaking authority on the SEC, the SEC had never issued a rule governing—let alone one prohibiting—transactions like the one at issue. It first announced the prohibition in the Federal Water adjudication.

The SEC based its decision entirely on equitable rules of fiduciary law developed by the courts. Those fiduciary rules, as the SEC interpreted them, prohibited the management shareholders from trading in the securities of the

4. *See* FDA v. Wages & White Lion Invs., L.L.C., 604 U.S. 542, 565, 582 (2025); *see also, e.g.*, Shalala v. Guernsey Mem'l Hosp., 514 U.S. 87, 96 (1995).

company during its reorganization. The officers and directors sought review in the U.S. Court of Appeals for the D.C. Circuit, which set aside the SEC's order.[5] The SEC's appeal of the D.C. Circuit's decision resulted in the first of the Supreme Court's two *Chenery* decisions—*Chenery I*, decided in 1943.[6]

In *Chenery I*, the Court ruled that the SEC's order could not "stand" because the judicial precedents that the SEC relied on did not prohibit the transaction. The Court recognized that the act's "fair and equitable" standard did not bind the SEC to "settled judicial precedents." The Court acknowledged that the SEC might have relied on its accumulated experience and expertise in adopting a policy prohibiting the challenged transaction. But the SEC had not adopted any such policy, grounding its decision only in judicial precedents that did not support it. Judicial review was limited accordingly. A reviewing court may judge the "propriety" of an agency's action, the Court held in announcing what would become known as the *Chenery I* doctrine, "solely by the ground invoked by the agency" at the time. The Court then remanded the matter to the SEC, which became standard practice when a court rejects an agency's basis for a decision.[7] Nowhere did the Court say what exactly the SEC might do on remand.

Dicta in the Court's *Chenery I* decision, written by Justice Frankfurter, suggested that policymaking of the sort contemplated by the Court would take the form of an ex ante "general rule" that the SEC would then apply in an adjudication.[8] Justice Frankfurter noted that "before transactions" like the one before the SEC could be "outlawed, they must fall under the ban of some standards of conduct prescribed" by Congress or the agency.[9] Congress had not prescribed any such standard; nor, Justice Frankfurter emphasized, had the SEC done so by exercising its rulemaking authority.[10]

On remand, the SEC again disapproved a reorganization plan much the same as the plan at issue in *Chenery I*. This time, though, the SEC drew

5. Chenery Corp. v. SEC, 128 F.2d 303 (D.C. Cir. 1942).
6. SEC v. Chenery Corp. (*Chenery I*), 318 U.S. 80 (1943). *Chenery I* is addressed in Chapter 22.
7. *See, e.g.*, Christopher J. Walker, *The Ordinary Remand Rule and the Judicial Toolbox for Agency Dialogue*, 82 Geo. Wash. L. Rev. 1553 (2014).
8. 318 U.S. at 92.
9. *Id.* at 92–93.
10. *See id.* at 93.

not on judicially developed fiduciary law but on what the Court called the SEC's "accumulated experience in dealing with utility reorganizations" and "informed view of statutory requirements" in concluding that the proposed transaction was "detrimental to the public interest or the interest of investors" and "would result in an unfair or inequitable distribution of voting power among Federal Water's security holders." Again, the D.C. Circuit refused to uphold the SEC's order.[11]

Before the Supreme Court in *Chenery II*, Federal Water's management argued that the SEC was required to approve the transaction so that the company could "realize a profit through" its stock purchases. In its view, the SEC could promulgate a prospective general rule "outlawing such profits" that would govern "future utility reorganizations," but it could not adopt a new decisional rule with retroactive effect in an adjudication.

Upholding the SEC's order, the Court held that the "absence of a general rule" did not affect the SEC's authority to decide whether the proposed reorganization plan complied with the "standards" that the SEC was required to apply. The SEC, in fact, would have been "unjustified" in approving a transaction inconsistent with those standards. Although the Court acknowledged that *Chenery I* had "recognized the possibility" that the SEC might have exercised its rulemaking powers, the decision had not "implied" that the absence of a rule deprived the agency of authority to act. Any such requirement would "stultify the administrative process."

In the most cited part of its decision, the Court acknowledged that the SEC had "less reason to rely upon ad hoc adjudication to formulate new standards of conduct" because, unlike a court, it "had the ability to make new law prospectively through the exercise of its rule-making powers." The Court also acknowledged that when "filling the interstices" of the statute the SEC was implementing, it "should" do so "as much as possible" through the "quasi-legislative promulgation of rules to be applied in the future."

Still, the Court was unwilling to impose "any rigid" requirement that the SEC proceed by "general rule." To do so, the Court explained, would render "the administrative process inflexible and incapable of dealing with many

11. Chenery Corp. v. SEC, 154 F.2d 6 (D.C. Cir. 1945).

of the specialized problems" that it must address. Sometimes an agency will not have foreseen a problem. Sometimes it "may not have had sufficient experience with a particular problem to warrant rigidifying its tentative judgment into a hard and fast rule." And sometimes an agency could not have "capture[d]" a "specialized" and "var[ied]" problem "within the boundaries of a general rule." In short, the Court recognized "a very definite place for case-by-case evolution of statutory standards." The Court concluded, in its most oft-quoted sentence, that "the choice . . . between proceeding by general rule or by individual, ad hoc litigation is one that lies primarily in the informed discretion of the administrative agency." This formulation encapsulates the *Chenery II* doctrine.

The Court largely brushed aside the objection that the SEC had applied its new policy retroactively to deprive management shareholders of rights they otherwise would have enjoyed as securities holders. A decision in any adjudication—judicial or administrative—of "first impression has retroactive effect." As the Court stated:

> [R]etroactivity must be balanced against the mischief of producing a result which is contrary to a statutory design or to legal and equitable principles. If that mischief is greater than the ill effect of the retroactive application of the new standard, it is not the type of retroactivity which is condemned by law.

With little analysis, the Court concluded that the balance of interests favored the SEC.

This aspect of the Court's opinion was the target of Justice Jackson's impassioned dissent, joined by Justice Frankfurter, the author of *Chenery I*. Justice Jackson identified as the "basic assumption" of *Chenery I*—reasonably so given Justice Frankfurter's language there—that the SEC could prohibit the Federal Water reorganization plan only on the authority of a preexisting rule. Allowing the SEC to apply a "new standard of conduct" in an adjudication "brings the Court squarely against the invalidity of retroactive law-making." Justice Jackson went so far as to accuse the Court of sanctioning "administrative authoritarianism"—the "power to decide without law."

The *Chenery II* Doctrine in the Supreme Court

Not until its 1969 decision in *NLRB v. Wyman-Gordon Co.* did the Court return to the issue addressed in *Chenery II*.[12] What, exactly, the Court decided in that fractured decision is not altogether clear. The plurality opinion and the dissent together might be read to require rulemaking for certain—not clearly specified—policies. Some lower courts read it that way.[13] But the Court largely foreclosed that interpretation of *Wyman-Gordon* five years later in *NLRB v. Bell Aerospace*, where it reaffirmed the principle announced in *Chenery II* that the choice between rulemaking and adjudication lies within the agency's "informed discretion."[14] The Court suggested that an agency would be denied the choice only when it sought to impose liability on a party in an adjudication for conduct it had taken in "good-faith reliance" on the agency's earlier "pronouncements."[15]

Bell Aerospace was the last case in which the Court addressed the *Chenery II* doctrine in a holding. Several times since, the Court has cited it approvingly in dicta, most recently in *FDA v. Wages & White Lion Investments L.L.C.*[16] One distinguished critic of the doctrine has described it as "black-letter administrative law."[17]

Limits on Agency Discretion to Choose?

Bell Aerospace followed *Chenery II* in seemingly recognizing the possibility that a court might find an agency to have abused its discretion by forgoing rulemaking. But only a few outlier lower court decisions—none of

12. 394 U.S. 759 (1969).
13. *See, e.g.*, 1 Kristin E. Hickman & Richard J. Pierce, Jr., Administrative Law Treatise § 4.9 (6th ed. 2019); Magill, *supra* note 2, at 1407 & n.80; *see also* Ronald A. Cass, *Models of Administrative Action*, 72 Va. L. Rev. 363, 382–83 (1986).
14. 416 U.S. 267 (1974); *see, e.g.*, Cass, *supra* note 13, at 383–84. *But cf.* Morton v. Ruiz, 415 U.S. 199 (1974).
15. *Bell Aerospace*, 416 U.S. at 295.
16. 604 U.S. 542, 565, 582 (2025); *see also, e.g.*, Martin v. OSHRC, 499 U.S. 144, 154 (1991).
17. Aaron L. Nielson, *Three Wrong Turns in Agency Adjudication*, 28 Geo. Mason L. Rev. 657, 667 (2021).

them recent—actually have done so.[18] Most courts have not even required agencies to explain their choice of policymaking form, despite the reason-giving requirement that generally attends agency action under the APA.[19]

Post-*Chenery II* lower court decisions have given agencies wide latitude to apply new policies established in adjudicative decisions retroactively,[20] even when implementing vague, ambiguous, and open-ended statutory provisions. Most courts have not attempted to identify a place along the "adjudicative spectrum from pure application of law . . . to pure law creation"[21] at which to demarcate permissible from impermissible retroactivity in adjudication.[22] (Whether courts might establish justiciable standards to draw that line is a debated question.[23]) Although the law disfavors retroactive application of legislative rules,[24] it favors the retroactive application of decisional rules announced in agency adjudications.[25]

Courts have recognized one important limitation on agency choice of form: An agency may not apply a rule retroactively when doing so would, in the D.C. Circuit's terms, "work a manifest injustice."[26] Courts have used various multifactor tests to identify unfair retroactivity; variance in their formulation—not to mention their application—abounds even within the D.C. Circuit.[27] A common formulation asks whether a decisional rule merely clarifies an existing rule, applying it to new facts, in which case an agency may apply it retroactively; or whether it substitutes new law for "old law that was reasonably clear," in which case the agency may not apply it

18. *See, e.g.*, Ford Motor Co. v. FTC, 673 F.2d 1008 (9th Cir. 1981); *see generally* 1 Hickman & Pierce, *supra* note 13, § 4.9; Magill, *supra* note 2, at 1408.

19. *See* Magill, *supra* note 2, at 1414–15. *But cf.* Lisa Schultz Bressman, *Beyond Accountability: Arbitrariness and Legitimacy in the Administrative State*, 78 N.Y.U. L. Rev. 461, 535–36 (2003).

20. *See, e.g.*, AT&T v. FCC, 454 F.3d 329, 332 (D.C. Cir. 2006).

21. Abner S. Greene, *Adjudicative Retroactivity in Administrative Law*, 8 Sup. Ct. Rev. 261, 265 (1992).

22. *But cf.* De Niz Robles v. Lynch, 803 F.3d 1165, 1173 (10th Cir. 2015) (Gorsuch, J.).

23. *Compare* 1 Hickman & Pierce, *supra* note 13, § 4.9, *and* Russell L. Weaver & Linda D. Jellum, Chenery II *and the Development of Federal Administrative Law*, 58 Admin. L. Rev. 815, 824–26 (2006), *with* Magill, *supra* note 2, at 1424.

24. *See* Bowen v. Georgetown Univ. Hosp., 488 U.S. 204 (1988).

25. *See, e.g.*, *AT&T*, 454 F.3d at 332.

26. *E.g.*, *id.*; Epilepsy Found. v. NLRB, 268 F.3d 1095, 1103 (D.C. Cir. 2001).

27. *See* Williams Nat'l Gas Co. v. FERC, 3 F.3d 1544, 1554 (D.C. Cir. 1993).

retroactively.[28] This test is mainly concerned with protecting reliance interests. Sometimes courts will even ask whether a party actually relied on an existing policy to its detriment.[29] This retroactivity limitation might reside in the prohibition against arbitrary and capricious decision-making,[30] but it may also be understood as a freestanding, equitably based limitation on unfair retroactive decision-making.[31]

Sometimes agencies will deny their own decision's retroactive effect, relying on much the same standard established by the courts.[32] Although courts usually do not defer to an agency's decision to give a decision rule retroactive effect, they sometimes give deference to an agency's decision not to apply a rule retroactively. In the latter situation, the court typically will demand that the agency explain why it departed from the presumption that a decision rule applies in the case announcing the rule. Agencies do not always carry this burden.[33]

When a court forecloses an agency from applying a decision rule retroactively, or the agency declines to do so of its own accord, the rule will usually be applied prospectively: The agency will treat the decision announcing the policy as a precedent that controls the outcome of future cases involving the same issue but unrelated parties. Of course, a party in a future case may always ask the agency to overrule the precedent.

A final question arises: Is prospective-only application allowed in adjudication—or is it really an impermissible form of rulemaking? The plurality opinion and the dissenting opinions in *NLRB v. Wyman-Gordon*

28. Verizon Tel. Cos. v. FCC, 269 F.3d 1098, 1109 (D.C. Cir. 2011) (citations and internal quotation marks omitted); *see, e.g.*, *AT&T*, 454 F.3d at 332; *Epilepsy Found.*, 268 F.3d at 1102–03; *Willams Nat'l Gas*, 3 F.3d at 1553–54. The foundational case is *Retail, Wholesale & Department Store Union v. NLRB*, 466 F.2d 380, 390 (D.C. Cir. 1972).

29. *See, e.g.*, Qwest Servs. Corp. v. FCC, 509 F.3d 531, 540 (D.C. Cir. 2007); *AT&T*, 454 F.3d at 332.

30. *See* Bressman, *supra* note 19, at 535 n.348; *see also* Daniel T. Deacon, Chenery II *Revisited*, 92 Geo. Wash. L. Rev. 1050, 1093 (2024).

31. *See, e.g.*, Cassell v. FCC, 154 F.3d 478, 486 (D.C. Cir. 1998); *see also* John F. Manning, *Non-Legislative Rules*, 72 Geo. Wash. L. Rev. 893, 908 (2004). *But cf.* De Niz Robles v. Lynch, 803 F.3d 1165, 1177 (10th Cir. 2015) (due process); *see also* Greene, *supra* note 21, at 266–67.

32. *See, e.g.*, Sanitary Truck Drivers & Helpers Loc. 350 v. NLRB, 45 F.4th 38 (D.C. Cir. 2022); Total Sec. Mgmt. Ill. 1, LLC, 364 N.L.R.B. 1532 (2016).

33. *See, e.g.*, *Qwest Servs.*, 509 F.3d at 539–40.

Co. together might have been read to say "no."[34] But no such general limitation seems to have taken hold in case law. To the contrary, a court's finding that a decisional rule may not be applied retroactively usually carries the implication that it can (and even should) be applied prospectively.[35] Sometimes an agency decision will note explicitly that its holding will be applied only prospectively.[36]

Conclusion

When the Court decided *Chenery II* in 1947, most agencies established policy by adjudication, not rulemaking. It was not until the early 1970s that rulemaking became the predominate form of agency policymaking. Today only a few agencies—most notably the NLRB—establish significant policy by adjudication with any regularity. But policymaking by adjudication at least in more modest forms retains a central place in agency governance, and despite continued objections to the *Chenery II* doctrine from some critics of the administrative state,[37] the Supreme Court is unlikely to revisit it.

Bibliography

Ronald A. Cass, *Models of Administrative Action*, 72 Va. L. Rev. 363 (1986).

Daniel T. Deacon, Chenery II *Revisited*, 92 Geo. Wash. L. Rev. 1050 (2024).

Abner S. Greene, *Adjudicative Retroactivity in Administrative Law*, 1991 Sup. Ct. Rev. 261 (1992).

Gary Lawson & Joseph Postell, *Against the* Chenery II *"Doctrine,"* 99 Notre Dame L. Rev. 47 (2023).

---

34. *See* 394 U.S. 759 (1969); *see also* Bowen v. Georgetown Univ. Hosp., 488 U.S. 204, 221 (1988) (Scalia, J., concurring).

35. *See, e.g.*, *De Niz Robles*, 803 F.3d at 1177 n.8; Greene, *supra* note 21, at 300 n.125.

36. *See, e.g.*, Total Sec. Mgmt. Ill. 1, LLC , 364 N.L.R.B. 1532, 1532, 1543 (2016).

37. *See, e.g.*, Gary Lawson & Joseph Postell, *Against the* Chenery II *"Doctrine,"* 99 Notre Dame L. Rev. 47 (2023); Nielson, *supra* note 17.

M. Elizabeth Magill, *Agency Choice of Policymaking Form*, 71 U. Chi. L. Rev. 1383 (2024).

Aaron L. Nielson, *Three Wrong Turns in Agency Adjudication*, 28 Geo. Mason L. Rev. 657 (2021).

Antonin Scalia, *Back to Basics: Making Law Without Making Rules*, Regulation, July/Aug. (1981).

Roy A. Schotland, *A Sporting Proposition*—SEC v. Chenery, *in* Administrative Law Stories 169 (Peter L. Strauss ed., 2006).

Cass R. Sunstein & Adrian Vermeule, *The Morality of Administrative Law*, 131 Harv. L. Rev. 1924 (2018).

Russell L. Weaver, Chenery II*: A Forty-Year Retrospective*, 40 Admin. L. Rev. 161 (1988).

Chapter 3

Board of Regents v. Roth, 408 U.S. 564 (1972); *Perry v. Sindermann*, 408 U.S. 593 (1972)

William Jordan

Goldberg v. Kelly[1] represented the high point of a broadly applicable conception of constitutional due process as a bulwark against abuse by government officials. *Board of Regents of State Colleges v. Roth* marked a retreat from that broad concept, to be followed a few years later by *Mathews v. Eldridge*.[2] *Perry v. Sindermann*, decided the same day as *Roth*, indicated that the retreat was not yet a rout, but the U.S. Supreme Court again interpreted due process protections more narrowly than suggested by previous decisions. *Roth* also suggested the possibility of due process protections against government harm to an individual's reputation, but the Court later significantly retreated from that suggestion.

1. 397 U.S. 254 (1970). The case is the subject of Chapter 4.
2. 424 U.S. 319 (1976). *Roth* addressed the availability of due process protections, while *Mathews v. Eldridge* addressed the nature of procedures required if due process attaches. *Mathews* is the subject of Chapter 8.

The Road to *Roth*

The Due Process Clauses of the Fifth and 14th Amendments provide that "no person shall be . . . deprived of life, liberty, or property, without due process of law."[3] In 1951, Justice Frankfurter described due process as "respect enforced by law for that feeling of just treatment which . . . cannot be imprisoned within the treacherous limits of any formula" and "a profound attitude of fairness between . . . the individual and government."[4] In language we will see again, he said that the Court had recognized "the right to be heard before being condemned to suffer grievous loss of any kind."[5] As described in Chapter 4 on *Goldberg*, the 1960s saw a dramatic expansion of government entitlements, adding to those already created during the New Deal. So too, employment expanded at all levels of government, particularly in state universities and colleges. The loss of either a statutory entitlement such as welfare or a government job could certainly qualify as a "grievous loss" under Frankfurter's conception of due process.

But the Due Process Clause refers only to deprivation of "life, liberty, or property," indicating that due process protections do not apply unless government action affects one of those interests. Was the clause intended to ensure basic fairness in any interactions between individuals and the state, as Frankfurter's "grievous loss" language suggests? Or was it limited to interactions involving interests fitting neatly into one of those three categories?

Goldberg left this unclear. Writing for the Court, Justice Brennan recognized statutory entitlements as a form of property, but he also said a welfare beneficiary's entitlement to due process "is influenced by the extent to which he may be 'condemned to suffer grievous loss.'"[6]

3. This is the language of the Fifth Amendment. U.S. CONST. amend. V. The 14th Amendment is slightly different, providing that "nor shall any State deprive any person of life, liberty, or property, without due process of law." U.S. CONST. amend. XIV, § 1. For ease of reference, this entry refers simply to the "Due Process Clause."

4. Joint Anti-Fascist Refugee Comm. v. McGrath, 341 U.S. 123, 162 (1951).

5. *Id.* at 168.

6. *Goldberg*, 397 U.S. at 263.

Roth Requires a State-Recognized Property Interest

Board of Regents v. Roth held that due process protections apply only to interests "within the Fourteenth Amendment's protection of liberty and property," rejecting broader protection of the individual against governmental abuse. David Roth was hired as an untenured assistant professor of political science at Wisconsin State University-Oshkosh for a fixed term of one year. No "statutory or administrative standards" defined eligibility for reemployment the following year. State law left the decision about whether to rehire an untenured professor to the "unfettered discretion of university officials."

Without stating reasons for its decision, the university told Roth that he would not be rehired for the following year. Roth sued, arguing the university was punishing him for statements critical of the university. He asserted violations of his right to due process under the 14th Amendment and free speech under the First Amendment.

Relying upon a pre-*Goldberg* decision,[7] the district court ruled for Roth after balancing his interest in continued employment against the university's interest in declining to rehire him without a hearing or statement of reasons. The court of appeals affirmed.

Emphasizing that "we must look not to the 'weight' but to the nature of the interest at stake," the Supreme Court emphatically rejected a balancing approach in determining the applicability of due process to government action affecting an individual. Instead, the government action must affect the individual's interest in life, liberty, or property. As to property, the Court described due process protection as "a safeguard of the security of interests that a person has already acquired in specific benefits." A tenured position would qualify, as would employment during the term of a contract. But a "unilateral expectation" is not enough. There must be a "legitimate claim of entitlement" of the sort "upon which people rely in their daily lives." Roth's untenured position, with no mutual expectation of continued employment, was not enough.

---

7. *See* Cafeteria & Rest. Workers Union, Loc. 473 v. McElroy, 367 U.S. 886 (1961).

In reaching this conclusion, the Court held that property rights are "not created by the Constitution." They are defined by "existing rules or understandings that stem from an independent source such as state law."

Perry v. Sindermann and the Concept of Entitlement Property

Much like David Roth, Robert Sindermann held a one-year position in the Texas state college system. But Sindermann had held such positions for a decade in the system and under four successive one-year contracts at his then-current institution, which had no formal tenure system. Unlike Roth, Sindermann claimed that statements by college officials had created a de facto tenure system, that he qualified for tenure under those statements, and that written system-wide guidelines provided that a teacher employed in the system for seven or more years has "some form of job tenure."

In *Perry v. Sindermann*, the Court recognized that this sort of arrangement could constitute a property interest under the Due Process Clause: "A person's interest in a benefit is a 'property' interest for due process purposes if there are such rules or mutually explicit understandings that support his claim of entitlement to the benefit and that he may invoke at a hearing." Even without "an explicit contractual provision," a teacher could have a property interest in reemployment. This would be a matter of the state common law of contracts, which "long has employed a process by which agreements, though not formalized in writing, may be 'implied.'" Considering Sindermann's factual claims, the Court held that Sindermann was entitled the "opportunity" to prove at a trial the "legitimacy of his claim of . . . entitlement [to his job] in light of 'the policies and practices of the institution.'" If he prevailed, he would be entitled to an explanation for his non-retention and a due process hearing to challenge those reasons.

Implications of *Roth/Sindermann* for Claiming Property Interests

Goldberg expanded due process property to statutory entitlements. *Roth/Sindermann* expanded it to include both formal and de facto implied contracts with government. But both recognize a significant limitation. They in effect allow government to control the availability of the constitutional right to due process. The legislature or government entity that created the entitlement can decide to eliminate it. Thus, in 1996 for example, Congress enacted welfare reform legislation conferring discretion on state agencies and making benefits subject to fiscal constraints. In doing so, Congress eliminated the previous entitlement to welfare payments and probably in effect removed payment terminations or denials from the ambit of the Due Process Clause.[8] Similarly, public colleges and universities can avoid due process requirements by saying to employees nothing about their prospects for future reemployment or explicitly stating that, as in *Roth*-like situations, nontenured faculty hold only one-year appointments with no agreement as to reemployment the following year.[9]

Thus, this seeming due process explosion to a significant extent retained the right-privilege distinction in another guise. The legislature or government entity can simply eliminate the entitlement, thereby eliminating due process protection against abuse in implementing the employment or benefit program at issue.

In *Arnett v. Kennedy*,[10] decided two years after *Roth* and *Sindermann*, then-Justice Rehnquist sought to give government actors control over the procedures available to those deprived of entitlements. *Arnett* involved a non-probationary federal employee who could be dismissed only for cause. He was thus comparable to a tenured professor protected by due process under *Roth* and *Sindermann*. In *Arnett*, however, a statute provided specific procedural rights for such an employee subject to dismissal. The employee argued that the limited procedures violated due process. For a three-Justice plurality, Justice Rehnquist wrote that when a substantive right (in this case employment) is "inextricably intertwined" with certain procedures, the person seeking to protect the right must "take the bitter with the sweet."[11]

8. *See* Personal Responsibility and Work Opportunity Reconciliation Act of 1996, Pub. L. No. 104-193, § 103(a)(l), 110 Stat. 2105, 2113 (codified at 42 U.S.C. § 601(b)); Richard J. Pierce, Jr., *The Due Process Counterrevolution of the 1990s?*, 96 Colum. L. Rev. 1973, 1990–91 (1996).

9. *See* Carol Herrnstadt Shulman, *Employment of Nontenured Faculty: Some Implications of* Roth *and* Sindermann, 51 Denv. L.J. 215 (1974).

10. 416 U.S. 134 (1974).

11. *Id.* at 154.

Once again, the legislature or government entity would control the procedures available to protect against government abuse. The "bitter with the sweet" principle never achieved a majority. The Court explicitly rejected it in *Cleveland Board of Education v. Loudermill*,[12] declaring that rights to life, liberty, and property "cannot be deprived except pursuant to constitutionally adequate procedures."[13] Thus, federal and state legislatures and entities can create or eliminate entitlements, but they cannot dictate procedures less than the minimum required by due process.

With the *Roth/Sindermann* importation of contract concepts into the due process arena, does due process apply to the millions of government contracts of various kinds? So far the Court has applied the contract reasoning only to employment contracts, and most lower courts have declined to apply it to other government contracts.[14]

Liberty Interest in Reputation and the Name-Clearing Hearing Under *Roth*

In *Board of Regents v. Roth*, the Court also considered the argument that the state university's refusal to rehire Roth infringed upon his liberty interest by harming his standing in the community. The Court rejected this argument because the university had given no reason for its action, so "there is no suggestion whatever that the respondent's 'good name, reputation, honor, or integrity' is at stake." The Court noted that "there is no suggestion the State, in declining to reemploy the respondent, imposed on him a stigma or other disability that foreclosed his freedom to take advantage of other employment opportunities."

The Court's reference to stigma suggested that a governmental statement harmful to an individual's reputation could infringe a liberty interest in violation of the Due Process Clause. Edward Davis made just this argument in *Paul v. Davis*[15] in response to a city police chief's inclusion of his name

12. 470 U.S. 532 (1985).
13. *Id.* at 541.
14. *See* 1 Kristin E. Hickman & Richard J. Pierce, Jr., Administrative Law Treatise § 7.4 (7th ed. 2024).
15. 424 U.S. 693 (1976).

and photograph on a list of "ACTIVE SHOPLIFTERS" widely distributed to local businesses. Davis asserted that the designation would "inhibit him" from shopping and "seriously impair his future employment opportunities."[16]

In *Paul v. Davis*, the Court rejected the argument that mere harm to reputation infringes upon an individual's liberty interest protected by the Due Process Clause. Refusing to constitutionalize the tort of defamation, the Court limited the reach of the *Roth* "stigma" concept to situations in which any defamation occurred "in the course of the termination of employment." Outside that context, a defamatory government statement triggers due process only if it "distinctly alter[s] or extinguishe[s]" "a right or status previously recognized by state law."[17] The Court distinguished *Wisconsin v. Constantineau*,[18] in which the plaintiff's name had been included on a list of known harmful drinkers of alcohol. There, the Court had found infringement of a liberty interest because alcohol vendors were forbidden from selling alcohol to anyone on the list. This was the denial of a preexisting right to purchase alcohol. Mere damage to reputation, as in *Paul v. Davis*, did not meet this test.

Despite this narrowing of its potential reach, *Roth* left the valuable legacy of a name-clearing hearing for those subject to dismissal from government employment. If, in dismissing an employee, a government makes any charge that would harm the employee's "good name, reputation, honor, or integrity," the employee has a right to "an opportunity to clear his name."

Conclusion

The *Roth/Sindermann* doctrine has prompted much criticism to the effect that due process rights should not be determined by the states, but by the Constitution through the federal courts, generally through some form of "grievous loss" analysis.[19] Indeed, one commentary has argued that *Roth*'s

16. *Id.* at 697.
17. *Id.* at 711.
18. 400 U.S. 433 (1971).
19. *See, e.g.*, William W. Van Alstyne, *Cracks in "The New Property": Adjudicative Due Process in the Administrative State*, 62 Cornell L. Rev. 445 (1977); Hickman & Pierce, *supra* note 14, § 7.4.

insistence upon a specific life, liberty, or property interest was the real due process revolution, narrowing previously broader protections against government abuses.[20] In defense of the doctrine, however, one commentator has argued that it was necessary to protect the effective exercise of administrative discretion, which would otherwise collapse under the administrative and judicial review burdens imposed by broader applicability of the Due Process Clause.[21]

The future may look very different, however, depending upon future appointments to the Supreme Court. In 2015, a plurality of the Court—Justices Scalia and Thomas and Chief Justice Roberts—presaged significant narrowing of the reach of the Due Process Clause. In *Kerry v. Din*,[22] an American citizen living in the United States challenged the federal government's refusal to explain why it had denied a visa to her husband, an Afghan citizen who lived in that country. The plaintiff argued that the denial of her husband's visa deprived her of her right to live with her husband in this country. The plurality found no such general constitutional right and refused to extend the "liberty" interest to this situation. Indeed, reaching back to the Magna Carta as discussed by Coke and Blackstone, the plurality limited the Due Process Clause to narrow traditional concepts of property and liberty and a version of due process as referring only to "the law of the land."[23] If this understanding of due process should prevail, it could eliminate the *Goldberg* principle that government entitlements are a form of property, and perhaps even the *Paul v. Davis* principle that government statements effectively altering one's legal standing impinge upon liberty interests. With the appointments of Justices Gorsuch, Kavanaugh, and Barrett, the due process landscape could change dramatically over time.

20. *See* Sidney A. Shapiro & Richard E. Levy, *Government Benefits and the Rule of Law: Toward a Standards-Based Theory of Due Process*, 57 ADMIN. L. REV. 107 (2005).
21. *See* Peter N. Simon, *Liberty and Property in the Supreme Court: A Defense of* Roth *and* Perry, 71 CALIF. L. REV. 146 (1983).
22. 576 U.S. 86 (2015).
23. HICKMAN & PIERCE, *supra* note 14, § 7.4.

Bibliography

1 Kristin E. Hickman & Richard J. Pierce, Jr., Administrative Law Treatise § 7.4 (7th ed. 2024).

Jeffrey S. Lubbers, *Constitutional and Statutory Foundations*, *in* A Guide to Federal Agency Adjudication 245, 246–47 (Jeremy S. Graboyes ed., 3d ed. 2023).

Jerry L. Mashaw, Due Process in the Administrative State (1985).

Richard J. Pierce, Jr., *The Due Process Counterrevolution of the 1990s?*, 96 Colum. L. Rev. 1973 (1996).

Edward L. Rubin, *Due Process and the Administrative State*, 72 Calif. L. Rev. 1044 (1984).

Section of Admin. L. & Regul. Prac., Am. Bar Ass'n, A Blackletter Statement of Federal Administrative Law pt. 1, § II (2d ed. 2013).

Sidney A. Shapiro & Richard E. Levy, *Government Benefits and the Rule of Law: Toward a Standards-Based Theory of Due Process*, 57 Admin. L. Rev. 107 (2005).

Carol Herrnstadt Shulman, *Employment of Nontenured Faculty: Some Implications of* Roth *and* Sindermann, 51 Denv. L.J. 215 (1974).

Peter N. Simon, *Liberty and Property in the Supreme Court: A Defense of* Roth *and* Perry, 71 Calif. L. Rev. 146 (1983).

William W. Van Alstyne, *Cracks in "The New Property": Adjudicative Due Process in the Administrative State*, 62 Cornell L. Rev. 445 (1977).

Chapter 4

Goldberg v. Kelly, 397 U.S. 254 (1970)

Kathryn Kovacs

Goldberg v. Kelly is among the most significant administrative law decisions because it marks the constitutionalizing of administrative procedure. In *Goldberg*, the U.S. Supreme Court for the first time applied the Constitution's 14th Amendment's Due Process Clause to an agency adjudication regarding a statutory benefit. In addition, the Court proclaimed itself the arbiter of what process satisfies the Constitution. After *Goldberg*, a legislature may create a statutory entitlement, but the Supreme Court reserves the power to determine the process by which that entitlement may be withdrawn.

The Rising Tide

The New Deal ushered in a vast expansion of government functions. Agencies changed as the government took on a wider role in solving societal problems and providing benefits to individuals. Many of the social welfare programs that have become entrenched in our law originated in this era. This expansion of government functions raised accompanying concerns about how agencies make decisions that affect people's lives.

The 14th Amendment parallels the Fifth Amendment by providing that a state may not "deprive any person of life, liberty, or property without due process of law."[1] Traditionally, the Supreme Court had assumed that the

1. U.S. Const. amend. IV, § 1.

Due Process Clauses only applied to common-law "rights," not to statutory "privileges," and that, when it applied, it required a hearing resembling a full civil trial. That traditional model did not fit well in the post-New Deal world of agency adjudications; it was simply too rigid for the volume and variety of agency decisions and decision-making contexts in the expanded administrative state.

The 1960s saw the onset of the so-called War on Poverty. One of the major strikes in that war was Professor Charles A. Reich's seminal article, "The New Property."[2] Reich argued that the government had become a significant source of wealth and thus many government entitlements should be considered property and protected against deprivation without due process. Armed with that analysis, welfare advocates relied upon *Goldberg* as part of the fight against poverty and the societal ills poverty foments.[3]

The plaintiffs, led by John Kelly, filed their claims against various New York state and city officials under 42 U.S.C. § 1983, alleging that the city had terminated their welfare benefits without notice or a hearing prior to the termination. A three-judge panel of the district court held for the plaintiffs. The court found "one overpowering fact" controlling: "a welfare recipient is destitute." The court thought it would be unconscionable to cut off welfare benefits "in the face of this kind of 'brutal need' without a prior hearing of some sort . . . unless overwhelming considerations justify it." The trial court concluded that the city's concerns did not override the plaintiffs' needs, and thus the procedures the city provided did not satisfy due process.

New York City Commissioner of Social Services Jack Goldberg appealed to the Supreme Court. The Court had ample means to avoid a decision on the due process issue. The case may have been deemed moot because by the time it reached the Court, most, if not all, of the plaintiffs had been restored to the welfare rolls or received a fair hearing. Alternatively, the Court might have avoided the constitutional issue by focusing on the relevant federal statute, which required the state to provide a "fair hearing" before finally terminating welfare benefits. Finally, the Court might have at least delayed its consideration to give the federal Department of Health, Education, and

2. Charles A. Reich, *The New Property*, 73 Yale L.J. 733 (1964); *see also* Charles A. Reich, *Individual Rights and Social Welfare: The Emerging Legal Issues*, 74 Yale L.J. 1245 (1965).
3. *See* Richard J. Pierce, Jr., *The Due Process Counterrevolution of the 1990s?*, 96 Colum. L. Rev. 1973, 1974–76 (1996).

Welfare time to implement its then-new regulations, which required that welfare payments be continued until the recipient was given notice and an opportunity for a conference.[4] None of these issues, however, prevented the Court from reaching the constitutional issue.

The High-Water Mark

The Supreme Court affirmed the trial court's judgment in favor of the plaintiffs by a vote of five to three.[5] Narrowly, the Court's holding concerned timing. The city already provided a full hearing after terminating a person's welfare benefits. The Court held that the city had to provide an evidentiary hearing before terminating benefits. The "crucial factor," the Court said, was that terminating aid could deprive recipients "of the very means by which to live" while awaiting a hearing. The city's countervailing interests did not override the plaintiffs' "desperate" need.

Two elements of *Goldberg* make it among the most important Supreme Court decisions in administrative law. First, *Goldberg* definitively eliminated the traditional distinction between rights and privileges under the Due Process Clauses. The Court had already made a statement to that effect in 1961.[6] Indeed, both the defendants and the federal government appearing as amici curiae conceded that the 14th Amendment's Due Process Clause applied to the termination of welfare benefits.[7] Nonetheless, *Goldberg* put the nail in the coffin of the rights-privileges distinction.[8]

The Court's analysis of this issue was unclear. Justice Brennan, writing for the Court, indicated that termination of welfare benefits triggers the Due Process Clause because welfare benefits "are a matter of statutory

4. Following President Nixon's inauguration, the Department had postponed the effective date of those regulations until July 1, 1970, several months after the Court decided *Goldberg*. Chief Justice Burger in his dissent questioned why the Court went forward in light of the new regulations.

5. Justice Blackmun did not fill the seat left empty when Justice Fortas resigned until after the Court decided *Goldberg*.

6. *See* Cafeteria & Rest. Workers Union v. McElroy, 367 U.S. 886, 897–98 (1961).

7. *See* Brief for the United States as Amicus Curiae at 6, Wheeler v. Montgomery, 397 U.S. 280 (1970), Goldberg v. Kelly, 397 U.S. 254 (1970) (Nos. 14 & 62).

8. *See* William W. Van Alstyne, *The Demise of the Right-Privilege Distinction in Constitutional Law*, 81 HARV. L. REV. 1439 (1968).

entitlement for persons qualified to receive them." In a footnote, Justice Brennan quoted from Professor Reich and suggested that welfare should be regarded as property even though it did not qualify as such under the common law. Justice Brennan then stated that termination of welfare benefits "involves state action that adjudicates important rights." In the same paragraph, Justice Brennan asserted that a welfare beneficiary's entitlement to due process "is influenced by the extent to which he may be 'condemned to suffer grievous loss.'" This paragraph sowed confusion about when government benefits qualify as property under the Due Process Clauses. The Court elucidated that issue in *Board of Regents v. Roth*[9] and *Perry v. Sindermann*,[10] which are addressed in their own chapters.

Despite that temporary confusion, the Court's abandonment of the rights-privileges distinction, accompanied by its holding that due process applies to the termination of welfare benefits, imported the Due Process Clauses into the modern administrative state. *Goldberg* was the first time the Court applied due process to a government benefit that previously would have been considered a mere privilege. Thus, *Goldberg* subjected a wide variety of administrative decisions to due process analysis and opened the floodgates to due process claims against state and federal administrative agencies.

A second element of *Goldberg* warrants its inclusion in the canon of administrative law opinions: The Court in *Goldberg* repudiated the traditional assumption that due process requires a trial-type hearing whenever it applies. Instead, the Court in *Goldberg* established itself as the arbiter of what process is sufficient under the Due Process Clauses. The Court declined the solicitor general's request that the Court defer to the secretary of health, education, and welfare's "expert judgment" that the new regulations were "the most appropriate method for accomplishing the congressional directive."[11] Before terminating welfare benefits, the Court said, the city had to provide only "minimum procedural safeguards" tailored to the circumstances. Nonetheless, the process the Court ultimately required the city to provide in *Goldberg* resembled a full trial, lacking only government-appointed counsel and formal findings of fact.

9. 408 U.S. 564 (1972). *Roth* is the subject of Chapter 3.
10. 408 U.S. 593 (1972). *Perry* is the subject of Chapter 3.
11. Brief for the United States as Amicus Curiae, *supra* note 7, at 11.

The dissents, soon joined by academics, thought the Court had gone too far in requiring the city to provide such extensive process before terminating welfare benefits. Justice Black argued that the Court had intruded on Congress's constitutional authority by effectively legislating welfare termination procedures. He argued that the majority's opinion was ungrounded, based only on the Justices' sense of fairness, and hence would be unpredictable in its application. Justice Black also argued that the decision would end up harming the poor by spurring governments to avoid putting claimants on the welfare rolls initially. In sum, such determinations should be left to the legislature. Chief Justice Burger took the position that the Court should have stayed its hand and allowed the new regulations to take effect rather than rigidly constitutionalizing administrative procedure. Chief Justice Burger also expressed concern that the majority's decision would hurt the poor by redirecting funds away from welfare payments and towards hearings.[12]

The Receding Tide

Goldberg marked the start of the "due process revolution" in administrative law. Due process litigation increased, and the courts soon applied *Goldberg* to other government benefits. Federal, state, and local governments amended their statutory procedures to comply with *Goldberg* as well.[13]

Yet, *Goldberg* turned out to be the high-water mark of due process in administrative law. Within six years, four new Justices took the bench. Although it never overruled *Goldberg*, the Court soon began to back off from *Goldberg*, perhaps recognizing that requiring agencies to provide trial-type hearings before terminating any statutory entitlement would impose an intolerable burden. *Goldberg* remains the only administrative law case in which the Supreme Court has required an agency to provide a full hearing before terminating a statutory benefit. Since *Goldberg*, the Court has narrowed the scope of interests that trigger due process protection as well as the breadth of procedures required in cases where due process applies.

12. Justice Stewart also dissented, merely citing *Cafeteria & Restaurant Workers Union v. McElroy*, 367 U.S. 886 (1961). That citation indicates that Justice Stewart thought that the government's interests outweighed the plaintiffs' interests in a pre-termination hearing.

13. *See* Jason Parkin, *Adaptable Due Process*, 160 U. PA. L. REV. 1309, 1315–16, 1323–25 (2012).

The chapters on *Board of Regents v. Roth*[14] and *Mathews v. Eldridge*[15] address those developments.

The dissents turned out to be prescient. Among other things, states replaced social workers with clerks who applied rigid formulas, arguably making the welfare system even worse for claimants.[16] Then in 1996, Congress repealed the welfare program at issue in *Goldberg* and replaced it with a program that gives states wide policymaking discretion and explicitly provides no individual entitlement.[17] This is part of *Goldberg*'s legacy: legislative attempts to provide statutory benefits without triggering due process protection.

Nonetheless, *Goldberg v. Kelly* is remembered as the case that applied constitutional due process to administrative agencies and opened the doors to due process claims in administrative law. Though the Court has backed away from *Goldberg*, it has never shut that door. The Due Process Clauses remain a bulwark against agency overreaching, and the Court itself remains the arbiter of what process satisfies due process.

Bibliography

William J. Brennan, Jr., *Reason, Passion, and the Progress of the Law*, 10 Cardozo L. Rev. 3 (1988).

Henry J. Friendly, *Some Kind of Hearing*, 123 U. Pa. L. Rev. 1267 (1975).

Jerry L. Mashaw, Due Process in the Administrative State (1985).

Jerry L. Mashaw, *Management Side of Due Process: Some Theoretical and Litigation Notes on the Assurance of Accuracy, Fairness, and Timeliness in the Adjudication of Social Welfare Claims*, 59 Cornell L. Rev. 772 (1974).

Judith Resnik, *The Story of* Goldberg*: Why This Case Is Our Shorthand*, *in* Civil Procedure Stories 473 (Kevin M. Clermont ed., 2d ed. 2008).

14. 408 U.S. 564 (1972). *Roth* is the subject of Chapter 3.

15. 424 U.S. 319 (1976). *Mathews* is the subject of Chapter 8.

16. *See* William H. Simon, *The Invention and Reinvention of Welfare Rights*, 44 Md. L. Rev. 1 (1985).

17. Personal Responsibility and Work Opportunity Reconciliation Act of 1996, Pub. L. No. 104-193, § 103(a)(l), 110 Stat. 2105, 2113 (codified at 42 U.S.C. § 601(b)).

Edward L. Rubin, *Due Process and the Administrative State*, 72 CALIF. L. REV. 1044 (1984).

SECTION OF ADMIN. L. & REGUL. PRAC., AM. BAR ASS'N, A BLACKLETTER STATEMENT OF FEDERAL ADMINISTRATIVE LAW pt. 1, § II (2d ed. 2013).

Symposium, *The Legacy of* Goldberg v. Kelly*: A Twenty Year Perspective*, 56 BROOK. L. REV. 729 (1990).

Chapter 5

United States v. Florida East Coast Railway Co., 410 U.S. 224 (1973)

Emily Bremer

United States v. Florida East Coast Railway Co. has been described as one of the most "underrated" cases in the administrative law canon.[1] Its place in the canon was assured by its straightforward, blackletter law holding regarding the circumstances in which agencies must observe the formal rulemaking requirements of the Administrative Procedure Act (APA).[2] The case's legacy, however, reaches far beyond its precise holding. As a practical matter, *Florida East Coast Railway* all but eliminated formal rulemaking and made it easier for agencies to use informal rulemaking.[3] Scholars applaud the case for these desirable consequences, while critiquing the U.S. Supreme Court's flawed reasoning, which was a product of deeper defects in the Court's decision-making process.[4] Despite its difficulties, *Florida East Coast Railway* fundamentally altered administrative law's structure by paving the way for informal rulemaking to become administration's default policymaking tool.

---

1. Michael P. Healy, Florida East Coast Railway *and the Structure of Administrative Law*, 58 ADMIN. L. REV. 1039, 1039 (2006); *cf.* Henry J. Friendly, *"Some Kind of Hearing,"* 123 U. PA. L. REV. 1267, 1305 (1975).
2. *See* 5 U.S.C. §§ 556–557.
3. *See id.* § 553.
4. *See* Kent Barnett, *How the Supreme Court Derailed Formal Rulemaking*, 85 GEO. WASH. L. REV. ARGUENDO 1 (2017). For a defense of the decision, see Emily Bremer, *Blame (or Thank) the Administrative Procedure Act for* Florida East Coast Railway, 97 CHI.-KENT L. REV. 79 (2022).

The Dispute

Rulemaking, which under the APA is the "agency process for formulating, amending, or repealing a rule,"[5] comes in two principal forms: formal and informal. Formal rulemaking involves a trial-like evidentiary hearing governed by sections 556 and 557 of the APA. These procedures include oral argument, cross-examination, and a presiding official endowed with judge-like powers. In contrast, informal rulemaking uses the notice-and-comment procedures established by section 553 of the APA and fleshed out by a robust body of judicial decisions. (Informal rulemaking is sometimes called "notice-and-comment rulemaking.") An agency authorized to adopt rules determines which procedure it should use based on the language of its organic statute. This approach is mandated by section 553(c) of the APA, which provides that formal rulemaking must be used "[w]hen rules are required by statute to be made on the record after opportunity for an agency hearing."[6] In the absence of such a statutory requirement, the agency may use informal rulemaking. Whether conducted formally or informally, the product of any rulemaking is a "rule," which the APA defines as an "agency statement of general or particular applicability and future effect designed to implement, interpret, or prescribe law or policy or describing the organization, procedure, or practice requirements of an agency." This definition expressly includes a number of specific kinds of agency action, including ratemaking (i.e., "the approval or prescription for the future of rates"[7]).

The question presented in *Florida East Coast Railway* was whether the Interstate Commerce Commission (ICC) had to use formal rulemaking to adopt per diem charges on railroads to address a persistent, nationwide shortage of boxcars.[8] The ICC adopted these charges under section 1(14)(a) of the Esch Car Service Act (Esch Act), which authorized the agency, "after hearing, on a complaint or upon its own initiative without complaint, [to] establish reasonable rules, regulations, and practices with respect to car

5. 5 U.S.C. § 551(5).
6. *Id.* § 553(c).
7. *Id.* § 551(4).
8. Barnett, *supra* note 4, at 3.

service."[9] Both the ICC and the courts had consistently interpreted this provision, enacted in 1917, to require formal rulemaking.

In 1966, Congress directed the ICC to address the boxcar shortage, but without modifying the statute's "after hearing" language. The ICC was slow to implement this new statutory responsibility. At a 1969 congressional hearing, the ICC explained to impatient legislators that the Esch Act required the agency to conduct further formal proceedings before it could act. After the hearing, however, "[t]he Commission, now apparently imbued with a new sense of mission," tentatively adopted the per diem charges. The agency finalized this decision in 1970, without holding the further oral evidentiary hearings that it had once thought legally required and that multiple parties had requested. The railroads sued.

The Decision

A six-Justice majority of the Supreme Court upheld the Commission's use of written notice-and-comment rulemaking procedures against the railroads' challenge.[10] Writing for the majority, then-Justice Rehnquist reasoned that the statutory phrase "after hearing" was not "the equivalent of a statutory requirement that the rule 'be made on the record after opportunity for an agency hearing.'" Indeed, "the term 'hearing' as used [in the APA] does not necessarily embrace either the right to present evidence orally and to cross-examine opposing witnesses, or the right to present oral argument to the agency's decisionmaker." In rulemaking, an APA "hearing" may be formal, including these and other procedures identified in sections 556 and 557, or it may be informal and exclusively on paper, as contemplated by section 553. An APA "hearing" may even fall somewhere between these procedural poles, since section 556(d) suggests the possibility that a formal "hearing" may be conducted on paper. The agency's organic statute determines the proper procedure. Although the magic words "on the record" are not necessary to trigger the APA's formal rulemaking requirements, the statute must require

9. United States v. Allegheny-Ludlum Steel Corp., 406 U.S. 742, 757 (1972) (internal citation omitted).

10. *See* 1 Kristin E. Hickman & Richard J. Pierce, Jr., Administrative Law Treatise § 5.2 (7th ed. 2024).

more than just a "hearing." Applying this reasoning, the Court concluded that the Esch Act's "after hearing" language permitted the ICC to use an informal, written notice-and-comment proceeding under section 553 to make the factual determinations necessary to support the per diem charges.

Florida East Coast Railway's outcome was inevitable after the Court's decision a year earlier in *United States v. Allegheny-Ludlum Steel Corp.*[11] In *Allegheny-Ludlum*, the Court held that the same statutory provision did not require the ICC to use formal rulemaking to promulgate rules generally requiring railroads to return freight cars in the direction of the railroads that owned them after those cars were unloaded. With little discussion, the Court held that the "language of the Esch Car Service Act is insufficient to invoke" sections 556 and 557, particularly since the ICC's decision was an exercise of rulemaking rather than adjudicative authority.[12] *Allegheny-Ludlum* thus controlled the resolution of these core issues in *Florida East Coast Railway*.

Although *Allegheny-Ludlum* was a unanimous decision, *Florida East Coast Railway* was not. In the latter case, Justice Douglas dissented, joined by Justice Stewart. The dissent is "notoriously hard-to-follow,"[13] principally because it is unclear whether it is based on a different interpretation of the statutory term "hearing" or of the constitutional requirements of due process. The majority opinion is similarly afflicted, in both its affirmative reasoning and in its response to the dissent.[14] In any event, the dissent's principal objection was that the ICC's per diem charges were not purely legislative because they "impos[ed] on carriers by administrative fiat . . . a new financial liability." The dissent viewed this as adjudication. This distinguished the action from that at issue in *Allegheny-Ludlum* and required the agency to provide a formal hearing.

The Legacy

Florida East Coast Railway's legacy is broader than its holding. As Judge Friendly explained, "[i]f the case stood only for the proposition that the provision of the APA requiring trial-type procedures . . . should be limited

11. 406 U.S. at 742.
12. *Id.* at 757.
13. Barnett, *supra* note 4, at 3.
14. *See* 1 Hickman & Pierce, *supra* note 10, at 676; Bremer, *supra* note 4, at 109.

to the few statutes that used th[e] words [of section 553(c)] or something very much like them, the decision would be of relatively little moment."[15] But the opinion went further, redefining "hearing" as it appeared after the Esch Act. That term had long been interpreted to mean a formal, trial-like proceeding. *Florida East Coast Railway* held that, under the APA, "nothing more than notice and written comment is required if the action falls within the APA's expansive definition of rulemaking."[16]

As a practical matter, *Florida East Coast Railway* almost entirely eliminated formal rulemaking. It inspired judicial reluctance to require agencies to use trial-like, oral rulemaking hearings, which courts viewed as unnecessarily burdensome. Whether the case is understood as adopting a strict interpretation of section 553(c)[17] or "a presumption against formal rulemaking,"[18] its effect is clear. Today, few agencies use formal rulemaking at all, and still fewer do so with any regularity.

By vastly narrowing the circumstances in which formal rulemaking is required, *Florida East Coast Railway* aided the broader shift towards notice-and-comment rulemaking.[19] The case freed agencies to use informal, notice-and-comment rulemaking in a variety of regulatory contexts, including under statutes that previously had been interpreted to require formal hearings.[20] This endowed section 553 of the APA with newfound status as the presumptive source of rulemaking procedures. In *Vermont Yankee Nuclear Power Corp. v. Natural Resources Defense Council, Inc.*, decided a few years later, the Supreme Court explained that *Allegheny-Ludlum* and *Florida East Coast Railway* "held that generally speaking [section 553 of the APA] established the maximum procedural requirements which Congress was willing to have the courts impose upon agencies in conducting rulemaking procedures."[21] *Florida East Coast Railway* thus enabled informal rulemaking to become what it is today: the default device for agency policymaking.

15. *See* Friendly, *supra* note 1, at 1306.
16. *Id.* at 1307.
17. Harv. L. Rev. Ass'n, *III. Federal Statutes and Regulations: B. Review of Administrative Action*, 114 Harv. L. Rev. 369, 374 n.44 (2000) (internal citations omitted).
18. Emily Hammond Meazell, *Super Deference, the Science Obsession, and Judicial Review as Translation of Agency Science*, 109 Mich. L. Rev. 733, 757 n.127 (2011).
19. *See* Friendly, *supra* note 1, at 1273.
20. *Compare* Fed. Power Comm'n v. Nat. Gas Pipeline Co. of Am., 315 U.S. 575 (1942), *with* Phillips Petroleum Co. v. Fed. Power Comm'n, 475 F.2d 842 (10th Cir. 1973).
21. 435 U.S. 519, 524 (1978). The case is the subject of Chapter 25.

The overwhelming reaction to formal rulemaking's demise was "good riddance." When *Florida East Coast Railway* was decided, formal rulemaking was increasingly viewed as a burdensome, time-consuming, inefficient process particularly ill-suited to rulemaking.[22] In the years immediately preceding the Supreme Court's decision, the Administrative Conference of the United States adopted two recommendations against formal rulemaking: One criticized the Food and Drug Administration's use of the procedure in its infamous "Peanut Butter Rule,"[23] while the other more broadly urged that "Congress ordinarily should not impose mandatory procedural requirements other than those required by 5 U.S.C. § 553."[24] In the intervening decades, formal rulemaking has been subject to nearly unanimous "collective repudiation" by courts, agencies, scholars, and the bar.[25]

The Flaws

Although *Florida East Coast Railway* delivered a welcome policy outcome, the Court's reasoning is easy to critique. Some echoed Justice Douglas's dissent in the case and viewed the decision as "a sharp break with traditional notions of due process."[26] The Court seems to have misused authorities, citing judicial precedents and administrative materials for propositions they did not support.[27] It also seems to have violated traditional principles of statutory interpretation.[28] As Jonathan Siegel has explained, "[e]ven though the statutory requirement of a 'hearing,' in 1917," when the Esch Act was enacted, "would almost surely have been understood to require an oral

22. *See* Atl. Refin. Co. v. Pub. Serv. Comm'n of N.Y., 360 U.S. 378, 389 (1959); Robert W. Hamilton, *Rulemaking on a Record by the Food and Drug Administration*, 50 Tex. L. Rev. 1132 (1972).
23. Admin. Conf. of the U.S., *Rulemaking on a Record by the Food and Drug Administration*, 2 ACUS 42 (Dec. 7, 1971).
24. Admin. Conf. of the U.S., *Procedures for the Adoption of Rules of General Applicability*, 38 Fed. Reg. 19,792 (July 23, 1973).
25. Section of Admin. L. & Regul. Prac., Am. Bar Ass'n, Comments on H.R. 3010, The Regulatory Accountability Act of 2011, at 21 (2011), https://www.americanbar.org/content/dam/aba/administrative/administrative_law/commentson3010_final_nocover.authcheckdam.pdf.
26. *See* Henry J. Friendly, *Book Reviews*, 51 N.Y.U. L. Rev. 896, 901 (1976) (quoting Justice Douglas's dissent).
27. *See* Barnett, *supra* note 4, at 8–9.
28. Aaron L. Nielson, *In Defense of Formal Rulemaking*, 75 Ohio St. L.J. 237, 253 (2014).

evidentiary hearing, the Court read the requirement out of the statute before it, because the statute governed a rulemaking process, not an adjudication."[29] The decision is further muddied by the Court's failure to distinguish clearly between its statutory analysis and its due process analysis.

Digging below the surface of the Court's opinion, other research has identified several additional reasons to criticize the Court's decision-making process. First, *Allegheny-Ludlum* and *Florida East Coast Railway* arose under the Court's mandatory jurisdiction, and the Justices may have "hurriedly dispatched the formal rulemaking issue because they had little interest in these admittedly dry and inaccessible rulemaking cases."[30] Second, in *Allegheny-Ludlum*, the Court decided the procedural issue *sua sponte*, without the benefit of a lower court decision, briefing, or even oral argument.[31] Although rapidly issued and ill-considered, *Allegheny-Ludlum*'s consideration of the key issue effectively controlled the outcome of *Florida East Coast Railway*. One might reasonably wish that the Supreme Court had given more careful attention before deciding a matter so important to administrative law's fundamental structure.

Despite its many flaws, *Florida East Coast Railway* appears likely to remain solidly a part of the modern administrative state's legal foundation. Indeed, even those who have documented its defects generally have not called for it to be overturned. The decision is deeply ingrained in the fabric of administrative law. Moreover, support for the policy effects that are its primary legacy remains strong and widespread. The possibility of a formal rulemaking renaissance seems remote indeed.

Bibliography

Kent Barnett, *How the Supreme Court Derailed Formal Rulemaking*, 85 Geo. Wash. L. Rev. Arguendo 1 (2017).

Jack M. Beermann & Gary Lawson, *Reprocessing* Vermont Yankee, 75 Geo. Wash. L. Rev. 856 (2007).

29. Jonathan R. Siegel, *Textualism and Contextualism in Administrative Law*, 78 B.U. L. Rev. 1023, 1068 (1998).
30. Barnett, *supra* note 4, at 3.
31. *See id.* at 2, 4–5, 7, 15, 19, 21.

Emily Bremer, *Blame (or Thank) the Administrative Procedure Act for* Florida East Coast Railway, 97 CHI.-KENT L. REV. 79 (2022).

Henry J. Friendly, *Book Reviews*, 51 N.Y.U. L. REV. 896 (1976).

Henry J. Friendly, *"Some Kind of Hearing,"* 123 U. PA. L. REV. 1267 (1975).

Robert W. Hamilton, *Procedures for the Adoption of Rules of General Applicability: The Need for Procedural Innovation in Administrative Rulemaking*, 60 CALIF. L. REV. 1276 (1972).

Robert W. Hamilton, *Rulemaking on a Record by the Food and Drug Administration*, 50 TEX. L. REV. 1132 (1972).

Michael P. Healy, Florida East Coast Railway *and the Structure of Administrative Law*, 58 ADMIN. L. REV. 1039 (2006).

1 KRISTIN E. HICKMAN & RICHARD J. PIERCE, JR., ADMINISTRATIVE LAW TREATISE (7th ed. 2024).

Charles H. Koch, Jr., *Judicial Review of Administrative Discretion*, 54 GEO. WASH. L. REV. 469 (1986).

Emily Hammond Meazell, *Super Deference, the Science Obsession, and Judicial Review as Translation of Agency Science*, 109 MICH. L. REV. 733 (2011).

Aaron L. Nielson, *In Defense of Formal Rulemaking*, 75 OHIO ST. L.J. 237 (2014).

Edward Rubin, *It's Time to Make the Administrative Procedure Act Administrative*, 89 CORNELL L. REV. 95 (2003).

SECTION OF ADMIN. L. & REGUL. PRAC., AM. BAR ASS'N, A BLACKLETTER STATEMENT OF FEDERAL ADMINISTRATIVE LAW pt. 2, § I.B (2d ed. 2013).

Jonathan R. Siegel, *Textualism and Contextualism in Administrative Law*, 78 B.U. L. REV. 1023 (1998).

Chapter 6

Portland Cement Association v. Ruckelshaus, 486 F.2d 375 (1973)

Linda Jellum

Portland Cement is not the most stirring case in administrative law. Regardless, the case is important because it augments the Administrative Procedure Act (APA) requirements for agency rulemaking in a critical respect. In the case, the U.S. Court of Appeals for the D.C. Circuit held that agencies must disclose the scientific data and methodology upon which they rely to formulate rules.

Portland Cement's holding has never been challenged, but it remains susceptible to a successful challenge before the U.S. Supreme Court in light of subsequent case law. Its holding is arguably contrary to the language of APA section 553 and to the holding of *Vermont Yankee Nuclear Power Corp. v. Natural Resources Defense Council, Inc.*[1] In *Vermont Yankee*, the Supreme Court held that courts may not impose rulemaking procedures on agencies in addition to those in the APA and enabling statutes.[2] Moreover, the Court more recently reaffirmed that it meant what it had said in *Vermont Yankee*: no more judicially imposed procedures.[3]

Thus, it is very possible that if *Portland Cement* is challenged before the Supreme Court it will be overruled. Indeed, in *American Radio Relay*

1. 435 U.S. 519, 524 (1978). The case is the subject of Chapter 25. Whether the *Portland Cement* rule is sound as a matter of policy is another question. The American Bar Association (ABA) has recommended that Congress codify the *Portland Cement* rule as an amendment to the APA. *See* ABA, House of Delegates Resolution 106B (adopted Feb. 8, 2016).
2. *Vermont Yankee*, 435 U.S. at 523–25.
3. *See* Perez v. Mortg. Bankers Ass'n, 575 U.S. 92, 100 (2015).

League, Inc. v. FCC,[4] a dissenting Judge Kavanaugh argued it should be overruled. He rejected *Portland Cement*'s holding as contrary to both the text of APA section 553 and *Vermont Yankee*.[5] His appointment to the Supreme Court enhances the likelihood that the decision will not survive much longer.

Case Background

In 1970, Congress passed the Clean Air Act (1970 CAA). With the 1970 CAA, Congress brought the federal government into the job of regulating air quality. The 1970 CAA authorized the development of comprehensive federal and state regulations to limit emissions from both stationary and mobile sources of air pollution.

When the 1970 CAA was enacted, multiple federal agencies were tasked with regulating various aspects of the environment. Hence, on December 2, 1970, President Nixon established the Environmental Protection Agency (EPA) by executive order to consolidate federal environmental activities into one agency. Consequently, the EPA was now responsible for administering the 1970 CAA.

One section of the CAA directed the EPA's administrator to promulgate "standards of performance" to govern air pollutant emissions from new sources of pollution. The 1970 CAA further defined these "standard[s] of performance" as "standard[s] for emissions of air pollutants which reflect[] the degree of emission limitation *achievable* through the application of the best system of emission reduction which . . . the Administrator determines has been *adequately demonstrated*."[6]

On August 3, 1971, the EPA's first administrator, William D. Ruckelshaus (the named defendant), published proposed standards of performance to cap

4. *See* 524 F.3d 227, 246–47 (D.C. Cir. 2008) (Kavanaugh, J., concurring in part and dissenting in part).

5. *See id.* at 246 (noting that *Portland Cement* "cannot be squared with the text of § 553" and hence "stands on a shaky legal foundation (even though it may make sense as a policy matter in some cases)"). For academic critiques, see Kathryn E. Kovacs, *Rules About Rulemakings and the Rise of the Unitary Executive*, 70 ADMIN. L. REV. 515, 538–40 (2018); Jack M. Beermann & Gary Lawson, *Reprocessing* Vermont Yankee, 75 GEO. WASH. L. REV. 856, 894 (2007).

6. 42 U.S.C. § 1857c-6 (1973).

emissions from Portland cement plants.[7] The proposed regulation included a background document, in which the EPA stated that the standards of performance were "based on stationary source testing conducted by the [EPA] and/or contractors." The agency did not disclose the location or methodology used in the testing.

After issuing its proposed standards, the EPA had to act quickly because the 1970 CAA required the agency to issue its final performance standards within 90 days of issuing its notice of proposed rulemaking. After receiving more than 200 comments, the EPA promulgated the final regulation with the new standards on December 16, 1971.

When promulgating the final regulation, the EPA repeated its statement from the background document about the testing, concluding that the testing proved the standards were achievable, but again offered little information about the testing methodology.

The Portland Cement Association (the named petitioners) and several cement companies challenged the final performance standards on a number of grounds, including that the testing was flawed.

In *Kennecott Copper Corp. v. EPA*—which was unrelated to *Portland Cement*—the D.C. Circuit had directed "the Administrator to supply an implementing statement that will enlighten the court as to the basis on which he reached [a different proposed] standard."[8] In *Kennecott*, the court had directed the EPA to explain its reasoning, but not to disclose its data; still, as a result, the EPA had to be considerably more forthcoming than it had been in the past.

Because of the requirement in *Kennecott* that the EPA explain its reasoning more fully, the agency issued a supplemental statement regarding the new cement standards of performance on March 21, 1972. This supplementary statement was issued while the case was pending and disclosed that the testing involved a particular type of filter and, more importantly, that additional testing had been conducted during the comment period. A month later, the EPA finally disclosed the dates, locations, and methodology of both the initial and the comment-period testing.

7. "Portland cement" refers to the most common type of cement, which is manufactured from limestone and clay and hardens under water. The name comes from the cement's similarity to Portland stone, which is quarried on the Isle of Portland in Dorset, England.
8. 462 F.2d 846, 850 (D.C. Cir. 1972).

Once the cement companies obtained full information regarding the testing, they offered an expert's scathing critique of the testing process. The petitioners moved the court to remand so that the EPA could consider their expert's criticism. The court granted the motion; however, the EPA never responded to the criticism. Instead, it merely added the expert's criticism to the administrative record and held firm on its new standards. In hindsight, that was not the agency's smartest decision.

Holding and Reasoning

The EPA's failure to respond to the expert's criticism did not sit well with the D.C. Circuit. The court was explicit that it did not expect the EPA to respond to every comment, but the prior remand should have made it abundantly clear to the EPA that the court viewed the expert's criticism as important. Because the EPA had failed to respond to the criticism, the court remanded again, asking the EPA to take a "hard look" at the problem.[9] "Hard look," the court said, included the obligation to comment on matters the court had identified as potentially significant. In addition to chiding the EPA for failing to respond to the expert's criticism, the court offered the dicta for which this case is known in administrative circles.

Writing for a unanimous panel, Judge Leventhal said that the EPA's decision-making process contained a "critical defect." The petitioners had been unable to obtain the test results and the procedures used for determining the EPA's standards in a timely fashion. While the short, statutory time frame had created some difficulty for the EPA, the court recommended that agencies disclose information as it became available.

The court reasoned that an agency's failure to disclose information created three problems: one for potential commenters, one for the agency, and, finally, one for reviewing courts. First, for the commenters: "[A] prerequisite to the ability to make meaningful comment is to know the basis upon which the rule is proposed." Here, the petitioners did not know this information and, thus, could not comment meaningfully.

9. After the second remand, the court affirmed the EPA's new standards of performance. *See* Portland Cement Ass'n v. Train, 513 F.2d 506 (D.C. Cir. 1975).

Second, for the agency: "It is not consonant with the purpose of a rule-making proceeding to promulgate rules on the basis of inadequate data, or on data that, [in] critical degree, is known only to the agency." In short, rules are better when data is complete and disclosed.

Third, for the reviewing court: "[T]o be more than a meaningless exercise, [judicial review] requires enough steeping in technical matters to determine whether the agency has exercised a reasoned discretion." Thus, to be able to review an agency's decision, courts have to know the information upon which the agency relied.

Even though the court's directive was merely dicta and lacked support in precedent or the APA, it quickly became the law of the land.[10]

Relevance to Administrative Law

One of only two cases in this book not decided by the Supreme Court, *Portland Cement* occupies an especially important place in administrative law for several reasons.

First, the law in many circuits is that agencies must disclose the theories, data, methodology, and studies relied upon[11] to make rules. When an agency fails to disclose this information, a court is likely to find that the public was deprived of the opportunity to comment meaningfully, that the agency did not engage in reasoned decision-making, and that judicial review is exceedingly difficult. As a consequence, the court is likely to make the agency try again.

Is the *Portland Cement* doctrine a good one as a matter of policy? On the one hand, it furthers public participation and government accountability in the rulemaking process. While neither the APA nor case law requires agencies to disclose *all* the information underlying a proposed rule, *Portland Cement* and its progeny require agencies to disclose information to the

10. *See, e.g.*, Chamber of Com. of U.S. v. SEC, 443 F.3d 890, 908 (D.C. Cir. 2006); Solite Corp. v. EPA, 952 F.2d 473, 499–500 (D.C. Cir. 1991); Lloyd Noland Hosp. & Clinic v. Heckler, 762 F.2d 1561 (11th Cir. 1985); United States v. Nova Scotia Food Prods. Corp., 568 F.2d 240, 251–52 (2d Cir. 1977); Ethyl Corp. v. EPA, 541 F.2d 1, 48–49 (D.C. Cir. 1976).
11. *See* Banner Health v. Burwell, 55 F. Supp. 3d 1, 10 (D.D.C. 2014) (refusing to apply the *Portland Cement* doctrine when the agency did not actually rely on the undisclosed material).

extent necessary for the public to comment meaningfully, for the agency to engage in reasoned decision-making, and for the court to review the agency's reasoning process.[12] The outcome should be a better rule for everyone.

On the other hand, do-overs slow down the rulemaking process, which may not be in either the public's or government's interest. Consider whether it is likely that "Congress, in providing for notice and comment under the APA, . . . intended to subject the agencies—and the public on whose behalf they regulate—to [an] interminable back-and-forth" process.[13] Likely, not.

Moreover, it is possible that this information is available from the agency by way of another process, such as a Freedom of Information Act[14] request. If so, then there may be no need for *Portland Cement*'s disclosure mandate. Thus, at a minimum, courts need to balance the public's need for disclosure with the agency's need to complete a rulemaking. At a maximum, the *Portland Cement* doctrine contributes to rulemaking ossification.

Second, there is an interesting historical point. Judge Leventhal, who wrote the opinion, is the same judge who coined the term "hard look" review. In doing so, he was describing the level of scrutiny an agency should give to information before it.[15] However, his descriptive term has been commandeered. Today "hard look" review is also used to describe the level of scrutiny judges should themselves give to agency reasoning.[16]

In *Portland Cement*, Judge Leventhal relied on his original meaning to chastise the EPA for failing to take a "hard look" at an expert comment critical of the EPA's testing, one the court strongly hinted the agency should consider on remand. Judge Leventhal viewed the court and the agency as partners, both attempting to further the public interest. Hence, he believed more judicial oversight—some would call it judicial activism—furthered the administrative process. With the Supreme Court having become increasingly conservative, his collaborative approach is unlikely to prevail.

---

12. However, if the agency can demonstrate that the public was aware of all the relevant information and able to comment had it wished, the agency may well still prevail.
13. Int'l Fabricare Inst. v. EPA, 972 F.2d 384, 399 (D.C. Cir. 1992) (citation omitted).
14. 5 U.S.C. § 552.
15. *See, e.g.*, Pikes Peak Broad. Co. v. FCC, 422 F.2d 671 (D.C. Cir. 1969); Nat. Res. Def. Council, Inc. v. Morton, 458 F.2d 827 (D.C. Cir. 1972).
16. *See* Vermont Yankee Nuclear Power Corp. v. Nat. Res. Def. Council, Inc., 435 U.S. 519, 557–58 (1978). The case is the subject of Chapter 25.

Third, and finally, this case provides yet one more example of what some commentators see as the D.C. Circuit's judicial activism in administrative law cases. On a number of occasions, the nation's "administrative law court"[17] has created new procedural rules untethered to the APA, which the Supreme Court subsequently rejected.[18]

For example, in *Alaska Professional Hunters Ass'n v. FAA*, the D.C. Circuit held that "[w]hen an agency has given its regulation a definitive interpretation, and later significantly revises that interpretation, the agency has in effect amended its rule, something it may not accomplish without notice and comment."[19] The court reasoned that because APA section 551(5) defines "rulemaking" as including the process of modifying a rule, the interpretive rule exception in APA section 553(b)(3)(A) did not apply. The court's holding appeared to violate *Vermont Yankee*, and, sure enough, the Supreme Court overruled it.[20]

Similarly, in *Landry v. FDIC*,[21] the D.C. Circuit held that administrative law judges (ALJs) at the Federal Deposit Insurance Corporation were not inferior officers because they could not issue final decisions. The court refused to follow *Freytag v. Commissioner*,[22] in which the Supreme Court had held that special trial judges (STJs) in the tax court were inferior officers because of the powers they wielded. Importantly, the powers ALJs have are virtually identical to the powers STJs have. Not surprisingly, the Supreme Court squarely rejected the D.C. Circuit's position in *Landry* when the issue presented itself in another case.[23]

Portland Cement may be one more example of a D.C. Circuit decision on the precipice. Judge Kavanaugh is now Justice Kavanaugh. Given his

---

17. Patricia M. Wald, *The Contribution of the D.C. Circuit to Administrative Law*, 40 ADMIN. L. REV. 507, 534 (1988).
18. *See, e.g.*, Cass R. Sunstein & Adrian Vermeule, *Libertarian Administrative Law*, 82 U. CHI. L. REV. 393 (2015).
19. 177 F.3d 1030, 1034 (D.C. Cir. 1999).
20. Perez v. Mortg. Bankers Ass'n, 575 U.S. 92, 100 (2015) (holding that the *Paralyzed Veterans'* doctrine "[was] contrary to the clear text of the APA's rulemaking provisions, and it improperly impose[d] on agencies an obligation beyond the 'maximum procedural requirements' specified in the APA").
21. 204 F.3d 1125, 1134 (D.C. Cir. 2000).
22. 501 U.S. 868 (1991).
23. *See* Lucia v. SEC, 585 U.S. 237 (2018).

earlier criticism that *Portland Cement*'s disclosure requirement is untethered to the APA and violates *Vermont Yankee*, and given the Supreme Court's overwhelming reaffirmance of the principle of that case, *Portland Cement*'s days may be numbered.

Bibliography

Matthew S. Brooker, Note, *Taking the Path Less Travelled: FOIA's Impact on the Tension Between the D.C. Circuit and* Vermont Yankee, 102 VA. L. REV. 1101 (2016).

Samuel Estreicher, *Pragmatic Justice: The Contributions of Judge Harold Leventhal to Administrative Law*, 80 COLUM. L. REV. 894 (1980).

William F. Pedersen, Jr., *Formal Records and Informal Rulemaking*, 85 YALE L.J. 38 (1975).

SECTION OF ADMIN. L. & REGUL. PRAC., AM. BAR ASS'N, A BLACKLETTER STATEMENT OF FEDERAL ADMINISTRATIVE LAW pt. 2, § IV.A–B (2d ed. 2013).

Cass R. Sunstein, *In Defense of the Hard Look: Judicial Activism and Administrative Law*, 7 HARV. J. L. & PUB. POL'Y 51 (1984).

Chapter 7

Withrow v. Larkin, 421 U.S. 35 (1975)

Michael Asimow

Regulatory agencies typically enjoy combined functions, meaning that a single agency adopts regulations, investigates possible violations, issues complaints, adjudicates liability, and determines the sanction. Since combined function agencies emerged in the late 19th century, many people have questioned their legitimacy.[1] Viewed globally, systems of combined functions, checked only by deferential judicial review, are rare. Many countries (including Canada and the United Kingdom) separate enforcement from adjudication by establishing adjudicatory tribunals. In Europe, administrative decisions are subject to *de novo* review by administrative courts.[2]

Combined function agencies are typically required by the Administrative Procedure Act (APA)[3] or by procedural regulations[4] to maintain a system of internal separation of functions. Under internal separation, agency adversaries (such as prosecutors, investigators, and advocates) cannot serve as decision makers or give off-the-record advice to decision makers. These

1. *See, e.g.*, Martin H. Redish & Kristin McCall, *Due Process, Free Expression, and the Administrative State*, 94 Notre Dame L. Rev. 297 (2018).
2. *See* Michael Asimow, *Five Models of Administrative Adjudication*, 63 Am. J. Compar. L. 3 (2015).
3. *See* 5 U.S.C. § 554(d).
4. Agencies that hold evidentiary hearings but are not covered by the APA adjudication provisions typically require internal separation of functions in their procedural regulations. *See* Michael Asimow, Admin. Conf. of the U.S., Sourcebook on Federal Administrative Adjudication Outside the Administrative Procedure Act (2019).

arrangements are based on concern that adversaries might have acquired a will to win that could cause them to be biased as adjudicators or advisers. A further concern is that adversaries might rely on non-record evidence that they learned about in their investigations.

The role of agency heads remains problematic in a system of internal separation. Due process requires neutral decision makers. Is due process offended by an agency structure that allows the agency heads to combine the functions of investigation, prosecution, and adjudication? The leading case of *Withrow v. Larkin* answered that question firmly in the negative, but it left many unanswered questions about the interface between due process and combined functions.

The Story of Duane Larkin

The *Withrow* case involved a physician named Duane R. Larkin who practiced in both Michigan and Wisconsin. The case arose from the intense political and legal controversy surrounding the abortion issue in the early 1970s. Abortion became legal in Wisconsin in 1970[5] but only became legal in Michigan in 1973 after *Roe v. Wade*.[6] Larkin operated abortion clinics in both states and was apparently a pioneer in making legal abortion available.

In Wisconsin, Larkin was hounded by law enforcement authorities and private litigation.[7] A federal district court in 1972 ordered prosecutors to stop pursuing charges against Larkin, rejecting claims by the Wisconsin attorney general that state rather than federal courts should decide on the legality of abortion laws. In May 1972, a legislator asked the state medical society to revoke Larkin's license because he advertised abortion services. Mary Carpenter of Milwaukee filed a suit against Larkin on behalf of unborn children, seeking $1 million in damages. Carpenter also claimed that his clinic was a public nuisance. Larkin filed suit to stop Carpenter's

5. *See* Babbitz v. McCann, 310 F. Supp. 293 (E.D. Wis. 1970), *appeal dismissed*, 400 U.S. 1 (1970).
6. *See* 410 U.S. 113 (1973).
7. *See* Brief of Appellee at 8–21, Withrow v. Larkin, 421 U.S. 35 (1975) (No. 73-1573); Email from Mary Ziegler, Professor of Law, Florida State University College of Law, to chapter author Michael Asimow (Mar. 26, 2018) [hereinafter Ziegler Email] (on file with author).

nuisance suit. Big players in the national abortion controversy were involved in this litigation.[8]

Journalistic reports on the Wisconsin and Michigan abortion clinics Larkin owned or worked in were rather negative. Milwaukee abortion referral consultants would not refer patients to Larkin's clinic because he would not let them inspect his facility.[9] A reporter claiming to be pregnant and seeking an abortion reported that Larkin was brusque and would not speak to her directly. Conditions in the examining room were unhygienic.[10] In January 1976, after losing the U.S. Supreme Court case, Larkin surrendered his license to practice medicine in Wisconsin because he was no longer practicing there. He died in July 1976, about a year after losing the Supreme Court case.

Administrative Proceedings Against Larkin

On June 20, 1973, in the midst of all the legal controversy in Wisconsin, the Wisconsin Medical Examining Board sent Larkin a notice that it would hold an investigatory hearing to determine whether he had engaged in conduct unbecoming a medical licensee and conduct detrimental to the best interests of the public. The specific charges were that, between 1971 and 1973, Larkin operated an abortion clinic under a false name and delegated the performance of abortions to a non-licensed physician, while splitting fees with that person.

Larkin claimed that the other doctors working at the clinic were properly licensed, but that both he and the other doctors used false names as a method of self-protection against abortion protesters.[11] This excuse seems plausible and suggests that the reasons cited by the Wisconsin Board might have been a pretext for getting rid of an unwelcome abortion provider.

---

8. *See* Ziegler Email, *supra* note 7. Larkin was also a litigant before the Supreme Court of Michigan, seeking an order clarifying Michigan abortion law after *Roe v. Wade* was decided. *4 Abortion Cases Pending Before State High Court*, TRAVERSE CITY REC.-EAGLE, Feb. 1, 1973, at 26.

9. *See Inside Detroit-Area Abortion Clinics*, DET. FREE PRESS, Feb. 4, 1973, at 63.

10. *See Only 1 Clinic in 12 Found Adequate*, DET. FREE PRESS, Sep. 10, 1974, at 4.

11. *See Inside Detroit-Area Abortion Clinics*, *supra* note 9, at 63.

Under the Wisconsin statute as it existed in 1973, the Wisconsin Medical Examining Board could suspend the license of a physician for up to six months if it determined that a violation of the medical licensing law had occurred. The Board could then petition the district attorney to file a judicial complaint seeking revocation of the license or pursuing criminal prosecution of the licensee. This was a rather primitive regulatory scheme; modern licensing statutes give regulatory agencies power to both suspend and revoke professional licenses, subject to judicial review.

The Board held an investigatory hearing on July 12, 1973, at which Larkin's attorney was present. Larkin attempted to obtain a temporary restraining order to prevent the Board from holding the investigatory hearing, but the federal district court denied it. Although not required by statute, the Board then informed Larkin that it would hold a contested (or trial-type) hearing on October 4, 1973, to determine whether to suspend his license.

This time, the three-judge district court granted a preliminary injunction preventing the Board from conducting the contested hearing. It filed a brief opinion holding that the Board violated due process by investigating Larkin and then adjudicating to suspend his license. After holding another investigatory hearing, the Board notified the district attorney to institute an action for the revocation of Larkin's license to practice.

Based on Larkin's complaint, the district court assumed that the heads of the Medical Examining Board personally investigated Larkin's case and then held a hearing on the issue of whether to suspend his license. The Supreme Court decided the case under the same assumption. In fact, the Court knew that this assumption was false; the Board's staff members performed the investigation, not the agency heads, although the heads made the decision to hold a hearing on the suspension issue.

Withrow v. Larkin in the Supreme Court

In a unanimous decision authored by Justice White, the Supreme Court reversed the lower court decision, holding that the injunction was improper because Larkin had no chance to prevail on the merits. The opinion stated:

> That is not to say that there is nothing to the argument that those who have investigated should not then adjudicate. The issue is substantial, it

is not new, and legislators and others concerned with the operations of administrative agencies have given much attention to whether and to what extent distinctive administrative functions should be performed by the same persons. No single answer has been reached. Indeed, the growth, variety, and complexity of the administrative processes have made any one solution highly unlikely. . . .

It is not surprising, therefore, to find that '[t]he case law, both federal and state, generally rejects the idea that the combination [of] judging [and] investigating functions is a denial of due process. . . .' . . . Similarly, our cases, although they reflect the substance of the problem, offer no support for the bald proposition applied in this case by the District Court that agency members who participate in an investigation are disqualified from adjudicating. The incredible variety of administrative mechanisms in this country will not yield to any single organizing principle.[12]

This decision was hardly surprising. It is supported by the principle of necessity, meaning that due process cannot be used to disqualify the only decision makers empowered to enforce the law.[13] Previous Supreme Court decisions are consistent with *Withrow* on this point. For example, in *Cement Institute*, the Court held that the heads of the Federal Trade Commission could investigate the basing point pricing system and conclude that it was illegal, then prosecute the respondents for employing that very system. Otherwise, the Court noted, "[i]f the Commission's opinions expressed in congressionally required reports would bar its members from acting in unfair trade proceedings, it would appear that opinions expressed in the first basing point unfair trade proceeding would similarly disqualify them from ever passing on another."[14] Similarly, shortly after the *Withrow* decision, the Court decided that a school board could conduct contract negotiations

12. *See also* 2 Kenneth Culp Davis, Administrative Law Treatise § 13.02, at 175 (1958).
13. The Court cited with approval a lower court case that allowed the Civil Aeronautics Board to investigate a crash (as it was required to do by statute) and then to review the decision of its trial examiner suspending the pilot's license. *See* Pangburn v. CAB, 311 F.2d 349 (1st Cir. 1962).
14. FTC v. Cement Inst., 333 U.S. 683, 702 (1948).

with teachers and later adjudicate the discharge of the striking teachers.[15] These decisions are solidly based on the principle of necessity.

When Combination of Functions Offends Due Process

The *Withrow* decision left open the possibility that other instances of combined functions could violate due process. It cited (but withheld approval of) several lower court cases that so held.[16] And in *Goldberg v. Kelly*, which applied due process to hearings in welfare revocation cases, the Court specifically noted that "prior involvement in some aspects of a case will not necessarily bar a welfare official from acting as a decisionmaker. He should not, however, . . . participate[] in making the determination under review."[17]

What distinguishes the cases in which a combination of functions does or does not violate due process? It appears to be the principle of necessity as well as a desire to avoid a large-scale disruption of state and federal administrative processes, such as would occur if agency heads were barred from investigating and then adjudicating the same case.[18] However, a lower-level staff member, who has previously engaged in adversary functions in a case, could be disqualified from serving as an administrative judge in that case or from furnishing advice in that case. The agency could always find an uninvolved staff member to hear and decide the case or to furnish needed

15. Hortonville Joint Sch. Dist. v. Hortonville Educ. Ass'n, 426 U.S. 482 (1976). Similarly, the U.S. Court of Appeals for the D.C. Circuit rejected a due process attack on a Securities and Exchange Commission (SEC) decision to impose sanctions after the SEC had prosecuted the respondent in court. *See* Blinder, Robinson & Co. v. SEC, 837 F.2d 1099, 1107 (D.C. Cir. 1988).

16. *See, e.g.*, Amos Treat & Co. v. SEC, 306 F.2d 260 (D.C. Cir. 1962) (one of the SEC members had previously engaged in an investigation of charges pending before the Commission); Trans World Airlines, Inc. v. CAB, 254 F.2d 90 (D.C. Cir. 1958) (agency head signed brief in favor of one of the parties prior to becoming agency head).

17. Goldberg v. Kelly, 397 U.S. 254, 271 (1970). This case is the subject of Chapter 4. Similarly, in probable cause parole revocation hearings, the decision maker can be a parole officer, but not the one responsible for supervising and rearresting the parolee. *See* Morrissey v. Brewer, 408 U.S. 471 (1972).

18. *See* Richardson v. Perales, 402 U.S. 389, 410 (1971) (rejecting a due process attack on the function of Social Security administrative law judges who present the government's side of the case and then adjudicate it).

advice to the agency heads.[19] Similarly, if a single member of a multi-headed commission engaged in adversarial functions, that member can be disqualified while the remaining members of the commission can hear the case. But if all of the members of the commission are disqualified, the agency could not decide the case, and misconduct might then go unpunished.

By the same token, if the agency heads decide, on the basis of a staff investigation, that the agency should issue a complaint, they are not disqualified from adjudicating that complaint. As the Court in *Withrow* pointed out, "there is no incompatibility between the agency filing a complaint based on probable cause and a subsequent decision, when all the evidence is in, that there has been no violation of the statute."[20] Otherwise, a useful and conventional administrative process (requiring that agency heads sign off on a complaint before it is issued) would be prohibited.

Interpretation of the APA's Separation-of-Functions Provision

A final puzzle left by the *Withrow* decision is the interpretation of the "agency head" exception to the separation-of-functions provision in the APA. That provision reads:

> An employee or agent engaged in the performance of investigative or prosecuting functions for an agency in a case may not, in that or a factually related case, participate or advise in the decision, recommended decision, or agency review pursuant to section 557 of this title, except as witness or counsel in public proceedings. This subsection does not apply . . . (C) to the agency or a member or members of the body comprising the agency.[21]

19. *See* Michael Asimow, *When the Curtain Falls: Separation of Functions in the Federal Administrative Agencies*, 81 Colum. L. Rev. 759, 779–88 (1981); Doe v. Mia. Univ., 882 F.3d 579, 601 (6th Cir. 2018); Stone v. FDIC, 179 F.3d 1368 (Fed. Cir. 1999); Walker v. City of Berkeley, 951 F.2d 182 (9th Cir. 1991).

20. *But see* Andrew N. Vollmer, *Accusers as Adjudicators in Agency Enforcement Proceedings*, 52 U. Mich. J.L. Reform 103 (2018). For my response, see Michael Asimow, *Greenlighting Administrative Prosecution*, 75 Admin. L. Rev. 227, 258–61 (2023).

21. 5 U.S.C. § 554(d).

In *Withrow*, the Court cited the (C) exception in support of its position that due process does not prohibit agency heads from investigating a case and then adjudicating it. But the scope of the (C) exception has never been clarified. Consistent with the *Withrow* dictum, the (C) exception seems to allow agency heads personally to engage in investigation of a case, approve the prosecution, and then adjudicate the case. But does the (C) exception also permit staff adversaries to advise the agency heads off the record?

The better view is that it does not. The statute says that adversaries cannot "advise in the decision, recommended decision, or *agency review*."[22] If the staff adversaries could advise agency heads off the record during the "agency review" process, that language in section 554(d) would be meaningless. This is the interpretation of the *Attorney General's Manual on the Administrative Procedure Act*.[23]

Although the principle that due process is not offended by the commingling of investigative, prosecutorial, and adjudicatory functions has been firmly established for nearly 50 years, litigants have begun to challenge the principle with increasing frequency in recent years.[24] Whether the Supreme Court will revisit *Withrow* remains to be seen. In a recent case, Justice Gorsuch, joined by Justice Thomas, raised due process concerns about the commingling of functions in federal regulatory agencies, but he did not cite *Withrow*. Justice Gorsuch was concerned with the larger question whether, consistent with the Due Process Clause and other constitutional provisions, Congress can assign adjudicatory authority over certain cases to federal regulatory agencies.[25]

Bibliography

Michael Asimow, Admin. Conf. of the U.S., Sourcebook on Federal Administrative Adjudication Outside the Administrative Procedure Act (2019).

22. *Id.* (emphasis added).
23. Tom C. Clark, U.S. Dep't of Just., Attorney General's Manual on the Administrative Procedure Act 56 (1947); Asimow, *supra* note 19, at 766–68.
24. *See, e.g.*, Axon Enterprises, Inc. v. FTC, 598 U.S. 175, 180 (2022).
25. *See* SEC v. Jarkesy, 603 U.S. 109, 141 (2024) (Gorsuch, J., joined by Thomas, J., concurring).

Michael Asimow, *Five Models of Administrative Adjudication*, 63 Am. J. Compar. L. 3 (2015).

Michael Asimow, *Greenlighting Administrative Prosecution*, 75 Admin. L. Rev. 227 (2023).

Michael Asimow, *When the Curtain Falls: Separation of Functions in the Federal Administrative Agencies*, 81 Colum. L. Rev. 759 (1981).

Tom C. Clark, U.S. Dep't of Just., Attorney General's Manual on the Administrative Procedure Act (1947).

2 Kenneth Culp Davis, Administrative Law Treatise § 13.02 (1958).

Richard J. Pierce, Jr., *Constitutional Foundations*, *in* A Guide to Federal Agency Adjudication 33 (Jeremy S. Graboyes ed., 3d ed. 2023).

Martin H. Redish & Kristin McCall, *Due Process, Free Expression, and the Administrative State*, 94 Notre Dame L. Rev. 297 (2018).

Section of Admin. L. & Regul. Prac., Am. Bar Ass'n, A Blackletter Statement of Federal Administrative Law pt. 1, § IV (2d ed. 2013).

Section of Admin. L. & Regul. Prac., Am. Bar Ass'n, A Guide to Federal Agency Adjudication (Jeremy S. Graboyes ed., 3d ed. 2023).

Andrew N. Vollmer, *Accusers as Adjudicators in Agency Enforcement Proceedings*, 52 U. Mich. J. L. Reform 103 (2018).

Chapter 8

Mathews v. Eldridge, 424 U.S. 319 (1976)

Jeffrey S. Lubbers

In *Mathews v. Eldridge*, the U.S. Supreme Court established the three-part balancing test for determining what process is due when there has been a finding that the federal or state government has deprived a person of life, liberty, or property under the Fifth or 14th Amendments to the Constitution. As such, it is one of the most influential, oft-cited,[1] and important cases in constitutional and administrative law. With respect to federal administrative agency adjudication, it forms the applicable standard for determining whether informal adjudications (i.e., hearings not subject to the formal adjudication provisions of the Administrative Procedure Act) are constitutionally adequate.

The backdrop of the *Mathews* case was the "due process revolution" reflected in cases like *Goldberg v. Kelly*[2] and *Perry v. Sindermann*,[3] which expanded the notion of property deprivation to include government termination of welfare benefits and government employment, respectively. At the same time, the Court was also recognizing a broader conception of liberty deprivation to include government stigmatic actions in *Wisconsin*

1. As of January 6, 2025, the *Mathews* decision was cited 19,251 times in cases appearing in Westlaw's database. But, interestingly, it was misspelled as "Matthews" in 1,537 (8 percent) of those cases. Law review writers were even more error-prone, with 10.1 percent (593 of 5,870) of the articles containing the mistake.
2. 397 U.S. 254 (1970). The case is the subject of Chapter 4.
3. 408 U.S. 593 (1972). The case is the subject of Chapter 3.

v. Constantineau[4] and *Board of Regents v. Roth*,[5] and prison discipline in *Wolff v. McDonnell*.[6] *Goldberg* not only expanded the notion of property to include welfare benefits, it also required a pre-termination hearing and then spelled out a set of required procedures that amounted to a trial-type hearing. In so doing, the Court stressed the welfare recipients' "brutal need" for the benefits—that "termination of aid pending resolution of a controversy over eligibility may deprive an eligible recipient of the very means by which to live while he waits."[7] But, given the ongoing expansion of notions of liberty and property, how could the *Goldberg* trial-type formal hearing be applied to every situation where a liberty or property deprivation was found?

The answer became apparent a year before *Mathews* was decided, in *Goss v. Lopez*,[8] where the Court expanded notions of liberty and property deprivations to encompass a ten-day suspension of a public high school student. This expansion was closely contested, as a four-member minority decried the "judicial intervention in the operation of our public schools," and found the ten-day suspension to be de minimis.[9] Nonetheless, the majority required a "hearing," but one that was decidedly informal and tailored to the educational context, requiring "that the student be given oral or written notice of the charges against him and, if he denies them, an explanation of the evidence the authorities have and an opportunity to present his side of the story."[10]

A year later, *Mathews v. Eldridge* addressed these questions in a context that was far closer to *Goldberg*—revocation of Social Security disability benefits. By that point, there was no question that such benefits, as entitlements to eligible beneficiaries, were property. The sole question was whether a federal agency's informal, largely written, pre-termination and oral post-termination hearing procedures met the demands of due process.

4. 400 U.S. 433 (1971).
5. 408 U.S. 564 (1972). The case is the subject of Chapter 3. The Court later made clear that injury to reputation was not enough; it had to be accompanied by some change in the plaintiff's legal status. *See* Paul v. Davis, 424 U.S. 693 (1976).
6. 418 U.S. 539 (1974).
7. *Goldberg*, 397 U.S. at 264.
8. 419 U.S. 565 (1975).
9. *Id.* at 585, 586 (Powell, J., dissenting).
10. *Id.* at 581.

The Social Security Benefits Claim in *Mathews*

On June 2, 1968, George Eldridge had been awarded Social Security disability benefits after a hearing by a Social Security hearing examiner (now known as an administrative law judge, or ALJ). The Social Security Administration (SSA), or more specifically the state agency with which it contracted to carry out such reviews, then embarked on a series of reviews of his medical condition, including sending him a questionnaire, which he answered by contending that he continued to be disabled. After the state agency reviewed his answers and medical evidence, it notified him of its conclusion that the evidence in his case indicated that he was able to work (no longer disabled) as of May 1972. He was provided notice of the reasons for the conclusion and allowed an opportunity to obtain and submit additional information to SSA, but was also told that under the law, unless reversed, he would receive benefits only through June. Eldridge's written reply to SSA disputed one characterization of his medical condition but otherwise indicated that the agency already had enough evidence to establish his continuing disability. In response, the SSA, on July 7, 1972, advised him that it accepted the state agency's conclusion, but that he had a right to request reconsideration by the SSA within six months of that date.

Instead of doing so, he filed suit in federal district court challenging the constitutionality of these procedures, citing *Goldberg v. Kelly*. The district court agreed with Eldridge and ordered a pre-termination hearing (and continued payments of benefits) à la *Goldberg*.[11] The U.S. Court of Appeals for the Fourth Circuit affirmed, simply adopting the district court's opinion.[12] But the Supreme Court reversed in a 6–2 opinion by Justice Powell. Justice Brennan, who had authored *Goldberg*, dissented, joined by Justice Marshall. Justice Stevens did not participate.

The Court first dispensed with the government's defense that Eldridge's case should be dismissed for failure to exhaust administrative remedies—specifically, his failure to request reconsideration (which, if denied, could also have led to a further ALJ hearing on the matter). The Court held that

11. *See* Eldridge v. Weinberger, 361 F. Supp. 520 (W.D. Va. 1973).
12. *See* Eldridge v. Weinberger, 493 F.2d 1230 (4th Cir. 1974).

although Eldridge concededly had not exhausted the internal review procedures, the claimant's challenge was not only a collateral one, unrelated to the merits of his claim, but that his interest in having this issue promptly resolved was so great it would allow for an exception to the usual exhaustion requirements in this case. The Court did not pause long over the issue of whether back benefits could have been awarded to Eldridge to "make him whole"—an indication that the Court was eager to decide this constitutional issue.[13]

The *Mathews* Balancing Test

As for the constitutional claim, both parties agreed that "[t]he dispute centers upon what process is due prior to the initial termination of benefits, pending review." After carefully reviewing the SSA's procedures in benefits revocations cases, the Court began its legal analysis by putting *Goldberg* in its place: "In only one case, *Goldberg v. Kelly*, has the Court held that a hearing closely approximating a judicial trial is necessary. In other cases requiring some type of pretermination hearing as a matter of constitutional right[,] the Court has spoken sparingly about the requisite procedures." Then the Court announced the test that would be used henceforth and that became known as the "*Mathews* balancing test," stating:

> [I]dentification of the specific dictates of due process generally requires consideration of three distinct factors: First, the private interest that will be affected by the official action; second, the risk of an erroneous deprivation of such interest through the procedures used, and the probable value, if any, of additional or substitute procedural safeguards; and finally, the Government's interest, including the function involved and the fiscal and administrative burdens that the additional or substitute procedural requirement would entail.

---

13. The Court merely averred that "Eldridge has raised at least a colorable claim that because of his physical condition and dependency upon the disability benefits, an erroneous termination would damage him in a way not recompensable through retroactive payments."

Application of the Balancing Test in *Mathews* Itself

In applying its new test, Justice Powell took pains to distinguish the Social Security context from the welfare context in *Goldberg*.

Factor 1: The private interest that will be affected by the official action. It is clear that the private interest affected has to be carefully analyzed and that it is not necessarily the importance of the entitlement per se. As Justice Powell stated in both *Mathews* and *Goldberg*, because the recipients would be awarded back benefits if they prevailed, their sole interest at the stage of their due process challenge "is in the uninterrupted receipt of this source of income pending final administrative decision on [their] claim."

But Justice Powell distinguished the facts in *Goldberg*, pointing out that "[i]t was emphasized there that welfare assistance is given to persons on the very margin of subsistence." The Court conceded that, due to the "typically modest resources of the family unit of the physically disabled worker," the disruption of benefits may cause significant hardship. In contrast to welfare benefits, however, "[e]ligibility for disability benefits . . . is not based upon financial need," suggesting that disabled workers could still obtain income from welfare or other sources while they litigated their eligibility before SSA.

These distinctions are at best debatable. The Court acknowledged that the delay between the interruption of benefits could be lengthy, approximately a full year. Moreover, people with a disability by definition are not working and have (or at least had) a very serious long-term health problem, and in that sense may be even worse off than welfare recipients. Indeed, they may not qualify for welfare and at the same time are ineligible for SSA's own needs-based program, the Supplemental Security Income (SSI) program, which has the same definition of disability.[14]

Factor 2: The risk of an erroneous deprivation of such interest through the procedures used, and the probable value, if any, of additional or substitute procedural safeguards. Here the Court concentrated on "the fairness and reliability of the existing [SSA] pretermination procedures, and the probable value, if any, of additional procedural safeguards." It began

14. A disability beneficiary who was already receiving SSI benefits would be eligible for a pre-termination hearing under *Goldberg* regarding those benefits because SSI is a needs-based entitlement program.

with a very managerial focus: "To be sure, credibility and veracity may be a factor in the ultimate disability assessment in some cases. But procedural due process rules are shaped by the risk of error inherent in the truthfinding process as applied to the generality of cases, not the rare exceptions."

Again, comparing the case to *Goldberg*, the Court concluded that "[t]he potential value of an evidentiary hearing, or even oral presentation to the decisionmaker, is substantially less in this context than in *Goldberg*." Why? Because it found that the required medical assessment of the worker's condition is "a more sharply focused and easily documented decision than the typical determination of welfare entitlement" where "issues of witness credibility and veracity often are critical to the decisionmaking process."

But, again, this is quite debatable. Welfare cases can turn on many non-credibility issues such as income stream and legal issues. And disability cases can raise many credibility issues: Does the recipient have real back pain or is he faking? What kind of work can she actually do?

The Court conceded that there was a significant reversal rate for revocation cases appealed to ALJs, but discounted that factor because of the open-file system used in the administrative review process that allowed recipients to submit new evidence throughout the appeal. And, notably in its discussion of this prong of the test, the Court concentrated solely on the value of accuracy (risk of error). It omitted discussion of other process values—acceptability, dignity, and right to be heard—that suffused the *Goldberg* opinion.

Factor 3: The government's interest, including the function involved and the fiscal and administrative burdens that the additional or substitute procedural requirement would entail. Finally, the Court considered "the administrative burden and other societal costs that would be associated with requiring, as a matter of constitutional right, an evidentiary hearing upon demand in all cases prior to the termination of disability benefits."

The Court's analysis of these considerations in *Mathews* is 179 degrees different from that in *Goldberg*. The Court was heavily influenced by the cost of inevitably having more hearings and of continuing to pay benefits to recipients who later turn out to be ineligible after their hearing. It also considered the incentive that pre-termination hearings will give for appellants to prolong their appeals. That this had turned out to be an outcome of the *Goldberg* case was doubtless not lost on the majority.[15] In the end the Court deferred to the agency on its judgment that the procedure is sufficient. This is all very different from *Goldberg*, which also factored in the larger public interest—the social value of continuing payments until after an oral hearing for persons previously determined to be eligible. Indeed, this factor proved to be so politically important that Congress and SSA later mandated pre-termination ALJ hearings in these cases notwithstanding that *Mathews* held they were not constitutionally mandated.[16]

Ultimately, *Goldberg* was not overruled, but it was essentially limited to needs-based welfare cases, which themselves largely disappeared with "welfare reform" in the 1990s. One could argue that the recitation of the various grounds on which Social Security is supposedly different from welfare represented a polite way of breaking away from it without conspicuously overruling it only six years later.

---

15. *See generally* Jason Parkin, *Adaptable Due Process*, 160 U. PA. L. REV. 1309 (2012). According to Professors Levin and Asimow, "*Goldberg* triggered a massive increase in hearings. . . . However, nearly half of clients who request a hearing never follow through on their request, which suggests that the request for hearing was being used to keep the checks coming as much as possible." MICHAEL ASIMOW & RONALD M. LEVIN, STATE AND FEDERAL ADMINISTRATIVE LAW 25–26 (4th ed. 2014). And Professor Mashaw points to other responses to the decision by administrators that were harmful to beneficiaries as a whole:

> One was to tighten up and slow down the initial eligibility determination process. Another was to generalize and objectify the substantive eligibility criteria so that messy subjective judgments about individual cases would not have to be made and defended. This move led to the realization that professional social welfare workers were no longer needed. Costs could be reduced further by lowering the quality of the staff and by depersonalizing staff-claimant encounters. If these reactions were not sufficient to restore fiscal balance, then payment levels could be reduced or allowed to remain stable in the face of rising prices . . . . Moreover, because hearings presumably protected the claimants' interests, internal audit procedures were skewed to ignore nonpayment and underpayment problems and concentrate on preventing over-payments and payments to ineligibles.

JERRY L. MASHAW, DUE PROCESS IN THE ADMINISTRATIVE STATE 42 (1985).

16. In 1983, Congress added section 223(g) of the Social Security Act, 42 U.S.C. § 423(g), allowing recipients to elect "in such manner and form and within such time as the Commissioner of Social Security shall by regulations prescribe" to have the payment of such benefits continue until a negative decision was made after hearing. This provision was amended several times to allow continuing payments pending the SSA rulemaking. In 1988 SSA finally completed its rulemaking process by issuing a regulation specifying certain deadlines by which such recipients had to make their election. *See* 20 C.F.R. § 404.1597a (1988).

Justice Brennan, not surprisingly, was not happy. In a terse dissent, he labeled as "speculative" the Court's "consideration that a discontinuance of disability benefits may cause the recipient to suffer only a limited deprivation." Indeed, he pointed out that "in the present case, it is indicated that because disability benefits were terminated there was a foreclosure upon the Eldridge home and the family's furniture was repossessed, forcing Eldridge, his wife, and their children to sleep in one bed."

Mathews's Legacy—Two Views

Since *Mathews* was decided, the Supreme Court and the lower courts have applied it to a multitude of different procedural due process claims.[17] On the one hand, it has been criticized as allowing judges to make decisions based on their "subjective value choices" and for "containing a utilitarian bias that denigrates the intrinsic worth of constitutional rights."[18] On the other hand, as Cynthia Farina concludes at the end of her *Rashomon*-like book chapter "The Stories of *Mathews v. Eldridge*," it "has given lawyers a structure for telling the story of their clients (and the people like them) in a way that judges can locate, and assess, within the constitutional framework." As she put it, "[p]erhaps that is not, after all, such a modest accomplishment."[19]

Bibliography

Michael Asimow & Ronald M. Levin, State and Federal Administrative Law (4th ed. 2014).

Jerome A. Barron & C. Thomas Dienes, Constitutional Law in a Nutshell (11th ed. 2024).

17. *See, e.g.*, Hamdi v. Rumsfeld, 542 U.S. 507 (2004) (persons detained as "enemy combatants"); City of Los Angeles v. David, 538 U.S. 715 (2003) (person seeking a refund of a state fee for towing his illegally parked car); Brock v. Roadway Express, Inc., 481 U.S. 252 (1987) (employer ordered to reinstate an employee before his claim of retaliatory discharge was adjudicated); Ingraham v. Wright, 430 U.S. 651 (1977) (students subject to corporal punishment administered by public school officials).

18. Jerome A. Barron & C. Thomas Dienes, Constitutional Law in a Nutshell 352 (11th ed. 2024).

19. Cynthia R. Farina, *Due Process at Rashomon Gate: The Stories of* Mathews v. Eldridge, *in* Administrative Law Stories 229, 257 (Peter L. Strauss, ed. 2006).

Cynthia R. Farina, *Due Process at Rashomon Gate: The Stories of* Mathews v. Eldridge, *in* ADMINISTRATIVE LAW STORIES 229 (Peter L. Strauss, ed. 2006).

Jeffrey S. Lubbers, *Constitutional and Statutory Foundations*, *in* A GUIDE TO FEDERAL AGENCY ADJUDICATION 245 (Jeremy S. Graboyes ed., 3d ed. 2023).

JERRY L. MASHAW, DUE PROCESS IN THE ADMINISTRATIVE STATE (1985).

Jerry L. Mashaw, *The Supreme Court's Due Process Calculus for Administrative Adjudication in* Mathews v. Eldridge*: Three Factors in Search of a Theory of Value*, 44 U. CHI. L. REV. 28 (1976).

Jason Parkin, *Adaptable Due Process*, 160 U. PA. L. REV. 1309 (2012).

SECTION OF ADMIN. L. & REGUL. PRAC., AM. BAR ASS'N, A BLACKLETTER STATEMENT OF FEDERAL ADMINISTRATIVE LAW pt. 1, § I.D (2d ed. 2013).

Adrian Vermeule, *Deference and Due Process*, 129 HARV. L. REV. 1890 (2016).

Chapter 9

Sierra Club v. Costle, 657 F.2d 298 (D.C. Cir. 1981)

Jeremy Graboyes

It is tempting to think of agency rulemaking as an algorithmic process. An agency confronts a problem. It seeks information—on its own and from the public—and, after neutrally analyzing the information, it arrives at an incontrovertible solution that it implements through a rule.

That is rarely how rulemaking works, however, especially when many people are affected by a rule and there are deep divisions regarding the extent of the problem, the meaning of the information, and the nature of the solution. Instead, regulated entities, regulatory beneficiaries, trade groups, public interest groups, career policymakers, and elected politicians all jostle to influence the agency and determine the outcome of its rulemaking.

Sierra Club v. Costle provides the perfect case study to understand the dynamics of public participation and political involvement in agency rulemaking. It is the story of a high-profile rulemaking, a leaked draft rule, and a dynamic campaign by industry and environmental groups, the White House, other agencies, and members of Congress to shape decision-making by the young Environmental Protection Agency (EPA). Judge Wald's opinion remains the canonical statement on major points of law, including the "questionable utility" of the concept of ex parte contacts in informal rulemaking and the proper role for the White House and members of Congress in agency policymaking.

Setting Emissions Standards for Coal-Powered Generators

The Clean Air Act (CAA) is one of the most important environmental laws and the principal federal statute regulating air quality. First enacted in 1955, the act was substantially amended in December 1970, the same month President Nixon established the EPA by executive order.

An important amendment directed the EPA to establish performance standards for air pollutant emissions by stationary sources (i.e., "any building, structure, facility, or installation which emits or may emit any air pollutant"). The EPA determined that large coal-fired generators were stationary sources and, in December 1971, issued a new source performance standard (NSPS) for them. Operators could satisfy the NSPS by burning coal with a low sulfur content.

In 1976, the Sierra Club and the Oljato and Red Mesa Chapters of the Navajo Tribe petitioned the EPA to revise the NSPS. They claimed that, due to technological advancements, the agency should revise the NSPS to require a 90 percent reduction in sulfur dioxide emissions. In 1977, while the EPA was still considering the petition, a new law required the agency to revise the NSPS for electric power plants by August 1978.

Revising the NSPS for large coal-fired generators was bound to be controversial. The 1970s was a decade of energy crises, and coal remained the leading fuel for generating electricity. Coal was also the bedrock of several regional economies. At the same time, coal-burning electric power plants were emitting more than 18 million tons of sulfur dioxide—a pollutant responsible for respiratory illnesses—each year.

When it was clear the EPA would miss the deadline for revising the NSPS, the Sierra Club sued. A consent decree required the agency to issue a proposed rule in September 1978 and a final rule within the following six months. After additional delays, the agency finally issued a final revised NSPS in June 1979 requiring a 70–90 percent reduction in sulfur dioxide emissions.

Utilities and environmental groups alike objected to the NSPS. Utilities thought it was too stringent, and environmental groups thought it was not stringent enough. After the EPA denied petitions to reconsider the NSPS in February 1980, industry and environmental groups sought judicial review of the revised standard.

The "Ex Parte Blitz"

The EPA's rulemaking is best remembered for the "ex parte blitz" that took place between the close of the comment period in January 1979 and the publication of the revised NSPS six months later.

The EPA circulated a draft NSPS for interagency review in February 1978 that would have established an emissions limit stricter than what the final rule ended up requiring. At some point after the comment period ended, the draft was leaked. Given the significance of the rulemaking, and with so many communications circulating within EPA and throughout the executive branch, the agency was "hardly operating in an insulated bureaucratic environment."[1]

After the leak, there was a flurry of communications between EPA and persons outside the agency. The Environmental Defense Fund (EDF) called it an "ex parte blitz." The agency received more than 300 written submissions during this period, many of them from coal- and utility-industry representatives and members of Congress advocating on their behalf.

EPA officials also met with outside entities to discuss the rulemaking on several occasions. They met with Energy Department officials, for example, and attended White House briefings. EPA officials also met with coal-industry representatives and environmental groups. And at the invitation of Senate Majority Leader Robert Byrd of West Virginia, the EPA administrator attended a meeting at Senator Byrd's office with the senator, National Coal Association officials, and President Carter's domestic affairs advisor.

Written comments and materials associated with all but two meetings were added to the rulemaking docket. But the EPA did not notify the public that it was docketing the materials, nor did it officially reopen the comment period. (Reopening the comment period would have meant further delaying the publication of final rules—a matter already under judicial supervision.) EDF objected.

1. *See* Bruce A. Ackerman & William T. Hassler, *Beyond the New Deal: Coal and the Clean Air Act*, 89 YALE L.J. 1466, 1543 (1980).

"Ex Parte Contacts" and Informal Rulemaking

The Administrative Procedure Act (APA) describes two principal modes for rulemaking: formal and informal. Both require agencies to publish notice of a proposed rule in the *Federal Register*. Formal rulemaking requires agencies to hold a trial-like hearing on the record, just as in an adjudication. Informal rulemaking requires only that agencies give interested persons "an opportunity to participate in the rule making through submission of written data, views, or arguments with or without opportunity for oral presentation."[2]

Some statutes limit communications between agency officials and persons outside the agency during rulemakings. These communications are often called "ex parte contacts," borrowing a term from the judicial context. The APA prohibits ex parte communications in formal rulemaking. The APA does not address ex parte contacts in informal rulemaking.

There is a general consensus that it would be undesirable to categorically prohibit ex parte contacts in informal rulemaking. As the Administrative Conference of the United States (ACUS) stated in a 1977 recommendation:

> A general prohibition applicable to all agencies against the receipt of private oral or written communications is undesirable, because it would deprive agencies of the flexibility needed to fashion rulemaking procedures appropriate to the issues involved, and would introduce a degree of formality that would, at least in most instances, result in procedures that are unduly complicated, slow, and expensive, and, at the same time, perhaps not conducive to developing all relevant information.[3]

Private communications, particularly face-to-face meetings, can "facilitate a more candid and potentially interactive dialogue of key issues," "satisfy the natural desire of interested persons to feel heard," and "be an indispensable avenue for agencies to obtain the information necessary to develop sound, workable policies."[4]

---

2. 5 U.S.C. § 553.
3. ACUS, Recommendation 77-3, Ex Parte Communications in Informal Rulemaking Proceedings, 42 Fed. Reg. 54,253 (Oct. 5, 1977).
4. ACUS, Recommendation 2014-4, "Ex Parte" Communications in Informal Rulemaking, 79 Fed. Reg. 35,993 (June 25, 2014).

Still, there are concerns associated with ex parte contacts, particularly those that take place after a comment period has ended. Issuing rules based on nonpublic information undermines transparency norms and may erode public confidence in agency decision-making. Overreliance on nonpublic information that has not been vetted publicly may affect the quality of rules. Nondisclosure of significant information may also undermine judicial review of agency rules.

One possible solution is to prohibit ex parte contacts altogether. Another approach that balances the benefits of ex parte contacts with concerns over their occurrence is to require that agencies disclose "significant new information" received through ex parte contacts. ACUS has recommended this latter approach, and many statutes and agency rules today employ it.

"Ex Parte Contacts" Under the CAA and the NSPS Rulemaking

Although the CAA contains its own procedures for rulemaking, they largely mirror the procedures for informal rulemaking under the APA. The EPA must publish a notice of proposed rulemaking (NPRM) and "allow any person to submit written comments, data, or documentary information." The agency must also "give interested persons an opportunity for the oral presentation of data, views, or arguments."[5]

Unlike the APA, however, the CAA contains specific requirements for maintaining a public rulemaking docket. Inspired by a law review article by an EPA attorney,[6] the CAA requires the EPA to establish a docket, open for public inspection, when it revises an NSPS. The docket must contain, among other materials, all written submissions received during the public comment period, the transcripts of any oral presentations, and "all documents which become available after the proposed rule has been published and which the Administrator determines are of central relevance to the rulemaking." If an objection of "central relevance to the outcome of the rule"

5. 42 U.S.C. § 7607(d) (1981).
6. William F. Pedersen, Jr., *Formal Records and Informal Rulemaking*, 85 Yale L.J. 38 (1975).

arises after the public comment period, the administrator must convene a proceeding for reconsideration of the rule.[7]

The CAA thus contains a framework for handling written comments received after the close of a comment period without restricting the agency from receiving or considering them. In *Sierra Club*, the U.S. Court of Appeals for the D.C. Circuit found that this framework "accords well with the realities of Washington administrative policymaking, where rumors, leaks, and overreactions by concerned groups abound, particularly as the time for promulgation draws near." Absent an objection of central relevance to the rule or an inability for interested persons to respond to written comments, the D.C. Circuit declined to find any procedural defect with the EPA's handling of documents received after the comment period.

The CAA does not explicitly address, however, oral communications with persons outside the agency that take place after a comment period has ended. EDF asked the D.C. Circuit to extend its decision in *HBO v. FCC* to the NSPS rulemaking. In *HBO*, the court made the seemingly broad holding that once an agency engaged in informal rulemaking issues an NPRM, agency officials should refuse to discuss substantive matters related to the rulemaking with interested private parties.[8] Within a few months of deciding *HBO*, the D.C. Circuit had declined to extend *HBO*'s holding to "informal rulemaking of the general policymaking sort," limiting it to rulemaking that determines "conflicting private claims to a valuable privilege."[9] The court reiterated this holding again in *Sierra Club*.

The court ultimately held the EPA was free to meet with persons outside the agency after the close of the comment period but generally should handle such communications like "documents" received during the same period.

Intra-Executive Communications

Presidential involvement in rulemaking had been "substantial" during the Carter administration,[10] and the president and his staff had participated

7. 42 U.S.C. § 7607(d) (1981).
8. *See* HBO v. FCC, 567 F.2d 9 (D.C. Cir. 1977).
9. Action for Children's Television v. FCC, 564 F.2d 458 (D.C. Cir. 1977).
10. Kenneth Culp Davis, *Presidential Control of Rulemaking*, 56 Tul. L. Rev. 849, 851 (1982).

in at least one meeting with EPA officials related to the rulemaking. The agency had neglected to add information about a meeting with the president and his staff to the rulemaking docket.

Although the court had held that the rulemaking docket should generally reflect oral communications that take place after the end of the comment period, it found unique interests at stake in contacts with the president. Rulemaking is no mere "rarified technocratic process," the court's opinion suggests, and political considerations may well be relevant to its outcome. Given separation-of-powers principles and the U.S. Supreme Court's holding in *Vermont Yankee Nuclear Power Corp. v. Natural Resources Defense Council*,[11] the court held that courts should "tread with extraordinary caution in mandating disclosure beyond that already required by statute."

Of course, an agency must be able to offer a reasoned justification for its rule, and the rule must have some factual support in the record. An agency may also be required by statute or rule to docket intra-executive communications. The CAA, for example, states that the EPA may not base a rule on "any information or data which has not been placed in the docket." The court held that the EPA would be required to docket intra-executive communications that include "information or data" that is otherwise unavailable in the docket.

As the D.C. Circuit noted, this holding is consistent with a 1980 ACUS recommendation that agencies should generally be free to receive written or oral communications from the president, presidential advisors, the Executive Office of the President, and other administrative bodies without docketing them. Agencies should, however, docket any intragovernmental communications that "contain material factual information (as distinct from indications of governmental policy) pertaining to or affecting a proposed rule."[12]

Though grounded in the CAA, the D.C. Circuit's distinction between "'hard' data and analysis, which must be placed in the record, and 'soft'

---

11. 435 U.S. 519 (1978). The case is the subject of Chapter 25.

12. ACUS, Recommendation 80-6, Intragovernmental Communications in Informal Rulemaking Proceedings, 45 Fed. Reg. 86,407 (Dec. 31, 1980); *see also* Paul R. Verkuil, *Jawboning Administrative Agencies: Ex Parte Contacts by the White House*, 80 COLUM. L. REV. 943 (1980).

political arguments, which need not be disclosed," has been applied more generally.[13]

Congressional Pressure

The D.C. Circuit also paid particular attention to meetings between EPA officials and Senator Byrd, which EDF alleged amounted to improper congressional pressure on the agency.

In an earlier case, *D.C. Federation of Civil Ass'ns v. Volpe*, the D.C. Circuit had held that agencies may not make a decision based "in whole or in part on pressures emanating from [an individual member of Congress]" because such a decision would take into account "considerations that Congress could not have intended to make relevant."[14] That case involved a situation in which the chair of a key congressional committee threatened to withhold funding for a project unless an agency reached a certain decision.

In *Sierra Club*, the D.C. Circuit held that to overturn an administrative rulemaking based on congressional pressure, two conditions must be met. First, the content of pressure on an agency official must be "designed to force him to decide upon factors not made relevant by Congress in the applicable statute." Second, the agency's decision "must be affected by those extraneous considerations."

The court found critical differences between the situations in *Sierra Club* and *D.C. Federation of Civil Ass'ns*. Far from threatening the EPA, the court held, Senator Byrd merely requested a meeting, focused on the substance of the proposed rule, and aired his already well-known views. Describing the role for members of Congress in agency rulemaking, the court concluded:

> We believe it is entirely proper for Congressional representatives vigorously to represent the interests of their constituents before administrative agencies engaged in informal, general policy rulemaking, so long as individual Congressmen do not frustrate the intent of Congress as a whole as expressed in statute, nor undermine applicable rules of procedure.

---

13. *See* Richard A. Nagareda, *Ex Parte Contacts and Institutional Roles: Lessons from the OMB Experience*, 55 U. Chi. L. Rev. 591, 620 (1988).
14. 459 F.2d 1231, 1247 (D.C. Cir. 1971).

Significance

Sierra Club is important for three reasons. First, it established that the concept of ex parte contacts is of "questionable utility" in most informal rulemaking—at least for courts on judicial review. Recognizing that too much secrecy can raise fundamental concerns about agency rulemaking, ACUS has recommended best practices for regulating and, when appropriate, disclosing communications that occur after comment periods have ended. Congress and agencies have paid heed.[15]

Second, the case cemented the White House's position at the center of executive branch policymaking. The decision was issued in April 1981, only four months after the Paperwork Reduction Act established the Office of Information and Regulatory Affairs and just two months after Executive Order No. 12,291 directed agencies to submit major rules and accompanying regulatory impact analyses to the Office of Management and Budget for review.[16] Judge Wald's opinion was read at the time as "definitively establish[ing] the legality of White House regulatory review,"[17] and *Sierra Club* is still cited as the "canonical" case on political involvement in agency rulemaking.[18] This legacy has not been uncontroversial.[19] Executive Order No. 12,866 addresses ex parte communications.

15. *See* Sidney A. Shapiro, *Two Cheers for* HBO*: The Problem of the Nonpublic Record*, 54 ADMIN. L. REV. 853, 859–67 (2002).

16. For the current policy on Office of Management and Budget (OMB) regulatory review, see Executive Order No. 12,866, which addresses OMB-related ex parte contacts.

17. Jim Tozzi, *OIRA's Formative Years: The Historical Record of Centralized Regulatory Review Preceding OIRA's Founding*, 63 ADMIN. L. REV. 37, 58–61 (2011); *see also* Christopher G. DeMuth & Douglas H. Ginsburg, *White House Review of Agency Rulemaking*, 99 HARV. L. REV. 1075, 1082 (1986); C. Boyden Gray, *Presidential Involvement in Informal Rulemaking*, 56 TUL. L. REV. 863, 867 (1982); Paul R. Verkuil, *Symposium on Presidential Control of Rulemaking: Introduction*, 56 TUL. L. REV. 811, 814 (1982).

18. *See, e.g.*, Michael A. Livermore, *Political Parties and Presidential Oversight*, 67 ALA. L. REV. 45, 60 (2015); Neomi Rao, *Removal: Necessary and Sufficient for Presidential Control*, 65 ALA. L. REV. 1205, 1223–24 (2014); Peter Strauss, *Legislation That Isn't—Attending to Rulemaking's Democracy Deficit*, 98 CALIF. L. REV. 1351, 1363 (2010); Peter Strauss, *Presidential Rulemaking*, 72 CHI.-KENT L. REV. 965, 968 (1997); Kathryn A. Watts, *Proposing a Place for Politics in Arbitrary and Capricious Review*, 119 YALE L.J. 2, 38–39 (2009).

19. *See, e.g.*, Lisa Heinzerling, *Classical Administrative Law in the Era of Presidential Administration*, 92 TEX. L. REV. 171, 177–80 (2014); *see also* Sidney A. Shapiro & Richard Murphy, *Constraining White House Political Control of Agency Rulemaking Through the Duty of Reasoned Explanation*, 48 U.C. DAVIS L. REV. 1457, 1472–77 (2015).

Finally, *Sierra Club* helped clarify the role members of Congress may play in agency rulemaking, and comments like those made by Senator Byrd more than 40 years ago continue to shape congressional oversight of the executive branch.[20]

Bibliography

BRUCE A. ACKERMAN & WILLIAM T. HASSLER, CLEAN COAL/DIRTY AIR, OR HOW THE CLEAN AIR ACT BECAME A MULTIBILLION-DOLLAR BAIL-OUT FOR HIGH-SULFUR COAL PRODUCERS AND WHAT SHOULD BE DONE ABOUT IT (1981).

Lisa Heinzerling, *Classical Law in the Era of Presidential Administration*, 92 TEX. L. REV. 171 (2014).

Sidney A. Shapiro, *Two Cheers for* HBO: *The Problem of the Nonpublic Record*, 54 ADMIN. L. REV. 853 (2002).

Peter L. Strauss, *Legislation That Isn't—Attending to Rulemaking's Democracy Deficit*, 98 CALIF. L. REV. 1351 (2010).

Jim Tozzi, *OIRA's Formative Years: The Historical Record of Centralized Regulatory Review Preceding OIRA's Founding*, 63 ADMIN. L. REV. 37 (2011).

Paul R. Verkuil, *A Judge of Character*, 52 ADMIN. L. REV. 11 (2000).

20. *See, e.g.*, Jack M. Beermann, *Congressional Administration*, 43 SAN DIEGO L. REV. 61, 131–34 (2006); Jamelle C. Sharpe, *Judging Congressional Oversight*, 65 ADMIN. L. REV. 183, 209–10 (2013); MORTON ROSENBERG & JACK H. MASKELL, CONG. RSCH. SERV., RL32113, CONGRESSIONAL INTERVENTION IN THE ADMINISTRATIVE PROCESS: LEGAL AND ETHICAL CONSIDERATIONS 28–30 (2003).

PART II

Prerequisites to Judicial Review

Chapter 10

Abbott Laboratories v. Gardner, 387 U.S. 136 (1967)

Ronald Levin

A request for judicial review of an agency action may be turned away if the party seeking review has gone to court prematurely.[1] For example, if the party files for review while the agency's proceeding is under way, the petition or complaint might be dismissed on the basis of principles of finality or exhaustion.[2] But an additional type of prematurity must also be considered. The implementation of an administrative program often takes place in a series of discrete steps. Thus, even when the agency has taken "final" action with respect to one of those steps, the government may argue that judicial intervention should await the completion of one or more additional steps. For example, the government might argue that a particular rule should not be open to challenge in court as soon as it has been promulgated; instead, an affected person should wait until the agency has taken action to implement the rule. Such arguments amount to saying that the rule is not *ripe* for review. The framework that courts use in evaluating such contentions was definitively set forth in the U.S. Supreme Court's 1967 decision in *Abbott Laboratories v. Gardner*, commonly called *Abbott Labs*.

---

1. *See* A Guide to Judicial and Political Review of Federal Agencies 7–15 (Michael E. Herz et al. eds., 2d ed. 2015); Section of Admin. L. & Regul. Prac., Am. Bar Ass'n, A Blackletter Statement of Federal Administrative Law pt. 4, § II (2d ed. 2013).
2. See Bennett v. Spear, 520 U.S. 154 (1997), which is the subject of Chapter 14.

The *Abbott Labs* Litigation

The *Abbott Labs* case grew out of the 1962 amendments to the Food, Drug, and Cosmetic Act. This legislation set forth a new requirement for the labeling and advertising of prescription drugs: A drug's generic name must be "printed prominently and in type at least half as large as that used thereon for" the drug's brand name. The Food and Drug Administration (FDA) implemented this statute with a rule providing that a drug's generic name "shall accompany each appearance of such [brand] name." Pharmaceutical companies considered this so-called "every time" requirement burdensome, unnecessary, and unlawful. They filed suit to challenge its validity. The district court agreed with their contentions, but the U.S. Court of Appeals for the Third Circuit ordered the complaint dismissed on two grounds: that Congress had forbidden judicial review of an FDA rule under these circumstances; and that the case was nonjusticiable, or, as we would say today, unripe for review. However, the Supreme Court reversed the Third Circuit holding and held that the companies' suit could proceed.

Preclusion

A threshold question was whether Congress, by providing for judicial review of other types of FDA rules, had impliedly forbidden the courts to entertain a case of this nature. The Administrative Procedure Act (APA) recognizes this type of government defense in section 701(a)(1), which provides that the general right of judicial review afforded by the APA does not apply "to the extent that . . . statutes preclude judicial review." The Court rejected the government's defense in broad language, stating that the APA embodies a "basic presumption favoring judicial review" and that "only upon a showing of 'clear and convincing evidence' of a contrary legislative intent should the courts restrict access to judicial review." In subsequent years, the Court's "presumption" has not been dispositive in every case,[3] but courts have adhered to it in a wide variety of contexts.[4] Indeed, courts often adopt

3. *See, e.g.*, Thunder Basin Coal Co. v. Reich, 510 U.S. 200 (1994).
4. *See, e.g.*, Kucana v. Holder, 558 U.S. 233 (2010); Bowen v. Mich. Acad. of Fam. Physicians, 476 U.S. 667 (1986).

strained interpretations of preclusion statutes in order to avoid concluding that judicial review is unavailable, especially when constitutional values[5] or statutory limitations[6] are at stake.

The Ripeness Analysis in *Abbott Labs*

After dispensing with the preclusion argument, the Court turned to the key issue of whether the controversy was ripe for review. The weight of judicial authority at that time held that the validity of a rule could usually not be contested in a "pre-enforcement" suit. Instead, a regulated party that wanted to dispute the validity of a rule would have to wait until the agency applied it in a particular case.[7] In the context of *Abbott Labs*, this would have meant that the only way the manufacturers could contest the rule would be by violating it and then defending against the FDA's enforcement action on the basis that the rule was unlawful.

Abbott Labs rejected this restrictive approach in favor of a more flexible mode of analysis. Under the Court's framework for assessing the ripeness of a challenge to a rule, a reviewing court should take into account the fitness of the issue for immediate review and the hardship that deferral of review would impose on challengers. The premise of this approach was that the implications of a rule can become clearer over time, so that postponement of review would enable a court to evaluate its legality and rationality in a more informed way. Yet deferral of review would often come at a cost to persons who must live under the rule while such experience is developing, and sometimes that cost is too high.

In this instance, the Court concluded that experience with the "every time" rule in a particular case would shed little if any additional light on its validity, because the parties had argued their positions entirely on the basis of competing accounts of what Congress had intended. Meanwhile, deferral of review would impose hardship on the manufacturers. They would

5. *See, e.g.*, Demore v. Kim, 538 U.S. 510, 517 (2003); Webster v. Doe, 486 U.S. 592, 603 (1988).

6. *See* Sackett v. EPA, 566 U.S. 120 (2012); Traynor v. Turnage, 485 U.S. 535 (1988).

7. *See* Ronald M. Levin, *The Story of the* Abbott Labs *Trilogy: The Seeds of the Ripeness Doctrine*, *in* Administrative Law Stories 431, 442–43 (Peter L. Strauss ed., 2006).

have to begin to comply immediately, at significant expense, with a rule that they regarded as unlawful, or else risk incurring serious civil and criminal penalties.

Pre-Enforcement Review After *Abbott Labs*

Abbott Labs has had a major impact on judicial review. Pre-enforcement review is now commonplace in the federal courts. A party may still challenge the validity of a rule in an enforcement proceeding,[8] but most regulated entities prefer to sue directly, to avoid exposure to liability for not complying with the agency's rule.

Although the Court did not directly say that courts should be predisposed to allow pre-enforcement review, its ripeness test has often had that result, because of the way it has interacted with other trends in administrative law that were developing at around the same time. One such trend was agencies' increasing reliance on rulemaking to make important regulatory decisions.[9] Faced with the issuance of rules that would be very expensive to implement, regulated entities could argue strongly to the courts that they ought to have an opportunity to test the legality of such rules before being required to comply with them.

Moreover, at around the same time as *Abbott Labs*, courts adopted the principle that they should evaluate the factual and policy basis for a rule by looking exclusively at a record compiled during the rulemaking proceeding.[10] This development meant that many disputes about factual and policy issues could be deemed "fit" for judicial review as soon as the rule was promulgated.

Another advantage of pre-enforcement review was that it enables beneficiaries of regulation to seek judicial review of whether a rule provides them with adequate protection.[11] Such appeals could not, by their nature,

---

8. *See* 5 U.S.C. § 703.

9. *See* Antonin Scalia, Vermont Yankee*: The APA, the D.C. Circuit, and the Supreme Court*, 1978 SUP. CT. REV. 345, 376.

10. *See* Admin. Conf. of the U.S., Recommendation 2013-4, The Administrative Record in Informal Rulemaking, 78 Fed. Reg. 41,358, 41,358–59 (June 14, 2013).

11. *See, e.g.*, Cottonwood Env't L. Ctr. v. U.S. Forest Serv., 783 F.3d 1075, 1083–84 (9th Cir. 2015); *In re* Polar Bear Endangered Species Act Listing, 720 F.3d 354, 359 (D.C. Cir. 2013).

be postponed until an enforcement stage because the beneficiaries would not themselves be the targets of enforcement. (Beneficiaries who contend that a rule wrongly deprives them of benefits, however, may have greater difficulty overcoming a ripeness defense because of the difficulty they may face in demonstrating that postponement of review would cause hardship to them.[12])

The shift towards pre-enforcement judicial review is not universally acclaimed. Critics argue, for example, that such review leads courts to overemphasize process and prediction, as opposed to waiting to find out how rules would work out in practice. Moreover, the judicial stays that often accompany pre-enforcement review can cause the implementation of a desirable rule to be delayed for months or years.[13] On the whole, however, these criticisms have not prevailed.[14]

A broader criticism of *Abbott Labs* has been that the APA contains a self-contained body of principles governing judicial review; therefore, the argument goes, ripeness and other case law doctrines that may operate to detract from the statutory right to judicial review are fundamentally illegitimate.[15] This view has never made headway, probably because the federal courts regularly hold, in a wide range of circumstances, that the APA was intended to coexist with principles of equitable discretion. *Abbott Labs* expressly described ripeness as an outgrowth of those principles.

Exclusive Pre-Enforcement Review

Indeed, the norm of pre-enforcement review has become so entrenched that Congress has provided in some enabling statutes—especially in the environmental area—that a rule may be challenged *only* within a short period

12. *See* Reno v. Cath. Soc. Servs., Inc., 509 U.S. 43, 57–61 (1993).
13. *See, e.g.*, JERRY L. MASHAW, GREED, CHAOS, AND GOVERNANCE 177–80 (1997).
14. *See, e.g.*, Richard J. Pierce, Jr., *Seven Ways to Deossify Rulemaking*, 47 ADMIN. L. REV. 59, 88–93 (1995); Mark Seidenfeld, *Playing Games with the Timing of Judicial Review: An Evaluation of Proposals to Restrict Pre-Enforcement Review of Agency Rules*, 58 OHIO ST. L.J. 85 (1997).
15. *See* John F. Duffy, *Administrative Common Law in Judicial Review*, 77 TEX. L. REV. 113 (1998).

following its promulgation, such as 60 days.[16] Such requirements give an especially powerful impetus to the goal of determining promptly whether a rule will or will not go into effect.

In practice, however, courts do not enforce these provisions as strictly as their language seems to invite. Judges recognize that such rules typically continue over time to exert influence over persons who may not have been able to contest them at the time of promulgation. Thus, defendants in enforcement proceedings are sometimes allowed to bring challenges after the statutory deadline, especially when they allege that the rule is unconstitutional or beyond the agency's statutory authority.[17] With regard to factual, discretionary, and procedural issues, however, the preclusion provisions usually are enforced.[18]

Lack of Ripeness

Although *Abbott Labs* changed the landscape of administrative law, the doctrine of ripeness has by no means faded away. Indeed, in a case decided on the same day as *Abbott Labs*, the Court reached a contrasting result. In *Toilet Goods Ass'n v. Gardner*,[19] cosmetics manufacturers challenged an FDA regulation that required them to make their factories, including proprietary formulas, accessible for inspection by FDA personnel. Applying the *Abbott Labs* framework, the Court held that the rule was unripe for review. The manufacturers' objections were not yet appropriate for judicial resolution, because the Court had no idea whether or how the FDA would order inspections, nor how the agency would justify them. These practical issues could only be assessed on an evidentiary record, which did not yet exist. The Court also was unpersuaded that deferral of review would impose hardship on the industry. The rule did not require manufacturers to alter

16. *See* Frederick Davis, *Judicial Review of Rulemaking: New Patterns and New Problems*, 1982 DUKE L.J. 279, 300–08; *see also* Corner Post, Inc. v. Bd. of Governors of Fed. Rsrv. Sys., 603 U.S. 799, 814 (2024).

17. *See* Adamo Wrecking Co. v. United States, 434 U.S. 275, 278–85 (1978); Ronald M. Levin, *Statutory Time Limits on Judicial Review of Rules: Verkuil Revisited*, 32 CARDOZO L. REV. 2203, 2220, 2224–29 (2011).

18. *See* Levin, *supra* note 17, at 2218–19, 2224.

19. 387 U.S. 158 (1967).

their primary conduct. If the FDA ever did find that a manufacturer had violated the rule, it would merely suspend certifying the company's products as suitable for sale, and the company could seek judicial review at that time. The Court said that the plaintiffs had not shown that this alternative would cause significant inconvenience.

More recently, the Court upheld a ripeness defense in *Ohio Forestry Ass'n v. Sierra Club*.[20] In that case, environmentalists brought suit to challenge a Forest Service rule that set forth a plan for logging and clearcutting of forest lands. The Court found, however, that dismissal of the suit would cause no immediate harm to the plaintiffs. Several further steps in the administrative process would have to occur before any trees could be cut, so plaintiffs could renew their challenge after those steps occurred. The Court also noted that these subsequent steps were designed to enable the agency to refine its policies and formulate site-specific proposals. Immediate judicial review could hinder the agency's ability to take those actions and would "threaten[] the kind of 'abstract disagreements over administrative policies' that the ripeness doctrine seeks to avoid."

Even more recently, the Court upheld a ripeness defense in *Trump v. New York*.[21] This was a challenge to a presidential memorandum that declared a policy of excluding undocumented aliens from the calculations that would be used to apportion congressional seats following the 2020 census. The memorandum directed the secretary of commerce to furnish population figures that would facilitate this policy. States that were at risk of losing a congressional seat and some of their federal funding under this policy sued to prevent implementation of the memorandum, but the Court ordered dismissal on the basis of a lack of ripeness (and also lack of standing). The Court emphasized that there was considerable uncertainty about whether the secretary could supply the requested population figures at all, whether and to what extent the president would actually make use of the figures, and how these adjustments would alter federal funding decisions that depend on census data. The Court said that these uncertainties militated against immediate adjudication of the dispute, especially since the plaintiffs would suffer no concrete harm from such postponement.

20. 523 U.S. 726 (1998).
21. 592 U.S. 125 (2020).

The courts have been relatively willing to find judicial review proceedings to be unripe when litigants have asked them to review the validity of interpretive rules or statements of general policy—otherwise known as guidance documents. Because these documents lack the force of law, the government is often able to argue successfully that they do not give rise to the kind of hardship for private persons that would warrant immediate judicial review. For example, in *National Park Hospitality Ass'n v. Department of the Interior*,[22] a rule issued by the department stated that concessionaires that operate in national parks were not entitled to invoke the dispute resolution procedures of the Contract Disputes Act. The concessionaires filed suit to contest the rule, but the Court found the suit to be unripe. The act was actually administered by other adjudicators, and the rule merely stated the department's opinion; concessionaires could and sometimes did choose not to follow it. Realistically speaking, however, some guidance documents do exert substantial and unwelcome influence on regulated persons' conduct. Thus, litigation challenging the validity of such documents does sometimes survive a ripeness defense.[23] In any event, the significance of this doctrinal issue has waned in recent years. Guidance documents are increasingly found not to be final agency action,[24] so that questions about the timeliness of such challenges tend to be resolved on the basis of finality rather than ripeness.

In sum, ripeness analysis depends on a balancing of competing factors and can vary from case to case. The legacy of *Abbott Labs*, however, is that—at least in cases involving rules that have the force of law—modern courts strike the balance in favor of pre-enforcement review much more readily than they once did.

Bibliography

Nicholas Bagley, *The Puzzling Presumption of Reviewability*, 127 HARV. L. REV. 1285 (2014).

22. 538 U.S. 803 (2003); *see also* Am. Tort Reform Ass'n v. OSHA, 738 F.3d 387 (D.C. Cir. 2013).
23. *See, e.g.*, Aviators for Safe & Fairer Regul., Inc. v. FAA, 221 F.3d 222, 225–26 (1st Cir. 2000); Nat'l Automatic Laundry & Cleaning Council v. Shultz, 443 F.2d 689 (D.C. Cir. 1971).
24. See Bennett v. Spear, 520 U.S. 154 (1997), which is the subject of Chapter 14.

Frederick Davis, *Judicial Review of Rulemaking: New Patterns and New Problems*, 1981 Duke L.J. 279.

John F. Duffy, *Administrative Common Law in Judicial Review*, 77 Tex. L. Rev. 113 (1998).

Ronald M. Levin, *Statutory Time Limits on Judicial Review of Rules: Verkuil Revisited*, 32 Cardozo L. Rev. 2203 (2011).

Ronald M. Levin, *The Story of the* Abbott Labs *Trilogy: The Seeds of the Ripeness Doctrine*, *in* Administrative Law Stories 431 (Peter L. Strauss ed., 2006).

Jerry L. Mashaw, Greed, Chaos, and Governance (1997).

Richard J. Pierce, Jr., *Seven Ways to Deossify Rulemaking*, 47 Admin. L. Rev. 59 (1995).

Daniel B. Rodriguez, *The Presumption of Reviewability: A Study in Canonical Construction and Its Consequences*, 45 Vand. L. Rev. 743 (1992).

Section of Admin. L. & Regul. Prac., Am. Bar Ass'n, A Blackletter Statement of Federal Administrative Law pt. 4, § II.C (2d ed. 2013).

Mark Seidenfeld, *Playing Games with the Timing of Judicial Review: An Evaluation of Proposals to Restrict Pre-Enforcement Review of Agency Rules*, 58 Ohio St. L.J. 85 (1997).

Chapter 11

Association of Data Processing Service Organizations, Inc. v. Camp, 397 U.S. 150 (1970)

Kevin Stack

Ass'n of Data Processing Service Organizations, Inc. v. Camp more dramatically reformulated the law of standing than any single decision in the past five decades—and caused as many decades of confusion.

The Standing Dispute and the Supreme Court's Resolution

The litigation presented a classic case of competitor standing. The comptroller general had revised its manual for national banks to permit them to offer data processing services and equipment incidental to their banking services. An association of data processing businesses as well as a Minnesota company sued the comptroller general, arguing that this revision violated the National Bank Act, which gives national banks only "incidental powers as shall be necessary to carry on the business of banking." The data processing plaintiffs invoked Administrative Procedure Act (APA) section 10(a), codified at 5 U.S.C. § 702, for their cause of action. The district court dismissed the suit for lack of standing, and the U.S. Court of Appeals for the Eighth Circuit affirmed. The U.S. Supreme Court reversed the lower courts, explicitly overruling the so-called "legal rights" or "legal interest" analysis that had applied in some standing cases and introducing a new framework to all cases for review of administrative action.

In an eight-page opinion written by Justice Douglas, the *Data Processing* Court introduced a new, two-tiered inquiry—first, whether the plaintiff alleged an "injury in fact," and, second, whether the plaintiff asserted an interest that falls arguably within the "zone of interest" protected by statute—that continues to structure standing law. Applying these new tests, the *Data Processing* Court held that the data processing plaintiffs had standing to challenge the comptroller general's decision because they had alleged an economic injury and their interests fell generally within those the banking statutes sought to protect even though those statutes conferred no legal rights to data processers. Justice Brennan, joined by Justice White, concurred in the result but dissented in a companion case on the ground that the only standing question is the constitutional one of injury.

The Decision's Seismic Shift of Standing Law

The many repetitions of these two new tests—injury in fact and zone of interest—since *Data Processing* can obscure the seismic shift they both represented. At the time of the suit, standing law offered two primary paths for potential plaintiffs challenging government action, neither of which offered hope to the data processing plaintiffs.

First, a plaintiff could obtain standing by alleging that the government's conduct violated a "legal right" belonging to them. Allegations that the government had violated common-law rights of the plaintiff—whether by infringing property, breaching contract, or acting in a tortious manner—clearly satisfied the legal rights (also called legal interest) inquiry.[1] Statutes, too, could create legal rights. For instance, a competitor who alleged that an agency has violated a statutory duty, such as a duty of fair treatment to all railroad carriers,[2] had standing. But mere economic loss and increased competition was not sufficient when the competitor could not locate a duty the agency owed to it.[3]

---

1. *See* Tenn. Elec. Power Co. v. Tenn. Valley Auth., 306 U.S. 118 (1939); Elizabeth Magill, *Standing for the Public: A Lost History*, 95 Va. L. Rev. 1131, 1135–39 (2009).
2. *See* Chicago Junction Case, 264 U.S. 258, 259–62 (1924).
3. *See* Alexander Sprunt & Son, Inc. v. United States, 281 U.S. 249, 255 (1930) (holding that shippers by water lacked standing to challenge an Interstate Commerce Commission decision

Second, even if the plaintiff could not satisfy the legal rights test, a plaintiff could obtain standing if Congress had included a "special statutory review provision" authorizing review in court for those "adversely affected" or "aggrieved" by the agency's action.[4] The Supreme Court established this route to standing in *FCC v. Sanders Bros. Radio Station*[5] in which a radio station challenged a Federal Communications Commission (FCC) decision to license another station in the same market. Although the existing station had no legal right under the communications statute or common law to be free from competition, the communications statute included a special statutory review provision. The *Sanders Bros.* Court held that denying standing would deprive that special provision of any operative force, and accordingly granted the competitor station standing. In this framework, merely being "aggrieved"—which includes almost any allegation of injury—is sufficient to authorize the plaintiff to effectively "stand for the public."[6]

This prior law did not provide the data processing plaintiffs standing. As the lower courts noted, the National Bank Act did not include a special statutory review provision, so the mere allegation of being aggrieved or adversely affected was not sufficient. Nor, as the lower court also held, did the plaintiffs satisfy the legal rights test. The common law grants no right to be free from increased competition, and the National Bank Act created rights and duties only for banks, not for data processing companies. Without a legal right or interest created by statute or the common law, as the Eighth Circuit concluded, "the complaint resolves itself into an attempt merely to show 'a common concern for obedience to law.'"[7]

In reaching this conclusion, the lower courts heeded the prevailing view that the APA's section 702 did not change the standing analysis. Section 702

---

adjusting rates for railroad where the shippers did not allege "a right of his own . . . violated by the order").

4. FCC v. Sanders Bros. Radio Station, 309 U.S. 470, 476 (1940) (holding that Communication Act's provision for suit by persons "aggrieved or whose interests are adversely affected" authorizes suit by a competitor); *see* Magill, *supra* note 1, at 1139–42.

5. 309 U.S. 470.

6. *See* Magill, *supra* note 1, at 1144; William A. Fletcher, *The Structure of Standing*, 98 Yale L.J. 221, 230 (1988). The Court later characterized the decision as giving private litigants standing "only as representatives of the public interest." *See* Scripps-Howard Radio, Inc. v. FCC, 316 U.S. 4, 14–15 (1942).

7. *See* Ass'n of Data Processing Serv. Orgs. v. Camp, 406 F.2d 837, 843 (8th Cir. 1969) (quoting L. Singer & Sons v. Union Pac. R.R., 311 U.S. 295, 304 (1940)).

provides that "[a] person suffering legal wrong because of agency action, or adversely affected or aggrieved by agency action within the meaning of a relevant statute, is entitled to judicial review thereof."[8] The district court treated the provision as it had long been understood—namely, that it "did not by its passage create any legal rights which did not otherwise exist,"[9] but merely directed attention to whether the "relevant statute" created standing,[10] either by creating a legal right or in a special statutory review provision.

The Supreme Court's *Data Processing* decision rolled over these frameworks in its twin holdings. It pronounced that the "first question" of standing is whether the plaintiff has suffered an "injury in fact, economic or otherwise." The Court implied that this requirement was a matter of Article III's case-or-controversy limitation on the jurisdiction of federal courts—an understanding of the source of the requirement that Justices Brennan and White endorsed, and was settled by later doctrine.[11] Although the Court had previously stated plaintiffs must have a personal stake sufficient to ensure adversarial presentation,[12] the Supreme Court had never, prior to *Data Processing*, formulated that stake in terms of the plaintiff establishing an "injury in fact."[13] The *Data Processing* Court had "no doubt" that the plaintiff's allegations of loss of profits, including from two alleged cancelled agreements for data services, satisfied this injury-in-fact test. The test thus appeared to be lenient. Competitors would have an easy time satisfying it, as would, at least in principle, a greater number of regulatory beneficiaries. But the transformation of this formulation was fundamental: the mere allegation of some injury or adverse effect, previously sufficient only when Congress had enacted a special statutory review provision, now seemed to

8. 5 U.S.C. § 702.
9. Ass'n of Data Processing Serv. Orgs. v. Camp, 279 F. Supp. 675, 677 (D. Minn. 1968).
10. *See* Fletcher, *supra* note 6, at 255.
11. *See* Schlesinger. v. Reservists Comm. to Stop the War, 418 U.S. 208, 219 (1974) (holding that case-or-controversy requirement requires "injury in fact"). The leading case on Article III's injury-in-fact requirement is *Lujan v. Defenders of Wildlife*, 504 U.S. 555 (1992), which is the subject of Chapter 13.
12. *See, e.g.*, Flast v. Cohen, 392 U.S. 83, 88 (1968).
13. *See* Magill, *supra* note 1.

take its place as part of the constitutional requirements for standing under Article III.[14]

Data Processing's second renovation was that plaintiffs must also allege that the interest they seek to protect is "arguably within the zone of interests to be protected or regulated by the statute or constitutional guarantee in question." *Data Processing* implied that the zone-of-interest test elaborated section 702's provision for review of persons "aggrieved by agency action within the meaning of a relevant statute."[15] This transformed section 702 by reading it as including its own, generally applicable test—the zone-of-interest test—to supplant the prior inquiry into whether a relevant statute created a legal right or included a special statutory review provision. In applying this test, the *Data Processing* Court read section 702's reference to a "relevant statute" expansively; it held that plaintiffs fell within the zone of interest of section 4 of the Bank Services Corporation Act of 1962, an entirely separate act from the National Bank Act upon which the plaintiffs based their complaint.

What amounts to an interest within the zone also "has not proved self-explanatory."[16] To be distinct from the legal rights test it was replacing, the zone of interests had to be broader than those with legal rights created by the statute. *Data Processing*, especially when read in company with its companion decision, *Barlow v. Collins*,[17] contemplates the reviewing court looking at the purposes of the act, whether explicit in its stated purposes

14. *See* Cass R. Sunstein, *Injury in Fact, Transformed*, 2021 Sup. Ct. Rev. 349, 358–60 (arguing the injury-in-fact inquiry has no historical, statutory, or constitutional foundation).
15. 5 U.S.C. § 702. *See* Section of Admin. L. & Regul. Prac., Am. Bar Ass'n, A Black-letter Statement of Federal Administrative Law pt. 4, § IV.E (2d ed. 2013). The *Data Processing* Court confused the source of the test by also implying it was a prudential rule of "self-restraint." The Court subsequently clarified that the zone-of-interest test glosses section 702. *See* Clarke v. Secs. Indus. Ass'n, 479 U.S. 388, 395 (1987). It has also held that it "applies to all statutorily created causes of action; that it is a 'requirement of general application,'" beyond the APA cases. Lexmark Int'l v. Static Control Components, Inc., 572 U.S. 118, 129 (2014) (quoting Bennett v. Spear, 520 U.S. 154, 163 (1997)). *See* Sunstein, *supra* note 14, at 358–60 (arguing the injury-in-fact inquiry has no historical, statutory, or constitutional foundation).
16. *Clarke*, 479 U.S. at 396.
17. 397 U.S. 159 (1970). The opinion for the Court was also authored by Justice Douglas.

and provisions[18] or implied from its provisions and legislative history, to find a congressional intent to protect the plaintiffs. Thus, in its initial form, the zone-of-interest test imagined a delicate inquiry under section 702 to determine the existence of a set of interests that Congress sought the underlying statutory scheme to protect but did so without conferring legal rights upon the plaintiffs.

Impact of Standing for Challenging Administrative Action

Data Processing's two new tests, at least in their original formulations, enlarged standing for plaintiffs challenging administrative action. By blurring—or simply ignoring—the distinction between standing for those with and without special statutory review provisions, *Data Processing* appeared to level-up many would-be plaintiffs to the status of plaintiffs previously protected by a special statutory review provision; the mere allegation of injury would be enough to establish standing (i.e., to show that Congress had some purpose to benefit the plaintiff). But once that distinction between these two types of standing was obscured, any tightening of what counts as an "injury in fact" as part of the constitutional inquiry would level-down all plaintiffs, even those Congress specifically sought to authorize to sue.

The ensuing developments are familiar. Over the next three decades, the Court increased the demands for establishing constitutional standing, splintering and recasting the inquiry into three sub-elements. To meet the constitutional test for standing, the plaintiff must now allege a "concrete and particularized injury . . . that is fairly traceable" to the defendant's alleged unlawful conduct and that would be "redressed by a favorable judicial decision."[19] As the Court has recognized, these requirements make it "substantially more difficult"[20] for statutory beneficiaries to establish standing than for plaintiffs who are regulated. Just as important, in *Lujan v. Defenders of Wildlife* the Court also read these tests to preclude standing even when

18. *See, e.g.*, *id.* at 164 (examining stated purposes of statute and drawing implications from statutory provisions and legislative history); *Lexmark*, 572 U.S. at 131 (construing zone of interest in non-APA case with reference to Congress's stated purposes).
19. *See Lexmark*, 572 U.S. at 125.
20. Lujan v. Defenders of Wildlife, 504 U.S. 555, 562 (1992).

Congress had authorized it through a special statutory review provision,[21] though it has more recently waffled on this important question.[22]

Following *Data Processing*, the Court has also limited which statutory provisions are relevant to determining the zone of interest. It has restricted that inquiry to whether the plaintiff is within the zone of interest of the particular statutory provision the plaintiff invoked as a basis of the claim.[23] The definition of what interests fall within the zone has been an evolving story, to say the least. The greatest point of clarity is still *Clarke v. Securities Industry Ass'n*,[24] where the Court read the zone-of-interest inquiry in light of the question of the reviewability of agency action. Characterizing the inquiry as "not meant to be especially demanding," the *Clarke* Court emphasized that there need not be a showing of a congressional intent to benefit the plaintiff and that the test should exclude only those plaintiffs whose interests are "so marginally related to or inconsistent with the purposes implicit in the statute that it cannot reasonably be assumed that Congress intended to permit the suit." *Clarke* suggested that "[t]he essential inquiry" is very similar to the reviewability question of "whether Congress intended for a particular class of plaintiffs to be relied upon to challenge an agency's disregard of the law."[25] The Court's recent treatment in *Lexmark International v. Static Control Components*, a non-APA case, picks up this same theme.[26]

---

21. *See id.*
22. *Compare* Massachusetts v. EPA, 549 U.S. 497, 516 (2007) (quoting *Lujan*, 504 U.S. at 580) (Kennedy, J., concurring) ("Congress has the power to define injuries and articulate chains of causation that will give rise to a case or controversy where none existed before."), *with* Summers v. Earth Island Inst., 555 U.S. 488, 497 (2009) ("the requirement of injury in fact is a hard floor of Article III jurisdiction that cannot be removed by statute").
23. *See* Bennett v. Spear, 520 U.S. 154, 175–76 (1997); Jonathan R. Siegel, *Zone of Interests*, 92 GEO. L.J. 317, 336–37 (2004) (examining the resolution of the "relevant statute" question). *Bennett* is the subject of Chapter 14.
24. 479 U.S. 388 (1987).
25. *Id.* at 399.
26. *See* 572 U.S. 118, 130–31 (2014) (holding that Congress authorizes only plaintiffs with a cause of action to sue under the Lanham Act); *see also* Nat'l Credit Union Admin. v. First Nat'l Bank & Tr. Co., 522 U.S. 479, 492 (1998) (holding that commercial bank's status as competitor to credit union drew them within the zone of interest of a statute that imposed limits on credit union membership).

Criticism of the Decision and Its Legacy

The *Data Processing* opinion has been sharply criticized from virtually all corners. For many critics, its essential error was, as Richard Stewart puts it, "wantonly destroying pre-existing law that was sound in principle, reasonably coherent, and capable of accommodating desirable extensions of standing."[27] In this regard, the failure to distinguish between suits where the statute has specially authorized aggrieved parties to appear in court and those where it did not, combined with the development of "injury in fact" as a constitutional matter, set in motion (as Elizabeth Magill argues) the challenge to Congress's power to authorize access to courts for those aggrieved by agency action.[28]

The zone-of-interest inquiry has also been a focus of rebuke. Some, including Justice Brennan, Justice White, and Kenneth Culp Davis,[29] advocated for the test to be abandoned, with the only standing question being the constitutional inquiry. The courts' vacillations in applying the test lend support to Jonathan Siegel's criticism that the inquiry is an unworkable one.[30]

The distinction *Data Processing* makes between standing and the merits has also been subject to withering criticism. If the zone-of-interest inquiry amounts to asking whether the plaintiff has a legally protected interest, then, as Justice Breyer and Richard Stewart argued, the inquiry converges with whether the plaintiff has a claim on the merits. William Fletcher and Lee Albert go one step further, contending that the question of standing is only a question of the merits—whether Congress has authorized review in a statutory case or the Constitution permits it in a constitutional case.[31] More charitably to *Data Processing*, Cass Sunstein has suggested that the adoption of the zone-of-interest test can at least be seen as a step away from conceiving standing within a private law model of monitoring duties

---

27. Richard B. Stewart, *Standing for Solidarity*, 88 YALE L.J. 1559, 1566 (1979).
28. *See* Magill, *supra* note 1, at 1134.
29. *See* Ass'n of Data Processing Serv. Orgs. v. Camp, 397 U.S. 150, 167–78 (1970) (Brennan, J., concurring in result in *Data Processing* and dissenting from Court's opinion in *Barlow v. Collins* on ground that the question is Article III standing); KENNETH CULP DAVIS, ADMINISTRATIVE LAW OF THE SEVENTIES § 22.02.11, at 509 (Supp. 1976). Davis subsequently changed his view.
30. *See* Siegel, *supra* note 23, at 359.
31. Fletcher, *supra* note 6, at 239, 251.

owed to particular persons and toward a public law model of policing the government's fidelity to the law.[32]

The legacy of *Data Processing* for administrative law is decidedly mixed. One could imagine that the framework it announced, despite its inattention to prior law and rough execution, would have done more to overcome the asymmetry between the regulated and regulatory beneficiaries in access to courts. But to do so, it needed to recognize and preserve Congress's power to create rights to challenge agency action in court. *Data Processing* did neither. As a consequence, those same asymmetries reemerged. But they now arise from the abstract elaboration of what counts as suitable and redressable injuries and interests, as opposed to the more specific, manageable, transparent question of whether Congress had created a right for the plaintiff, if aggrieved by agency action, to sue.

Bibliography

Lee A. Albert, *Standing to Challenge Administrative Action: An Inadequate Surrogate for Claim for Relief*, 83 Yale L.J. 425 (1974).

Kenneth Culp Davis, *The Liberalized Law of Standing*, 37 U. Chi. L. Rev. 450 (1970).

A Guide to Judicial and Political Review of Federal Agencies (Michael E. Herz et al. eds., 2d ed. 2015).

William A. Fletcher, *The Structure of Standing*, 98 Yale L.J. 221 (1988).

Yoon-Ho Alex Lee, *A Model of the Zone-of-Interest Test*, 2024 J. L. Econ. & Org. 1.

Ronald M. Levin, *The Administrative Law Legacy of Kenneth Culp Davis*, 42 San Diego L. Rev. 315 (2005).

Elizabeth Magill, *Standing for the Public: A Lost History*, 95 Va. L. Rev. 1131 (2009).

Section of Admin. L. & Regul. Prac., Am. Bar Ass'n, A Blackletter Statement of Federal Administrative Law pt. 4, § IV.D–E (2d ed. 2013).

32. *See* Cass R. Sunstein, *Standing and the Privatization of Public Law*, 88 Colum. L. Rev. 1432, 1446–47 (1988).

Jonathan R. Siegel, *Zone of Interests*, 92 GEO. L.J. 317 (2004).

Richard B. Stewart, *Standing for Solidarity*, 88 YALE L.J. 1559 (1979) (book review).

Peter L. Strauss, *Changing Times: The APA at Fifty*, 63 U. CHI. L. REV. 1389 (1996).

Cass R. Sunstein, *Injury in Fact, Transformed*, 2021 SUP. CT. REV. 349.

Cass R. Sunstein, *Standing and the Privatization of Public Law*, 88 COLUM. L. REV. 1432 (1988).

Chapter 12

Heckler v. Chaney, 470 U.S. 821 (1984)

Bijal Shah

The Administrative Procedure Act (APA) permits judicial review of any "final agency action."[1] Furthermore, the APA expressly defines "agency action" to include an agency's "failure to act,"[2] and requires reviewing courts to "set aside agency action" that is "arbitrary, capricious, an abuse of discretion, or otherwise not in accordance with law."[3] In *Heckler v. Chaney*, the U.S. Supreme Court nonetheless held that an agency's refusal to initiate enforcement proceedings is not ordinarily subject to judicial review. More specifically, the Court determined that the administrative exercise of discretion as to whether to investigate or prosecute allegations of statutory violations is exempt from review under APA section 701(a)(2), which states that an action "committed to agency discretion by law" is categorically exempt from the general rule that agency action is subject to judicial review. The Court made this determination despite its own declaration that section 701(a)(2) applies only rarely, when a statute provides no law for the judiciary to apply.[4] For this reason, *Heckler* is a leading decision on judicial review of administrative nonenforcement of the law.

1. 5 U.S.C. § 704.
2. *Id.* § 551(13).
3. *Id.* § 706(2)(A). The APA also requires the reviewing court to "compel agency action unlawfully withheld or unreasonably delayed." *Id.* § 706(1).
4. *See* Citizens to Preserve Overton Park, Inc. v. Volpe, 401 U.S. 402, 410 (1971) ("The legislative history of the Administrative Procedure Act indicates that [§ 701(a)(2)] is applicable in those rare instances where 'statutes are drawn in such broad terms that, in a given case,

Facts and Holding

The controversy in *Heckler* arose when death row inmates sought judicial review of the Food and Drug Administration (FDA) denial of their petition to enforce laws forbidding the misuse of drugs by state officials administering capital punishment. The essence of the prisoners' petition was that the lethal injection of a mix of prescription drugs was unapproved and caused unnecessary pain and suffering, and therefore administrative action should be taken to ban the use of these drugs for human execution. The FDA refused to act, citing, among other reasons, its "inherent discretion to decline to pursue certain enforcement matters." The question before the Court was whether the FDA's refusal to take enforcement action against the use of certain drugs in implementing the death penalty was reviewable as a potential abuse of administrative discretion. Ultimately, the Court held both that there is a presumption of unreviewability of agency decisions not to undertake enforcement action and that this presumption was not overcome here because there was no clear standard for courts to apply to the FDA's determination not to bring an enforcement action in this situation.

The Supreme Court's Rationale

Fundamentally, *Heckler* established "that an agency's decision not to prosecute or enforce, whether through civil or criminal process, is a decision generally committed to an agency's absolute discretion." First, the Court noted that the administrative exercise of prosecutorial discretion often turns on "a complicated balancing of a number of factors that are peculiarly within [the agency's] expertise," including the availability of scarce resources and whether enforcement against certain violations is consistent with the agency's priorities. Since the agency is "far better equipped than the courts to deal with the many variables involved in the proper ordering of its priorities," the Court determined that it is within the agency's province to decide not to act. In addition, the Court indicated that when an agency "refuses to act it generally does not exercise its *coercive* power over an individual's liberty

there is no law to apply.'") (citing S. Rep. No. 752, at 26 (1945)). The case is the subject of Chapter 24.

or property rights, and thus does not infringe upon areas that courts often are called upon to protect."

The Court also acknowledged that an agency's decision not to act "has traditionally been 'committed to agency discretion'" and "that the Congress enacting the APA did not intend to alter that tradition." As an initial matter, *Heckler* built on precedent suggesting that an agency's exercise of prosecutorial discretion merits some protection from judicial inquiry.[5] Moreover, the Court announced that the choice not to enforce a law is generally unsuitable for judicial review primarily because

> an agency's refusal to institute proceedings shares to some extent the characteristics of the decision of a prosecutor in the Executive Branch not to indict—a decision which has long been regarded as the special province of the Executive Branch, inasmuch as it is the Executive who is charged by the Constitution to "take Care that the Laws be faithfully executed."

For these reasons, the Court held that the agency's decision not to act in this instance was a legitimate example of an action committed to administrative discretion under section 701(a)(2) and was exempt from "the 'common law' of judicial review of agency action."

Subsequent Judicial Interpretations

A number of Supreme Court decisions have sought to articulate the contours of *Heckler*'s conclusion that an agency's discretion is at its height when it decides not to bring an enforcement action.[6] In one case, the Court decided

5. When an agency exercises prosecutorial discretion in clear violation of its governing statute, its decision is reviewable by Article III courts. *See, e.g.*, Leedom v. Kyne, 358 U.S. 184 (1958). Even in those cases, however, judicial review must focus on the agency's reasons for its decision and may not entail a wide-ranging factual inquiry. *See* Dunlop v. Bachowski, 421 U.S. 560 (1975).

6. *See, e.g.*, Young v. United States *ex rel.* Vuitton et Fils S.A., 481 U.S. 787, 817 (1987) (citing *Heckler* in observing that "the discretion our system allows to prosecutors . . . is so broad that we ordinarily find decisions not to prosecute unreviewable") (Scalia, J., concurring). In this and other cases, the Court has limited judicial efforts to control administrative prosecutorial discretion. *See, e.g.*, *Dunlop*, 421 U.S. 560; United States v. Armstrong, 517 U.S. 456, 465 (1996).

that Congress can alter the presumption that "agency enforcement decisions have 'traditionally been "committed to agency discretion"' . . . with a statute that explicitly indicates the contrary."[7] In another, the Court reiterated the need for concrete standards before judicial review of agency exercises of discretion may be triggered. More specifically, in *Webster v. Doe*, the Court emphasized that APA section 701(a)(2) "requires careful examination of the statute on which the claim of agency illegality is based"[8] in order to determine whether, as noted in *Heckler*, the court has a "meaningful standard against which to judge the agency's exercise of discretion."[9] In this way, *Webster* emphasized that both clauses of section 701(a)—that is, both section 701(a)(1), which precludes judicial review if a statute does so, and section 701(a)(2)—are circumscribed by legislation, as opposed to a more general concept of "law" in section 701(a)(2). *Webster* also suggested that even if a statute fails to permit "application of any meaningful judicial standard of review," the courts can nonetheless consider a "colorable constitutional claim" related to agency nonenforcement.[10] Additionally, in *Lincoln v. Vigil*, the Court affirmed more generally *Webster*'s requirement that there be a "meaningful" statutory basis for judicial oversight of agency action.[11]

Other Supreme Court cases have refined *Heckler* to include or exclude specific forms of administrative nonenforcement. For instance, soon after *Heckler* was issued, the Court concluded in *ICC v. Brotherhood of Locomotive Engineers* that most agency refusals to respond to petitions to reopen and reconsider an agency order are not reviewable as a result of section 701(a)(2), unless the petition alleges new evidence or changed circumstances.[12] More recently, however, in *Massachusetts v. EPA*, the Court declared that there are limits to the exemption from judicial review for agencies' refusal to take action and, in particular, that courts may review an agency's negative response to a petition to initiate rulemaking because such petitions involve legal analysis that is rightly subject to judicial review.[13] In addition,

7. FEC v. Akins, 524 U.S. 11, 26 (1998).
8. 486 U.S. 592, 600 (1988).
9. *Id.* (citing Heckler v. Chaney, 470 U.S. 821, 830 (1984)).
10. *Id.* at 600, 603.
11. 508 U.S. 182, 191 (1993).
12. 482 U.S. 270 (1987).
13. 549 U.S. 497 (2007) (finding the Environmental Protection Agency's refusal to avoid regulating greenhouses gasses under the Clean Air Act in response to a petition for rulemaking to be arbitrary and capricious).

it is worth noting that the U.S. Court of Appeals for the Ninth Circuit and other courts of appeals have recognized that *Heckler* does not bar judicial review when an agency's regulation (as opposed to statute alone) provides the judiciary with law to apply[14] and that the U.S. Court of Appeals for the D.C. Circuit's application of *Heckler* has been inconsistent.[15]

Scholarly Reception

According to some scholars, *Heckler* represented an enlargement of the areas of administrative policymaking deemed unreviewable[16]—despite the Court's general support of "a robust presumption in favor of judicial review"[17]—and one that allowed for deregulation to be accomplished by an agency's *lack* of action.[18] Some scholars suggest that by carving out broader areas of agency autonomy from judicial scrutiny, *Heckler* "renounce[d] [previous judicial] distrust of agency autonomy and expertise."[19] Others argue that *Heckler* facilitated a more unitary executive model of administration[20] and

14. *See, e.g.*, Socop-Gonzalez v. INS, 208 F.3d 838 (9th Cir. 2000).
15. *See, e.g.*, Crowley Caribbean Transp., Inc. v. Peña, 37 F.3d 671, 675–76 (D.C. Cir. 1994) (general enforcement policies reviewable); Ass'n of Irritated Residents v. EPA, 494 F.3d 1027, 1030 (D.C. Cir. 2007) (certain polluter consent decrees unreviewable); Sierra Club v. Jackson, 648 F.3d 848, 856 (D.C. Cir. 2011) (agency's failure to prevent construction of unlawful pollution-emitting facilities unreviewable); Cook v. FDA, 733 F.3d 1, 7 (D.C. Cir. 2013) (agency's refusal to prevent importation of unlawful medications reviewable).
16. *See, e.g.*, Ronald M. Levin, *Understanding Unreviewability in Administrative Law*, 74 Minn. L. Rev. 689, 692–93 (1990).
17. Zachary S. Price, *Seeking Baselines for Negative Authority: Constitutional and Rule-of-Law Arguments over Nonenforcement and Waiver*, 8 J. Legal Analysis 235, 246 (2016).
18. *See, e.g.*, Harold J. Krent, *Reviewing Agency Action for Inconsistency with Prior Rules and Regulations*, 72 Chi.-Kent L. Rev. 1187, 1192–93 (1997); Stephen G. Wood et al., *Regulation, Deregulation, and Re-Regulation: An American Perspective*, 1987 B.Y.U. L. Rev. 381, 417. *But see* Daniel E. Walters, *The Judicial Role in Constraining Presidential Nonenforcement Discretion: The Virtues of an APA Approach*, 164 U. Pa. L. Rev. 1911, 1929 (2016).
19. Richard M. Thomas, *Prosecutorial Discretion and Agency Self-Regulation:* CNI v. Young *and the Aflatoxin Dance*, 44 Admin. L. Rev. 131, 142 (1992); *see also* Cass R. Sunstein, *Reviewing Agency Inaction After* Heckler v. Chaney, 52 U. Chi. L. Rev. 653, 683 (1985); Eric Biber, *The Importance of Resource Allocation in Administrative Law*, 60 Admin. L. Rev. 1, 16 (2008) (suggesting that *Heckler* is a symbol of "judicial deference to agency resource allocation").
20. *See* Lisa Schultz Bressman, *Judicial Review of Agency Action: An Arbitrariness Approach*, 79 N.Y.U. L. Rev. 1657, 1678 (2004) (suggesting that *Heckler* is particularly salient when it allows the president more control over agency enforcement action); Kate Andrias, *The*

may even problematically exclude judicial oversight of agency nonenforcement by artificially hinging Article III review of agency inaction on explicit, or even precise, legislative sanction.[21] Scholars have also raised concerns about how broadly *Heckler* should be construed[22] and about its impact on the proper constitutional and administrative separation of powers.[23]

Bibliography

Ashutosh Bhagwat, *Three Branch Monte*, 72 NOTRE DAME L. REV. 157 (1996).

Eric Biber, *The Importance of Resource Allocation in Administrative Law*, 60 ADMIN. L. REV. 1 (2008).

Eric Biber, *Two Sides of the Same Coin: Judicial Review of Administrative Agency Action and Inaction*, 26 VA. ENV'T L.J. 461 (2008).

Lisa Schultz Bressman, *Judicial Review of Agency Action: An Arbitrariness Approach*, 79 N.Y.U. L. REV. 1657 (2004).

Mary M. Cheh, *When Congress Commands a Thing to Be Done: An Essay on* Marbury v. Madison, *Executive Inaction, and the Duty of the Courts to Enforce the Law*, 72 GEO. WASH. L. REV. 253 (2003).

President's Enforcement Power, 88 N.Y.U. L. REV. 1031, 1120 (2013) (suggesting that under *Heckler*, judicial review "is even less likely when a presidential decision is at issue, at least when the decision is understood as properly within the President's power to make").

21. *See, e.g.*, Kenneth Culp Davis, *"No Law to Apply,"* 25 SAN DIEGO L. REV. 1 (1988); Mary M. Cheh, *When Congress Commands a Thing to Be Done: An Essay on* Marbury v. Madison, *Executive Inaction, and the Duty of the Courts to Enforce the Law*, 72 GEO. WASH. L. REV. 253, 279 (2003) (suggesting that by "sound[ing] a retreat from the judicial review of executive refusals to enforce the law [*Heckler* represents a] serious breach of *Marbury* [*v. Madison*]'s core principles"); Bressman, *supra* note 20, at 1692–93 (noting that agency inaction, like agency action, can also be the result of arbitrary administrative decision-making); *see generally* Jim Rossi, *Waivers, Flexibility, and Reviewability*, 72 CHI.-KENT L. REV. 1359 (1997).

22. Cass R. Sunstein & Adrian Vermeule, *The Law of "Not Now": When Agencies Defer Decisions*, 103 GEO. L.J. 157, 171–72 (2014) (noting that *Heckler* left unclear how to define and apply the principle that agencies may not abdicate their statutory duties).

23. *See* Price, *supra* note 17, at 247 (questioning the impact of *Heckler*'s "impulse to insulate a quintessentially executive form of decision—the choice not to enforce a particular law in a particular case—from . . . judicial oversight"); Ashutosh Bhagwat, *Three Branch Monte*, 72 NOTRE DAME L. REV. 157, 158 (1996) ("The main consequence, then, of a rule against review of enforcement decisions is to encourage agencies to make law using their enforcement powers rather than other reviewable avenues such as rulemaking.").

Kenneth Culp Davis, "*No Law to Apply*," 25 San Diego L. Rev. 1 (1988).
Harold J. Krent, *Reviewing Agency Action for Inconsistency with Prior Rules and Regulations*, 72 Chi.-Kent L. Rev. 1187 (1997).
Ronald M. Levin, *Understanding Unreviewability in Administrative Law*, 74 Minn. L. Rev. 689 (1990).
Zachary S. Price, *Seeking Baselines for Negative Authority: Constitutional and Rule-of-Law Arguments over Nonenforcement and Waiver*, 8 J. Legal Analysis 235 (2016).
Jim Rossi, *Waivers, Flexibility, and Reviewability*, 72 Chi.-Kent L. Rev. 1359 (1997).
Section of Admin. L. & Regul. Prac., Am. Bar Ass'n, A Blackletter Statement of Federal Administrative Law pt. 3, § V (2d ed. 2013).
Cass R. Sunstein, *Reviewing Agency Inaction After* Heckler v. Chaney, 52 U. Chi. L. Rev. 653 (1985).
Cass R. Sunstein & Adrian Vermeule, *The Law of "Not Now": When Agencies Defer Decisions*, 103 Geo. L.J. 157 (2014).
Richard M. Thomas, *Prosecutorial Discretion and Agency Self-Regulation:* CNI v. Young *and the Aflatoxin Dance*, 44 Admin. L. Rev. 131 (1992).
Daniel E. Walters, *The Judicial Role in Constraining Presidential Nonenforcement Discretion: The Virtues of an APA Approach*, 164 U. Pa. L. Rev. 1911 (2016).
Stephen G. Wood et al., *Regulation, Deregulation, and Re-Regulation: An American Perspective*, 1987 B.Y.U. L. Rev. 381.

Chapter 13

Lujan v. Defenders of Wildlife, 504 U.S. 555 (1992)

Adam J. White

The Constitution vests the "judicial Power" in a "Supreme Court, and in such inferior courts as the Congress may from time to time ordain and establish,"[1] and it further provides for the "judicial Power" to extend to various kinds of "cases" and "controversies."[2] From the very beginning, the U.S. Supreme Court has understood that these provisions circumscribe the power of Congress and the courts, preventing the courts from deciding matters not presented to them in the proper form, issuing advisory opinions,[3] or deciding purely "political questions."[4] But how should the courts distinguish those matters from the genuine "cases" and "controversies" that the Constitution subjects to their jurisdiction?

In *Lujan v. Defenders of Wildlife*, the Supreme Court consolidated previous standards into a modern doctrine of constitutional "standing," under which a plaintiff may bring suit in federal court only if they have suffered an actual injury caused by the challenged conduct and redressable by the court. The Court's decision was seminal, in that it announced the modern framework that continues to guide courts' assessment of their own jurisdiction over cases. But it also raised many questions that have required further judicial elaboration.

1. U.S. Const. art. III, § 1.
2. *Id.* § 2.
3. *See* Letter from Supreme Court Justices to President George Washington (Aug. 8, 1793).
4. Baker v. Carr, 369 U.S. 186 (1962).

Background

Lujan arose from the U.S. secretary of the interior's promulgation of a rule concluding that section 7 of the Endangered Species Act (ESA) applies only to actions within the United States or on the high seas, and not in foreign territory. Section 7 requires that "any action authorized, funded, or carried out by" federal agencies must not "jeopardize" endangered or threatened species. The Interior Department had previously concluded in a 1978 rule that the ESA applies with full force in foreign territory; but in 1983 the Department reversed course and concluded that this prohibition applies only in U.S. territory and on the high seas.

The interior secretary's rule was challenged in federal district court by environmental groups—including Defenders of Wildlife, which identified two of its members who claimed to be individually harmed by the interior secretary's rule. Each member's injury pertained to a foreign infrastructure project funded in part by the U.S. government: the first member alleged that she had visited Egypt in 1986 to observe Nile crocodiles that might someday be harmed by the Nile River's Aswan High Dam; the second alleged that she had visited Sri Lanka in 1981 to observe the habitat of endangered Asian elephants and leopards, which might someday be harmed by a project funded by the U.S. Agency for International Development. Both members alleged that they might someday return to those sites, but neither had any specific plans to do so.

The Court's Holding and Analysis

The Court's analysis began from first principles. Emphasizing the courts' particular place among our Constitution's three branches of government, Justice Scalia's opinion for the six-Justice majority presented the elements characteristic of "those disputes which are appropriately resolved through the judicial process"—that is, of "the doctrine of standing." Noting but setting aside "merely prudential considerations" that might also bear on standing, the Court focused on "the core component of [constitutional] standing," which it characterized as "an essential and unchanging part of the case-or-controversy requirement of Article III" of the Constitution.

Marshalling precedents touching on various aspects of standing, the Court explained that "the irreducible constitutional minimum" of standing comprises three elements: (1) "injury in fact"; (2) "a causal connection between the injury and the conduct complained of"; and (3) a "likelihood" that the injury will be "redressed by a favorable decision" by the courts.

Each element involved a measure of further nuance.

First and foremost, an "injury in fact" is an "invasion of a legally protected interest" that is both "concrete and particularized," not common to the general population, and "actual or imminent," not "conjectural" or "hypothetical."

Second, as to the causal connection between that injury and the action challenged in court, the injury must be "fairly" "traceable" to the challenged action and not caused by the independent act of a third party.

Finally, while the plaintiff need not show with absolute certainty that the court can ultimately remedy their injury, they must show that it is at least "likely," not "merely speculative," that the injury could be redressed by the court.

The Court emphasized that the plaintiff bears the burden of showing their standing, although the requisite level of proof varies as the case progresses, corresponding to the plaintiff's general burdens throughout a case. At the pleading stage, to survive a motion to dismiss for lack of standing, the plaintiff need only make factual allegations satisfying standing's elements. Later, if faced with a motion for summary judgment against them, the plaintiff must go beyond "mere allegations" and instead provide actual evidence, such as affidavits.

But in the case at hand, the Court held that the plaintiffs had failed to provide evidence sufficient to overcome the interior secretary's motion for summary judgment; indeed, the Court emphasized that the plaintiffs had failed even to allege facts necessary for standing. The Court focused primarily on their failure to demonstrate injury: their description of previous trips to the overseas sites, and their general allegations of personal affinity for those sites, "plainly contain no facts . . . showing how damage to the species will produce 'imminent' injury" to either individual.

The Court also rejected the argument that the plaintiffs had suffered a judicially cognizable "procedural injury" sufficient for standing: statutes granting citizens a right to sue cannot themselves create constitutional standing when the plaintiff lacks his or her own "concrete injury" from the challenged action.

A four-Justice plurality—Justice Scalia, with Chief Justice Rehnquist and Justices White and Thomas—further concluded that the plaintiffs had failed to show causation or redressability. Justices Kennedy and Souter declined to join that part of the majority opinion; Justice Kennedy wrote separately (with Justice Souter), primarily to urge that Congress still has latitude to "define injuries and articulate chains of causation" that can provide standing for citizen suits. Justices Stevens and Blackmun (with Justice O'Connor) both wrote separately to disagree with the Court's standing analysis.

Commentators' Reactions

Observers immediately recognized the potential ramifications of the Court's holding. "This is one more nail in the coffin of citizen standing," one environmental lawyer in the case told the *New York Times*.[5] Just a year later, Professor Gene Nichol echoed such sentiments in a *Duke Law Journal* symposium: *Lujan* was Justice Scalia's "most important opinion in federal courts law." Professor Nichol predicted it would "mark a transformation in the law of standing," but he concluded that its denigration of Congress's power to unilaterally vest citizens with standing was "difficult to square with the language and history of Article III [of the Constitution], with the injury requirement itself, with more modest visions of judicial power, and with time-honored notions of public law litigation."[6] Professors Richard Pierce and Cass Sunstein, among others, shared such views.[7] Sunstein, in particular, observed that although *Lujan* "settled some important questions," it also "left many issues open, and it raised at least as many new ones."[8] Such

5. Linda Greenhouse, *Court Limits Legal Standing in Suits*, N.Y. TIMES, June 13, 1992, at 12.
6. Gene R. Nichol, Jr., *Justice Scalia, Standing, and Public Law Litigation*, 42 DUKE L.J. 1141, 1142–43 (1993).
7. *See* Richard J. Pierce, Jr., Lujan v. Defenders of Wildlife*: Standing as a Judicially Imposed Limit on Legislative Power*, 42 DUKE L.J. 1170 (1993); Cass R. Sunstein, *What's Standing After* Lujan*? Of Citizen Suits, "Injuries," and Article III*, 91 MICH. L. REV. 163 (1992).
8. Sunstein, *supra* note 7, at 223.

new issues included the question of how far plaintiffs might have to go to show concrete "injuries" in the impairment of their future plans,[9] or injuries caused by agency actions that allegedly exacerbate public health risks.[10]

But others applauded the decision, including then-litigator John Roberts, who wrote that *Lujan* was "a sound and straightforward decision applying the Article III injury requirement" that rightly eschewed other "nonconstitutional concept[s] of injury."[11]

Subsequent Issues and Further Elaboration

As Sunstein observed, the Court's formulation of standing's requirements of injury, causation, and redressability left open significant questions about what each requirement specifically entailed, and whether prior precedents' own specific terms remained intact. To fully explore all of those ramifications would require a treatise,[12] But several issues merit particular consideration, beginning with questions about what constitutes an "injury" sufficient for standing.

On the overarching question of whether or how individual plaintiffs could show an "actual," "concrete" injury to their own interests caused by governmental action affecting the environment, the Court would subsequently emphasize that plaintiffs do suffer an actionable injury "when they aver that they use the affected area and are persons 'for whom the aesthetic and recreational values of the area will be lessened' by the challenged activity."[13] Such allegations (or, if the stage in litigation requires it, evidence) of plaintiffs' reasonable concerns suffices where the plaintiffs' showings in *Lujan* failed so long as the plaintiff details specific ways in which their own activities or plans are impacted by the government's action.[14] But with respect to economic injuries, the U.S. Court of Appeals for the D.C. Circuit

9. *Id.* at 227.
10. *Id.* at 228.
11. John G. Roberts, Jr., *Article III Limits on Statutory Standing*, 42 Duke L.J. 1219, 1219–20 (1993).
12. *See, e.g.*, 2 Kristin E. Hickman & Richard J. Pierce, Jr., Administrative Law Treatise § 18.4 (7th ed. 2024).
13. Friends of the Earth, Inc. v. Laidlaw Env't Servs. (TOC), Inc., 528 U.S. 167, 183 (2000).
14. *See id.* at 180–84.

has observed that "'courts routinely credit' assertions founded on basic economic logic in upholding standing."[15]

And while *Lujan* requires an actual injury that is particularized and not merely a generalized grievance, the Court would subsequently conclude that even a "widely shared" injury suffices for standing so long as it is concrete and not merely "abstract and indefinite." Thus, in *FEC v. Akins*,[16] the Court held that plaintiffs had standing to challenge an agency action depriving the public of information when that deprivation affected the plaintiff directly, even if many other people were also affected by the agency's action.

In several cases after *Lujan* addressing whether a particular harm is sufficiently "concrete" to satisfy Article III's injury requirement, the Court has drawn a distinction between tangible harms such as physical or tangible economic injury, which it has said always qualify as Article III injuries, and intangible harms such as the improper disclosure of information, which it has said only sometimes qualify. The Court has emphasized that the latter harms qualify as Article III injuries when, as tangible harms do, they "bear a close relationship to harms traditionally recognized as providing a basis for lawsuits in American courts."[17] This reliance on historical tradition seems to have become an especially prominent feature of the Court's Article III jurisprudence, just as it has been in other areas of constitutional law.

Because *Lujan* held that Congress cannot vest standing in an individual who otherwise lacks standing simply by granting the individual procedural rights in the agency's proceedings, some questions arose about the extent to which procedural injuries would suffice for standing in the aftermath of *Lujan*. The Court would reiterate this point years later in *Summers v. Earth Island Institute*, stressing that "deprivation of a procedural right without some concrete interest that is affected by the deprivation—a procedural right *in vacuo*—is insufficient to create Article III standing." Thus, a plaintiff's deprivation of procedural rights can support standing only when the procedural deprivation "injures him in a concrete and personal

15. Shays v. FEC, 414 F.3d 76, 90 (D.C. Cir. 2005) (quoting United Transp. Union v. ICC, 891 F.2d 908, 912 n.7 (D.C. Cir. 1989)).
16. 524 U.S. 11 (1998).
17. TransUnion LLC v. Ramirez, 594 U.S. 413 (2021); *see* Spokeo, Inc. v. Robins, 578 U.S. 330 (2016). For a critique of *TransUnion*, see Cass Sunstein, *Injury-in-Fact Transformed*, 2021 Sup. Ct. Rev. 349.

way."[18] As the D.C. Circuit has explained, "the plaintiff must show that the government act performed without the procedure in question will cause a distinct risk to a particularized interest of the plaintiff. The mere violation of a procedural requirement thus does not permit any and all persons to sue to enforce the requirement."[19]

Even where a plaintiff shows injury, *Lujan*'s causation element may still remain unsatisfied. Where the injury and the challenged action are separated by independent actions of third parties, the causal chain is broken.[20] But in that situation, the key word is "independent": If the challenged action had a "determinative or coercive effect upon" the intervening third party, then the causal chain may remain intact.[21] Moreover, in cases involving an injury from deprivation of procedural rights, the "normal standards" for causation and redressability are "relaxed," precisely because it is impossible to know whether judicial relief requiring the agency to obey procedural requirements will actually change the agency's ultimate action.[22]

Finally, the Court returned to the "redressability" requirement in later cases, emphasizing that a plaintiff's own prior injuries are not redressed by forward-looking declaratory or injunctive relief, or by civil penalties paid to the government.[23]

Other subsequent developments have helped to situate *Lujan* and progeny into broader principles of constitutional or federal law. In *Steel Co.*, the Court held that courts must resolve questions of constitutional standing before reaching merits issues. In *Massachusetts v. EPA*, the Court announced that states are "entitled to special solicitude in our standing analysis," at least in cases where "quasi-sovereign" interests are implicated by federal agency actions under statutes affording procedural rights to the states.[24]

Finally, the Court's observation in *Lujan* that "each element [of standing] must be supported in the same way as any other matter on which the plaintiff bears the burden of proof" raised a practical question: What burden of

18. Summers v. Earth Island Inst., 555 U.S. 488, 497 (2009) (quoting Lujan v. Defenders of Wildlife, 504 U.S. 555, 580–81 (1992) (Kennedy, J., concurring)).
19. Fla. Audubon Soc'y v. Bentsen, 94 F.3d 658, 664 (D.C. Cir. 1996) (en banc).
20. *See, e.g.*, Murthy v. Missouri, 603 U.S. 43 (2024).
21. Bennett v. Spear, 520 U.S. 154, 169 (1997). The case is the subject of Chapter 14.
22. *Fla. Audubon Soc'y*, 94 F.3d at 678.
23. *See* Steel Co. v. Citizens for a Better Env't, 523 U.S. 83 (1998).
24. 549 U.S. 497, 520 (2007).

proof is placed upon petitioners directly appealing agency action through a petition for review in a circuit court? According to the D.C. Circuit, "[t]he petitioner's burden of production in the court of appeals is accordingly the same as that of a plaintiff moving for summary judgment in the district court: it must support each element of its claim to standing 'by affidavit or other evidence,'" except in cases where the petitioner's standing is "self-evident."[25] In at least one case, the D.C. Circuit has allowed petitioners to introduce new evidence of standing, even after the close of briefing, because the petitioners "reasonably believed their standing [was] self-evident" at the outset of briefing.[26]

Bibliography

Jonathan H. Adler, *Stand or Deliver: Citizen Suits, Standing, and Environmental Protection*, 12 DUKE ENV'T L. & POL'Y F. 39 (2001).

William W. Buzbee, *Standing and the Statutory Universe*, 11 DUKE ENV'T L. & POL'Y F. 247 (2001).

Gene R. Nichol, Jr., *Justice Scalia, Standing, and Public Law Litigation*, 42 DUKE L.J. 1141 (1993).

Richard J. Pierce, Jr., Lujan v. Defenders of Wildlife*: Standing as a Judicially Imposed Limit on Legislative Power*, 42 DUKE L.J. 1170 (1993).

John G. Roberts, Jr., *Article III Limits on Statutory Standing*, 42 DUKE L.J. 1219 (1993).

Antonin Scalia, *The Doctrine of Standing as an Essential Element of the Separation of Powers*, 17 SUFFOLK U. L. REV. 881 (1983).

SECTION OF ADMIN. L. & REGUL. PRAC., AM. BAR ASS'N, A BLACKLETTER STATEMENT OF FEDERAL ADMINISTRATIVE LAW pt. 4, § IV (2d ed. 2013).

Cass R. Sunstein, *Standing Injuries*, 1993 SUP. CT. REV. 37.

Cass R. Sunstein, *What's Standing After* Lujan*? Of Citizen Suits, "Injuries," and Article III*, 91 MICH. L. REV. 163 (1992).

25. Sierra Club v. EPA, 292 F.3d 895, 899–900 (D.C. Cir. 2002).
26. Am. Libr. Ass'n v. FCC, 401 F.3d 489, 492 (D.C. Cir. 2005).

Chapter 14

Bennett v. Spear, 520 U.S. 154 (1997)

William Funk

Under the Administrative Procedure Act (APA), only "final agency action" is subject to judicial review.[1] The test the U.S. Supreme Court set forth for final agency action in *Bennett v. Spear* has become the standard metric by which federal courts determine whether an agency action is reviewable under the APA as "final agency action."

Facts and Holdings

In 1992, the Fish and Wildlife Service issued a biological opinion (BO) to the Bureau of Reclamation in which it concluded that the current operation of the Bureau's Klamath Project would likely jeopardize the continued existence of two species of suckers listed as endangered under the Endangered Species Act (ESA). Under that act, federal agencies are prohibited from jeopardizing the continued existence of listed species. Consequently, in the BO the Service identified "reasonable and prudent measures"—the imposition of minimum water levels in the lakes—by which the Bureau could operate the project without jeopardizing the suckers. The Bureau notified the Service that it would follow those recommended measures. Several ranchers and irrigation districts reliant upon water from the Klamath Project believed such a change in the operation of the project would adversely affect them, and they brought suit against the Service challenging the BO under both the

1. 5 U.S.C. § 704.

ESA's citizen suit provision and the APA. Specifically, the plaintiffs claimed that the BO's jeopardy determination and the reasonable and prudent measures violated section 7 of the ESA and the APA's prohibition of agency action that is "arbitrary, capricious, an abuse of discretion or otherwise not in accordance with law."[2] In addition, they alleged that the imposition of minimum water levels was an implicit determination of critical habitat for the suckers. This determination, they argued, was both arbitrary and capricious and a violation of section 4 of the ESA because it failed to take into consideration the economic impact of such a determination.

The U.S. District Court for the District of Oregon dismissed the suit for lack of Article III standing as well as not being within the zone of interests of the ESA.[3] The U.S. Court of Appeals for the Ninth Circuit affirmed the dismissal, but solely under the zone-of-interests test.[4] The Supreme Court, in a unanimous opinion by Justice Scalia, reversed and remanded. In so doing, it found that the plaintiffs had Article III standing, that they were within the zone of interests under both the ESA and the APA, and that the BO was final agency action under the APA.

The first issue was whether the plaintiffs, who had sued under both the ESA and APA, were within the zone of interests of the ESA. The Court looked to the ESA claim initially because the APA only applies when "there is no other adequate remedy in a court."[5] The lower court had believed that, because the plaintiffs were not interested in protecting endangered species, they were not within the zone of interests of the ESA. The Supreme Court, however, said that the plain language of the ESA's citizen suit provision, which provides that "any person may commence a civil suit," was sufficient to express Congress's intent to expand the zone of interests to anyone who could satisfy Article III standing, whether or not they were environmentalists.

The Court then turned to whether the plaintiffs satisfied Article III standing. Because the case had been dismissed at the pleading stage, the plaintiffs needed only to make "general factual allegations," because courts are to "presum[e] that general allegations embrace those specific facts that

2. *Id.* § 706(2)(A).
3. *See* Bennett v. Plenert, No. 93-6076-HO, 1993 WL 669429, at *1 (D. Or. Nov. 18, 1993).
4. *See* Bennett v. Plenert, 63 F.3d 915 (9th Cir. 1995). On the zone-of-interest test, see Data Processing Serv. Org. v. Camp, 397 U.S. 150 (1970). The case is the subject of Chapter 11.
5. 5 U.S.C. § 704.

are necessary to support the claim." Thus, their general allegation that the Bureau would reduce the total water allocated due to the BO sufficed to include the presumed fact that the general reduction would result in the plaintiffs' receiving less water, thereby injuring them. The government then argued that any such injury would be neither "fairly traceable" to the Service's BO nor "redressable" by a favorable judicial ruling because the Bureau retained ultimate responsibility for determining whether to follow the BO, and here the suit was against the Service. By law, a BO issued by the Service is only advisory, provided as part of interagency consultation; the actual decision as to how to proceed in any given case is by law left to the action agency.[6] The Supreme Court was not convinced. First, it noted that the BO "has a powerful coercive effect on the action agency," and agencies rarely take action inconsistent with a jeopardy determination in a BO. Second, it said that a BO that includes "reasonable and prudent alternatives" to avoid jeopardy "alters the legal regime to which the action agency is subject." This occurs because the BO includes what is known as an "incidental take statement," which is nothing less than an authorization to "take" a limited number of listed species under terms set out in the statement if the agency adopts the reasonable and prudent alternatives. Absent such an authorization, any "take" of a listed species is unlawful. Only if the Bureau adopted the reasonable and prudent alternatives in the BO would the deaths of endangered suckers be lawful. Given "the virtually determinative effect" of a BO, the Court concluded that the plaintiffs had met their burden of alleging that their injury is "fairly traceable" to the Service's BO and that it would "likely" be redressed by a finding that the BO is unlawful.

The government argued that the plaintiffs could not sue under the ESA's citizen suit provision. That provision has two relevant subsections. Subsection (A) allows suits against anyone alleged to be "in violation" of the ESA or regulations thereunder. The other, subsection (C), allows for suit against the secretary of the interior for an alleged failure "to perform any act or duty under section 1533 of this title which is not discretionary with the Secretary."[7] The government maintained that the secretary was neither "in violation" of the ESA nor had he failed to perform any nondiscretionary

6. *See* 16 U.S.C. § 1536(a).
7. *See id.* § 1540(g)(1).

function. The Court said that the ESA's requirement in section 1533 that the secretary consider the economic impact of designating critical habitat was a nondiscretionary duty. It allowed that how the secretary might use that information was a matter of his discretion, but it said that "[i]t is rudimentary administrative law that discretion as to the substance of the ultimate decision does not confer discretion to ignore the required procedures of decisionmaking," citing *SEC v. Chenery Corp.*[8] The plaintiffs' other claim—that the secretary had violated section 7 of the ESA—could not be brought under subsection (C), because the creation of the BO is not performed under section 1533.

The Court thus turned to whether these other claims could be brought under subsection (A), which authorizes suits against anyone in violation of the ESA or its regulations. The government asserted that the secretary's actions could not be deemed to be "in violation" of the ESA within the meaning of this provision. Rather, the purpose of subsection (A) was to enable private parties to enforce the substantive provisions of the ESA against regulated parties. The Court agreed. It noted that to read this provision to allow a suit against the secretary alleging some legal fault with the secretary's implementation of the statute would make subsection (C) superfluous. Congress clearly wished to limit suits against the secretary to only those situations involving nondiscretionary duties.

Having determined that the plaintiffs could sue under the ESA's citizen suit provision regarding the secretary's alleged failure to consider the economic impact of designating critical habitat, but not their other claims, the Court turned to the question whether these other claims could be brought under the APA. The Court first asked whether the plaintiffs' claims were within the zone of interests of the applicable portions of the ESA. The Court noted that the answer to this question was not to be found in the citizen suit provision of the ESA. Nor was the answer to be found "by reference to the overall purpose of the Act in question." Rather, one must look to the "substantive provisions . . . the alleged violations of which serve the gravamen of the complaint." And it quoted from *Lujan v. National Wildlife Federation*: "the plaintiff must establish that the injury he complains of . . . falls within the 'zone of interests' sought to be protected *by the statutory*

8. 318 U.S. 80 (1943). *Chenery I*, as it is known, is the subject of Chapter 22.

provision whose violation forms the legal basis for his complaint."[9] Here the plaintiffs had argued that the Service had not used the "best scientific and commercial data available," as required by the ESA. The Court noted that this requirement undoubtedly served the overall goal of species preservation, but it also served the objective of avoiding needless economic dislocation, inasmuch as economic consequences are explicitly a concern of the ESA.[10] Thus, the Court concluded that the requirement to use the best scientific and commercial data was intended at least in part "to prevent uneconomic (because erroneous) jeopardy determinations." Consequently, the plaintiffs' claim that they are injured by such an erroneous determination put it squarely within the zone of interests of that provision.

The government's last argument to avoid the merits was to say that the BO was not "final agency action" within the meaning of the APA[11] and therefore was not reviewable. The government cited *Franklin v. Massachusetts*[12] for the proposition that one agency's recommendation to another agency is not final agency action, and here, it said, the BO was simply the Service's recommendation to the Bureau. In *Franklin*, Massachusetts had challenged the secretary of commerce's report to the president tabulating the results of the decennial census, which would result in Massachusetts losing a congressional seat if the president accepted that report. The Court held that there was no final agency action because the president was under no duty to accept that report. As a result, the Court said that the report carried "no direct consequences" and served "more like a tentative recommendation than a final and binding determination." The Court in *Bennett*, however, found that case distinguishable.

No one doubted that the BO was the consummation of the Service's decision-making process, one of the requirements for "final agency action." The second requirement, the Court said, is that the action "must be one by which 'rights or obligations have been determined,' or from which 'legal consequences will flow.'" The Court said, drawing on its earlier discussion of standing, that the BO and accompanying incidental take statement "alter[ed] the legal regime to which the action agency is subject," by authorizing the

9. 497 U.S. 871, 883 (1990).
10. *See* 16 U.S.C. § 1536(h).
11. 5 U.S.C. § 704.
12. 505 U.S. 788 (1992).

Bureau to take endangered species if the Bureau adopted the reasonable and prudent measures recommended by the Service. These "direct and appreciable legal consequences" were sufficient to meet the second requirement for "final agency action."

Because the lower courts had erred in finding all of the claims unreviewable, the Court remanded the case for a determination on the merits.

Test for Final Agency Action and Its Implications

The Court's decision in *Bennett* made no notable contribution to the law of standing or zone of interests. Its opinion on those issues was entirely consistent with past decisions. Not so its opinion on final agency action. In stating that final agency action must be action by which rights or obligations have been determined or from which legal consequences will flow, the Court broke new ground. As authority for that statement, it quoted from one case: *Port of Boston Marine Terminal Ass'n v. Rederiaktiebolaget Transatlantic.*[13] But that case did not involve review under the APA at all. Instead, it involved review under the Hobbs Administrative Orders Act (often just known as the Hobbs Act).[14] Under that act, "final orders" from certain agencies under particular statutes are reviewable in courts of appeal, and the Court in that case used the language quoted in *Bennett* to describe such orders. The Court in *Bennett*, moreover, ignored both earlier and later cases under the APA that had used a different test for the second requirement for finality. *Abbott Laboratories v. Gardner*[15] has generally been considered the classic statement of finality, and its articulation of the second part of the finality test provided that "the impact of the [agency action] upon the petitioners [must be] sufficiently direct and immediate as to render the issue appropriate for judicial review," such as having a "direct effect on the day-to-day business" of a person. This test, focusing on the practical rather than legal effects of the agency action, was utilized and

13. 400 U.S. 62 (1970).
14. *See* 28 U.S.C. § 2342.
15. 387 U.S. 136 (1967). The case is the subject of Chapter 10.

reiterated in both *Franklin v. Massachusetts* and *Dalton v. Specter*.[16] Each of these cases was an APA case.

Despite *Bennett*'s seeming deviation from the then-prevailing test, the Supreme Court and lower courts have uniformly cited *Bennett*'s test. The difference between the two tests might not seem that consequential because usually any agency action that has practical and direct effects on a person's day-to-day business activities will stem from an action that has legal consequences. But not always. Interpretive rules and statements of policy do not determine rights or obligations, nor do they have legal consequences, although they often have significant practical consequences. If the *Bennett* test is applied, interpretive rules and agency statements of policy will not be final agency actions and consequently not subject to judicial review.[17]

Recently, the Supreme Court has demonstrated some awareness of the two differing lines of precedent for final agency action. In *U.S. Army Corps of Engineers v. Hawkes Co.*,[18] the Court was faced with a decision by the Corps of Engineers that Hawkes Co.'s property was subject to its jurisdiction. The Corps, however, represented this decision as merely its interpretation of its regulations as applied to a particular person; the agency action did not require the person to do anything or forbid the person from doing anything. The government argued that under *Bennett* there was no legal effect and therefore no final agency action. The Court unanimously rejected that argument. The Chief Justice, after citing *Bennett* for the test for finality, wrote that there was a legal effect. Under a memorandum of understanding (MOU) between the Corps and the Environmental Protection Agency (EPA), if the Corps had found to the contrary—that the property was not subject to its jurisdiction—then both the Corps and EPA would have formally agreed not to bring an enforcement action against Hawkes for a period of years. Thus, a "negative" determination would clearly have a legal effect. Consequently, according to the Court, a "positive" determination was a denial of that legal protection, thereby having its own legal effect.

16. 511 U.S. 462 (1994).
17. *See, e.g.*, Ctr. for Auto Safety v. Nat'l Highway Transp. Admin., 452 F.3d 798 (D.C. Cir. 2006). *See generally* Ronald M. Levin, *Rulemaking and the Guidance Exemption*, 70 ADMIN. L. REV. 263 (2018).
18. 578 U.S. 590 (2016).

The Court could have stopped there, but the Chief Justice's opinion went on, stressing the "pragmatic approach" the Court has taken with respect to questions of finality. He then discussed *Frozen Food Express v. United States*,[19] in which the Court had found the agency action reviewable because of the "immediate and practical impact" on the regulated parties. This two-part justification, citing both legal and practical effects of the agency action, resulted in warring concurrences by Justices Ginsburg and Kagan. Justice Ginsburg wrote to say that in her view the immediate and practical impacts of the Corps' action were sufficient to meet the finality requirement, and she contended that *Bennett* had not changed this historical test to require actual legal effects. Justice Kagan, replying to Justice Ginsburg, expressed her view that the legal effect resulting from the Corps/EPA MOU was necessary to finality; practical impacts were not enough.

Whatever uncertainty *Hawkes* might have suggested as to the proper test for finality, subsequent lower court cases have routinely cited the *Bennett* test for finality.

Bibliography

William Funk, *Final Agency Action After* Hawkes, 11 N.Y.U. J. L. & LIBERTY 285 (2017).

William Funk, *Make My Day! "Dirty Harry" and Final Agency Action*, 46 ENV'T L. 313 (2016).

Stephen Hylas, *Final Agency Action in the Administrative Procedure Act*, 92 N.Y.U. L. REV. 1644 (2017).

Gwendolyn McKee, *Judicial Review of Agency Guidance Documents: Rethinking the Finality Doctrine*, 60 ADMIN. L. REV. 371 (2008).

SECTION OF ADMIN. L. & REGUL. PRAC., AM. BAR ASS'N, A BLACKLETTER STATEMENT OF FEDERAL ADMINISTRATIVE LAW pts. 1, 4, §§ I.F & II.A (2d ed. 2013).

19. 351 U.S. 40 (1956).

PART III

Legal Interpretation in Administrative Law

Chapter 15

Skidmore v. Swift & Co., 323 U.S. 134 (1944)

Kathryn Watts

Before the U.S. Supreme Court overturned the *Chevron* doctrine[1] in *Loper Bright Enterprises v. Raimondo*,[2] agencies frequently issued interpretations of statutes that courts determined did not warrant *Chevron* deference. For example, an agency might have set forth an interpretation of a statute in an interpretive rule, which lacks the force and effect of law and thus fell outside of *Chevron*'s domain.[3] In addition, agencies sometimes issued interpretations of their own regulations that were ineligible for *Auer* deference.[4] In these situations where neither *Chevron* nor *Auer* deference applied, *Skidmore* operated as a fallback. But now that the Court has overturned the *Chevron* doctrine, *Skidmore* will occupy an even more important—indeed, a critical—place in judicial review of agency interpretations of the statutes they administer.

Skidmore calls upon the courts to give weight to an agency's views, even though the agency's views do not bind the courts, if the court finds

1. *See* Chevron v. Nat'l Res. Def. Council, 467 U.S. 837 (1984). The case is the subject of Chapter 16.
2. 603 U.S. 369 (2024). The case is the subject of Chapter 21.
3. *See* United States v. Mead Corp., 533 U.S. 218 (2001); Christensen v. Harris Cnty., 529 U.S. 576 (2000); *see also* Thomas W. Merrill & Kristin E. Hickman, Chevron*'s Domain*, 89 Geo. L.J. 833 (2001). *Mead* is the subject of Chapter 18.
4. *See* Christopher v. SmithKline Beecham Corp., 567 U.S. 142 (2012). *Auer* deference is named after *Auer v. Robbins*, 519 U.S. 452 (1997), the subject of Chapter 17. The Court modified *Auer* in *Kisor v. Wilkie*, 588 U.S. 558 (2019), which is the subject of Chapter 19.

the agency's views persuasive.[5] The precise amount of weight accorded to an agency's views under *Skidmore* depends on a variety of context-specific factors, including the consistency of the agency's views, the thoroughness of the agency's consideration, and other factors that bear on the overall persuasiveness of the agency's interpretation. As a result, a court's application of *Skidmore* can result in an agency interpretation being given no, some, or substantial weight. *Skidmore*, in other words, creates a sliding scale of deference. It does not operate in a rigid or a one-size-fits-all manner.

The Origins of the *Skidmore* Case

In 1938, Congress enacted the Fair Labor Standards Act (FLSA), which, among other things, gave workers the right to overtime compensation in certain circumstances. The act created the Office of the Administrator of the Wage and Hour Division within the Department of Labor (DOL), and it empowered the administrator to bring lawsuits seeking injunctions to restrain violations of the act. However, the act did not give the administrator the power to adjudicate alleged violations of the act. Instead, Congress placed that responsibility with the courts.

After the FLSA went into effect, Jim Skidmore and six other employees of the Swift & Company packing plant in Fort Worth, Texas, filed suit in federal district court seeking unpaid overtime compensation. The employees asserted that they were entitled to approximately $77,000 under the FLSA from Swift for time that they had spent in the company's fire hall waiting to be called in case of a fire alarm. During the time that the employees spent waiting on the company's premises, the employees were free to sleep, to play dominos or pool, and to listen to the radio. Yet the employees asserted that this time spent waiting in the fire hall constituted compensable working time for purposes of the FLSA's overtime pay provisions.

In 1942, the district court ruled against the employees, finding that the time the employees spent waiting did not constitute working hours within the meaning of the FLSA. In so ruling, the district court judge took note of

5. *See* Section of Admin. L. & Regul. Prac., Am. Bar Ass'n, A Blackletter Statement of Federal Administrative Law pt. 3, § II.D (2d ed. 2013).

an interpretive bulletin that had been issued by the administrator in 1939. The administrator's interpretive bulletin took a fairly flexible position on the question of waiting time, explaining that the facts of a given employment situation may suggest that an employee is not working at all times during which he is subject to take an emergency call. Although the district court stated that the "Administrator's ruling on this subject strikes me as right,"[6] the judge found that the time the plaintiffs had spent waiting in the fire hall fell outside the scope of the FLSA's overtime provisions.

On appeal, the U.S. Court of Appeals for the Fifth Circuit affirmed. It also pointed to the administrator's interpretive bulletin, noting that it thought the administrator's interpretation was "correct."[7] The case then went up to the U.S. Supreme Court.

The Supreme Court's 1944 Decision in *Skidmore*

In 1944, the Supreme Court reversed the Fifth Circuit in a unanimous opinion written by Justice Jackson. In its opinion, the Court provided the lower courts with important guidance as to how they should treat an agency's interpretation of a statute that, even though not controlling on the courts, represents the agency's informed judgment. The Court explained that even when an agency view is not binding, the courts should nonetheless give it weight depending on its thoroughness, validity, and consistency, as well as "all those factors which give it the power to persuade, if lacking power to control."

Applying these principles to the case at hand, the Supreme Court explained that Congress had charged the courts, not the administrator, with determining whether a particular case falls inside or outside of the FLSA's coverage. As a result, the administrator's views set forth in the interpretive bulletin and other informal formats were "not controlling" on the courts. Nonetheless, the Supreme Court made clear that the administrator's views constituted a "body of experience and informed judgment to which the courts and litigants may properly resort for guidance."

6. Skidmore v. Swift & Co., 53 F. Supp. 1020, 1021 (N.D. Tex. 1942).
7. Skidmore v. Swift & Co., 136 F.2d 112 (5th Cir. 1943).

Although the district court had properly taken note of the administrator's views in its decision, the Supreme Court concluded that the district court's fairly rigid approach in the case was in tension with the administrator's more flexible views. More specifically, the Supreme Court faulted the district court for failing to assess the particular facts of the employment relationship at hand to determine whether, in this case, the time the plaintiffs had spent waiting did or did not constitute working time. The Court, accordingly, reversed the judgment and remanded for further proceedings.

Skidmore's Continuing Importance

Even though *Skidmore* was decided by the Supreme Court more than seven decades ago, it remained an important decision even after *Chevron*. One reason involved the Supreme Court's rulings in *Christensen v. Harris County*[8] and *United States v. Mead Corp.*[9] These two decisions narrowed the universe of agency interpretations entitled to *Chevron* deference. In doing so, they increased the universe of agency interpretations eligible only for weight under *Skidmore*, not *Chevron* deference.

Specifically, in 2000 in *Christensen*, the Supreme Court declined to give *Chevron* deference to a DOL opinion letter that lacked the force and effect of law. The Court explained that the opinion letter was entitled to respect under *Skidmore* to the extent it was persuasive. Yet, in the end, the Court found the opinion letter unpersuasive.

Subsequently, in 2001 in *Mead*, the Supreme Court declined to afford *Chevron* deference to an interpretation contained in a U.S. Customs Service ruling letter on the ground that there was "no indication that Congress intended such a ruling to carry the force of law."[10] Nonetheless, the Supreme Court disagreed with the lower court's determination that the ruling letter was entitled to no deference at all. Rather, the Court remanded the case, instructing that the lower court apply *Skidmore* to determine how much weight, if any, to give to the ruling letter.

8. 529 U.S. 576.
9. 533 U.S. 218 (2001). The case is the subject of Chapter 18.
10. *Mead*, 533 U.S. at 221.

The Court's opinions in *Christensen* and *Mead* made clear that even when *Chevron* deference was inapplicable because, for example, an agency interpretation lacks the force of law, *Skidmore* remained a fallback. Furthermore, because *Mead* involved direct review of a tariff ruling issued by the U.S. Customs Service, it made clear that *Skidmore* applies to cases involving direct review of agency action, not just cases like *Skidmore* and *Christensen* that involved federal court cases between private parties.

A second development that also underscored *Skidmore*'s continuing vitality after *Chevron*—and that clarified *Skidmore*'s reach—involves the Supreme Court's 2012 decision in *Christopher v. SmithKline Beecham Corp.*[11] In that case, the Court declined to give *Auer* deference to the DOL's interpretation of its own regulations because DOL's interpretation had changed and created a risk of unfair surprise. Nonetheless, even after finding that *Auer* deference was inapplicable, the Court went on to consider whether DOL's interpretation warranted a measure of respect under *Skidmore*. Here, the Court noted that whether weight should be given to DOL's interpretation turned on "the thoroughness evident in its consideration, the validity of its reasoning, its consistency with earlier and later pronouncements, and all those factors which give it power to persuade."[12] Ultimately, the Court found DOL's interpretation "quite unpersuasive" and declined to give it *Skidmore* weight. Nonetheless, the Court's opinion in *Christopher* made clear that *Skidmore* can come into play not only as a fallback to *Chevron* deference, but also to *Auer* deference.[13] In other words, *Skidmore* can be applied not just to an agency's interpretation of a statute, but also to an agency's interpretation of its own regulations.

But now that agency interpretations of statutes will no longer command *Chevron* deference as a result of *Loper Bright Enterprises*, *Skidmore* is sure to assume much greater importance than it did in the post-*Chevron* world. As explained in Chapter 21, the court in *Loper Bright Enterprises* emphasized that, although courts may not defer to agency interpretations of ambiguous statutes, as *Chevron* required them to do, courts must consider those interpretations under *Skidmore*.

11. 567 U.S. 142 (2012).
12. *Id.* at 159.
13. *See also* Gonzales v. Oregon, 546 U.S. 243, 255–56 (2006).

What Is *Skidmore* Deference? Lingering Questions

When determining whether and to what extent to give weight to an agency's views under *Skidmore*, the courts will consider a variety of factors, such as the thoroughness of the agency's consideration, the validity of its reasoning, and the consistency of the agency's views. Sometimes these context-specific factors can prompt a court to dismiss an agency's view as unpersuasive and to decline to give any weight to an agency's views. In contrast, at other times these factors can lead a court to find an agency view highly persuasive and to give it significant weight. In this sense, *Skidmore* operates along a continuum or a sliding scale.

Although the doctrine is easily described, some lingering questions remain as to what, exactly, it requires of courts. First, debate has erupted over whether *Skidmore* is most properly labeled as a deference doctrine or as something else. The crux of this debate centers around the fact that, under *Chevron*, the courts had to defer to (i.e., "accept") an agency's reasonable interpretation of statutory ambiguity (subject to the exceptions noted earlier). Yet, under *Skidmore*, the courts must merely take seriously (i.e., "consider") an agency's views. The courts, in other words, are not bound to adhere to (i.e., to "defer" to) an agency's views under *Skidmore*.[14] For this reason, at least one scholar has suggested that *Skidmore* is most properly labeled as "*Skidmore* weight" rather than "*Skidmore* deference."[15]

Second, precisely because *Skidmore* does not mandate a rigid or a one-size-fits-all type of deference, it can be difficult to predict just how much weight, if any, a court will give to an agency's views under *Skidmore*. The amount of weight will increase or decrease based on a number of highly contextual factors, including the consistency of the agency's views;[16] whether the agency's interpretation was adopted around the time that the statute itself was enacted;[17] the existence of congressional approval or acquiescence;[18]

14. *See, e.g.*, Alaska Dep't of Env't Conservation v. EPA, 540 U.S. 461, 487 (2004).
15. Peter L. Strauss, *Deference Is Too Confusing—Let's Call Them* "Chevron *Space" and* "Skidmore *Weight*," 112 Colum. L. Rev. 1143 (2012).
16. *See, e.g.*, Fed. Express Corp. v. Holowecki, 522 U.S. 389, 399 (2008); *In re* Daley, 717 F.3d 506, 509 (6th Cir. 2013).
17. *See, e.g.*, EEOC v. Arabian Am. Oil Co., 499 U.S. 244, 257 (1991); Udall v. Tallman, 380 U.S. 1, 16 (1965).
18. *See, e.g.*, Bob Jones Univ. v. United States, 461 U.S. 574, 599 (1983).

the agency's expertise;[19] and the thoroughness evident in the agency's consideration.[20] These factors bear on the overall persuasiveness of the agency's interpretation and, as a result, can prompt a court to give no weight, some weight, or a lot of weight to an agency's interpretation. For this reason, it is difficult to quantify with any precision the amount of weight that a court will give to an agency view under *Skidmore*. This uncertainty may become especially pronounced in the aftermath of *Loper Bright Enterprises*.

Bibliography

Kristin E. Hickman & Matthew D. Krueger, *In Search of the "Modern"* Skidmore *Standard*, 108 COLUM. L. REV. 1235 (2007).

Richard W. Murphy, *A "New" Counter-*Marbury*: Reconciling* Skidmore *Deference and Agency Interpretive Freedom*, 56 ADMIN. L. REV. 1 (2004).

SECTION OF ADMIN. L. & REGUL. PRAC., AM. BAR ASS'N, A BLACKLETTER STATEMENT OF FEDERAL ADMINISTRATIVE LAW pt. 3, § II.D (2d ed. 2013).

Peter L. Strauss, *Deference Is Too Confusing—Let's Call Them* "Chevron *Space" and* "Skidmore *Weight*," 112 COLUM. L. REV. 1143 (2012).

Peter L. Strauss, *In Search of* Skidmore, 83 FORDHAM L. REV. 789 (2014).

Jamie A. Yavelberg, *The Revival of* Skidmore v. Swift*: Judicial Deference to Agency Interpretations After* EEOC v. Aramco, 42 DUKE L.J. 166 (1992).

19. *See, e.g.*, *Fed. Express Corp.*, 522 U.S. at 403.

20. *See, e.g.*, Arobelidze v. Holder, 653 F.3d 513, 520 (1st Cir. 2011); Doe v. Leavitt, 552 F.3d 75, 81 (1st Cir. 2009).

Chapter 16

Chevron v. Natural Resources Defense Council, 467 U.S. 837 (1984)

Kent Barnett and Christopher J. Walker

Until June 2024, it was a bedrock principle of federal administrative law that a reviewing court, under the holding of *Chevron v. Natural Resources Defense Council*, must defer to a federal agency's reasonable interpretation of an ambiguous statute that the agency administers. The *Chevron* deference doctrine had been a cornerstone of judicial review of agency action since the U.S. Supreme Court issued the *Chevron* decision in 1984, and the decision itself is one of the most cited Supreme Court decisions of all time. Indeed, as of this writing, *Chevron* has been cited in more than 100,000 sources available on Westlaw, including in more than 18,500 judicial decisions and 22,000 law review articles and other secondary sources.

This cornerstone doctrine was both untouchable and yet, as recent indications from federal judges and Justices suggest, vulnerable to attack or constraint. Indeed, last term in *Loper Bright Enterprises v. Raimondo*, the Court declared that "*Chevron* is overruled. Courts must exercise their independent judgment in deciding whether an agency has acted within its statutory authority, as the [Administrative Procedure Act] requires."[1] What follows describes how *Chevron* deference operated before *Loper Bright* (a case that has its own chapter in this book). Understanding *Chevron* remains necessary to understanding this difficult area of law.

1. 603 U.S. 369, 412 (2024). The case is the subject of Chapter 21.

In *Chevron*, the Supreme Court articulated a now-famous two-step framework for judicial deference to agency statutory interpretations. First, the reviewing court determines whether the statutory provision at issue is ambiguous. To determine whether "Congress had an intention on the precise question at issue," as the *Chevron* Court explained in footnote nine, the court must "employ[] traditional tools of statutory construction." If the statute is unambiguous, that is the end of the matter, and no deference is afforded. If the statute is ambiguous, however, the reviewing court proceeds to the second step and assesses whether the agency's interpretation is reasonable. As the *Chevron* Court explained in footnote 11, the reviewing "court need not conclude that the agency construction was the only one it permissibly could have adopted to uphold the construction, or even the reading the court could have reached if the question had arisen in a judicial proceeding." Instead, the agency's interpretation need only be "permissible" or reasonable.

Despite the apparent simplicity of this two-step framework, courts, litigants, and scholars over the past three decades have struggled with, and even argued against, *Chevron* deference on a number of fronts. We briefly summarize those developments here, beginning with steps one and two and then looking at the threshold question of whether to apply the *Chevron* deference framework at all. The chapter concludes with a brief summary of the current calls to eliminate *Chevron* deference entirely and return to *Chevron*'s theoretical foundation.

Step One: What Counts as an Ambiguity?

The Supreme Court has been far from clear—one might say ambiguous—as to how *Chevron*'s first step should operate. *Chevron* itself called for reliance on "traditional tools of statutory construction," and it relied on statutory text, historical development of the Clean Air Act, and legislative history of relevant amendments as tools. Yet over the decades, the Court has arguably turned the first step into a purely textual inquiry, meaning that step one has become a textualist, as opposed to an intentionalist, inquiry. Questions abound about which interpretive tools should apply at step one, including whether courts should use substantive canons such as constitutional avoidance and clear-statement rules to resolve ambiguity. Other questions concern the degree of ambiguity required to advance to the second step. Courts have often suggested that any silence or ambiguity is enough. More recently, however, the Supreme Court has applied more textual and contextual tools to eliminate ambiguity and has suggested perhaps a less-agency-friendly "clear enough" standard.[2]

What is clear, however, is that, of the two steps, the first is the most outcome determinative, at least as *Chevron* is applied in the federal courts of appeals. In our empirical study of all published *Chevron* decisions in the circuit courts from 2003 through 2013, we found that federal agencies only prevailed 39 percent of the time when the circuit courts found the statute unambiguous at step one. If the circuit courts reached step two, by contrast, federal agencies prevailed 94 percent of the time.[3]

Step Two: When Is an Interpretation Unreasonable?

Whereas much ink has been spilt regarding *Chevron* step one, the same is not true for step two. The Supreme Court has provided little guidance on this reasonableness inquiry, which may partly explain why federal courts seldom reject an agency's interpretation at step two. The Court originally suggested some sort of hypertextualist inquiry but, increasingly, has embraced a second step that involves an inquiry into an agency's reasoned decision-making similar to arbitrary-and-capricious review under the Administrative Procedure Act (APA).[4]

Among the circuit courts, however, three distinct approaches to step two have emerged: (1) a more searching textualist or structuralist inquiry into the statutory ambiguity in light of the whole statute; (2) an enhanced purposivist or contextualist inquiry; and (3) an APA-like arbitrary-and-capricious review.[5] Unlike the Supreme Court, the circuit courts have

2. *See, e.g.*, Wis. Cent. Ltd. v. United States, 585 U.S. 274, 283 (2018).
3. *See* Kent Barnett & Christopher J. Walker, Chevron *in the Circuit Courts*, 116 Mich. L. Rev. 1, 33 fig.2 (2017).
4. *See, e.g.*, Judulang v. Holder, 565 U.S. 42, 52 n.7 (2011).
5. *See* Kent Barnett & Christopher J. Walker, Chevron *Step Two's Domain*, 93 Notre Dame L. Rev. 1441 (2018).

generally not embraced a hypertextualist inquiry when rejecting an agency's statutory interpretations at step two. Instead, the predominant circuit court approach has applied arbitrary-and-capricious review, while others have embraced a more purposivist inquiry into congressional intent. *Chevron* step two is fertile ground for more theoretical and doctrinal development.

Step Zero: When Does *Chevron* Apply?

Uncertainty exists not only as to *how*, but also *when Chevron* applies. The *Chevron* Court indicated that the two-step framework applied to all interpretations concerning a statute that an agency administers. But the Court has indicated that not all interpretive issues are suitable for deference. In other words, there is a threshold, "step zero" inquiry regarding the *Chevron* framework.

Most notably, the Court has confirmed that *Chevron*'s framework does not apply to questions of "deep 'economic and political significance' that [are] central to [the] statutory scheme" at issue.[6] Such questions, although rare, concern, for example, an Internal Revenue Service (IRS) interpretation of "an Exchange established by the State"[7] and the attorney general's statutory interpretation implicating "medical judgments" outside of their expertise.[8] Otherwise, the Court has given little guidance regarding this "major questions" exception to *Chevron* deference.

Relatedly, the uncertainty as to when *Chevron* applies extends to the method by which the agency must provide its interpretation. After *Chevron*, the Court has clarified in two leading decisions that *Chevron* applies only to agency statutory interpretations with the "force of law."[9] Those interpretations are usually the product of notice-and-comment rulemaking or "formal" adjudication. But less formal interpretations may also occasionally qualify, such as interpretive rules or policy statements.[10] This indeterminacy

6. King v. Burwell, 576 U.S. 473, 486 (2015).
7. *Id.* at 485–86.
8. Gonzales v. Oregon, 546 U.S. 243, 266–67 (2006).
9. United States v. Mead Corp., 533 U.S. 218 (2001); Christensen v. Harris Cnty., 529 U.S. 576 (2000). *Mead* is the subject of Chapter 18.
10. *See, e.g.*, Barnhart v. Walton, 535 U.S. 212 (2022).

over which agency actions have the force of law has led to the "*Mead* puzzle," as lower courts attempt to determine which agency actions suffice. In 2022, for instance, the Supreme Court noted that *Chevron* did not apply to "[t]he scope of judicial review" because it was "hardly the kind of question that the Court presumes that Congress implicitly delegated to an agency."[11]

Revisiting *Chevron*'s Theoretical Foundation

Before considering recent calls to eliminate *Chevron* deference, it is helpful to revisit the doctrine's theoretical foundation. The Court has regularly grounded deference in a theory of congressional delegation. Under this theory, courts must defer to an agency's interpretation because there is "a 'presumption that Congress, when it left ambiguity in a statute meant for implementation by an agency, understood that the ambiguity would be resolved, first and foremost, by the agency, and desired the agency (rather than the courts) to possess whatever degree of discretion the ambiguity allows.'"[12] In other words, under this congressional delegation theory, it would arguably violate separation of powers for courts to displace federal agencies—the entities Congress has charged with implementing the statute—as the primary resolvers of those statutory ambiguities.

Although the Court has failed to provide a robust normative basis for the congressional delegation theory, it has suggested that the delegation theory resides in four separate comparative advantages of agencies over courts: (1) expertise, (2) deliberative process, (3) political accountability, and (4) national uniformity or stability in federal law.

First, agency expertise is considered one of the bedrock rationales for *Chevron* deference. Congress delegates interpretive authority to agencies, instead of generalist courts, at least in part because those agencies are more expert than courts in the subject matter. Second, while the *Chevron* decision itself did not focus on the value of the deliberative process involved in the agency crafting its statutory interpretation, subsequent decisions have so

11. Smith v. Berryhill, 587 U.S. 471, 486 (2019).
12. Nat'l Cable & Telecomms. Ass'n v. Brand X Internet Servs., 545 U.S. 967, 982 (2005) (quoting Smiley v. Citibank (S.D.), N.A., 517 U.S. 735, 740–41 (1996)).

focused.[13] In other words, certain agency procedures, such as notice-and-comment rulemaking, may better address the democratic deficits involved in lawmaking delegation than traditional judicial review.

Third, the *Chevron* Court expressly embraced a political accountability rationale for *Chevron* deference: "Judges are not experts in the field, and are not part of either political branch of the Government."[14] Agencies, by contrast, are part of a political branch (the executive) and report back to another political branch (the legislature). Accordingly, it makes sense for Congress to delegate policymaking implementation to more politically accountable agencies than Article III courts. Finally, more recently the Court has recognized the "stabilizing purpose of *Chevron*," in that the agency can set a uniform interpretation of ambiguous federal law that the lower federal courts can only displace when deemed unreasonable.[15]

The Rise of *Chevron* Skeptics

Perhaps because of *Chevron*'s evolving or uncertain theoretical grounding, it has opened itself up to existential challenge. In recent years, we have seen a growing call from the federal bench, Congress, and within the legal academy to eliminate *Chevron* deference. In 2015, Justice Thomas expressed constitutional concerns about *Chevron* deference.[16] In 2016, Republicans in Congress followed suit by introducing the Separation of Powers Restoration Act, which would amend the APA to require courts to review *de novo* all agency statutory and regulatory interpretations.[17] Some circuit judges subsequently expressed concerns about these deference doctrines, culminating in an extensive discussion of now-Justice Gorsuch's skepticism of *Chevron* deference at the Senate Judiciary Committee hearing on his nomination to the Supreme Court.[18] More recently, in one of his last opinions on the

13. *See, e.g.*, *Mead*, 533 U.S. at 229. The case is the subject of Chapter 18.
14. *See, e.g.*, Kent Barnett et al., *Administrative Law's Political Dynamics*, 71 Vand. L. Rev. 1463 (2018).
15. City of Arlington v. FCC, 569 U.S. 290, 307 (2013).
16. *See* Michigan v. EPA, 576 U.S. 743, 760–64 (2015) (Thomas, J., concurring).
17. *See* H.R. 4768, 114th Cong. § 2 (2016); S. 2724, 114th Cong. § 2 (2016).
18. *See, e.g.*, Waterkeeper All. v. EPA, 853 F.3d 527, 539 (D.C. Cir. 2017) (Brown, J., concurring in judgment); Egan v. Delaware River Port Auth., 851 F.3d 263, 278 (3d Cir. 2017)

Court, Justice Kennedy joined Justices Thomas and Gorsuch in expressing constitutional concerns about *Chevron* deference, at least with respect to how it has been applied in the lower courts.[19] And Justice Kennedy's replacement—Justice Kavanaugh—has similarly expressed doubts about *Chevron*'s future.[20]

In addition to the statutory argument that *Chevron* deference is not consistent with the text of section 706 of the APA, the predominant arguments against *Chevron* deference fall into two main categories. First, contrary to the vesting in Article I of all legislative powers in Congress, *Chevron* deference encourages members of Congress to delegate broad lawmaking power to federal agencies and thus frustrate the values of the nondelegation doctrine. Second, *Chevron* deference interferes with the federal judiciary's constitutional role under Article III to exercise independent judgment to "say what the law is."[21]

This rise of *Chevron* skeptics culminated in the Court overruling *Chevron* in *Loper Bright* in June 2024. *Loper Bright* has its own chapter in this book (see Chapter 21).

Bibliography

Aditya Bamzai, *The Origins of Judicial Deference to Executive Interpretation*, 126 Yale L.J. 908 (2017).

Nicholas R. Bednar & Kristin E. Hickman, Chevron's *Inevitability*, 85 Geo. Wash. L. Rev. 1392 (2017).

Jack M. Beermann, *End the Failed* Chevron *Experiment Now: How* Chevron *Has Failed and Why It Can and Should Be Overruled*, 42 Conn. L. Rev. 779 (2010).

Cary Coglianese, Foreword, Chevron's *Interstitial Steps*, 85 Geo. Wash. L. Rev. 1339 (2017).

(Jordan, J., concurring in judgment); Gutierrez-Brizuela v. Lynch, 834 F.3d 1142, 1149 (10th Cir. 2016) (Gorsuch, J., concurring).

19. *See* Pereira v. Sessions, 585 U.S. 198, 219–21 (2018).

20. *See* Brett M. Kavanaugh, Book Review, *Fixing Statutory Interpretation*, 129 Harv. L. Rev. 2118, 2150–54 (2016).

21. Marbury v. Madison, 5 U.S. (1 Cranch) 137, 177 (1803).

William N. Eskridge, Jr. & Lauren E. Baer, *The Continuum of Deference: Supreme Court Treatment of Agency Statutory Interpretations from* Chevron *to* Hamdan, 96 GEO. L.J. 1083 (2008).

Cynthia R. Farina, *Statutory Interpretation and the Balance of Power in the Administrative State*, 89 COLUM. L. REV. 452 (1989).

Abbe R. Gluck & Lisa Schultz Bressman, *Statutory Interpretation from the Inside—An Empirical Study of Congressional Drafting, Delegation, and the Canons: Part I*, 65 STAN. L. REV. 901 (2013).

THOMAS W. MERRILL, THE CHEVRON DOCTRINE: ITS RISE AND FALL, AND THE FUTURE OF THE ADMINISTRATIVE STATE (2022).

Thomas W. Merrill, *The Story of* Chevron*: The Making of an Accidental Landmark*, *in* ADMINISTRATIVE LAW STORIES 399 (Peter L. Strauss ed., 2006).

Thomas W. Merrill & Kristin E. Hickman, Chevron*'s Domain*, 89 GEO. L.J. 833 (2001).

Antonin Scalia, *Judicial Deference to Administrative Interpretations of Law*, 1989 DUKE L.J. 511.

SECTION OF ADMIN. L. & REGUL. PRAC., AM. BAR ASS'N, A BLACKLETTER STATEMENT OF FEDERAL ADMINISTRATIVE LAW pt. 3, § II.B–C (2d ed. 2013).

Matthew C. Stephenson & Adrian Vermeule, Chevron *Has Only One Step*, 95 VA. L. REV. 597 (2009).

Peter L. Strauss, *"Deference" Is Too Confusing—Let's Call Them* "Chevron *Space" and* "Skidmore *Weight,"* 112 COLUM. L. REV. 1143 (2012).

Cass R. Sunstein, Chevron *as Law*, 107 GEO. L.J. 1613 (2019).

Cass R. Sunstein, Chevron *Step Zero*, 92 VA. L. REV. 187 (2006).

Chapter 17

Auer v. Robbins, 519 U.S. 452 (1997)

Jennifer Mascott

The U.S. Supreme Court's decision in *Auer v. Robbins* rose to prominence for the principle that courts should defer to agency interpretations of their own regulations. Under *Auer*, an agency's interpretation of the legal scope and effect of its prior acts is "controlling unless plainly erroneous or inconsistent with the regulation." Originating in case law from at least as early as the mid-20th century, this principle has also been applied to legal interpretations of prior agency actions residing in policy statements, interpretive rules, and adjudicative determinations.[1] As explained in the next chapter, the Supreme Court significantly narrowed the availability of *Auer* deferential review in *Kisor v. Wilkie* in 2019.[2] But a general *Auer* deference framework remains in place.

Auer deference to interpretations of regulations can be viewed as a companion principle to the *Chevron* deference that, until recently, applied to agency interpretations of ambiguous statutes.[3] Until the Court's narrowing of the doctrine in *Kisor*, however, the related *Auer* and *Chevron* deference principles bore some important distinctions.

1. *See, e.g.*, Udall v. Tallman, 380 U.S. 1, 3–4 (1965).
2. *See* 588 U.S. 558 (2019). The case is the subject of Chapter 19.
3. *See* Chevron U.S.A., Inc. v. Nat. Res. Def. Council, Inc., 467 U.S. 837 (1984). The case is the subject of Chapter 16.

For example, the Supreme Court had indicated in *United States v. Mead*[4] in 2001 that *Chevron* deference applies only to agency interpretations issued through sufficiently formal procedures such as notice-and-comment rulemaking. The Court did not correspondingly impose that threshold limitation on *Auer* deference, which *Auer* itself had applied to an interpretation first delivered in the Supreme Court briefs in the case. This initial distinction between *Chevron* and *Auer* regarding the two frameworks' threshold formality requirements for the imposition of deference may be due to the distinct justifications that had initially motivated the *Chevron* and *Auer* deference regimes. *Auer* authority had been described as law-reporting in contrast to the lawmaking power that *Chevron* indicated Congress delegates to agencies when it enacts broadly worded statutes leaving policymaking gaps for agencies to fill.[5]

In addition, prior to *Kisor*, some courts had suggested that the *Auer* standard was even more deferential to agency interpretations than *Chevron* deference.[6] *Chevron* deference itself, however, was sufficiently generous that courts had frequently affirmed agency interpretations when applying either *Auer* deference to an agency's interpretations of its own prior legal acts such as regulations or *Chevron* deference to an agency's statutory interpretation.[7]

The Facts Underlying *Auer* and the Doctrine's Application

In *Auer v. Robbins*, a lieutenant and sergeants working for the St. Louis Police Department sued members of the city board of police commissioners for overtime pay under the federal Fair Labor Standards Act (FLSA). The act requires certain employers to pay time and a half for each hour worked beyond 40 hours in a given week. But the FLSA also exempts numerous

4. 533 U.S. 218 (2001). The case is the subject of Chapter 18.
5. *Compare* Jeffrey A. Pojanowski, *Revisiting* Seminole Rock, 16 Geo. J. L. & Pub. Pol'y 87, 96 (2018), *with Chevron*, 467 U.S. at 843–44.
6. *See* C.F. Commc'ns Corp. v. FCC, 128 F.3d 735, 738 (D.C. Cir. 1997); Paradissiotis v. Rubin, 171 F.3d 983, 987 (5th Cir. 1999); *see also Udall*, 380 U.S. at 16.
7. *See, e.g.*, *Mead*, 533 U.S. at 227; *see also* Cynthia Barmore, Auer *in Action: Deference After* Talk America, 76 Ohio St. L.J. 813 (2015); Kent H. Barnett & Christopher J. Walker, Chevron *in the Circuit Courts*, 116 Mich. L. Rev. 1 (2017).

classes of employees from these overtime requirements, including those "employed in a bona fide executive, administrative, or professional capacity."

The secretary of labor had promulgated regulations establishing that employees qualified for these senior exempt categories if they earned a certain minimum income on a "salary or fee basis." The secretary in turn defined "'salary basis'" to mean regular payments of "a predetermined amount" that are "not subject to reduction because of variations in the quality or quantity of the work performed."[8] But the regulations provided an exception to this limitation, ensuring that employees subject to penalties just for safety-related infractions would remain within the "salary basis" standard. And the secretary further expounded in his Supreme Court brief that the regulatory scheme transformed an otherwise exempt senior employee category into a non-overtime-exempt position only where there was an "actual practice" of punishing the employees with a pay reduction or an employment policy that made the deduction likely.

As in many cases involving agency interpretations of legal requirements, the secretary's overtime pay interpretation was challenged as an unlawful application of both the relevant statute and the accompanying regulations. Regarding interpretation of the statute, the police commissioner board argued that even a regular practice of imposing disciplinary pay reductions should not remove senior professional employees from overtime-exempt status. In the board's view, pay adjustments are one of the few disciplinary alternatives available to government employers, and the availability of this disciplinary tool should not be treated like a standard pay variation in the private sector. The Court readily rejected this argument under *Chevron* deference, finding that it was reasonable to subject public and private employers to the same overtime rules. The Court, however, ultimately found for the board because it deferred to the secretary's regulatory interpretation that the disciplinary pay reduction principle was not applicable to the senior employees at issue.

The interpretive analysis for which *Auer* is best known comes in the part of the opinion affirming lower court findings in favor of the board based on deference to the secretary's interpretation of his own salary-basis

8. 29 C.F.R. § 541.118(a) (1996).

regulations. The secretary had concluded that the employee petitioners were not "'subject to'" regular pay deductions and therefore were senior salaried employees, ineligible for mandatory overtime pay. In an amicus brief filed at the Court's request, the secretary "interpret[ed] the salary-basis test" to exclude only employees who "'as a practical matter'" were subject to disciplinary payment penalties and concluded that the lieutenant and sergeants at issue in the case were not.

In affirming the secretary's amicus brief interpretation, the Court stated: "Because the salary-basis test is a creature of the Secretary's own regulations, his interpretation of it is, under our jurisprudence, *controlling unless plainly erroneous or inconsistent with the regulation*." The Court found that standard "easily met here" as the secretary's interpretation fit "comfortably" within the meaning of the salary-basis regulation. Presumably because of the Court's decision to defer to the secretary's interpretation, the Court engaged in abbreviated interpretive work. The Court noted simply that dictionaries define "'subject to' to mean 'prone; disposed.'" The Court then explained that the secretary's "as a practical matter" standard was "usefully illustrated" by this case. The police manual provision on disciplinary pay reductions applied just in the abstract to all departmental employees—both to the more senior-level petitioners as well as to junior-level staff. This nominal applicability did not "effectively communicate" that pay deductions were indeed anticipated for employees at the professional level of the petitioners.

One additional component of the Court's deference bears note. The petitioners had requested that the Court apply the interpretative canon that fair labor statutory exemptions should be construed against employers. But the Court rejected application of the canon to the secretary's interpretation of a regulation versus a statute, because the secretary had the power to write the initial regulation as broadly or narrowly as he wished. This conclusion suggests that typical canons of construction embodying substantive presumptions generally should not apply to agency administrators' interpretations of the rules that they create.

Petitioners had also more generally objected to the application of deference because the secretary's interpretation had appeared in a legal brief. The Court dismissed this concern since the Court had asked the secretary to submit the brief containing the challenged interpretation. The Court thus concluded that the secretary's position in this case was not an attempt to create a new post hoc defense of regulatory action and that there was no reason to doubt the agency's "fair and considered judgment."

Origins of *Auer* Deference

The concept of deference to an agency's interpretation and application of its regulations did not originate with *Auer* in 1997. The doctrine has deeper roots, from as early as 1945, that are in tension with the Court's broad application of deference in *Auer* and its progeny.

In *Bowles v. Seminole Rock*,[9] decided the year before enactment of the Administrative Procedure Act, the Court reviewed a challenge to the implementation of World War II-era price regulations. The Court said perhaps even more clearly than it did in *Auer* that "a court must necessarily look to the administrative construction of the regulation if the meaning of the words used is in doubt." That construction then "becomes of controlling weight unless it is plainly erroneous or inconsistent with the regulation."[10]

But the manner of applying the standard in the two cases differed. The *Seminole Rock* Court applied fairly exacting review to the relevant agency interpretation despite several phrases in the opinion suggesting nearly automatic deference to an agency's interpretive view.[11] The Court began by describing its own "read" of "the plain words of the regulation," which it detailed extensively. The Court explained that the relevant regulatory text could be interpreted either to adopt the highest price of goods *sold* in March 1942 regardless of their delivery date, or to adopt the highest sales price for only those goods that were actually *delivered* that month. The Court concluded that the fact of delivery was the operative element in the rule, so for purposes of the rule "the highest price charged for an article delivered

9. 325 U.S. 410 (1945).
10. *Id.* at 413–14.
11. In what would become an oft-cited formulation, the Court stated most notably that "the ultimate criterion" for choosing between competing regulatory interpretations is the relevant agency's "administrative interpretation, which becomes of controlling weight unless it is plainly erroneous or inconsistent with the regulation." *Id.* at 414.

during March, 1942 [wa]s the seller's ceiling price regardless of the time when the sale or charge was made."[12]

The Court noted, only then, that even if lingering interpretive doubts remained, they would be "removed by reference to the administrative construction" of the rule issued by the Office of Price Administration (OPA). The OPA administrator's interpretation had been uniform throughout the Office's "countless explanations" of the rule.[13] The Court's own understanding of the regulation in conjunction with OPA's consistency compelled adherence to the challenged regulatory interpretation. Still, the Court was unwilling to definitively conclude that the regulation was lawful. The Court noted its assessment did not guarantee that the agency's underlying regulation was within the proper scope of statutory authority, just that the agency's subsequent interpretation was consistent with the four corners of the regulation.

Subsequent Narrowing of *Auer* Deference

In the years after *Auer*, the Court repeatedly clarified and narrowed the contours of the deference regime's application. For example, the determination in *Auer* to give weight to an agency interpretation in a litigation brief was walked back in part 15 years later in *Christopher v. SmithKline Beecham Corp.*[14] There, writing for the Court, Justice Alito declined to rely on the Department of Labor's brief interpreting overtime requirements, partly on the ground that an agency's litigating position often will be calculated and likely does not reflect a neutral view of the law. Unlike in *Auer*, in *Christopher* the Court had not solicited the brief. Further, the relevant agency interpretation appeared for the first time after the Supreme Court had granted review in the case, and it reversed a long-standing agency view on which private interests had heavily relied. In *Christopher*, the Court left open the possibility that *Auer* typically would apply to positions "advanced in a legal brief," but noted that this general rule would not uniformly apply,

12. *Id.*
13. *Id.* at 417–18.
14. 567 U.S. 142 (2012).

such as in *Christopher* where the new position created "unfair surprise."[15] Foreshadowing limitations that the Court would impose more broadly and with the support of more Justices a few years later in *Kisor*, the Court in *Christopher* further specified that *Auer* deference would not apply where the new interpretation "conflicts with a prior interpretation," the interpretation appears to be "nothing more than a convenient litigating position," or the position is a "*post hoc* rationalization . . . to defend past agency action."[16]

Lower federal courts soon noted the Court's clarification of limits on the *Auer* regime. One empirical study issued several years after *Christopher* indicated that the rate at which courts grant *Auer* deference to an agency's interpretation of its regulations declined from 82.3 percent in 2011 and 2012 to 70.6 percent as of 2014.[17]

Even prior to its 2012 limitations on litigating positions in *Christopher*, the Court in *Gonzales v. Oregon* in 2006 indicated that it would grant only *Chevron* and not *Auer* deference if a regulation merely "parroted," or restated, the terms of the underlying statute.[18] In other words, if the substantive content of the regulation and interpretation were merely identical, the agency could not use the alleged "reinterpretation" of the regulation through an informal interpretation as a roundabout means to receive greater-than-*Chevron* deference. Finally, in 2019, the Court in *Kisor* rejected litigants' request that the Court overrule *Auer* deference entirely by instead formalizing and strengthening many of these limitations. *Kisor* is the subject of Chapter 19 of this book.

Bibliography

Cynthia Barmore, Auer *in Action: Deference After* Talk America, 76 Ohio St. L.J. 813 (2015).

John F. Manning, *Constitutional Structure and Judicial Deference to Agency Interpretations of Agency Rules*, 96 Colum. L. Rev. 612 (1996).

15. *Id.* at 155–56 (internal quotation omitted).
16. *Id.* at 155 (internal quotations omitted).
17. *See* Barmore, *supra* note 7, at 827.
18. 546 U.S. 243, 256–57 (2006) (internal quotation omitted).

Aaron L. Nielson, *Beyond* Seminole Rock, 105 GEO. L.J. 943 (2017).

Jeffrey A. Pojanowski, *Revisiting* Seminole Rock, 16 GEO. J. L. & PUB. POL'Y 87 (2018).

SECTION OF ADMIN. L. & REGUL. PRAC., AM. BAR ASS'N, A BLACKLETTER STATEMENT OF FEDERAL ADMINISTRATIVE LAW pt. 3, § III (2d ed. 2013).

Cass R. Sunstein & Adrian Vermeule, *The Unbearable Rightness of* Auer, 84 U. CHI. L. REV. 297 (2017).

Chapter 18

United States v. Mead Corp., 533 U.S. 218 (2001)

Jack Beermann

United States v. Mead Corp. was the U.S. Supreme Court's most important pronouncement on *Chevron*'s domain[1]—that is, when an agency's statutory interpretation would receive deference under the now-overruled *Chevron* doctrine.[2] In *Mead*, the Court declined to afford *Chevron* deference to the U.S. Customs Service's interpretation of the Harmonized Tariff Schedule of the United States (HTSUS) contained in a Customs Service ruling letter. To understand why requires a brief look back at the origins of the *Chevron* doctrine and an examination of the process by which the Customs Service issues ruling letters.[3]

As Chapter 21 explains, the Court overruled *Chevron* deference in *Loper Bright Enterprises v. Raimondo*.[4] But *Mead*, like *Chevron*, remains a foundational case for understanding the relationship between court and agency in interpreting statutes.

1. *See* Thomas W. Merrill & Kristin E. Hickman, Chevron*'s Domain*, 89 Geo. L.J. 833 (2001).
2. *See* Chevron U.S.A., Inc. v. Nat. Res. Def. Council, Inc., 467 U.S. 837 (1984). The case is the subject of Chapter 16.
3. *See* Section of Admin. L. & Regul. Prac., Am. Bar Ass'n, A Blackletter Statement of Federal Administrative Law pt. 3, § II.B, C (2d ed. 2013).
4. 603 U.S. 369, 412 (2024). The case is the subject of Chapter 21.

Basis for *Chevron* Deference

In a decision that is familiar to anyone interested in administrative law, the *Chevron* Court held that courts should defer to reasonable agency interpretations of ambiguous provisions in the statutes they administer. The Court's primary justification for *Chevron* deference was congressional intent to delegate interpretive authority to the administering agency. Perhaps most controversially, the *Chevron* Court did not confine *Chevron* deference to cases of express congressional delegation of interpretive authority to the administering agency. Rather, it found intent to delegate implicit in ambiguity, apparently reasoning that Congress's meta-intent is to prefer agency to judicial interpretation of ambiguous statutes. Although critics and defenders of *Chevron* deference such as the late Justice Scalia characterized this as "fictional, presumed intent,"[5] by the time the *Mead* case arrived at the Supreme Court, intent to delegate interpretive authority, explicit and implicit, was firmly in place as the theoretical basis for *Chevron* deference.

Background of *Mead*

The *Mead* litigation arose out of the Customs Service's counterintuitive determination that loose-leaf day planning pages imported by Mead, which purchasers would insert into reusable notebooks each year, were subject to a four percent tariff under the HTSUS's category of "Diaries . . . bound." This determination was embodied in a "Headquarters ruling letter" that the Court characterized as "short on explanation." Mead appealed this ruling within the agency, and Customs Headquarters reaffirmed its decision in another unpublished letter, which the Court characterized as "carefully reasoned." Mead's appeal to the Court of International Trade was similarly unsuccessful, but the U.S. Court of Appeals for the Federal Circuit agreed with Mead that Customs ruling letters should receive no deference and that Mead's loose-leaf day planning inserts were neither "diaries" nor "bound," which meant that they were not subject to the four percent tariff that Customs had imposed.

5. Antonin Scalia, *Judicial Deference to Administrative Interpretation of Law*, 1989 Duke L.J. 511, 517; *see also* Lisa Schultz Bressman, Chevron*'s Mistake*, 58 Duke L.J. 549, 562 (2009).

Issues in the Supreme Court

The Supreme Court granted the government's petition for certiorari to address whether the Customs Service's determination that Mead's day planners were subject to the four percent tariff was entitled to deference on judicial review. The government argued that the Customs Service's decision was entitled to deference because it was the "formal interpretation of a statute adopted by the agency that has been 'charged with responsibility for administering the provision' by Congress."[6] The government also relied upon a long history and strong tradition of deference to executive branch decisions relating to the administration of the tariff laws.

Although the government argued that *Chevron* and related doctrines provided the appropriate standard of deference, the government also urged the Court to reject the Federal Circuit's "no deference" determination, even if it agreed that *Chevron* did not apply, and, at a minimum, to apply the so-called *Skidmore*[7] factors to determine the degree of deference that the Customs Service's decision should receive.

By contrast, the Mead Corporation argued that the Customs Service's decision should receive no deference primarily because classifying loose-leaf day planners as "diaries, bound" contravened the plain and unambiguous language of the HTSUS. That is, Mead argued that, under *Chevron* step one, the Customs Service's interpretation was not entitled to any deference because Congress's intent was clear. Mead also argued that the Customs Service's interpretation should not receive *Chevron* deference because, the clarity of the statute aside, it was embodied in an informally issued ruling letter and was not the product of formal adjudication or notice-and-comment rulemaking.

In *Mead*, the Court relied heavily on the Court's then-recent decision in *Christensen v. Harris County*, in which the Court rejected an argument for affording *Chevron* deference to a Department of Labor opinion letter construing the Fair Labor Standards Act. That opinion letter was formulated in response to an inquiry by one of the parties and did not purport to be binding. In *Christensen*, the Court reasoned that *Chevron* deference

6. Brief for Petitioner at 19, United States v. Mead Corp., 533 U.S. 218 (2001) (No. 99-1434), 2000 WL 977426, at *19.

7. *See* Skidmore v. Swift & Co., 323 U.S. 134 (1944). The case is the subject of Chapter 15.

was not appropriate for "an interpretation contained in an opinion letter, [as opposed to] one arrived at after, for example, a formal adjudication or notice-and-comment rulemaking."[8] *Christensen* did not actually foreclose *Chevron* deference for the Customs Service's ruling letter in *Mead* because the ruling letter was an actual, binding decision on the transaction, not a mere expression of the agency's opinion.

The Supreme Court's Decision

Although the Customs Service's ruling letter constituted a binding decision, the Court, in an opinion by Justice Souter, came down firmly against *Chevron* deference for the Customs Service's ruling letter, largely on the second ground argued for by Mead: that an informally arrived at decision is not entitled to the same level of deference as an agency determination made pursuant to formal adjudication or notice-and-comment rulemaking. While that conclusion seems sensible, given that more formal procedures usually lead to better reasoned decisions and are more likely to represent an agency's official position, explaining the decision within the *Chevron* framework was more complicated than may appear at first glance.

Recall that in *Chevron*, the Court justified the arguably new form of deference it recognized there on a theory of delegation: that whenever Congress leaves a gap or ambiguity in a statute, it thereby delegates primary interpretive authority to the agency administering the statute. On that understanding, it seems clear that the Customs Service had been delegated interpretive authority over the HTSUS. In *Mead*, however, the Court added a significant qualification to *Chevron*'s delegation theory: that congressional intent to delegate most likely exists only when Congress instructs an agency to employ a "relatively formal administrative procedure" such as rulemaking or formal adjudication. Because the Customs Service issued ruling letters without first conducting notice-and-comment rulemaking or a formal adjudication, its ruling letters were not subject to *Chevron* deference.

The *Mead* Court relied upon additional grounds for refusing to afford *Chevron* deference to the agency's ruling letter. It noted that Customs Service

8. Christensen v. Harris Cnty., 529 U.S. 576, 587 (2000).

classification rulings were subject to "independent review" in the Court of International Trade, which indicated that Congress did not intend for them to have the force of law. The Court also noted that Customs Service ruling letters were binding, but only as between the Customs Service and the particular importer that requested the letter; they could not be relied upon by other importers or the general public. The Court also observed that the Customs Service's 46 offices issued between 10,000 and 15,000 ruling letters each year, further indicating that they are not intended to have the force of law.

Although the Court rejected the Customs Service's claim for *Chevron* deference, the Court disagreed with the Federal Circuit's determination that ruling letters were entitled to no deference at all. Rather, the Court held that courts reviewing Customs Service ruling letters should apply the *Skidmore*[9] factors to determine whether and how much to defer to the agency's decision. Under *Skidmore*, the degree to which reviewing courts defer to agency legal constructions depends on numerous factors including "the thoroughness evident in its consideration, the validity of its reasoning, its consistency with earlier and later pronouncements, and all those factors which give it power to persuade, if lacking power to control."[10] The Court thus remanded the case to allow the lower courts to conduct a fresh review in light of the *Skidmore* factors.

On remand, the Federal Circuit reaffirmed its conclusion that Mead's loose-leaf day planners were neither "diaries" nor "bound."[11] This should not be surprising given that the Federal Circuit had previously determined, albeit on non-deferential review, that the dictionary meanings of "diary" and "bound" compelled the conclusion that the Customs Service's classification of Mead's day planners as "diaries, bound" was erroneous. Although the court of appeals acknowledged that the Supreme Court's remand required it to reconsider the Customs Service's contrary conclusions in light of the *Skidmore* factors, the court found the Service's reasoning and expertise insufficient to overcome the clear implications of the dictionary definitions of "diary" and "bound."

9. *Skidmore*, 323 U.S. 134. The case is the subject of Chapter 15.
10. *Id.* at 140.
11. Mead Corp. v. United States, 283 F.3d 1342 (Fed. Cir. 2002).

Questions and Concerns Raised by *Mead*

While the Court's decision not to afford *Chevron* deference to more than 10,000 Customs Service ruling letters issued by dozens of separate offices may seem sensible, the Court's reasoning left serious questions in its wake. First, as Justice Scalia noted in his forceful dissent, the Court did not establish a clear rule governing when *Chevron* applies. Rather than establish a requirement of either formal adjudication or notice-and-comment rulemaking for *Chevron* deference, the Court stated that "the want of that procedure here does not decide the case, for we have sometimes found reasons for *Chevron* deference even when no such administrative formality was required and none was afforded."[12] Cass Sunstein, agreeing with Justice Scalia, has lamented that *Mead* sacrificed the simplicity that would have prevailed had the Court concluded that *Chevron* applies regardless of the procedure used when an agency announces its interpretation of the statute it administers.[13]

A footnote in the *Mead* opinion expressed the Court's expectation that lower courts would develop an understanding of *Mead*'s requirements in a common-law fashion, "mak[ing] reasoned choices . . . the way courts have always done." Because the Court did not offer alternative factors that might justify *Chevron* deference in the absence of formal adjudication or notice-and-comment rulemaking, as Justice Scalia and others have noted, *Mead* potentially left lower courts at sea with regard to whether *Chevron* deference applies to any particular agency legal construction. Although Professor Kristin Hickman has argued that *Mead* has been relatively simple to apply at the Supreme Court and in the courts of appeals,[14] Professor Lisa Schultz Bressman has argued that *Mead* has significantly "muddled" judicial review of agency decisions. Bressman finds that lower courts have applied inconsistent approaches, especially when agencies seek *Chevron* deference in the absence of notice-and-comment rulemaking.[15] Hickman has also acknowledged that some of the more rigid applications of *Mead*

12. *See* Jack M. Beermann, *End the Failed* Chevron *Experiment Now: How* Chevron *Has Failed and Why It Can and Should Be Overruled*, 42 Conn. L. Rev. 779, 823–24 (2010).
13. Cass R. Sunstein, Chevron *Step Zero*, 92 Va. L. Rev. 187, 194 (2006).
14. Kristin E. Hickman, *The Three Phases of* Mead, 83 Fordham L. Rev. 527, 548 (2014).
15. Lisa Schultz Bressman, *How* Mead *Has Muddled Judicial Review of Agency Action*, 58 Vand. L. Rev. 1443, 1445–46 (2005).

have led to "questionable" results, consistent with the "'ugly and improbable structure' of which Justice Scalia has complained."[16]

In the main, courts followed *Mead*'s lead, applying *Chevron* only when the agency's statutory construction was arrived at through formal adjudication or notice-and-comment rulemaking—that is, applying what Hickman has aptly called a "rote version" of *Mead*.[17] With regard to any other potential indications of congressional intent that might have led reviewing courts to afford *Chevron* deference to agency legal conclusions, it is fair to say that Justice Souter's expectations regarding a reasoned body of case law never materialized.

Mead's shrinking of *Chevron*'s domain raised a set of more fundamental concerns. As Sunstein argued, agencies have greater expertise and are subject to more democratic accountability than federal courts.[18] The *Chevron* Court itself raised the specter of federal judges imposing their own "personal policy preferences" when they (non-deferentially) review agency constructions of ambiguous statutory provisions with policy implications. To *Mead*'s critics, by confining *Chevron*'s domain and reimposing more aggressive judicial review over a substantial swath of administrative decision-making, *Mead* threatened a return to all of the problems that led the Court to recognize *Chevron* deference in the first place.

In *Mead*, Justice Scalia also expressed concern over another potential consequence of a reduced domain for *Chevron* deference. He argued that the revival of *Skidmore* could "lead to the ossification of large portions of our statutory law." Justice Scalia's point here was that when a reviewing court upholds an agency's legal construction after applying *Chevron* deference, the agency remains free, at a later date, to substitute an alternative "reasonable" or "permissible" construction without having to convince the court to overrule its earlier decision. Under *Skidmore*, however, since the ultimate decision on the meaning of the agency's statute is determined by the reviewing court, once an agency's construction is affirmed on judicial review, the only way an agency can change its mind is to convince a court that its prior decision was incorrect.

16. Hickman, *supra* note 14, at 549–52 (quoting United States v. Home Concrete & Supply, LLC, 566 U.S. 478, 494 (2012) (Scalia, J., concurring)).
17. *Id.* at 549.
18. Sunstein, *supra* note 13, at 206.

This may be a valid concern, but it is not a necessary implication of *Skidmore* deference. If the reviewing court's initial decision was highly deferential to the agency under the *Skidmore* factors, then arguably an alternative construction offered later should also receive deference under *Skidmore*, thus allowing a similar range of flexibility as exists under *Chevron*.[19] Of course, the fact that the agency had changed its views would reduce the degree to which a reviewing court might defer.[20]

Conclusion

In *Mead*, the Supreme Court determined that decentralized, informally rendered agency decisions involving statutory construction should not receive the strong form of deference embodied in its *Chevron* doctrine. However, the Court did not rule out deference altogether, leaving it to the reviewing courts to determine whether, in light of the factors outlined in *Skidmore*, such decisions should receive at least some measure of deference. Although *Mead* raised numerous questions and concerns, courts did not generally find it terribly difficult to employ the decision and map out *Chevron*'s domain, even if *Mead* sometimes led to awkward or undesirable results. *Chevron* itself may have been the real culprit, creating so much uncertainty that reforming it would be much more fruitful than attempting to rationalize *Mead*. Indeed, the Supreme Court did just that—overruled *Chevron*—last term in *Loper Bright*.

Bibliography

Jack M. Beermann, *End the Failed* Chevron *Experiment Now: How* Chevron *Has Failed and Why It Can and Should Be Overruled*, 42 CONN. L. REV. 779 (2012).

Lisa Schultz Bressman, *How* Mead *Has Muddled Judicial Review of Agency Action*, 58 VAND. L. REV. 1443 (2005).

Evan J. Criddle, Chevron*'s Consensus*, 88 B.U. L. REV. 1271 (2008).

19. *See* Beermann, *supra* note 12, at 850.
20. *See* Skidmore v. Swift & Co., 323 U.S. 134, 140 (1944).

Kristin E. Hickman, *The Three Phases of Mead*, 83 FORDHAM L. REV. 527 (2014).

Ronald M. Levin, Mead *and the Prospective Exercise of Discretion*, 54 ADMIN. L. REV. 771 (2002).

THOMAS W. MERRILL, THE CHEVRON DOCTRINE: ITS RISE AND FALL, AND THE FUTURE OF THE ADMINISTRATIVE STATE (2022).

Thomas W. Merrill, *The* Mead *Doctrine: Rules and Standards, Meta-Rules, and Meta-Standards*, 54 ADMIN L. REV. 807 (2002).

SECTION OF ADMIN. L. & REGUL. PRAC., A BLACKLETTER STATEMENT OF FEDERAL ADMINISTRATIVE LAW pt. 3, § II.C (2d ed. 2013).

Cass R. Sunstein, Chevron *Step Zero*, 92 VA. L. REV. 187 (2006).

Adrian Vermeule, *Introduction:* Mead *in the Trenches*, 71 GEO. WASH. L. REV. 347 (2003).

Chapter 19

Kisor v. Wilkie, 588 U.S. 558 (2019)

Jennifer Mascott

In 2019, in the fractured *Kisor v. Wilkie* opinion reviewing the U.S. Court of Appeals for the Federal Circuit's deference to a determination of the U.S. Department of Veterans Affairs (VA), a five-member majority of the U.S. Supreme Court clarified several restrictions on the applicability of *Auer* deference to agency interpretations of regulations.[1] These limitations remove bite from the doctrine and make it less frequently applicable—more in line with threshold limitations that previously had applied primarily just to *Chevron* deference. Portions of the lead opinion by Justice Kagan, on behalf of four Justices in plurality, also included an analysis explicitly reaffirming the *Auer* deference regime's consistency with the Administrative Procedure Act's (APA's) legal standards for review, the Constitution, and procedural APA notice-and-comment rulemaking requirements. But Chief Justice Roberts, who constituted the fifth vote in the majority, declined to join those portions of Justice Kagan's opinion. Instead, he signed onto the Court's reliance on *stare decisis* to reaffirm the *Auer* precedent.

Significantly, the *Kisor* majority established that *Auer* deference will now apply only to interpretations that bear the mark of a formal authoritative agency position. That threshold limitation is similar to the limitation on deference to agency statutory interpretations that, before the Supreme Court

1. *See* Auer v. Robbins, 519 U.S. 452 (1997). The case is the subject of Chapter 17.

overruled the *Chevron* doctrine[2] in *Loper Bright Enterprises v. Raimondo*,[3] the Court had recognized in *United States v. Mead Corp.*[4]

In addition, *Auer* deference will be granted only to interpretations that are within an agency's substantive areas of expertise and that reflect its considered judgment. Finally, before even evaluating these factors, a court must first use all of the standard tools of interpretation to assess whether there is even any ambiguity or uncertainty in the regulation to justify the deference analysis. In *Kisor*, therefore, the Court built on its 2012 clarifications of the *Auer* deference scheme in *Christopher v. SmithKline Beecham Corp.*[5] *Kisor* arguably pared back the applicability of *Auer* deference to a nub. All nine Justices concurred in the judgment to remand the case for further proceedings to determine whether it would be appropriate to apply *Auer* deference in light of the Court's clarifications of the doctrine.[6]

Kisor: The Facts and Future

The Court concluded that *Auer* deference did not require affirming a VA determination that Kisor had not presented sufficiently "relevant" new service records to justify retroactive benefits. Kisor was a veteran of the Vietnam War who applied to the VA for disability benefits. In 1982, when he first applied, the VA denied his post-traumatic stress disorder (PTSD) benefits claim. In 2006, Kisor attempted to reopen his claim. The VA granted benefits at that time based on new documents. Kisor contended that the new award of benefits should be retroactive dating back to the time of his original application. But the agency declined, due to an agency rule permitting retroactive benefits only where the initial denial had overlooked "relevant official service department records." Because the new records concerned

2. *See* Chevron U.S.A., Inc. v. Nat. Res. Def. Council, Inc., 467 U.S. 837 (1984). The case is the subject of Chapter 16.
3. 603 U.S. 369 (2024). The case is the subject of Chapter 21.
4. 533 U.S. 218, 230 (2001). The case is the subject of Chapter 18.
5. 567 U.S. 142 (2012).
6. On remand, the Federal Circuit found that the agency adjudicator's interpretation did not merit *Auer-Kisor* deference but was nonetheless correct, as the only reasonable interpretation of the regulation. *See* Kisor v. Wilkie, 969 F.3d 1333, 1336 (Fed. Cir. 2020), *modified and reissued* as Kisor v. McDonough, 995 F.3d 1316, 1319 (Fed. Cir. 2021).

the fact of Kisor's participation during a Vietnam War operation and not the PTSD diagnosis, the agency concluded that the new records were not "relevant" under the rule. The Federal Circuit deferred under *Auer*.

In writing the lead opinion, which was not joined in its entirety by a majority of the Court, Justice Kagan noted that the only question before the Court was whether to overrule the deference regimes of *Auer* and *Seminole Rock*. The Court declined to eliminate *Auer* deference, but purported to "cabin[]" the "scope" of its applicability. Nonetheless, Justice Kagan clarified, when applied the deference would remain "potent."

Justice Kagan noted that many of the instructions her opinion provided were limitations that the Court had previously imposed on *Auer* deference in one form or another. In a portion of the opinion joined by only four Justices, Justice Kagan further described *Auer* as reflecting a presumption that Congress generally intends to delegate primary responsibility to agencies for addressing ambiguities in their own regulations. According to the plurality, in the typical absence of any statutory instruction on whether agencies or the courts are to resolve ambiguities, agencies have a rebuttable presumption of responsibility. Moreover, agencies are institutionally best equipped to address the policy questions arising under broad or ambiguous regulatory statutes.

The Chief Justice joined the four plurality Justices for the portions of the opinion delineating constraints on *Auer* deference. He emphasized, among other things, that the majority made clear that the threshold analysis requires courts to comprehensively apply relevant tools of statutory interpretation before deeming a regulation to be ambiguous and susceptible to more than one interpretation. The precise language and context of a regulation are relevant and must be given full consideration. The "core theory" of *Auer* is simply that where the law of a regulation runs out, "policy-laden choice is what is left over."

The Court laid to rest any continued notion that stronger deference might be applied under *Auer* than the degree of deference applied under *Chevron*. Rather, to be sustained under either deference regime, an agency's interpretation "must fall within the bounds of reasonable interpretation."

And even that level of deference will apply to regulatory interpretations only where certain criteria are met. Courts should not give dispositive weight to any agency interpretations that likely fail to "reflect an agency's authoritative, expertise-based, fair, or considered judgment." For example, as with the *Chevron* doctrine under *Mead*, a regulatory interpretation "must be the agency's 'authoritative' or 'official position,' not an ad hoc statement failing to reflect the agency's views." The Court found that the democratic accountability framework justifying *Chevron* deference was also relevant to the application of *Auer*. Consequently, any authority that Congress has delegated to agencies to regulate must be exercised by an official representative of the agency truly authorized to exercise power on its behalf. Lower courts should not grant the *Auer* benefit of the doubt, for example, to "official staff memoranda" not approved by the head of an agency, to a mid-level official's speech, or to an informal memorandum recording an employee's telephone conversation.

Next, courts should apply *Auer* deference only to those formal agency regulatory interpretations that involve an area within the agency's substantive expertise. When the interpretation strays from the subject areas in which Congress has granted the agency authority, then any separation-of-powers justification for *Auer* deference melts away. This element echoes both *Chevron* and the lesser *Skidmore* deference regime:[7] under *Mead* (pre-*Loper Bright*), *Chevron* deference applied only where Congress has authorized an agency to take formal action in the relevant subject area of interpretation. *Skidmore* deference applied to areas not subject to *Chevron* deference, where there are some other indicia that the relevant agency interpretation reflects expertise and reliability.

Courts also should give *Auer* deference to only those agency interpretations that "reflect fair and considered judgment," as the Court in *Christopher* earlier explained. New agency interpretations that disrupt expectations by changing policies midstream or creating conflict with positions on which regulated parties have relied provide insufficient fair warning to merit deference. *Auer* deference often will not apply to agency interpretations of regulations given these multiple constraints. Because the deference doctrine gives agencies "significant leeway" to define the meaning of their rules and to "fill out the regulatory scheme," courts should use care in its application.

7. *See* Skidmore v. Swift & Co., 323 U.S. 134 (1944). The case is the subject of Chapter 15.

Kisor was one of several key administrative law cases before the Supreme Court during the first Trump administration in which the government requested that the judiciary constrain administrative discretion.[8] Although the solicitor general opposed the overruling of *Auer* and *Seminole Rock* in *Kisor*, he had argued in his brief to the Court that the Court should impose many of the limits on *Auer* deference that the Court ultimately expressly adopted. For example, in line with the ultimate conclusion of a majority of the Court, the solicitor general suggested that an agency regulatory interpretation should receive deference only if it is the "considered judgment[] of the agency as a whole." Here, the agency determination receiving deference was that of an individual administrative judge within the VA.[9] The solicitor general had questioned whether the roughly 80,000 decisions issued annually by individual VA Board adjudicators, without precedential value, amounted to such decisions.

Relying on *stare decisis*, the Chief Justice wrote separately in addition to joining the parts of Justice Kagan's opinion that narrowed *Auer* deference. In his concurring opinion, he suggested that *Auer* deference under the *Kisor* Court's narrowing of the doctrine would not lead to the affirmance of significantly more agency regulatory interpretations than if the Court had overruled *Auer* and *Seminole Rock*.

In a separate concurring opinion joined in part by four Justices, Justice Gorsuch disagreed with the majority approach. He noted that there had not been a five-Justice majority to conclude that the *Auer* doctrine is grounded in law. Also, in contrast to Justice Kagan's suggestion that Congress has provided no instructions regarding deference to agency regulatory interpretations, Gorsuch identified the APA as requiring judges to decide all questions of law.[10]

Further, Justice Gorsuch suggested that *Auer* is in tension with constitutional principles. For example, he concluded that by assigning executive officials to aspects of the judicial role of interpretation, *Auer* interferes with

8. *See, e.g.*, Seila L. LLC v. CFPB, 591 U.S. 197, 208–09 (2020); Lucia v. SEC, 585 U.S. 237, 243–44 (2018). *Seila* is the subject of Chapter 34.

9. *Cf. Mead*, 533 U.S. at 233–34 (reasoning that the approximately 10,000 tariff classification rulings issued annually by the U.S. Customs Service should not merit *Chevron* deference).

10. *See* 5 U.S.C. § 706(2)(A).

judicial independence. Justice Kavanaugh joined most of the opinion but also wrote separately to note that the elimination of *Auer* deference would not interfere with agency policy discretion in implementing rules that contain open-ended terms like "practicable" or "reasonable."

More on *Auer*'s Origin Story

Four Justices suggested in *Kisor* that the roots of *Auer* deference extended even earlier than *Seminole Rock*, which Kisor had asked the Court to reexamine. The plurality opinion characterized the 1898 opinion in *United States v. Eaton* as an early progenitor of the doctrine.[11] Language in *Eaton* had suggested that an interpretation given to regulations "by the department charged with their execution . . . is entitled to the greatest weight." But the statement in *Eaton* did not stop with that phrase quoted by Justice Kagan. Rather, it also noted that the *Eaton* Court saw "no reason in this case to doubt [the] correctness" of the administrative interpretation—thereby implicitly suggesting that such cases of doubt might exist and therefore that an administrative interpretation would not always merit reliance. The *Eaton* decision also, prior to its pronouncement of administrative interpretive weight, had conducted its own extensive analysis of the correct meaning of the regulation and underlying statute. The Court announced "[t]he construction rendered necessary by a consideration of the text of the statute and the regulations" and the purpose of them. That construction matched the administrative interpretation.[12]

The Supreme Court's early treatment of *Seminole Rock* further suggests that the Court of that era also did not view *Seminole Rock* as effecting a significant new administrative deference regime. The Court cited the decision only three times in the first 20 years following its issuance in 1945. One of those times was in dissent.[13]

11. 169 U.S. 331 (1898).
12. *Id.* at 342–43.
13. *See* M. Kraus & Bros. v. United States, 327 U.S. 614, 622–23 (1946) (citing *Seminole Rock* for a procedural point not related to interpretive deference); Peters v. Hobby, 349 U.S. 331 (1955) (cited in dissent); Udall v. Tallman, 380 U.S. 1, 1 (1965).

It was not until 1965 that the Court relied on *Seminole Rock*'s analysis regarding deference to consistent executive branch interpretations. Even then, the Court did not employ the case to defer to an agency's interpretation of its own policymaking regulation. Rather, the Court in *Udall v. Tallman* evaluated an agency's interpretation of its authority to issue oil and gas leases under an executive order and a public land order. In contrast to *Auer*, which involved deference to an administrative policy choice imposing a new standard of behavior on regulated parties, the agency action in *Udall* had addressed allocation of governmental resources. The Interior Department had followed a long-standing nondiscretionary rule that a first-in-time oil and gas lease applicant must receive the lease so long as they satisfied eligibility criteria. The question underlying *Udall* was whether executive and agency orders purporting to withdraw lands from leasing availability altered the order of priority for eligible lease applicants. Ultimately the Supreme Court found the agency's determination regarding the orders' impact on applicant eligibility and priority to be reasonable. Therefore, the Court deferred to the agency, citing *Seminole Rock*. Judicial deference to the agency's long-standing position involving its own internal allocation and prioritization of government resources was of a very different nature than the determination in *Auer* addressing when private companies must pay out expensive overtime benefits.

Moreover, the Court cited *Seminole Rock* much more infrequently in the years following the decision than it cited *Auer* during the analogous time period—suggesting that the Court of that era viewed *Seminole Rock* as holding less significance. In particular, the Court cited *Seminole Rock* only a total of 21 times in the 52 years prior to deciding *Auer*; five of those citations were in dissent. By contrast, the Court cited *Auer* 28 times (only twice in dissent) in the much shorter 22-year period leading up to *Kisor*.

Kisor in the Lower Courts

In a handful of cases decided after *Kisor*, lower courts have declined to extend its principles of limited deference. Some have involved instances in which a court proceeds to apply *Auer* deference under the more limited terms of *Kisor* itself. In 2021, for example, the Supreme Judicial Court of Massachusetts, which had adopted *Auer* deference for state law questions, applied it to a state commission's amicus brief. Even though the U.S. Supreme Court had previously found litigation positions unsuitable for deference, the state court concluded that the brief was based on a previously adopted agency legal interpretation and the relevant ambiguity warranted *Auer* deference.[14]

In contrast, in 2022, the U.S. Court of Appeals for the Fourth Circuit held that *Kisor*'s limitations on *Auer* are inapplicable to the commentary accompanying the Federal Sentencing Guidelines. The U.S. Supreme Court concluded in 1993 that the commentary should be binding on federal courts whether or not the accompanying guidelines provision is ambiguous.[15] The Fourth Circuit concluded that the Supreme Court's unique deference framework for the guidelines commentary was unaffected by *Kisor* because it did not arise in the specific context of an executive branch agency interpreting "its own legislative rules."[16]

The U.S. Courts of Appeals for the Third Circuit sitting en banc and for the Sixth Circuit have concluded the opposite regarding the guidelines commentary. The Third and Sixth Circuits observed that the Supreme Court originally deferred to the guidelines commentary on the very ground that the Court found the commentary analogous to an agency's interpretation of its own legislative rules. Because the guidelines commentary received deference only under the umbrella of *Auer*, the Third and Sixth Circuits found that the *Auer* limitations from *Kisor* must apply to the sentencing context as well.[17]

Bibliography

Robert L. Glicksman, Kisor v. Wilkie*: A Reprieve for Embattled Administrative State?*, Geo. Wash. L. Rev. on the Docket (July 3, 2019), https://www.gwlr.org/kisor-v-wilkie-a-reprieve-for-embattled-administrative-state.

14. *See* DeCosmo v. Blue Tarp Redevelopment, LLC, 487 Mass. 690, 691, 699–707 (2021).
15. Stinson v. United States, 508 U.S. 35, 43–45 (1993).
16. United States v. Moses, 23 F.4th 347, 348–49 (4th Cir. 2022).
17. *See* United States v. Nasir, 17 F.4th 459, 469–72 (3d Cir. 2021) (en banc); United States v. Riccardi, 989 F.3d 476, 484–86 (6th Cir. 2021).

Edward L. Rubin, Auer, Chevron, *and the Future of* Kisor, 48 Fla. St. L. Rev. 719 (2021).
See also bibliography for Chapter 17 on *Auer v. Robbins*, 519 U.S. 452 (1997).

Chapter 20

West Virginia v. EPA, 597 U.S. 697 (2022)

Kristin Hickman

West Virginia v. EPA is the most prominent among several decisions in which the U.S. Supreme Court first embraced the "major questions doctrine" as such.[1] Some legal scholars and commentators speculated that the Court's decision in *West Virginia* could serve as a potential vehicle for reinvigorating the nondelegation doctrine[2] by replacing the intelligible principle standard.[3] The Court did not pursue that course. Although the major questions doctrine emerged from a strand of the Court's *Chevron* jurisprudence,[4] the Court did not cite *Chevron*[5] in deciding *West Virginia*. Instead, the Court recognized the major questions doctrine as a canon of statutory construction

1. The "major questions" label came from legal scholarship describing earlier Supreme Court jurisprudence.
2. *See* Chapter 32.
3. *See, e.g.*, Nathan Richardson, *The Supreme Court's New Threat to Climate Policy*, RESOURCES (Nov. 5, 2021), https://www.resources.org/common-resources/the-supreme-courts-new-threat-to-climate-policy/; LINDA TSANG & KATE R. BOWERS, CONG. RSCH. SERV., LSB10666, CONGRESS'S DELEGATION OF "MAJOR QUESTIONS": THE SUPREME COURT'S REVIEW OF EPA'S AUTHORITY TO REGULATE GREENHOUSE GAS EMISSIONS MAY HAVE BROAD IMPACTS 4 (2021); *see also* Brief of Amicus Curiae Americans for Prosperity in Support of Petitioners at 23–26, West Virginia v. EPA, 597 U.S. 697 (2022) (Nos. 20-1530, 20-1531, 20-1778 & 20-1780), 2021 WL 6118360, at *23–26 (arguing for overturning the intelligible principle standard).
4. *See* Chevron U.S.A., Inc. v. Nat. Res. Def. Council, Inc., 467 U.S. 837, 842–43 (1984). The case is the subject of Chapter 16.
5. *Id.*

independent of the *Chevron* framework. Yet the Court's explanation of when or how courts should apply the major questions doctrine raised as many questions as it answered.

Case Background

In 2015, the Obama administration's EPA issued regulations aimed at combating climate change by reducing carbon pollution from new and existing power plants. Labeled the Clean Power Plan, the regulations imposed requirements on existing power plants that included what the Environmental Protection Agency (EPA) described as "generation shifting from higher-emitting to lower-emitting" producers of electricity (i.e., from coal-fired plants to natural gas-fired plants). In support of these regulations, the EPA cited section 111 of the Clean Air Act. That provision authorizes the agency's administrator to establish ancillary standards for emissions from both new and existing power plants that reflect the "best system of emission reduction" that the EPA has determined to be "adequately demonstrated" in circumstances not covered by other Clean Air Act provisions. Justifying its regulations, the government maintained that the best system of emission reduction to combat climate change would be to require existing coal-fired power plants to either produce less electricity or subsidize the production of electricity by natural gas, wind, and solar sources.

Before the EPA's regulation could go into effect, West Virginia, other states, and regulated entities brought suit challenging its validity, and the Supreme Court stayed the regulation pending judicial review.[6] Under the Trump administration, the EPA revoked the Obama-era Clean Power Plan regulation on grounds that it exceeded statutory authority and replaced that regulation with the new Affordable Clean Energy rule. New York, other states, and pro-environmental advocacy groups challenged the revocation of the Clean Power Plan regulation as well as the validity of the Affordable Clean Energy rule, after which parties from among the original petitioners intervened to defend both of those actions. The U.S. Court of Appeals for the D.C. Circuit concluded that the Clean Air Act could reasonably be

6. West Virginia v. EPA, 577 U.S. 1126 (2016) (mem.).

read as including the Clean Power Plan's generation shifting approach and, thus, the EPA misunderstood the scope of its authority when it revoked and replaced that regulation with the Affordable Clean Energy rule. The Supreme Court disagreed and rejected the Obama-era EPA's interpretation of the Clean Air Act, concluding that the Clean Air Act did not authorize generation shifting as a system of emission reduction.

The Relevance of *Chevron*

At least before the D.C. Circuit, the government had claimed that its interpretation of the Clean Air Act was entitled to *Chevron* deference. The *Chevron* standard calls upon courts to defer to an administering agency's reasonable interpretation of ambiguous statutes. The Court has grounded *Chevron* deference in a theory that statutory ambiguity represents a congressional delegation of policymaking discretion to the administering agency.[7] If the meaning of a statute is clear, however, then no such delegation has occurred and deference is inappropriate because, as the *Chevron* Court observed, "the court, as well as the agency, must give effect to the unambiguously expressed intent of Congress."[8] Courts employ traditional tools of statutory interpretation to evaluate statutory clarity.

In several *Chevron* cases beginning at least in the 1990s, in addition to finding statutory clarity using traditional tools, the Court also suggested that the interpretive question was too important to conclude on the basis of mere statutory ambiguity that Congress intended to give the agency the power to resolve it.[9] In a few of those cases, the Court particularly mentioned the "vast economic and political significance" of the matter.[10] In *King*

7. *Chevron*, 467 U.S. at 842–43; *see also, e.g.*, United States v. Mead Corp., 533 U.S. 218, 226–27 (2001).

8. *Chevron*, 467 U.S. at 842–43.

9. *See, e.g.*, King v. Burwell, 576 U.S. 473, 485–86 (2015); FDA v. Brown & Williamson Tobacco Corp., 529 U.S. 120, 159–60 (2001); MCI Telecomms. Corp. v. Am. Tel. & Tel. Co., 512 U.S. 218, 231 (1994).

10. *See also* Stephen Breyer, *Judicial Review of Questions of Law and Policy*, 38 ADMIN. L. REV. 363, 370 (1986) (suggesting that a court is less likely to defer to an agency interpretation of a statute if "the legal question is an important one [because] Congress is more likely to have focused upon, and answered, major questions, while leaving interstitial matters to answer themselves in the course of the statute's daily administration").

v. Burwell in 2015, the Court rejected the availability of *Chevron* deference altogether and claimed for itself *de novo* review of an Internal Revenue Service (IRS) interpretation of the Affordable Care Act based on the interpretation's political and economic significance as well as the Court's skepticism that Congress intended the IRS to resolve such an important health policy question. In other *Chevron* cases, the Justices raised concerns about agencies pushing the interpretive limits of statutory ambiguity to pursue aggressive policy agendas, labeling the interpretive questions alternatively as "jurisdictional,"[11] as "elephants in mouseholes,"[12] or otherwise.

For several years prior to deciding *West Virginia v. EPA*, the Court had relied more heavily on traditional tools of statutory interpretation to discern statutory meaning, thereby avoiding finding statutory ambiguity. Whereas *Chevron* deference to agency interpretations by the Supreme Court was once common, by the time of its decision in *West Virginia*, the Court had not deferred to an agency's interpretation of a statute under the *Chevron* standard for six years.[13] In the months leading up to *West Virginia*, without citing *Chevron*, the Court issued opinions in two cases granting applications to stay executive actions addressing big problems—extending a nationwide moratorium on residential tenant evictions during continued pandemic conditions and imposing a COVID-19 vaccination-or-testing regime on virtually all employers with at least 100 employees—because the matters at stake were of vast political and economic significance and Congress had not clearly given the relevant agencies the authority they claimed through creative statutory interpretation.[14] According to the Court, if Congress wanted to give agencies such authority, it needed to do so more clearly.

11. *See, e.g.*, Miss. Power & Light v. Mississippi *ex rel.* Moore, 487 U.S. 354, 386–87 (1988) (Brennan, J., dissenting); *cf.* City of Arlington v. FCC, 569 U.S. 290, 312 (2013) (Roberts, C.J., dissenting).

12. *See, e.g.*, EPA v. EME Homer City Generation, LP, 572 U.S. 489, 528 (2014) (Scalia, J., dissenting) (quoting Whitman v. Am. Trucking Ass'ns, 531 U.S. 457, 468 (2001)); Gonzales v. Oregon, 546 U.S. 243, 267 (2006) (same).

13. *See* Cuozzo Speed Techs., LLC v. Lee, 579 U.S. 261 (2016).

14. *See* Ala. Ass'n of Realtors v. HHS, 594 U.S. 758 (2021) (per curiam); Nat'l Fed'n of Indep. Bus. v. OSHA, 595 U.S. 109 (2022) (per curiam).

The *West Virginia* Opinions

Writing for the Court in *West Virginia v. EPA*, Chief Justice Roberts combined these trends. He acknowledged that Congress often delegates policymaking authority to administrative agencies. Nevertheless, he recognized a category of "extraordinary cases" in which the text of the relevant statute had provided a "colorable" or "plausible" basis for an agency's claim of policymaking discretion, yet the Court had questioned whether Congress meant to make such a delegation. Invoking the major questions doctrine, Roberts echoed statements by the Court in prior cases about requiring Congress to "speak clearly if it wishes to assign to an agency decisions of vast economic and political significance." Applying that canon, he held that the Clean Air Act failed to give the EPA the authority necessary to support its actions. In other words, he said that Congress *did not* give the EPA the authority to adopt the regulations at issue, not that Congress *could not* grant the EPA that authority. He offered only limited guidance, however, regarding when or how courts should apply the major questions doctrine. He did not specify a particular threshold or methodology for evaluating the aforementioned economic or political significance. He identified as potentially relevant "the history and breadth of the authority that the agency has asserted" and "the extent to which the agency is relying on modest words, vague terms, or subtle devices" rather than direct and explicit delegations from Congress. He did not elaborate further regarding just how specific Congress must be in statutory text to pass muster. He did not mention *Chevron*.

In a concurring opinion joined by Justice Alito, Justice Gorsuch sought to provide that greater degree of clarity regarding the major questions doctrine's scope and application. Justice Gorsuch cast the major questions doctrine as a substantive canon of statutory interpretation grounded in constitutional separation-of-powers principles. He also maintained that, as a canon, the major questions doctrine functions as a clear statement rule rather than an ambiguity tiebreaker, meaning that courts need not make a preliminary finding of two "equally plausible interpretations of ambiguous [statutory] text" before applying it. Justice Gorsuch further provided a nonexclusive list of circumstances in which he said the major questions doctrine should apply: (1) "when an agency claims the power to resolve a matter of great political significance or end an earnest and profound debate across the country"; (2) when an agency "seeks to regulate a significant portion of the American economy or require billions of dollars in spending by private persons or entities"; or (3) "when an agency seeks to intrude into an area that is the particular domain of state law." In applying the major questions doctrine, Justice Gorsuch identified "several telling clues" for "what qualifies as a clear congressional statement authorizing an agency's action": (1) "the legislative provisions on which the agency seeks to rely with a view to their place in the overall statutory scheme"; (2) "the age and focus of the statute the agency invokes in relation to the problem the agency seeks to address"; (3) "the agency's past interpretations of the relevant statute"; and (4) whether "there is a mismatch between an agency's challenged action and its congressionally assigned mission and expertise."

Writing on behalf of the three dissenting Justices, Justice Kagan dramatically accused the majority of "strip[ping] [EPA] of the power Congress gave it to respond to 'the most pressing environmental challenge of our time.'" She offered a lengthy analysis of statutory text as supporting the EPA's Clean Power Plan regulation, arguing that it fell within the "wheelhouse" of EPA's expertise in addition to the provisions of the Clean Air Act. She also provided an extensive justification for administrative governance and congressional delegations of policymaking discretion based on comparative expertise and the demands of the modern age. She distinguished the cases on which the majority relied as establishing the major questions doctrine, claiming that those cases were distinguishable and involved merely "statutory construction of a familiar sort," and contending that "[t]he Court has never even used the term 'major questions doctrine' before." This last statement is best read as judicial hyperbole, as Justices had previously used the label in concurring and dissenting opinions,[15] and in doing so merely picked up what legal scholars and other lawyers for many years had dubbed the collection of *Chevron* and statutory interpretation cases on which the majority relied.[16]

---

15. *See, e.g.*, *Nat'l Fed'n of Indep. Bus.*, 595 U.S. at 122–26 (Gorsuch, J., concurring); DHS v. Regents of the Univ. of Cal., 591 U.S. 1, 52 (2020) (Thomas, J., concurring in the judgment in part and dissenting in part); Gundy v. United States, 588 U.S. 128, 167 (2019) (Gorsuch, J., dissenting).

16. *See, e.g.*, Abigail R. Moncrieff, *Reincarnating the "Major Questions" Exception to* Chevron *Deference as a Doctrine of Noninterference (or Why* Massachusetts v. EPA *Got It*

Subsequent Developments

The evolution of the major questions doctrine from its origins in *Chevron* analysis to a more robust and independent basis for rejecting agency interpretations of statutes has been discussed, debated, and criticized at great length by legal scholars. Key criticisms have been the Court's lack of more detailed guidance regarding just when or under what conditions the doctrine should apply and how precise Congress must be in drafting statutory text to avoid the doctrine. Although Justice Gorsuch's concurrence in *West Virginia v. EPA* offered greater specificity, only Justice Alito joined him in that opinion.

The Court again applied the major questions doctrine in *Biden v. Nebraska* to reject a Biden administration regulation canceling approximately $430 billion in student loan debt principal owed by roughly 43 million borrowers based on an interpretation of the HEROES Act permitting the Department of Education to "waive or modify" student loans.[17] Again, the Court highlighted the regulation's "staggering" economic and political significance and described the agency analysis of statutory text as "a wafer-thin reed on which to rest such sweeping power." On this occasion, Justice Barrett authored a concurring opinion seeking to explain the major questions doctrine more fully. The description she offered was different from that of Justice Gorsuch, however, in important ways. For example, she rejected Justice Gorsuch's characterization of the major questions doctrine as a clear statement rule, saying that she saw the doctrine instead as "an interpretive tool reflecting common sense" about how Congress drafts statutes and how courts should read statutory terms contextually. Importantly, the differences between the views regarding the major questions doctrine expressed by Justices Gorsuch and Barrett likely demonstrate why opinions of the Court have not been more thorough in explaining the doctrine's contours and parameters.

Wrong), 60 Admin. L. Rev. 593, 594–95 (2008); *see also* Abbe R. Gluck & Lisa Schultz Bressman, *Statutory Interpretation from the Inside—An Empirical Study of Congressional Drafting, Delegation, and the Canons, Part I*, 75 Stan. L. Rev. 901, 991–93 (2013) (documenting empirically awareness of the major questions doctrine among congressional drafters).

17. 600 U.S. 477 (2023).

Bibliography

Beau J. Baumann, *Americana Administrative Law*, 111 Geo. L.J. 465 (2023).

Samuel L. Bray, *The Mischief Rule*, 109 Geo. L.J. 967 (2021).

Natasha Brunstein & Donald L.R. Goodson, *Unheralded and Transformative: The Test for Major Questions After* West Virginia, 47 Wm. & Mary Env't L. & Pol'y Rev. 47 (2022).

Louis Capozzi, *The Past and Future of the Major Questions Doctrine*, 84 Ohio St. L.J. 191 (2023).

Daniel Deacon & Leah Litman, *The New Major Questions Doctrine*, 109 Va. L. Rev. 1009 (2023).

Alison Gocke, Chevron*'s Next Chapter: A Fig Leaf for the Nondelegation Doctrine*, 55 U.C. Davis L. Rev. 955 (2021).

Allison Orr Larsen, *Becoming a Doctrine*, 76 Fla. L. Rev. 1 (2024).

Ronald M. Levin, *The Major Questions Doctrine: Unfounded, Unbounded, and Cofounded*, 112 Calif. L. Rev. 899 (2024).

Aaron L. Nielson, *The Minor Questions Doctrine*, 169 U. Pa. L. Rev. 1181 (2021).

Richard L. Revesz & Max Sarinsky, *Regulatory Antecedents and the Major Questions Doctrine*, 36 Geo. Env't L. Rev. 1 (2022/2023).

Nathan D. Richardson, *Keeping Big Cases from Making Bad Law: The Resurgent "Major Questions" Doctrine*, 49 Conn. L. Rev. 355 (2016).

Joshua S. Sellers, *"Major Questions" Moderation*, 87 Geo. Wash. L. Rev. 930 (2019).

Mila Sohoni, *The Major Questions Quartet*, 136 Harv. L. Rev. 262 (2022).

Cass R. Sunstein, *There Are Two "Major Questions Doctrines,"* 73 Admin. L. Rev. 475 (2021).

Christopher J. Walker, *A Congressional Review Act for the Major Questions Doctrine*, 45 Harv. J. L. & Pub. Pol'y 773 (2022).

Daniel Walters, *The Major Questions Doctrine at the Boundaries of Interpretive Law*, 109 Iowa L. Rev. 465 (2024).

Ilan Wurman, *Importance and Interpretive Questions*, 110 Va. L. Rev. 909 (2024).

Chapter 21

Loper Bright Enterprises v. Raimondo, 603 U.S. 369 (2024)

Cary Coglianese and Katherine Shaw

In *Loper Bright Enterprises v. Raimondo*, the U.S. Supreme Court overruled its widely cited decision in *Chevron v. Natural Resources Defense Council.*[1] Under *Chevron*, courts were to defer to agencies' reasonable interpretations of ambiguities in statutes that Congress had charged these agencies to administer. For four decades, this approach—known as *Chevron* deference—provided the backdrop against which agencies, Congress, courts, and regulated entities operated. In overruling *Chevron*, the *Loper Bright* Court declared that the existence of an ambiguity in a statutory provision was, by itself, insufficient to justify judicial deference and that judges, not agency experts, should in these instances generally act as the primary interpreters of congressional enactments.

Although *Loper Bright* has been received by the legal community as having all the hallmarks of a watershed decision, it should not have come as a complete shock. Scholars and an increasing number of jurists had expressed serious doubts about *Chevron* in the years leading up to *Loper Bright.*[2] By June 2024, when *Loper Bright* was decided, the Supreme Court had not relied on *Chevron* for about eight years. Still, by overruling one of the most cited and discussed cases in administrative law, the Court has sparked extensive debate over whether it has set in motion changes that will have dramatic consequences for future administrative governance—both in terms

1. 467 U.S. 837 (1984). The case is the subject of Chapter 16.
2. *See* Buffington v. McDonough, 143 S. Ct. 14, 21 (2022) (Gorsuch, J., dissenting) (collecting cases).

of agencies' ability to act in the face of emergent or novel issues affecting the public and, more broadly, in the allocation of authority between Congress, agencies, and the courts.[3]

The Road to *Loper Bright: Chevron* and Its Critics

Chevron itself was not initially controversial when it was handed down in 1984. The Environmental Protection Agency (EPA) under the Reagan administration had at that time construed the word "source" in the Clean Air Act to encompass multiple points of emission at an industrial facility, thereby offering industrial facilities more flexibility in complying with pollution standards than if each smokestack or pipe needed to meet standards individually. The Court undertook to use all the "traditional tools of statutory construction"—text, legislative history, purpose—to determine whether a "source" meant an individual smokestack or if it meant an entire facility. But none of these traditional interpretive methods offered a clear answer.[4] This led the *Chevron* Court to articulate what became known as its famous "two-step" test and ultimately to defer to the EPA about how to understand the meaning of "source."

As detailed elsewhere in this volume,[5] the *Chevron* test called for a reviewing court first to determine whether a relevant statutory provision was ambiguous, relying upon traditional tools of statutory interpretation. If a court concluded that the statute's meaning was clear, that was the end of the inquiry, and the court obviously needed to give effect to the statute's unambiguous meaning. But if a court determined that the statute was silent or ambiguous as to the precise matter in question, the court was then supposed to proceed to step two, which called for assessing the reasonableness of the agency's interpretation. If the court reached step two and found that the agency's interpretation was a reasonable one, it was to defer to it, even if that interpretation differed from what the court might have decided if it were writing on a blank slate. This approach, the Court suggested, respected

3. Cary Coglianese & Daniel E. Walters, *The Great Unsettling: Administrative Governance After* Loper Bright, 77 ADMIN. L. REV. 1 (2025).
4. *Chevron*, 467 U.S. at 859–64.
5. *Chevron* is the subject of Chapter 16.

Congress's authority to delegate to agencies the power to administer congressionally created programs, which included the authority to "fill any gap left, implicitly or explicitly, by Congress."[6]

The *Chevron* Court explained that not only was deference at step two legally justified as necessary to honor the delegation that Congress had made to agencies, but it also made sense from a policy standpoint. After all, agency officials possessed "great expertise" and were "charged with responsibility for administering" statutory programs, while federal judges were "not experts in the field."[7] Moreover, federal judges "have no constituency," while agencies are accountable to the people via the president.[8] This meant that it was "entirely appropriate" for agencies, which are by design part of the political branches of government, to make policy choices in carrying out delegated authority, "resolving the competing interests which Congress itself either inadvertently did not resolve, or intentionally left to be resolved by the agency charged with the administration of the statute in light of everyday realities."[9]

Although *Chevron* was the most famous decision involving judicial deference to agency interpretations, it was hardly the only one. Much earlier cases such as *Gray v. Powell*[10] and *NLRB v. Hearst Publications*[11] applied deferential judicial review of agency interpretations long before *Chevron* announced its two-step test. In another early case, *Skidmore v. Swift*, the Court announced a form of deference (or "weight," in Peter Strauss's formulation[12]) under which courts, although not bound by the interpretations reached by agency actors, should under some circumstances be persuaded by those interpretations, reflective as they are of "a body of experience and informed judgment to which courts and litigants may properly resort for guidance."[13] *Skidmore* added, however, that "the weight of such a judgment in a particular case" depended on a number of factors, including "the

6. *Chevron*, 467 U.S. at 843.
7. *Id.* at 865.
8. *Id.* at 865–66.
9. *Id.*
10. 314 U.S. 402 (1941).
11. 322 U.S. 111 (1944).
12. Peter L. Strauss, *"Deference" Is Too Confusing—Let's Call Them* "Chevron *Space" and* "Skidmore *Weight,"* 112 Colum. L. Rev. 1143, 1146 (2012).
13. 323 U.S. 134, 140 (1944). The case is the subject of Chapter 15.

thoroughness evident in its consideration, the validity of its reasoning, its consistency with earlier and later pronouncements, and all those factors which give it power to persuade, if lacking power to control."[14]

These early cases were part of a long-standing practice of judicial deference to agency interpretations that preceded *Chevron*. But there is no question that after it was decided in 1984, *Chevron* eventually came to loom uniquely large in judicial consideration of statutes involving agency interpretations. By 2024, it had been cited in more than 18,000 cases and had captured the attention of administrative law scholars more than any other Supreme Court decision.[15]

Despite *Chevron*'s prominence—or perhaps because of it—the Court started in some respects to qualify or limit it in the decades leading up to *Loper Bright*. It announced a doctrinal framework under which only certain types of agency action were entitled to the deference announced in *Chevron*: typically only agency actions taken through notice-and-comment rulemaking or formal adjudication.[16] It also announced a principle, which eventually evolved into an increasingly important standalone "doctrine," whereby an agency action that raises issues of exceptional "economic and political significance" merits no *Chevron* deference.[17] The Court has emphasized that in such circumstances—the precise contours of which the Court has not defined—judges need not defer to the agency's interpretation purporting to justify such "major" action unless Congress had provided clear authority.[18]

Despite certain decisions circumscribing judicial deference, the Court also reinforced, if not expanded, interpretative deference to agencies in

---

14. *Id.*

15. *See* Christopher J. Walker, *Most Cited Supreme Court Administrative Law Decisions*, Yale J. on Regul.: Notice & Comment (Oct. 9, 2014), https://www.yalejreg.com/nc/most-cited-supreme-court-administrative-law-decisions-by-chris-walker/; Ronald A. Cass, Chevron—*Complicated, Start to Finish*, 23 Federalist Soc'y Rev. 265, 266 n.2 (2022) (collecting academic articles).

16. *See* United States v. Mead Corp., 533 U.S. 218 (2001). The case is the subject of Chapter 18.

17. FDA v. Brown & Williamson Tobacco Corp., 529 U.S. 120, 160 (2000); *see also* West Virginia v. EPA, 597 U.S. 697 (2022); Biden v. Nebraska, 600 U.S. 477 (2023). *West Virginia* is the subject of Chapter 20.

18. *Brown & Williamson*, 529 U.S. at 159 ("In extraordinary cases, . . . there may be reason to hesitate before concluding that Congress has intended . . . an implicit delegation.").

the years following *Chevron*. Justice Thomas, for example, authored a majority opinion in 2005 that essentially held that, under some conditions, an agency's interpretation of a statutory provision was entitled to *Chevron* deference even when that interpretation stood in some tension with a previous *judicial* decision involving the same statutory provision.[19] And Justice Scalia authored an opinion in 2013, joined by Justice Thomas and four other Justices, making clear that *Chevron* deference even applied to agencies' interpretations of statutory provisions granting them their own "jurisdictional" authority.[20] In an earlier unanimous opinion, Justice Scalia also affirmed that agency interpretations of not only their applicable statutes but also of their own regulations warranted judicial deference in the face of ambiguity.[21]

Despite these opinions by conservative Justices applying and even extending *Chevron*, in the years leading up to *Loper Bright* the *Chevron* doctrine had come under increasing fire by conservative critics within the legal academy and on the bench. By 2015, it appeared that Justice Thomas had changed his views. He raised concerns about *Chevron*'s consistency with the Constitution because he saw it calling for judges to abandon their role of saying what the law is.[22] Justice Gorsuch's 2017 confirmation hearing put a spotlight on *Chevron* because, as a judge on the U.S. Court of Appeals for the Tenth Circuit, Gorsuch had raised similar concerns.[23] Justice Kavanaugh, who joined the Court the following year, expressed similar doubts about *Chevron*.[24] The Court itself seemed, at least according to some accounts, to have abandoned *Chevron sub silentio*, because it had not expressly relied on the decision in a majority opinion since 2016.[25]

19. Nat'l Cable & Telecomms. Ass'n v. Brand X Internet Servs., 545 U.S. 967 (2005).
20. City of Arlington v. FCC, 569 U.S. 290 (2013).
21. Auer v. Robbins, 519 U.S. 452 (1997). The case is the subject of Chapter 17.
22. Michigan v. EPA, 576 U.S. 743, 760 (2015) (Thomas, J., concurring).
23. *See, e.g.*, Gutierrez-Brizuela v. Lynch, 834 F.3d 1142 (10th Cir. 2016).
24. Brett M. Kavanaugh, *Fixing Statutory Interpretation*, 129 Harv. L. Rev. 2118, 2150–54 (2016).
25. *See, e.g.*, Richard J. Pierce, Jr., *Is* Chevron *Deference Still Alive?*, Regul. Rev. (July 14, 2022), https://www.theregreview.org/2022/07/14/pierce-chevron-deference/.

The *Loper Bright* Decision

It was against this backdrop of increasing skepticism about *Chevron* that *Loper Bright Enterprises v. Raimondo* arrived at the Court.[26] The case involved a provision of the 1976 Magnuson-Stevens Fishery Conservation and Management Act (MSA). The MSA, which is administered by the U.S. Department of Commerce's National Marine Fisheries Service (NMFS), established regional fishery management councils to develop fishery management plans to achieve the statute's overall conservation and management goals. Those plans were to include, among other things, catch limits and gear requirements imposed on fishing operations. The MSA also contemplated the possibility of plans that required that "one or more observers be carried on board" ships "for the purpose of collecting data necessary for the conservation and management of the fishery." Once the councils developed their plans, NMFS could approve and promulgate the plans as regulations.

In 2013, the New England Fishery Management Council proposed a new plan to protect stocks of Atlantic herring that would require fishing boat operators to pay for observers on board should federal funding—which had previously covered the cost of such observers—become unavailable. NMFS promulgated the New England Council's plan as a final regulation several years later. Subsequently, Loper Bright Enterprises, a herring fishing business, together with several other similar businesses, challenged the rule under the Administrative Procedure Act (APA), arguing that the MSA did not authorize NMFS to require them to pay for observers required by a regional fishery management plan.[27] The government prevailed in both the district court and the court of appeals, with both courts relying in part on *Chevron*, finding both (1) the statute to be silent—or at the very least ambiguous—on the question of who must pay for observers, and (2) the agency's interpretation to be reasonable under *Chevron*'s second step.[28]

In a 6–3 opinion authored by Chief Justice Roberts, the Supreme Court rejected the lower courts' decisions and expressly overruled *Chevron*

---

26. The Court considered *Loper Bright* along with a companion case, *Relentless v. Department of Commerce*, which presented the Court with the same issues as *Loper Bright* and resulted in a joint opinion, which in the interest of space we refer to simply as *Loper Bright*. Justice Jackson did not participate in *Loper Bright* but did participate in *Relentless*.
27. Loper Bright Enters. v. Raimondo, 544 F. Supp. 3d 82, 107 (D.D.C. 2021).
28. *Id.*; Loper Bright Enters. v. Raimondo, 45 F.4th 359 (D.C. Cir. 2022).

deference. The Court reasoned that the *Chevron* framework was inconsistent with the "traditional understanding that questions of law were for courts to decide, exercising independent judgment," and that "agencies have no special competence in resolving statutory ambiguities." The *Loper Bright* Court concluded that the "traditional understanding of the judicial function" had been incorporated into the APA and that "[t]he deference that *Chevron* requires of courts reviewing agency action cannot be squared with the APA."

Although the Court's decision was grounded in the APA, the majority began its opinion with a recitation of passages from Article III of the U.S. Constitution, the *Federalist Papers*, and *Marbury v. Madison*—each extolling the unquestionable view that judges possess the responsibility to interpret statutes and say what the law means. *Chevron*, of course, never disavowed courts' role in interpreting statutes, but it did present the question of what that role should look like in situations in which Congress had delegated authority to agencies to carry out statutes and when judges conclude in good faith that provisions in those statutes are ambiguous. Although the *Chevron* decision had been handed down without any dissent and had stated that it was based on "well-settled principles," the *Loper Bright* majority claimed that *Chevron*'s articulation of mandatory deference to reasonable agency views at step two amounted to a "doctrinal shift" and "judicial invention" that "triggered a marked departure from the traditional approach." The majority noted the pre-*Chevron* decisions that involved deference to government agencies and concluded that the "traditional understanding" held that "[t]he views of the Executive Branch could inform the judgment of the Judiciary but did not supersede it."

Perhaps more than anything, the *Loper Bright* majority took issue with how *Chevron* had come to be characterized—at least by its critics—as "demand[ing] that courts mechanically afford *binding* deference to agency interpretations." It objected to the perception that lower courts had been much too willing over the years to find a statutory ambiguity at step one and then make an automatic, mechanical leap to mandatory judicial deference to the agency at step two. In the penultimate sentence of its opinion, the *Loper Bright* majority declared that courts "may not defer to an agency interpretation of the law *simply* because a statute is ambiguous" (emphasis added). It noted that "[c]ourts, after all, routinely confront statutory ambiguities in cases having nothing to do with *Chevron*—cases that do not involve agency interpretations or delegations of authority." In these instances, judges "understand that such statutes—no matter how impenetrable, do—in fact, must—have a single, best meaning." Judges have the responsibility, the majority stated, to "use every tool at their disposal to determine the best reading of the statute and resolve the ambiguity."

The *Loper Bright* majority was unsparing in its assessment of what the dissenting judges saw as *Chevron*'s core precept: namely, a presumption that favored agencies' interpretations in circumstances of statutory silence or ambiguity. As the Court stated in a 1996 decision, "Congress, when it left ambiguity in a statute meant for implementation by an agency, understood that the ambiguity would be resolved, first and foremost, by the agency, and desired the agency (rather than the courts) to possess whatever degree of discretion the ambiguity allows."[29] Such a presumption, the *Loper Bright* majority averred, was a fiction, and one that misunderstood the proper role of judges when it comes to interpreting laws administered by agencies.

Despite citations to *Marbury v. Madison* and paeans to the constitutional role of courts in matters of legal interpretation, the *Loper Bright* majority did not hold that the Constitution demanded *Chevron*'s overruling, as some advocates had urged it to do. But in concurring opinions in *Loper Bright*, two Justices did raise constitutional concerns. Justice Thomas insisted that not only did *Chevron* violate the APA but it "also violate[d] our Constitution's separation of powers." Justice Gorsuch leaned on preconstitutional history to support an argument that *Chevron* impermissibly "precludes courts from exercising the judicial power vested in them by Article III to say what the law is."

The majority opinion, by contrast, grounded its decision to overrule *Chevron* in the APA. It reasoned that section 706 of the APA, which directs reviewing courts to "decide all relevant questions of law" and "interpret . . . statutory provisions,"[30] must be understood as an instruction to courts to decide statutory interpretation questions on an independent basis, without being required to defer to agencies. On the majority's view, the APA in 1946

29. Smiley v. Citibank (S.D.), N.A., 517 U.S. 735, 740–41 (1996).
30. 5 U.S.C. § 706.

codified earlier practices that had accorded federal courts the responsibility of interpreting statutes, consistent with both founding-era expectations and *Marbury v. Madison*'s explicit pronouncement that courts would "say what the law is."[31] Claiming that neither *Chevron* nor any of its successor cases had sufficiently engaged with section 706, the majority declared that "*Chevron* cannot be reconciled with the APA."

The majority dismissed the notion that early cases such as *Gray v. Powell* and *NLRB v. Hearst Publications* had stood for anything like *Chevron* deference to executive branch interpretations of statutes. It reasoned that the Court in those earlier cases afforded nothing more than great *respect* for agency interpretations—not the kind of mandatory *deference* that *Chevron* demanded when conditions for reaching step two had been satisfied. That said, the majority did expressly acknowledge that the Court had properly concluded in early cases that Congress could adopt statutes that "empowered an agency to decide how a broad statutory term applied to specific facts found by the agency." The majority also accepted that "when a particular statute delegates authority to an agency consistent with constitutional limits, courts must respect the delegation, while ensuring that the agency acts within it." In such instances, the majority explained that judges "need only fulfill their obligations under the APA to independently identify and respect such delegations of authority, police the outer statutory boundaries of those delegations, and ensure that agencies exercise their discretion consistent with the APA."[32]

As to whether *stare decisis* compelled continuing adherence to what the majority opinion termed "the *Chevron* project," the majority concluded that it did not, reasoning that the *Chevron* test was both misguided and unworkable. It further claimed that *Chevron*'s fundamental indeterminacy had necessitated so many clarifications that a two-step test had been converted into a "dizzying breakdance." Under these circumstances, *Chevron*

31. 5 U.S. 137, 177 (1803).

32. To some readers, this articulation of judicial responsibility will seem close, if not conceptually identical, to the "well-accepted principles" that the *Chevron* Court had sought to articulate. *See, e.g.*, Adrian Vermeule, Chevron *by Any Other Name*, New Dig. (June 28, 2024), https://thenewdigest.substack.com/p/chevron-by-any-other-name; Cary Coglianese & David Froomkin, Loper Bright*'s Disingenuity*, 174 U. Pa. L. Rev. (forthcoming 2025).

had engendered no reliance interests of the sort that might counsel in favor of retaining it. From the majority's perspective, *Chevron*—by purportedly displacing the traditional primacy of the courts' role in statutory interpretation—actually *undermined* "the very 'rule of law' values that *stare decisis* exists to secure."

Three dissenting Justices argued that, in overruling *Chevron*, the Supreme Court undermined respect for Congress and its intentions in establishing administrative agencies and empowering them to carry out legislation. Justice Kagan, joined in dissent by Justices Sotomayor and Jackson, described the *Loper Bright* majority's decision as a power grab under which "a rule of judicial humility gives way to a rule of judicial hubris" and according to which "the majority turns itself into the country's administrative czar." She elaborated that, "[i]n one fell swoop, the majority . . . gives itself exclusive power over every open issue—no matter how expertise-driven or policy-laden—involving the meaning of regulatory law." On the merits, Justice Kagan reasoned:

> This Court has long understood *Chevron* deference to reflect what Congress would want, and so to be rooted in a presumption of legislative intent. Congress knows that it does not—in fact cannot—write perfectly complete regulatory statutes. It knows that those statutes will inevitably contain ambiguities that some other actor will have to resolve, and gaps that some other actor will have to fill. And it would usually prefer that actor to be the responsible agency, not a court. . . . Congress has conferred on that expert, experienced, and politically accountable agency the authority to administer—to make rules about and otherwise implement—the statute giving rise to the ambiguity or gap. Put all that together and deference to the agency is the almost obvious choice, based on an implicit congressional delegation of interpretive authority.

In addition to charging the majority with disregarding congressional delegations, the dissent insisted that the majority's conclusion about *Chevron* was not even required by the APA. According to Justice Kagan, section 706 did not specify that courts must possess *de novo* review when reviewing agency actions on statutory grounds—indeed it did not specify *any* standard of review at all—and thus the APA is compatible with *Chevron*.

Loper Bright's Unanswered Questions

Despite the *Loper Bright* majority's castigation of *Chevron* for being "byzantine" and prone to "inconsistencies" in how courts had applied it, the future of statutory decision-making under *Loper Bright* appears to be anything but clear.[33] *Loper Bright* leaves future courts to grapple with at least five sets of questions.

First, because *Loper Bright* states that judges must find the "best reading" of regulatory and administrative statutes through the "use [of] every tool at their disposal," courts will confront as squarely as ever the profound and perennial questions of statutory interpretation: What makes for a "best reading" of a statute? What tools are properly at courts' disposal? Specifically, what are the proper roles for text, history, purpose, and canons of construction? Admittedly, these have always been challenging questions, both in theory and application (even under *Chevron*), but *Loper Bright* does nothing to make them any less challenging. By purportedly imposing the full responsibility on judges alone to come to the "best" interpretations of statutes, *Loper Bright* would appear to increase the decision-making burden on judges.[34] After all, the statutes that agencies are called upon to implement are often exceedingly complex and technical—even, as a D.C. Circuit panel once put it in describing an environmental statute, sometimes truly "mind-numbing."[35]

Second, did *Loper Bright* really abandon the core logic of *Chevron* even as it overruled at least a caricature of *Chevron* deference? The majority opinion in *Loper Bright* still leaves open the possibility that the best reading of a statute will sometimes be that Congress gave the *agency* the authority or discretion to define general or ambiguous terms or to fill in gaps and silences. As noted earlier in this chapter, the majority did not disavow that statutes can explicitly delegate to or confer discretion on agencies to define

33. *See* Kristin E. Hickman & Richard J. Pierce, Jr., Administrative Law Treatise (7th ed. 2024-2 Supp. 2024) (noting that *Loper Bright* "creates a fair amount of uncertainty for future litigation").

34. *See, e.g.*, Abbe Gluck, *Overruling Chevron Without a Coherent Theory of Statutory Interpretation and the Court-Congress Relationship*, 62 Harv. Int'l L.J. 20 (2024) (arguing that *Loper Bright* only "raises more questions than it answers about the jurisprudential muddle that continues to characterize the Court's entire statutory-interpretation enterprise").

35. Am. Mining Cong. v. EPA, 824 F.2d 1177, 1189 (D.C. Cir. 1987).

or otherwise give meaning to statutory terms. Even as the majority repudiated the view that a statutory ambiguity *ipso facto* implies a delegation to the agency, it did not definitively rule out the possibility that an ambiguity *combined with* "other statutory circumstances"[36] could still leave courts duty-bound to defer to reasonable interpretations of agencies. The *Loper Bright* majority acknowledged, after all, that the best reading of a "statute's meaning may well be that the agency is authorized to exercise a degree of discretion." This can arise, the majority explained, in instances where statutes (1) "expressly" delegate to agencies the authority "to give meaning to a particular statutory term"; (2) "empower an agency to prescribe rules to 'fill up the details' of a statutory scheme"; or (3) authorize regulation "subject to the limits imposed by a term or phrase that 'leaves agencies with flexibility,' such as 'appropriate' or 'reasonable.'" In circumstances such as these, the majority accepted that Congress can delegate the authority to the agency to imbue an imprecise or ambiguous statute with specificity. It declared that in these circumstances judges "must respect the delegation"[37]—an obligation that seems akin to, if not the same as, the one articulated in *Chevron*.[38]

Third, what role will *Skidmore* play in the future? The *Loper Bright* majority indicated that, in exercising judgment about statutory meaning, "courts may—as they have from the start—seek aid from the interpretations of those responsible for implementing particular statutes." The so-called traditional understanding endorsed by the majority allows courts to give "the most respectful consideration"[39] and "great weight"[40] to the views of government agencies. Indeed, in citing *Skidmore* no fewer than five times, the majority affirmed that reviewing courts could still be guided by well-reasoned agency interpretations. It is not possible, however, to know exactly

36. United States v. Mead Corp., 533 U.S. 218, 229 (2001). The case is the subject of Chapter 18.
37. The Court did not address whether such delegations of discretionary authority might raise questions under the nondelegation or major questions doctrines.
38. For an initial effort to construct an analytic framework that purports to reconcile these parts of *Loper Bright* with an overruling of *Chevron*, see Kristin E. Hickman & Amy J. Wildermuth, *Harmonizing Delegation and Deference After* Loper Bright, N.Y.U. L. Rev. (forthcoming 2025).
39. Quoting United States v. Moore, 95 U.S. 760, 763 (1898).
40. Quoting United States v. Am. Trucking Ass'ns, Inc., 310 U.S. 534, 549 (1940).

when, or with how much weight, lower courts will be permitted to accord respect to agencies' views under *Skidmore*. The majority's favorable mention of *Skidmore*'s rationale for giving respect to "interpretations issued contemporaneously with the statute at issue" may well indicate that *Skidmore* deference will mostly come into play in the context of long-standing agency interpretations, rather than new ones.

Fourth, what is the precise retroactive effect of *Loper Bright*'s overruling of *Chevron*? The *Loper Bright* majority said that it was not displacing prior "agency actions" decided under *Chevron*, cautioning that the "holdings of those cases that specific agency actions are lawful—including the Clean Air Act holding of *Chevron* itself—are still subject to statutory *stare decisis* despite our change in interpretive methodology." But even if the "specific agency actions" are to remain unchallenged, are the *statutory interpretations* that underlay those prior court-approved actions immune from future consideration, unraveling, or reconsideration under a best-reading standard? Will new litigants come forward in the future—as the Court's decision in *Corner Post, Inc. v. Board of Governors of the Federal Reserve System*[41] now permits—to challenge the present or future application of those older interpretations?

Finally, what will come of *Kisor v. Wilkie*?[42] In *Kisor*, a case decided just five years before *Loper Bright*, the Court had been asked whether it should overrule *Auer* deference—that is, deference by courts to agencies' interpretations of their own ambiguous regulations under a framework similar to *Chevron*'s. The Court upheld *Auer* deference, albeit with some clarification or perhaps modification.[43] Even though Chief Justice Roberts in *Kisor* made a point of noting that *Auer* deference is different from *Chevron* deference,[44] can a distinction between *Auer* and *Chevron* really last long after *Loper Bright*? It is not hard to see the Court being asked again in the coming years to revisit its position on deference to agencies' interpretations of their own regulations.

41. 603 U.S. 799 (2024).
42. 588 U.S. 558 (2019). The case is the subject of Chapter 19.
43. *Id.* at 563.
44. *Id.* at 591 (Roberts, C.J., concurring).

Loper Bright and the Future of Administrative Law

Loper Bright has elicited a range of responses from lawyers and scholars. Some observers have predicted that the Court's decision would result in dramatic changes to administrative governance.[45] Others have suggested it would, at most, result in only modest effects.[46] Gauging the full impact of the Court's decision may take time. Still, it has taken no time at all for lawyers and lower courts to start citing the decision.[47] The very day *Loper Bright* was announced, a Texas judge cited it in issuing a preliminary injunction against a new Biden administration labor regulation expanding eligibility for overtime pay.[48] Within a week, three different federal judges, all citing *Loper Bright*, blocked implementation of a U.S. Department of Health and Human Services rule prohibiting discrimination in health care based on gender identity.[49] Of course, a key question is whether these judges—as well as the many other judges who will subsequently cite *Loper Bright* in many other future cases—would have reached the same or different results had the Supreme Court kept *Chevron* alive.[50]

Beyond that, the ultimate question presented by *Loper Bright* may be whether *agencies* will act differently under its logic than they would have had the Court not overruled *Chevron*. Will they act less responsively in the face of novel problems? Will they resist policy changes in the wake of future changes in presidential administration? Many factors will complicate the search for empirical answers to this ultimate question of *Loper Bright*'s impact, including the change in administration that occurred in the

45. *See, e.g.*, Steve Vladeck, *The Most Aggressive Restructuring of Government in Almost 90 Years*, CNN (July 2, 2024), https://www.cnn.com/2024/07/02/opinions/supreme-court-radically-restructures-government-vladeck/index.html.
46. *See, e.g.*, Nick Fromherz, *Professors, Don't Remove* Chevron *from Your Casebooks*, Yale J. on Regul.: Notice & Comment (July 11, 2024), https://www.yalejreg.com/nc/professors-dont-remove-chevron-from-your-casebooks-by-nick-fromherz/.
47. *See* Eli Sanders, *A Supreme Court Justice Warned That a Ruling Would Cause "Large-Scale Disruption." The Effects Are Already Being Felt*, ProPublica (Sep. 23, 2024), https://www.propublica.org/article/supreme-court-chevron-deference-loper-bright-guns-abortion-pending-cases; Robin Kundis Craig, *The Impact of* Loper Bright v. Raimondo*: An Empirical Review of the First Six Months*, 109 Minn L. Rev. 2671 (2025).
48. Texas v. DOL, 738 F. Supp. 3d 807, 812 (E.D. Tex. 2024).
49. *See* Sanders, *supra* note 47.
50. Coglianese & Walters, *supra* note 3.

months that followed the Court's decision. Still, as a doctrinal matter, *Loper Bright* has clearly shaken up discourse over at least the past 40 years of U.S. administrative and regulatory law. The aftershocks of this legal earthquake will include, if nothing else, considerable debate over the decision's meaning and legal implications for years, if not decades, to come. In time, *Loper Bright* may even find itself as widely cited and analyzed as *Chevron* had been in decades past.

Bibliography

Nicholas R. Bednar & Kristin E. Hickman, Chevron*'s Inevitability*, 85 GEO. WASH. L. REV. 1392 (2017).

Jack M. Beermann, *End the Failed* Chevron *Experiment Now: How* Chevron

Has Failed and Why It Can and Should Be Overruled, 42 CONN. L. REV. 779 (2010).

Ronald A. Cass, Chevron*—Complicated, Start to Finish*, 23 FEDERALIST SOC'Y REV. 265 (2022).

Cary Coglianese, Chevron*'s Interstitial Steps*, 85 GEO. WASH. L. REV. 1313 (2017).

Cary Coglianese & David Froomkin, Loper Bright*'s Disingenuity*, 174 U. PA. L. REV. (forthcoming 2025).

Cary Coglianese & Daniel E. Walters, *The Great Unsettling: Administrative Governance After* Loper Bright, 77 ADMIN. L. REV. 1 (2025).

Robin Kundis Craig, *The Impact of* Loper Bright v. Raimondo*: An Empirical Review of the First Six Months*, 109 MINN. L. REV. 2671 (2025).

Abbe Gluck, *Overruling* Chevron *Without a Coherent Theory of Statutory Interpretation and the Court-Congress Relationship*, 62 HARV. INT'L L.J. 20 (2024).

Michael Herz, Chevron *Is Dead; Long Live* Chevron, 115 COLUM. L. REV. 1867 (2015).

Kristin E. Hickman & Amy J. Wildermuth, *Harmonizing Delegation and Deference After* Loper Bright, N.Y.U. L. REV. (forthcoming 2025).

Thomas W. Merrill, *The Demise of Deference—And the Rise of Delegation to Interpret?*, 138 HARV. L. REV. 227 (2024).

Gillian E. Metzger, *The Supreme Court 2016 Term—Foreword: 1930s Redux: The Administrative State Under Siege*, 131 HARV. L. REV. 1 (2017).

Adrian Vermeule, *The Old Regime and the* Loper Bright *"Revolution,"* 2025 SUP. CT. REV. 235.

PART IV

Judicial Review on the Merits

Chapter 22

SEC v. Chenery Corp. (*Chenery I*), 318 U.S. 80 (1943)

Anna Shavers*

In *SEC v. Chenery* (*Chenery I*), Justice Frankfurter, writing for the U.S. Supreme Court and referring to a decision of the Securities and Exchange Commission, stated: "The Commission's action cannot be upheld merely because findings might have been made and considerations disclosed which would justify its order. . . . There must be such a responsible finding." Thus, the *Chenery* doctrine was established.[1] The Court has referred to it as "a simple but fundamental rule of administrative law."[2]

The *Chenery* doctrine requires a court, when reviewing an agency action, to examine the rationale presented by the agency for its action and, if no adequate explanation is provided, remand the case to the agency even if the court itself could discern an adequate explanation from the record that would support the agency's action. Whereas an appellate court may usually reject a lower court's reasoning and affirm the decision on other grounds found in the record, the Court explained in *Chenery I*, a court may not generally do so when reviewing agency action, for the "process of review requires that the grounds upon which the administrative agency acted be

*Editor's Note: At the time of her death, the author had prepared a substantially completed draft of this entry. The other editors of the book made some revisions—mostly stylistic—to the author's draft.

1. The "*Chenery* doctrine" is often used to refer both to the doctrine established by the decision discussed here and the doctrine established by *SEC v. Chenery Corp.* (*Chenery II*), 332 U.S. 194 (1947). As discussed in Chapter 2, the latter doctrine holds that agencies generally have discretion to choose between rulemaking and adjudication when establishing policy.

2. *Chenery II*, 332 U.S. at 196.

clearly disclosed and adequately sustained." The Court relied on the constitutional separation of powers in concluding that "an appellate court cannot intrude upon the domain which Congress has exclusively entrusted to an administrative agency."[3]

Facts and Holding

Chenery I resulted from an appeal from a Commission order approving, over management objections, a plan of reorganization of the Federal Water Service Corporation under the Public Utility Holding Company Act.[4] The Commission specifically based its order on principles of equity that the Court found invalid under "settled judicial doctrines." Before the Court, the Commission "contended" that its order could be sustained on an alternative ground. In a short opinion, however, the Court refused to consider that ground as a basis to sustain the order, since the "considerations" underlying it "were not those upon which . . . [the Commission's] action was based. Its action must be measured by what the Commission did, not by what it might have done." The Court then emphasized the limits of its holding:

> In finding that the Commission's order cannot be sustained, we are not imposing any trammels on its powers. We are not enforcing formal requirements. We are not suggesting that the Commission must justify its exercise of administrative discretion in any particular manner or with artistic refinement. We are not sticking in the bark of words. We merely hold that an administrative order cannot be upheld unless the grounds upon which the agency acted in exercising its powers were those upon which its action can be sustained.

On remand, the Commission reached largely the same result but on different grounds. The Court upheld the order in *Chenery II*, concluding that

3. *See also* Sidney A. Shapiro & Richard E. Levy, *Heightened Scrutiny of the Fourth Branch: Separation of Powers and the Requirement of Adequate Reasons for Agency Decisions*, 1987 Duke L.J. 387, 427–35.

4. *See* Roy A. Schotland, *A Sporting Proposition*—SEC v. Chenery, *in* Administrative Law Stories 169, 176–78 (Peter L. Strauss ed., 2016); Richard Murphy, Chenery *Unmasked: Reasonable Limits on the Duty to Give Reasons*, 80 U. Cin. L. Rev. 817, 832–35 (2012).

the Commission "has expressed its reasons with a clarity and thoroughness that admit of no doubt as to the underlying basis of its order."

Scope of the *Chenery I* Doctrine

Although *Chenery I* was decided before the enactment of the Administrative Procedure Act (APA) in 1946, it is clear that the principle it established applies to agency adjudicative decisions made under the APA's formal hearing procedures (often known as formal adjudications).[5] The agency action at issue in *Chenery I* was clearly a formal adjudication under the APA and subject to the APA's requirement that agency action be set aside when it is "arbitrary, capricious, an abuse of discretion, or otherwise not in accordance with law."[6] Similarly, the *Chenery I* doctrine applies to the now-infrequently used class of rulemakings subject to the APA's formal hearing procedures.

Of perhaps more significance given the prevalence of so-called informal agency action in the modern administrative state, the Supreme Court also extended the reach of the doctrine to informal adjudications in *Citizens to Preserve Overton Park v. Volpe*,[7] and to informal (notice-and-comment) rulemaking in *Motor Vehicle Manufacturers Ass'n v. State Farm Insurance Co.* In *State Farm*, the Court stated that an agency must "articulate a satisfactory explanation for its action."[8]

Reception of the *Chenery I* Doctrine

Courts have routinely applied the *Chenery I* doctrine's contemporaneous rationale principle to require that in reviewing any agency decision-making, "courts should not attempt to supply a reasoned basis for the action that

5. *See* 5 U.S.C. §§ 554, 556–57.
6. *Id.* § 706(2)(A) (2018).
7. *See* 401 U.S. 402 (1971). The case is the subject of Chapter 24.
8. Motor Vehicle Mfrs. Ass'n v. State Farm Ins. Co., 463 U.S. 29, 43 (1983). The case is the subject of Chapter 26. *See generally* Kathryn E. Kovacs, *Rules About Rulemaking and the Rise of the Unitary Executive*, 70 Admin. L. Rev. 515, 543–44 (2018); Kevin M. Stack, *The Constitutional Foundations of* Chenery, 116 Yale L.J. 952, 955 (2007).

the agency itself has not given."[9] The doctrine, however, is not without its critics.[10]

Several courts and commentators have raised concerns both about the Court's reasoning and its application in certain contexts.[11] Professor Kevin Stack has asserted that the doctrine has constitutional foundations, but has rejected the separation-of-powers rationale relied on by the Court, concluding that the nondelegation doctrine provides the best constitutional foundation for the *Chenery I* doctrine.[12] He suggests that the doctrine's post-rationalization prohibition on having "reviewing courts supply or substitute validating grounds for the action" is grounded in the nondelegation doctrine.[13]

While Professor Richard Murphy does not find the nondelegation doctrine justification convincing, he joins *Chenery I*'s critics in raising questions about the inability of courts to accept an agency's after-the-fact rationale even if it is supported by the record and well-reasoned.[14] In support of his position, he notes Judge Wald's observation:

> If I were to ease up on any aspect of reasoned decision making it would be on [*Chenery*'s] "post hoc rationalization" ban prohibiting government counsel from proffering any additional explanation for the agency action that has not been fully covered in the decision itself, even though the explanation may be a winner and everyone knows that the agency would be happy to accept it.[15]

9. Citizens Awareness Network, Inc. v. U.S. Nuclear Regul. Comm'n, 59 F.3d 284, 291 (1st Cir. 1995). For Judge Friendly's notable assessment of how lower courts had applied the *Chenery I* doctrine during its first two decades, see Henry J. Friendly, Chenery *Revisited: Reflections on Reversal and Remand of Administrative Orders*, 1969 DUKE L.J. 199.

10. *See generally* James D. Ridgway & David S. Ames, *Misunderstanding* Chenery *and the Problem of Reasons-or-Bases Review*, 68 SYRACUSE L. REV. 303, 336 (2018).

11. *See* Amy R. Motomura, *Rethinking Administrative Law's* Chenery *Doctrine: Lessons from Patent Appeals at the Federal Circuit*, 53 SANTA CLARA L. REV. 817 (2014); Murphy, *supra* note 4, at 867 (discussing immigration cases); Bryan C. Bond, Note, *Taking It on the* Chenery*: Should the Principles of* Chenery I *Apply in Social Security Disability Cases?*, 86 NOTRE DAME L. REV. 2157 (2011).

12. *See* Stack, *supra* note 8, at 974.

13. *Id.* at 1020.

14. *See* Murphy, *supra* note 4, at 819.

15. *Id.* at 818 (quoting Patricia M. Wald, *Judicial Review in a Time of Cholera*, 49 ADMIN. L. REV. 659, 666 (1997)).

As Professor Murphy notes, some courts have avoided the strictness of the contemporaneous-rationale rule by either relying on a harmless error rationale[16] or remanding to the agency for an adequate explanation without vacating the agency decision.[17] With respect to the remand-without-vacation approach used by the D.C. Circuit, Professor Murphy observes that some courts view this as inconsistent with the requirement of the APA that courts "*shall* . . . hold unlawful and set aside agency action" that is arbitrary and capricious.[18]

In evaluating the *Chenery I* doctrine, it is important to note that the APA contains no express requirement for contemporaneous agency explanations in informal adjudications or in informal rulemakings. In the case of informal rulemaking, the APA requires that agencies provide only "a concise general statement of their basis and purpose."[19] Today, however, it is common practice for agencies to provide detailed justifications and explanations for their rules. Some have described this as part of the ossification of rulemaking,[20] which "refers to the increasing time and resources needed to issue a rule."[21] Professor Murphy has noted that "notice-and-comment rulemaking, which was once easy and supposed to be so, is now a complex, time-consuming, resource-intensive procedural maze."[22] Professor Katherine E. Kovacs has concluded "the [h]ard-look doctrine is the prime culprit."[23] *Chenery I* has arguably played an important role in this development. As then-Judge Merrick Garland has stated, "[t]he origins of the hard look doctrine can be traced to the Supreme Court's [contemporaneous rationale

16. *See* Murphy, *supra* note 4, at 864; *see also* Nat'l Ass'n of Home Builders v. Defs. of Wildlife, 551 U.S. 644, 659 (2007); Mass. Trs. of E. Gas & Fuel Assocs. v. United States, 377 U.S. 235, 248 (1964); *Administrative Law*—Chenery *Avoidance—Fourth Circuit Vacates Environmental Approvals for the Atlantic Coast Pipeline*—Sierra Club v. U.S. Department of the Interior, *899 F.3d 260 (4th Cir. 2018)*, 132 Harv. L. Rev. 1104, 1107, 1110–11 (2019).

17. *See* Murphy, *supra* note 4, at 822, 868.

18. *Id.* at 868–69.

19. 5 U.S.C. § 553(c).

20. *See, e.g.*, Thomas O. McGarity, *Some Thoughts on "Deossifying" the Rulemaking Process*, 41 Duke L.J. 1385 (1992).

21. Kovacs, *supra* note 8, at 547 (citing Richard J. Pierce, Jr., *Rulemaking Ossification Is Real: A Response to Testing the Ossification Thesis*, 80 Geo. Wash. L. Rev. 1493, 1494 (2012)).

22. Richard Murphy, *Enhancing the Role of Public Interest Organizations in Rulemaking Via Pre-Notice Transparency*, 47 Wake Forrest L. Rev. 681, 687–88 (2012).

23. Kovacs, *supra* note 8, at 543.

requirement] holding in *SEC v. Chenery Corp.*"[24] Hard look judicial review requires a court to closely examine agency explanations for rationality.[25] Thus, agencies adopt procedures and spend considerable time explaining their decisions to avoid vacatur and remand of their decisions or attempt to make decisions in ways that will avoid the hard look review.

As Professor Nicholas Bagley has argued in a notable article, "[a]gencies may have a duty to explain themselves, but it doesn't follow that *Chenery I* was rightly decided or that hard-look review is indispensable."[26] This suggestion might be implemented by the Supreme Court revisiting the *Chenery I* doctrine and adopting the position it took in a pre-*Chenery* state administrative law decision: *Pacific States Box & Basket Co. v. White*, in which the Court gave extremely deferential review to an agency action and explained that courts should approve agency action whenever "any state of facts reasonably can be conceived that would sustain" the decision.[27] Another alternative would be for Congress to amend the APA to provide for judicial review of agency decision-making that is not limited by the Court-imposed contemporaneous rationale. Neither development is likely at this point.

Bibliography

Nicholas Bagley, *Remedial Restraint in Administrative Law*, 117 Colum. L. Rev. 253 (2017).

Henry J. Friendly, Chenery *Revisited: Reflections on Reversal and Remand of Administrative Orders*, 1969 Duke L.J. 199.

Merrick B. Garland, *Deregulation and Judicial Review*, 98 Harv. L. Rev. 507 (1985).

Kathryn E. Kovacs, *Rules About Rulemaking and the Rise of the Unitary Executive*, 70 Admin. L. Rev. 515 (2018).

24. Merrick B. Garland, *Deregulation and Judicial Review*, 98 Harv. L. Rev. 505, 526 (1985).

25. *See* Section of Admin. L. & Regul. Prac., Am. Bar Ass'n, A Blackletter Statement of Federal Administrative Law pt. 3, § II.D (2d ed. 2013); Jeffrey S. Lubbers, A Guide to Federal Agency Rulemaking 500 (6th ed. 2018).

26. Nicholas Bagley, *The Procedure Fetish*, 118 Mich. L. Rev. 345, 385 (2019).

27. 296 U.S. 176, 185 (1935).

Richard Murphy, Chenery *Unmasked: Reasonable Limits on the Duty to Give Reasons*, 80 U. CIN. L. REV. 817 (2012).

James D. Ridgway & David S. Ames, *Misunderstanding* Chenery *and the Problem of Reasons-or-Bases Review*, 68 SYRACUSE L. REV. 303 (2018).

Roy A. Schotland, *A Sporting Proposition*—SEC v. Chenery, *in* ADMINISTRATIVE LAW STORIES 169 (Peter L. Strauss ed., 2016).

SECTION OF ADMIN. L. & REGUL. PRAC., AM. BAR ASS'N, A BLACKLETTER STATEMENT OF FEDERAL ADMINISTRATIVE LAW pt. 3, § II.D (2d ed. 2013).

Sidney A. Shapiro & Richard E. Levy, *Heightened Scrutiny of the Fourth Branch: Separation of Powers and the Requirement of Adequate Reasons for Agency*, 1987 DUKE L.J. 387.

Kevin M. Stack, *The Constitutional Foundations of* Chenery, 116 YALE L.J. 952 (2007).

Christopher J. Walker, *The Ordinary Remand Rule and the Judicial Toolbox for Agency Dialogue*, 82 GEO. WASH. L. REV. 1553 (2014).

Chapter 23

Universal Camera Corp. v. NLRB, 340 U.S. 474 (1951)

Blake Emerson

Universal Camera is a landmark case on the judicial review of formal agency adjudication. It is also a foundation for the edifice of modern administrative law as a whole. In his opinion for the U.S. Supreme Court, Justice Frankfurter offered a candid assessment of the political origins of the Administrative Procedure Act (APA). While he read the statute to reject the heights of bureaucratic discretion during the New Deal, Justice Frankfurter nonetheless carved out significant space for agency autonomy. In doing so, he sketched many of the essential dynamics of contemporary administrative law: expertise as the basis for deference, the difficulties of defining the appropriate scope of judicial review, and the conflicting values implicated by internal agency procedure.

The Case

The National Labor Relations Board (NLRB) had ordered the Universal Camera Corporation to reinstate an employee with back pay, on the grounds that he had been unlawfully terminated in retaliation for his testimony at an NLRB hearing. In reaching this conclusion, the NLRB went against the factual findings of its own hearing examiner, who had first adjudicated the case. The NLRB sought enforcement of its order in federal court. The case thus raised the question of how a reviewing court should evaluate the sufficiency of the factual findings of an agency when there is evidence in the record to contradict those findings.

The Meaning of "Substantial Evidence"

Universal Camera offers the definitive, if open-ended, interpretation of the APA's "substantial evidence" test for judicial review of findings of fact in formal agency adjudication. The APA provides that a reviewing court must set aside agency orders issued after a formal evidentiary hearing if they are "unsupported by substantial evidence" on "the whole record."[1] Justice Frankfurter explained that this language meant that, in determining whether the evidence is substantial, a court must "take into account whatever in the record fairly detracts from its weight." Discrepancies between the factual findings of the initial adjudicator and those of the agency on issues, such as witness credibility, may therefore reduce the "substantiality" of the evidentiary record. This does not mean, however, that courts are permitted to weigh the evidence *de novo*. Given agencies' "experience" and "expertness" in their regulatory domain, a court may not "displace" an agency's choice "between two fairly conflicting views."

The opinion thus sets the upper and lower bounds of the scope of review for adjudicatory findings of fact. On the lower end, the court must ensure that the evidence is minimally sufficient to sustain the agency's order. On the upper end, however, the court cannot assume the fact-finding role that the legislature has assigned to the agency. It cannot supplant an agency's reasonable judgment as to the relative weight of the evidence with its own. Professor Louis Jaffe, shortly after the case was decided, defined this kind of review in terms of a basic notion of "fairness": a judge should set aside an agency's order "if as he conscientiously sees it the finding is not fairly supported by the record; or to phrase it more sharply, the judge must reverse if he cannot conscientiously escape the conclusion that the finding is unfair."[2]

1. 5 U.S.C. § 706.
2. Louis L. Jaffe, *Judicial Review: "Substantial Evidence on the Whole Record,"* 64 Harv. L. Rev. 1233, 1239 (1951).

After the "Era of Deference"

Although this standard of review might seem somewhat vague and otherwise unexceptional, it signified a changed legal and political environment. *Universal Camera* held that the APA's substantial evidence standard was identical with that of the Labor Management Relations Act of 1947 (known as the Taft-Hartley Act). The Taft-Hartley Act provided that the findings of the NLRB "with respect to questions of fact if supported by substantial evidence on the record considered as a whole shall be conclusive."[3] It is natural to read these two provisions as requiring the same sort of review. But reading the APA and the Taft-Hartley Act in tandem had wider implications.

The National Labor Relations Act of 1935 (NLRA, or the Wagner Act), which established the NLRB, had provided that "[t]he findings of the Board as to the facts, if supported by evidence . . . shall be conclusive."[4] Although the Court interpreted this provision of the Wagner Act to require "substantial evidence" to support the NLRB's findings, the scope of review was often quite narrow.[5] It required "more than a mere scintilla" of proof, but not much more.[6] If the NLRB's findings were supported by evidence in the record, considered in isolation, that would be sufficient to sustain them, any contrary evidence notwithstanding.

This approach had been part and parcel of the constitutional spirit of the New Deal, which Reuel Schiller has aptly described as an "era of deference."[7] The legislative response to the Great Depression gave birth to a plethora of new administrative institutions, such as the NLRB, the Securities and Exchange Commission, the Agricultural Adjustment Administration, the Farm Security Administration, the Works Progress Administration, and the Social Security Board. These efforts built upon the institutional and ideological legacy of the Progressive Era, which combined a faith in social science,

3. 29 U.S.C. § 160(e) (1951).
4. *Id.* (1935).
5. Wash., Va. & Md. Coach Co. v. NLRB, 301 U.S. 142, 147 (1937).
6. Consol. Edison Co. of N.Y. v. NLRB, 305 U.S. 197, 229 (1938).
7. Reuel E. Schiller, *The Era of Deference: Courts, Expertise, and the Emergence of New Deal Administrative Law*, 106 Mich. L. Rev. 399 (2007).

professionalism, and democratic policymaking to support the expansion of national administrative capacity.[8]

Progressives sought to protect individual liberty amidst vast governmental authority through fair administrative procedures, such as provision of "notice and a hearing" to individuals affected by agency action.[9] If agencies accorded such rudimentary process, the thinking went, their factual determinations ought to be accorded significant weight by courts.[10] The substantial evidence test originated in this effort to reconcile governmental power with private rights. It entered into administrative law in the early 20th century, as courts sought to respect the legislative mandate and procedural rigors of the Interstate Commerce Commission, while retaining authority to set aside its findings if unsupported by the record.[11] Justice Frankfurter himself articulated this progressive understanding of agency procedure and judicial review, arguing in 1927 that the "task of administrative law" was one of "fashioning instruments and processes at once adequate for social needs and the protection of individual freedom."[12]

The Wagner Act followed in the progressive tradition by creating an independent commission—the NLRB—that would have discretion to develop policy through adjudication. In upholding the constitutionality of the NLRA, the Court emphasized that "[t]he Act establishes standards to which the Board must conform. There must be complaint, notice and hearing. The Board must receive evidence and make findings. The findings as to the facts are to be conclusive, but only if supported by evidence."[13] The Court subsequently left the NLRB wide, but not unlimited,[14] latitude to implement the act.

In *Universal Camera*, Justice Frankfurter recognized that the winds had shifted with the APA and the Taft-Hartley Act, which amended the Wagner

8. *See* Blake Emerson, *Administrative Answers to Major Questions: On the Democratic Legitimacy of Agency Statutory Interpretation*, 102 MINN. L. REV. 2019, 2059–72 (2018).

9. *See* JOHN DICKINSON, ADMINISTRATIVE JUSTICE AND THE SUPREMACY OF LAW IN THE UNITED STATES 260 (1927).

10. *See* FRANK J. GOODNOW, SOCIAL REFORM AND THE CONSTITUTION 230 (1911).

11. *See, e.g.*, ICC v. Louisville & Nashville R.R. Co., 227 U.S. 88 (1913).

12. Felix Frankfurter, *The Task of Administrative Law*, 75 U. PA. L. REV. 614, 617 (1927).

13. NLRB v. Jones & Laughlin Steel Corp., 301 U.S. 1, 47 (1937).

14. *See, e.g.*, Phelps Dodge Corp. v. NLRB, 313 U.S. 177 (1941).

Act. He noted that the "contracted reviewing power" prescribed by the NLRA had been met with fierce criticism from employers who detected unfairness in the NLRB's adjudication of disputes. While Justice Frankfurter did not admit that such critiques had merit, he acknowledged "the climate of opinion thereby generated," which "stimulated pressures for legislative relief from alleged administrative excesses."

The Politics of Administrative Procedure

The "legislative relief" came with the APA. *Universal Camera*'s interpretation of the spirit of the APA is its most lasting contribution to administrative law, beyond its treatment of the substantial evidence test in particular. Justice Frankfurter noted that although the sponsors of the APA claimed that they were "reaffirming the substantial evidence test," they at the same time expressed with "equal clarity" their "disapproval of the manner in which the courts were applying their own standard."

"In all this," Justice Frankfurter famously noted, "Congress expressed a mood." The mood favored "stricter and more uniform practice" of judicial review. In light of the new legislation, "courts must now assume more responsibility for the reasonableness and fairness of Labor Board decisions than some courts have shown in the past." *Universal Camera* thus treated both the substantial evidence test and the APA as a whole as codifying a political "movement for enlarged review." Indeed, the APA had been forged in intense conflict over the legacy of the New Deal, as the conservative reaction against the welfare and regulatory state gained traction.[15] Failing to enact proposals that would have subjected a much wider range of administrative action to more searching judicial scrutiny, Congress nonetheless determined that some general procedural guidelines were necessary to order the variety of administrative forms, practices, and powers that had consolidated over the past decade.[16] *Universal Camera* recognized that

15. *See* George B. Shepherd, *Fierce Compromise: The Administrative Procedure Act Emerges from New Deal Politics*, 90 NW. U.L. REV. 1557 (1996).
16. *See* JOANNA L. GRISINGER, THE UNWIELDY AMERICAN STATE: ADMINISTRATIVE POLITICS SINCE THE NEW DEAL 73–91 (2012).

this statutory framework entailed an increased level of judicial scrutiny on administrative action.[17]

The APA was not, however, a complete reversal of the New Deal's regulatory posture or the scope it left for administrative policymaking. Justice Frankfurter emphasized that "the whole record formula" was not "intended to negative the function of the Labor Board as one of those agencies presumably equipped or informed by experience to deal with a specialized field of knowledge, whose findings within that field carry the authority of an expertness which courts do not possess and therefore must respect." *Universal Camera* indicated that the APA left intact the progressive legacy of agency autonomy underwritten by expert knowledge and procedural fairness. It represented a compromise position between judicially dominated classical constitutionalism and the New Deal's path towards executive-led social democracy. As Justice Jackson had put it a year earlier in *Sung v. McGrath*, the APA "settle[d] long-continued and hard-fought contentions, and enact[ed] a formula upon which opposing social and political forces have come to rest."[18] It is in this sense that the APA is sometimes understood as a *quasi*-constitutional statute, which has "codified the new public order."[19] The order would rest on the foundation of agencies' subject matter expertise, the quality of their decision-making processes, and their partial but not absolute accountability to political leadership and judicial control.

Talismans of Judicial Control

The formulas Justice Frankfurter deployed to describe the substantial evidence test were open-ended. As he admitted, "[t]here are no talismanic words that can avoid the process of judgment. The difficulty is that we cannot escape, in relation to this problem, the use of undefined defining terms." Justice Frankfurter recognized that the judicial task in this area could not be specified by some crisp delineation of jurisdiction. Rather, he

17. *See* Reuel E. Schiller, *Enlarging the Administrative Polity: Administrative Law and the Changing Definition of Pluralism*, 1945–1970, 53 VAND. L. REV. 1389, 1419–21 (2000).
18. 339 U.S. 33, 40 (1950).
19. WILLIAM N. ESKRIDGE, JR. & JOHN FEREJOHN, A REPUBLIC OF STATUTES: THE NEW AMERICAN CONSTITUTION 11 (2010).

counseled an attitude of qualified restraint in the face of legislative choice and administrative competence.[20]

While *Universal Camera*'s holding narrowly applies to judicial review of the factual findings in formal agency adjudication, its treatment of court-agency relations applies much more broadly. Agency action not governed by the substantial evidence test, such as an informal rulemaking or an informal adjudication, is to be set aside if it is "arbitrary" or "capricious."[21] This standard overlaps significantly with the substantial evidence test.[22] Indeed, in *Motor Vehicle Manufacturers Ass'n v. State Farm Mutual Automobile Insurance Co.*,[23] the paradigmatic application of arbitrary-and-capricious review of an agency rule, the Court incorporated the substantial evidence test into its analysis of an agency's rulemaking. Under this *State Farm* approach, "the agency must examine the relevant data and articulate a satisfactory explanation for its action including a 'rational connection between the facts found and the choice made.'"[24] Under both the substantial evidence and arbitrary-and-capricious standards, then, the agency must engage in "reasoned decisionmaking."[25] And the prevailing view is that when the specific question on judicial review is the adequacy of the agency's factual findings in an informal proceeding, whether a rulemaking or adjudication, the arbitrary-and-capricious standard demands the same evidentiary support as the substantial evidence standard does in the formal-proceeding context.[26]

Exactly how much "reason" is required, of course, remains an open question. Agencies win much more often than they lose according to both

---

20. *See* Alfred S. Neely, *Justice Frankfurter,* Universal Camera, *and a Jurisprudence of Judicial Review of Administrative Action*, 25 U. Tol. L. Rev. 1 (1994).

21. 5 U.S.C. § 706(2)(A).

22. *See* Thomas J. Miles & Cass R. Sunstein, *The Real World of Arbitrariness Review*, 75 U. Chi. L. Rev. 761, 763–64 (2008).

23. 463 U.S. 29 (1983). The case is the subject of Chapter 26.

24. *Motor Vehicle Mfrs. Ass'n*, 463 U.S. at 43 (quoting Burlington Truck Lines v. United States, 371 U.S. 156, 168 (1962)).

25. Allentown Mack Sales & Serv., Inc. v. NLRB, 522 U.S. 359, 374 (1998) (internal quotations omitted).

26. The most oft-cited decision remains *Ass'n of Data Processing v. Board of Governors*, 677 F.2d 677 (D.C. Cir. 1984) (Scalia, J.). That said, the record on which the agency may draw in an informal proceeding may be less confined than in a formal proceeding. *See, e.g.*, Phx. Herpetological Soc'y, Inc. v. Fish & Wildlife Serv., 998 F.3d 999, 1003 (D.C. Cir. 2021) (informal adjudication). *See also* Chapter 11.

the substantial evidence and the arbitrary-and-capricious tests.[27] The indeterminacy of these standards also leaves significant room for political ideology to influence courts' evaluation of agencies' handiwork.[28] With such flexible boundaries between judicial and administrative competence, courts and agencies often function as partners in the specification and implementation of legislative policy.[29]

The substantial evidence test has become a focal point for ongoing disagreement between the Justices about the institutional competence of courts and agencies. In *Allentown Mack Sales Service, Inc. v. NLRB*,[30] for instance, the Court considered whether the NLRB's determination that an employer lacked "objective reasonable doubt" concerning employee support for a union was supported by substantial evidence. Justice Scalia's opinion for the Court engaged in a searching review of how an administrative law judge (ALJ) had treated a manager's testimony on the subject, concluding that it was "quite impossible for a rational factfinder to avoid the conclusion that [the employer] had reasonable, good-faith grounds to doubt . . . the union's retention of majority support." Justice Breyer dissented from this assessment, however, arguing that the Court had shortchanged the Board's "specialized knowledge" and substituted its own "common understanding" for the Board's "expertise."

More recently, in *Biestek v. Berryhill*,[31] the Court hewed to a more deferential reading of "substantial evidence" in the context of Social Security Administration disability determinations. Affirming the pre-APA view that substantial evidence meant only "more than a mere scintilla," the Court held that a vocational expert's testimony on jobs a claimant might perform could constitute substantial evidence, even if the expert refused to share the data on which their testimony was based. Justice Kagan's opinion for the Court indicated that ALJs should have leeway to determine whether expert witnesses are "trustworthy" and should not be constrained to follow "categorical" rules concerning the evidence they can rely upon. Jus-

27. *See* David Zaring, *Reasonable Agencies*, 96 Va. L. Rev. 135, 139 (2010).
28. *See* Miles & Sunstein, *supra* note 22, at 767.
29. *See, e.g.*, Elizabeth Fisher et al., *Rethinking Judicial Review of Expert Agencies*, 93 Tex. L. Rev. 1681 (2015).
30. 522 U.S. 359.
31. 587 U.S. 97 (2019).

tice Sotomayor and Justice Gorsuch separately dissented, both concluding that in this particular case such testimony could not qualify as substantial evidence. Underlying the disagreements between the Justices in *Allentown Mack Sales* and *Biestek* are differing views of the degree to which judicial review of agency adjudication should adhere to the same standards as appellate review of trial court findings of fact, or whether agencies' expertise and statutory authority require courts to grant administrative fact finders somewhat greater leeway.[32] The progressive view that agency decision-making requires a recalibration of the balance between individual fairness and the efficient performance of public purposes, continues to contend with more traditional, common-law conceptions of the supremacy of judicial judgment.

Lineaments of Agency Appellate Process

Another critical aspect of *Universal Camera* is its treatment of the relationship between an agency's front-line adjudicators and its leadership.[33] The case holds that a reviewing court "should accord findings of the trial examiner the relevance that they reasonably command in answering the comprehensive question whether the evidence supporting the Board's order is substantial." Because the initial decision is part of the "whole record," the court must take those findings into account in evaluating the overall sufficiency of the agency's justification for its action.[34]

This does not mean that the standard of review becomes more intense when the agency on internal appeal contradicts the findings of the official who presided at the initial hearing.[35] Justice Frankfurter explicitly disavowed any more stringent requirement that the agency defer to the findings of hearing examiners (today called ALJs), or that they set their findings aside only under specified conditions. As he noted, the APA gives the agency on internal appeal "all the powers which it would have in making the

32. *See* Dickinson v. Zurko, 527 U.S. 150 (1999).
33. Elizabeth Magill & Adrian Vermeule, *Allocating Power Within Agencies*, 120 Yale L.J. 1032, 1067–71 (2011).
34. *See* A Guide to Judicial and Political Review of Federal Agencies 179–80 (Michael E. Herz et al. eds., 2d ed. 2015).
35. *See* Air Canada v. DOT, 148 F.3d 1142, 1151 n.15 (D.C. Cir. 1998).

initial decision."[36] But Justice Frankfurter nonetheless indicated that when the examiner and the agency disagree, the "evidence supporting a conclusion may be less substantial." This buttressed the independent judgment of ALJs within the administrative decision-making process, ensuring that the agency's action was grounded in empirical understandings of the case at hand rather than solely motivated by general policy considerations or other political interests.[37]

This holding has established some outer limits on the manner in which an agency handles the appeal and final disposition of a formal adjudicative decision. Today, agencies use a variety of appellate systems that accord varying weight to the decisions of the initial decision maker. Though many of these systems are not governed by the formal adjudication requirements of the APA, they are often governed by similar rules, such as confining the decision maker to the factual record developed at the evidentiary hearing. In all of these systems, the hearing functions as a primary point of contact between the agency and the persons it binds or otherwise affects. This interface between the government and the public is an important element of the broader accountability and legitimacy of the administrative system. The disposition of individual cases implicates due process considerations, such as provision of adequate notice and an evidentiary hearing.[38] At the same time, the adjudicative record furnishes building blocks from which agency policy can be formed and justified.[39] By requiring that the initial decision be taken relatively seriously by both the agency and the reviewing court, and yet disavowing any deference to that decision, *Universal Camera* ensured that individualized justice would be balanced against the broader policymaking and organizational interests of the agency.

The case in this way precluded the notion that the legitimacy of agency discretion stemmed exclusively from the political accountability of the agency's leadership. The interests of the affected individual and the findings of the official who heard their case had to be countenanced in the agency's

36. 5 U.S.C. § 557(b).
37. *See* Peter L. Strauss, Administrative Justice in the United States 345–46 (2d ed. 2002).
38. *See* Long v. Bd. Governors of the Fed. Rsrv. Sys., 117 F.3d 1145 (10th Cir. 1997); 5 U.S.C. §§ 554, 556.
39. *See* Charles H. Koch, Jr., *Policymaking by the Administrative Judiciary*, 56 Ala. L. Rev. 693 (2005).

judgment. To be sure, an agency's appellate system will usually allow its politically appointed leadership to weigh policy in reaching a final determination. But this top-down accountability must take seriously the bottom-up responsibility of the agency to the persons it confronts.

Conclusion

Universal Camera paved the way to our contemporary administrative landscape. It underscored that "specialized knowledge" and procedural fairness would be the bulwarks of administrative legitimacy. It interpreted the APA as a restriction on administrative authority that nonetheless would allow significant discretion to persist. It set the ambivalent tone for judicial review of agency action, insisting that the courts not displace reasonable administrative judgments, but step in if the record fell far short of justifying them. And it recognized that administrative adjudication procedures must balance due process concerns, empirical findings, and policy considerations. The interplay of these values continues to animate administrative law to this day.

Bibliography

JOANNA L. GRISINGER, THE UNWIELDY AMERICAN STATE: ADMINISTRATIVE POLITICS SINCE THE NEW DEAL (2012).

Louis L. Jaffe, *Judicial Review: "Substantial Evidence on the Whole Record,"* 64 HARV. L. REV. 1233 (1951).

Thomas J. Miles & Cass R. Sunstein, *The Real World of Arbitrariness Review*, 75 U. CHI. L. REV. 761 (2008).

Alfred S. Neely, *Justice Frankfurter,* Universal Camera, *and a Jurisprudence of Judicial Review of Administrative Action*, 25 U. TOL. L. REV. 1 (1994).

Reuel E. Schiller, *Enlarging the Administrative Polity: Administrative Law and the Changing Definition of Pluralism, 1945–1970*, 53 VAND. L. REV. 1389 (2000).

SECTION OF ADMIN. L. & REGUL. PRAC., AM. BAR ASS'N, A BLACKLETTER STATEMENT OF FEDERAL ADMINISTRATIVE LAW pt. 3, § IV (2d ed. 2013).

Christopher J. Walker, *Stages of Agency Adjudication Processes*, *in* A Guide to Federal Agency Adjudication 101 (Jeremy S. Graboyes ed., 3d ed. 2023).

Ralph Winter, *Judicial Review of Agency Decisions: The Labor Board and the Court*, 1968 Sup. Ct. Rev. 53.

David Zaring, *Reasonable Agencies*, 96 Va. L. Rev. 135 (2010).

Chapter 24

Citizens to Preserve Overton Park, Inc. v. Volpe, 401 U.S. 402 (1971)

Richard Murphy

Citizens to Preserve Overton Park can make a strong claim to being the most important administrative law opinion in the modern canon. In it, the U.S. Supreme Court (1) offered important guidance regarding the reviewability of agency action under the Administrative Procedure Act (APA); (2) embraced the "hard look" style of review of agency action for arbitrariness; and (3) effectively required agencies to produce records and contemporaneous explanations for their informal adjudications.

The Litigation and Its Background

Citizens to Preserve Overton Park, Inc. (Citizens) sued to block construction of a stretch of I-40 through Overton Park in Memphis, Tennessee. The Bureau of Public Roads had approved the route in 1956, and the Federal Highway administrator had also approved it in 1966. But, in that same year, Congress included in the Department of Transportation Act a provision that barred the secretary of transportation from approving projects that use public parkland unless "(1) there is no feasible and prudent alternative to the use of such land, and (2) such program includes all possible planning to minimize harm to such park." Congress reenacted this limitation in the Federal-Aid Highway Act of 1968.

In April 1968, the secretary announced that he agreed with local officials that I-40 should run through Overton Park. In November 1969, via an informal adjudication,[1] he announced final approval of the project's route and design. These announcements contained no factual findings or explanations detailing how the project satisfied the new statutory limits on building roads through parks.

Citizens contended that the secretary's action was invalid both due to his failure to issue formal findings and because he had improperly relied on the judgment of the Memphis City Council. Citizens also contended that the approved plan violated statutory requirements because "feasible and prudent" alternatives existed that avoided the park, and, even if there were no such alternatives, the plan did not sufficiently protect against harm to the park.

Reviewability Under the APA

The Supreme Court characterized the "threshold question" in the case as whether the petitioners were entitled to any review at all under the APA. Under the act, final agency actions are presumptively reviewable unless "statutes preclude review" or "agency action is committed to agency discretion by law."[2] Neither of these two exceptions to the presumption of reviewability applied to the secretary's action, which was therefore reviewable.

The Court indicated that statutory preclusion of judicial review requires "clear and convincing" evidence of a congressional intent to restrict access to the courts. Congress, however, had not provided any indication at all that it wished to preclude review of the agency action in *Overton Park*.

The Court explained that the exception for agency actions "committed to agency discretion by law" blocks judicial review "in those rare instances where 'statutes are drawn in such broad terms that in a given case there is no law to apply.'" Although the statutory provisions in *Overton Park* gave the secretary discretion to make determinations regarding the feasibility and

1. Administrative law parlance distinguishes between "formal" or "on-the-record" adjudications, which are subject to the record and explanatory requirements of 5 U.S.C. §§ 554, 556–57, and "informal" adjudications, which are not.

2. 5 U.S.C. § 701(a)(1), (2); *see generally* Harold H. Bruff, *Availability of Judicial Review*, *in* A GUIDE TO JUDICIAL AND POLITICAL REVIEW OF FEDERAL AGENCIES 1, 19–20 (Michael E. Herz et al. eds., 2d ed. 2015) [hereinafter GUIDE]; SECTION OF ADMIN. L. & REGUL. PRAC., AM. BAR ASS'N, A BLACKLETTER STATEMENT OF FEDERAL ADMINISTRATIVE LAW pt. 4, § III (2d ed. 2013) [hereinafter BLACKLETTER STATEMENT].

prudence of alternative routes, they also plainly indicated that Congress wished to give "paramount importance" to the protection of parkland. Given this much, the Court concluded that the secretary could approve construction of highways in parks only where "truly unusual factors" were present or where alternative routes would cause "extraordinary" disruption. There was, therefore, "law to apply," and the secretary's action was not committed to agency discretion by law.

Overton Park is one of the touchstone cases on the doctrine of reviewability, but one should take its discussion of the "no law to apply" principle with a grain of salt if only because, as Justice Scalia observed, there is always some law to apply if one looks hard enough.[3] It is therefore important to understand the "committed to agency discretion by law" exception to reviewability in light of the Supreme Court's later decisions in cases such as *Heckler v. Chaney*[4] and *Webster v. Doe.*[5] Still, *Overton Park* remains good law on the point that extreme levels of agency discretion cut against reviewability.

Embracing "Hard Look" Review for Arbitrariness

After determining that the secretary's action was reviewable, the Court turned to the problem of explicating the standard of review. The default standard of review under section 706 of the APA is the "arbitrary and capricious" standard, which instructs courts to review agency actions for arbitrariness unless section 706 instructs that a different standard should apply to the type of determination at issue.[6] The APA provides two alternative standards for review of factual determinations by agencies. Courts are to apply the "substantial evidence" standard to findings produced through formal, on-the-record proceedings.[7] Also, the APA instructs courts to set aside findings that are "unwarranted by the facts to the extent the facts are subject to trial de novo by the reviewing court."[8]

3. *See* Webster v. Doe, 486 U.S. 592, 608 (1988) (Scalia, J., dissenting).
4. 470 U.S. 821 (1985). The case is the subject of Chapter 12.
5. 486 U.S. 592.
6. 5 U.S.C. § 706(2)(A).
7. *Id.* § 706(2)(E).
8. *Id.* § 706(2)(F).

The Supreme Court rejected Citizens' contention that one of these two alternative standards should apply to the secretary's determinations regarding alternative routes and planning. The determinations were not the products of formal hearings "designed to produce a record that is to be the basis of agency action." The substantial evidence standard, which generally checks to determine whether an agency's findings have rational support in a formal administrative record, was therefore inapt.

As for *de novo* review, the Court held that the APA requires its application in just two circumstances. One is where "the action is adjudicatory in nature and the agency factfinding procedures are inadequate." "Independent judicial factfinding" may also be in order "when issues that were not before the agency are raised in a proceeding to enforce nonadjudicatory agency action." Courts almost never conclude that these criteria for triggering *de novo* review have been satisfied, and the practice has essentially vanished except in situations where a statute or constitutional provision requires it.[9]

As neither substantial evidence nor *de novo* review applied to the secretary's determinations, it followed that the APA's default standard of review for arbitrariness applied. At the time of the APA's passage in 1946, courts generally applied a lax form of arbitrariness review that asked whether "any state of facts reasonably can be conceived that would sustain" an agency action.[10] Arbitrariness review could thus resemble review of a jury verdict—asking whether an outcome fell within a range of reasonable possibilities rather than whether the decision maker actually chose an outcome using a reasonable decision-making process.

During the 1960s and 1970s, however, appellate courts had developed a "hard look" form of review for arbitrariness. In *Greater Boston Television Corp. v. FCC*,[11] Judge Leventhal characterized this approach as seeking to ensure that an agency has given "reasoned consideration to all the material facts and issues." To enable a court to conduct this task, an agency must "articulate with reasonable clarity its reasons for decision, and identify the significance of the crucial facts."[12] In other words, an agency has to provide a

9. *See* Ronald M. Levin & Jim Rossi, *Judicial Review of Issues of Fact*, *in* GUIDE, *supra* note 2, at 180–81; BLACKLETTER STATEMENT, *supra* note 2, pt. 3, § IV.B.
10. Pac. States Box & Basket Co. v. White, 296 U.S. 176, 185 (1935).
11. 444 F.2d 841 (D.C. Cir. 1970).
12. *Id.* at 851.

reviewing court with sufficient information to determine whether the agency thought about what it was supposed to think about in a reasonable way.

In *Overton Park*, the Supreme Court, without actually using the phrase "hard look," embraced this approach for review of the policy and factual determinations underlying informal adjudications—such as the secretary's decision to approve routing I-40 through the park. In a key sentence, the Court explained that, to determine whether an agency choice is arbitrary, "the court must consider whether the decision was based on a consideration of the relevant factors and whether there has been a clear error of judgment." Modern arbitrariness review thus insists not just that an agency action fall within a range of reasonable outcomes, but also that an agency demonstrate that it reached this outcome through reasoned decision-making.[13] Throwing darts is not allowed—even if the dart happens to land on a good result.

A little over a decade later, in another seminal opinion discussed in this volume, *Motor Vehicle Manufacturers Ass'n v. State Farm Mutual Automobile Insurance Co.*, the Supreme Court applied this same "hard look" approach to review of informal rulemaking.[14]

Over the decades, hard look review has generated an immense amount of scholarly commentary. Critics contend that this approach has contributed to, among other defects, an unhealthy "ossification" of agency action—particularly rulemaking. Defenders contend that careful judicial review is necessary to ensure sound and legitimate agency action.

Records and Contemporaneous Explanations for Informal Agency Adjudications

To conduct review of an agency action for reasoned decision-making, a court must know what information the agency considered in choosing that action and how the agency contemporaneously assessed that information. By its terms, however, the APA does not require that "informal" proceedings, like

13. For general discussion of judicial review of agency discretionary decisions under the arbitrariness standard, see Lisa Schulz Bressman & Glen Staszewski, *Judicial Review of Agency Discretion*, *in* Guide, *supra* note 2, at 195–231; Blackletter Statement, *supra* note 2, pt. 3, § V.

14. 463 U.S. 29 (1983). The case is the subject of Chapter 26.

the informal adjudicatory decision challenged in *Overton Park*, be based on information contained in a formal record.[15] Moreover, the APA does not expressly require agencies to give contemporaneous explanations for their decisions in informal adjudications.[16] For this very reason, the Supreme Court rejected Citizens' argument that the secretary's approval of the route for I-40 was invalid because of his failure to issue formal findings of fact supporting this action.

The Court solved the problem that the APA does not expressly impose a record requirement on informal agency actions by reasoning backwards from the requirements of judicial review. In short, agencies must supply records because, otherwise, courts could not conduct review for reasoned decision-making. This neat conclusion still left the problem of defining the record for informal proceedings. The Court essentially punted on this issue in *Overton Park*, asserting without elaboration that "there is an administrative record that allows the full, prompt review of the Secretary's action," but that, alas, "[t]hat administrative record is not, however, before us." Broadly speaking, in the aftermath of *Overton Park,* courts and agencies, absent other statutory instructions, have defined records for informal adjudications functionally as including those materials that an agency actively considered in making its decision.[17]

The Court also created strong incentives for agencies to offer contemporaneous explanations for their informal adjudications even though the APA does not expressly require them. It noted that the "bare record" for the secretary's action "may not disclose the factors that were considered or the Secretary's construction of the evidence." To fill this gap, the Court suggested that the secretary might be able to produce "formal findings" that would suffice for review but that these would need to be viewed "critically" as partaking of post hoc rationalization. The district court might also, however, require testimony from agency officials who participated in the decision.

For agency officials, the prospect of testifying about their decisions long after making them borders on nightmarish. The Court indicated that

---

15. *Cf.* 5 U.S.C. § 556(e) (defining record for formal proceedings).
16. *Cf. id.* § 557(c) (requiring explanations for formal actions).
17. *See* Levin & Rossi, *supra* note 9, at 182–85; BLACKLETTER STATEMENT, *supra* note 2, pt. 3, § IV.C.2.

agencies could avoid this possibility by making administrative findings at the same time that they take their actions. A reviewing court should generally accept such contemporaneous findings at face value and eschew further "inquiry into the mental processes of administrative decisionmakers" absent a "strong showing of bad faith or improper behavior" by the agency. Thus, as a practical matter, after *Overton Park*, an agency would be very unwise not to support its informal adjudications with contemporaneous explanations—even though *Overton Park* also held that informal adjudications do not require formal findings.

Two years later in *Camp v. Pitts*, the Court pulled back on *Overton Park*'s threat of intrusive evidentiary proceedings in district court.[18] The comptroller of the currency had denied an application for a bank charter. After concluding that the comptroller's explanation for this action was inadequate, the court of appeals ordered the district court to hold a *de novo* hearing on the matter. In reversing, the Court emphasized that, unlike in *Overton Park*, the comptroller had offered a contemporaneous explanation for his action, concluding that a new bank would be an "uneconomic venture" for the surrounding community. Under the doctrine of yet another seminal administrative law case, *SEC v. Chenery Corp.* (*Chenery I*), the Court held that the "Comptroller's action must, therefore, stand or fall on the propriety of that finding."[19] Where an agency's contemporaneous explanation proves inadequate, the reviewing court should generally vacate and remand to the agency rather than engage in further judicial proceedings. The *Camp* opinion thus discouraged the gathering of post hoc affidavits and testimony to explain agency action.[20] It also, however, left in place a basic element of the deal that *Overton Park* gave to agencies: if they wish to avoid vacation of their information adjudications, they should offer contemporaneous explanations for them.

18. 411 U.S. 138 (1973). *See* Harold J. Krent, *Ancillary Issues Concerning Agency Explanations*, *in* Guide, *supra* note 2, at 247–50; Blackletter Statement, *supra* note 2, pt. 3, § VI.

19. *Camp*, 411 U.S. at 143 (citing SEC v. Chenery Corp., 318 U.S. 80 (1943); the case is the subject of Chapter 22). *See* Krent, *supra* note 18, at 239–46; Blackletter Statement, *supra* note 2, pt. 3, § VI.

20. *Cf.* Levin & Rossi, *supra* note 9, at 185–89; Blackletter Statement, *supra* note 2, pt. 3, § IV.C.3 (discovery to expand the administrative record).

Bibliography

A GUIDE TO JUDICIAL AND POLITICAL REVIEW OF FEDERAL AGENCIES (Michael E. Herz et al. eds., 2d ed. 2015).

LELAND BECK, FINAL REPORT TO THE ADMINISTRATIVE CONFERENCE OF THE UNITED STATES ON AGENCY PRACTICES AND JUDICIAL REVIEW OF ADMINISTRATIVE RECORDS IN INFORMAL RULEMAKING (2013).

Richard McMillan, Jr. & Todd D. Peterson, *The Permissible Scope of Hearings, Discovery, and Additional Factfinding During Judicial Review of Informal Agency Action*, 1982 DUKE L.J. 333.

William F. Pedersen, Jr., *Formal Records and Informal Rulemaking*, 85 YALE L.J. 38 (1975).

Richard J. Pierce, Jr., *What Factors Can an Agency Consider in Making a Decision?*, 2009 MICH. ST. L. REV. 67.

SECTION OF ADMIN. L. & REGUL. PRAC., AM. BAR ASS'N, A BLACKLETTER STATEMENT OF FEDERAL ADMINISTRATIVE LAW pt. 3, § VI (2d ed. 2013).

Sidney A. Shapiro & Richard E. Levy, *Heightened Scrutiny of the Fourth Branch: Separation of Powers and the Requirement of Adequate Reasons for Agency Decisions*, 1987 DUKE L.J. 387.

Sidney A. Shapiro & Richard W. Murphy, *Arbitrariness Review Made Reasonable: Structural and Conceptual Reform of the "Hard Look,"* 92 NOTRE DAME L. REV. 331 (2016).

Matthew C. Stephenson, *A Costly Signaling Theory of "Hard Look" Judicial Review*, 58 ADMIN. L. REV. 753 (2006).

Peter L. Strauss, Citizens to Preserve Overton Park v. Volpe—*Of Politics and Law, Young Lawyers, and the Highway Goliath*, *in* ADMINISTRATIVE LAW STORIES 259 (Peter L. Strauss ed., 2006).

Peter L. Strauss, *Revisiting* Overton Park*: Political and Judicial Controls over Administrative Actions Affecting the Community*, 39 UCLA L. REV. 1251 (1992).

Patricia M. Wald, *Judicial Review in the Time of Cholera*, 49 ADMIN. L. REV. 659 (1997).

Chapter 25

Vermont Yankee Nuclear Power Corp. v. Natural Resources Defense Council, 435 U.S. 519 (1978)

Gillian Metzger

Vermont Yankee established that the procedures laid out in the Administrative Procedure Act (APA) generally represent the maximum procedural requirements a court can impose on an agency. Other statutes or agency regulations may impose additional procedures, and in some contexts further procedures may be constitutionally mandated. Possibly, courts can enforce compliance with long-established agency practice in the face of unexplained deviation. But *Vermont Yankee* made clear that a reviewing court cannot require additional procedures beyond those in the APA simply because the court believes such procedures "are 'best' or most likely to further some vague, undefined public good."

Declared in 1978, *Vermont Yankee*'s prohibition on judicial procedural inventiveness remains a centrally important principle of administrative law, reiterated most recently by the U.S. Supreme Court in *Perez v. Mortgage Bankers Ass'n.*[1] Yet *Vermont Yankee* did not succeed in protecting agency procedural discretion from judicial interference. Courts continue to impose procedural demands, either directly through broad readings of the APA or indirectly through substantive scrutiny of agency decision-making and deference doctrines. No doubt these procedural intrusions would have been

1. 575 U.S. 92 (2015).

broader without *Vermont Yankee*, but the decision's failure to curb judicial elaboration on the APA's requirements also reveals ongoing pressure on courts to respond to contemporary administrative realities.

The Lead Up to *Vermont Yankee*

Vermont Yankee arose against the background of the environmentalist movement, growing concerns about agencies being captured by the industries they regulate, and an explosion in rulemaking triggered by enactment of major environmental, health, and safety statutes in the 1960s and 1970s. Increasingly, environmental advocates began intervening in nuclear reactor licensing proceedings and raising environmental concerns as reasons for denying licenses. One such proceeding concerned an operating license for the Vermont Yankee Nuclear Power Corporation, in which environmental intervenors claimed that the environmental effects of transporting, reprocessing, and storing spent nuclear fuel had to be considered before the license could be granted. The Atomic Energy Commission (AEC) rejected this claim and awarded Vermont Yankee the license but also initiated a rulemaking on whether—and how—environmental effects of the nuclear fuel cycle should be considered in individual reactor proceedings. Although not required to do so by the informal rulemaking requirements set out in section 553 of the APA, the AEC held a hearing at which interested persons could testify and be questioned but refused to allow discovery or cross-examination. The AEC ultimately adopted a rule stipulating predetermined values for the effects of the nuclear fuel cycle that would be included in environmental impact statements for individual reactors.

The environmental intervenors challenged the new rule, as well as the agency's grant of Vermont Yankee's license, before the U.S. Court of Appeals for the D.C. Circuit. That court had emerged as the nation's administrative law court when Congress made it the center for challenges to regulations issued under the new federal environmental, health, and safety statutes. As its administrative docket grew, the D.C. Circuit began to subject agency decision-making to new scrutiny. This was in part a reaction to the dramatic expansion in the scope and impact of rulemaking under the new statutes, and in part a reflection of growing concern that agencies had become captured by the industries they regulate and were not functioning as impartial experts or defenders of the public interest. While agreeing on the need for greater oversight of agencies' actions, the D.C. Circuit's judges famously divided on the form this oversight should take. In particular, Judge Leventhal argued for enhanced substantive scrutiny of the basis and reasoning behind agency decisions, while Chief Judge Bazelon insisted that judges lacked the competence and expertise to assess the substance of agency decision-making and instead should mandate decision-making procedures that would ensure agency decisions were adequately scrutinized by the scientific community.

This division was evident in the D.C. Circuit's decision holding the fuel-cycle rule to be arbitrary and capricious.[2] The court concluded that the discussion the agency (now known as the Nuclear Regulatory Commission (NRC)) provided of the risks of long-term nuclear waste storage was conclusory and unexplained. But the court also emphasized that "many procedural devices for creating genuine dialogue" on the problems involved in waste disposal "were available to the agency."[3] As a result, it was unclear whether the D.C. Circuit was overturning the rule because the agency had failed to use adequate procedural mechanisms or because the agency had failed to produce an adequate record to support the rule. However, the fact that Chief Judge Bazelon wrote the panel opinion setting aside the rule—as well as a separate concurrence urging agencies to adopt innovative procedures that would better ensure accurate fact-finding on such a complex scientific issue as the nuclear fuel cycle—reinforced the decision's procedural dimension. Judge Tamm read the majority as imposing such a procedural mandate and therefore concurred in the judgment only, despite agreeing that the record was inadequate to sustain the rule. The appellate court also set aside the grant of a license to Vermont Yankee for the agency's failure to consider the fuel cycle's environmental effects.

Vermont Yankee in the Supreme Court

Along with another reactor operator whose license was overturned, Vermont Yankee filed a petition for certiorari seeking Supreme Court review. The federal government's response to the D.C. Circuit's decision was more

2. *See* Nat. Res. Def. Council, Inc. v. NRC, 547 F.2d 633 (D.C. Cir. 1976).
3. *Id.* at 647–55.

complicated. The solicitor general read the decision as holding that the record supporting the fuel-cycle rulemaking was inadequate—an erroneous determination in its view, but not one meriting further review. The NRC, by contrast, argued that the D.C. Circuit had imposed procedural requirements beyond those in section 553 of the APA and that it was important to have such a holding reversed by the Supreme Court. Yet the NRC also went ahead and reopened the fuel-cycle rulemaking for further proceedings while the petitions for certiorari were pending, in order to get reactor licensing resumed quickly.

The Supreme Court reversed in a unanimous opinion by seven Justices. Acknowledging that the basis of the D.C. Circuit's decision was somewhat unclear, the Court concluded that it had invalidated the fuel-cycle rule on procedural grounds. And in so holding, according to the Supreme Court, the lower court was clearly wrong. The Court described section 553 as, "generally speaking, . . . establish[ing] the maximum procedural requirements which Congress was willing to have the courts impose upon agencies in conducting rulemaking procedures." The Court acknowledged that in prior opinions it had suggested that due process might require additional procedures when an agency was making a *quasi*-judicial determination, and added that perhaps a court might reverse an agency's unjustified deviation from long-standing agency procedures. But those were rare exceptions. "Absent constitutional constraints or extremely compelling circumstances, the administrative agencies 'should be free to fashion their own rules of procedure and to pursue methods of inquiry capable of permitting them to discharge their multitudinous duties.'"

According to the Supreme Court, the legislative history of the APA made clear that while Congress viewed section 553 as setting out a minimum of rights and procedures, it intended that *agencies* and not courts would have "discretion [to] . . . determin[e] when extra procedural devices should be employed." A firm prohibition on judicial procedural inventiveness was thus necessary to respect the legislative compromises embedded in the APA. More than this, the Court insisted that such a prohibition was essential to preserve informal rulemaking as a viable procedure. Allowing a court to assess whether an agency had selected the procedures best suited to the issues at hand would render judicial review "totally unpredictable." Further, courts inevitably would assess the adequacy of an agency's procedures against the record produced rather than against the information the agency possessed when it made its procedural choices. In response to such uncertainty and "Monday morning quarterbacking," agencies "would undoubtedly adopt full adjudicatory procedures in every instance," and the "inherent advantages of informal rulemaking would be totally lost."

One of those advantages, the Court emphasized, was that informal rulemaking did not require that the resultant rule be justified exclusively on the record created during a rulemaking hearing. Hence, although an adequate record was required to avoid a rule being found arbitrary and capricious, additional hearing procedures could not be justified on that basis. Nonetheless, recognizing the possibility that the fuel-cycle rule lacked sufficient support in the record, the Court remanded to the D.C. Circuit for review of the adequacy of the NRC's justification for the rule.

Whether the Court's arguments were persuasive is a matter of debate. Writing in the aftermath of the decision, scholars disagreed on whether *Vermont Yankee* was a needed corrective for a troubling trend of judicial procedural intrusions in rulemaking or instead an unfortunate rejection of a salutary development in the lower courts.[4] They also debated whether the Supreme Court's own precedents were as clear as it proclaimed, and queried whether the D.C. Circuit's procedural adaptations were really at odds with the APA.[5]

Yet scholars broadly agree that the Supreme Court's *Vermont Yankee* opinion was a pointed takedown of the D.C. Circuit. The Court painted the appellate court as willfully blind to governing precedent and criticized it for forgetting the limited role of a reviewing court, going so far to describe the D.C. Circuit's decision in a companion case as "Kafkaesque." Not surprisingly, therefore, when the D.C. Circuit on remand invalidated the NRC's new version of the fuel-cycle rule as arbitrary for failing to address the

---

4. *Compare* Clark Byse, Vermont Yankee *and the Evolution of Administrative Procedure: A Somewhat Different View*, 91 Harv. L. Rev. 1823, 1823 (1978) (praising *Vermont Yankee*), *with* Richard B. Stewart, Vermont Yankee *and the Evolution of Administrative Procedure*, 91 Harv. L. Rev. 1805, 1814 (1978) (critiquing *Vermont Yankee*); *see also* Cass R. Sunstein & Adrian Vermeule, *Libertarian Administrative Law*, 82 U. Chi. L. Rev. 393, 397–401 (2015) (urging the Court to reassert *Vermont Yankee*'s prohibition on federal judges' inserting their policy preferences into administrative law).

5. *See* Antonin Scalia, Vermont Yankee*: The APA, the D.C. Circuit, and the Supreme Court*, 1978 Sup. Ct. Rev. 345, 359–63, 381; *cf.* Stewart, *supra* note 4, at 1814–15.

uncertainties of nuclear waste disposal, the Supreme Court again reversed.[6] The Court's sharp critique suggests that *Vermont Yankee* was in part an effort by the Court to rein in the D.C. Circuit's development of administrative law. This view is reinforced by the fact that the Court granted certiorari in the first place and did not dismiss the case when it became clear that the NRC had initiated a new rulemaking that might moot the challenge—something Justice Brennan repeatedly urged the Court to do.

Vermont Yankee over Time

In the years since, *Vermont Yankee* has assumed canonical status in administrative law. The Supreme Court made clear that the *Vermont Yankee* principle is not limited to the rulemaking context, holding in *Pension Benefit Guarantee Corp. v. LTV Corp.* (*PBGC*) that it applies to informal adjudication as well.[7] The Court recently reaffirmed *Vermont Yankee*'s "foundational" principle in *Perez v. Mortgage Bankers Ass'n*, in which the Court again overturned a novel D.C. Circuit procedural imposition.[8] At issue in *Perez* was the D.C. Circuit one-bite rule, which required agencies to use section 553's notice-and-comment procedures to issue a new interpretation of a regulation that deviates significantly from a previously adopted definitive interpretation. Emphasizing that section 553 expressly excludes interpretive rules from its notice-and-comment requirements, the Supreme Court invalidated the D.C. Circuit's approach as "contrary to the clear text of the APA's rulemaking provisions" and "improperly impos[ing] . . . an obligation beyond the 'maximum procedural requirements' specified in the APA," in violation of *Vermont Yankee*.[9]

Yet for all that, *Vermont Yankee* has not prevented courts from constraining agencies' procedural discretion so much as transformed the shape these constraints take. *Vermont Yankee* has not displaced decisions that read the APA's notice-and-comment requirements quite robustly, resulting in notice, disclosure, and response requirements well beyond those that the minimal

6. Balt. Gas & Elec. Co. v. Nat. Res. Def. Council, Inc., 462 U.S. 87 (1983).
7. 496 U.S. 633, 655 (1990).
8. 575 U.S. 92 (2015).
9. *Id.* at 100.

text of section 553 seems to demand.[10] In addition, before the Court overturned *Chevron* deference,[11] it had indicated that the availability of such deference may turn on an agency's use of notice-and-comment rulemaking procedures in promulgating the interpretation at issue, notwithstanding section 553's exemption for interpretive rules.[12] Moreover, scholars have long argued that the Court's development of sometimes quite searching or "hard look" review[13] of the basis and reasoning of agency decisions has served to impose procedural requirements of greater disclosure, response, and explanation.[14]

To some extent, these ongoing judicial procedural constraints can be squared with *Vermont Yankee*. In *PBGC*, for example, the Court argued that hard look review imposed "[a]t most . . . a general 'procedural' requirement of sorts by mandating that an agency take whatever steps it needs to provide an explanation that will enable the court to evaluate the agency's rationale at the time of decision," whereas what *Vermont Yankee* prohibited was judicial imposition of specific procedural requirements not found in the APA.[15] And doctrines elaborating on section 553's terms do not impose requirements like cross-examination that lack any textual toehold. Hence, the recent turn to more originalist readings of the APA[16] may not affect these procedure-expanding precedents.

Nonetheless, substantial tension remains, raising a question about why courts have continued to elaborate on the APA in the face of *Vermont Yankee*. In a prominent article on *Vermont Yankee*, then-Professor Antonin Scalia put the blame in part on the APA's limited procedural variants and the

10. *See* Am. Radio Relay League v. FCC, 524 F.3d 227, 245–48 (D.C. Cir. 2008) (Kavanaugh, J., concurring in part, concurring in the judgment in part, and dissenting in part). *See generally* Kathryn E. Kovacs, *Rules About Rulemaking and the Rise of the Unitary Executive Theory*, 70 Admin. L. Rev. 515, 532–45 (2018) (cataloguing such extra-textual requirements).
11. *See* Loper Bright Enters. v. Raimondo, 603 U.S. 369 (2024). The case is the subject of Chapter 21.
12. United States v. Mead Corp., 533 U.S. 218, 229–30 (2001). The case is the subject of Chapter 18.
13. Motor Vehicle Mfrs. Ass'n v. State Farm Mut. Auto. Ins. Co., 463 U.S. 29 (1983). The case is the subject of Chapter 26.
14. *See* Stewart, *supra* note 4, at 1816–17; Paul R. Verkuil, *Judicial Review of Informal Rulemaking: Waiting for* Vermont Yankee *II*, 55 Tul. L. Rev. 418, 419, 423–25 (1981).
15. *PBGC*, 496 U.S. at 654.
16. *See, e.g.*, Loper Bright Enters. v. Raimondo, 603 U.S. 369, 391–94 (2024). The case is the subject of Chapter 21.

stark choice it poses between formal and informal procedures.[17] Another driving force is the tremendous expansion in the scope and complexity of rulemaking over the second half of the 20th century, which makes the APA appear out of date and raises judicial concerns about unchecked agency power.[18] Such concerns still surface today in, for example, opinions that adopt narrow readings of section 553's policy statement and interpretive rule exemptions in the face of perceived administrative aggrandizement.[19] Absent congressional revision of the APA, *Vermont Yankee* thus represents a canonical administrative law principle that may always be honored, to some extent, in the breach, as courts struggle to harmonize the APA's requirements with the contemporary realities of administrative government.

Bibliography

Jack M. Beermann & Gary Lawson, *Reprocessing* Vermont Yankee, 75 GEO. WASH. L. REV. 856 (2007).

Clark Byse, Vermont Yankee *and the Evolution of Administrative Procedure: A Somewhat Different View*, 91 HARV. L. REV. 1823 (1978).

Kenneth Culp Davis, *Administrative Common Law and the* Vermont Yankee *Opinion*, 1980 UTAH L. REV. 3.

Kathryn E. Kovacs, *Rules About Rulemaking and the Rise of the Unitary Executive Theory*, 70 ADMIN. L. REV. 515 (2018).

Gillian E. Metzger, *Embracing Administrative Common Law*, 80 GEO. WASH. L. REV. 1293 (2012).

Gillian E. Metzger, *The Story of* Vermont Yankee*: A Cautionary Tale of Judicial Review and Nuclear Waste*, *in* ADMINISTRATIVE LAW STORIES 125 (Peter L. Strauss ed., 2006).

Richard J. Pierce, Jr., *Waiting for* Vermont Yankee II, 57 ADMIN. L. REV. 669 (2005).

17. *See* Scalia, *supra* note 5, at 382–86.

18. *See id.* at 375–86, 404–08; Gillian E. Metzger, *Embracing Administrative Common Law*, 80 GEO. WASH. L. REV. 1293, 1320–21, 1329 (2012).

19. *See, e.g.*, Texas v. United States, 809 F.3d 134 (5th Cir. 2015), *aff'd by an evenly divided court*, 579 U.S. 547 (2016). *See generally* Ronald M. Levin, *Rulemaking and the Guidance Exemption*, 70 ADMIN. L. REV. 263 (2018).

Antonin Scalia, Vermont Yankee*: The APA, the D.C. Circuit, and the Supreme Court*, 1978 SUP. CT. REV. 345.

Richard B. Stewart, Vermont Yankee *and the Evolution of Administrative Procedure*, 91 HARV. L. REV. 1805 (1978).

Cass R. Sunstein, *"Practically Binding": General Policy Statements and Notice-and-Comment Rulemaking*, 68 ADMIN. L. REV. 491 (2016).

Cass R. Sunstein & Adrian Vermeule, *Libertarian Administrative Law*, 82 U. CHI. L. REV. 393 (2015).

Paul R. Verkuil, *Judicial Review of Informal Rulemaking: Waiting for* Vermont Yankee II, 55 TUL. L. REV. 418 (1981).

Chapter 26

Motor Vehicle Manufacturers Association v. State Farm Insurance, 463 U.S. 29 (1983)

Reeve Bull

Under the Administrative Procedure Act (APA), an agency's action is to be held unlawful and set aside if, among other things, it is "arbitrary, capricious, an abuse of discretion, or otherwise not in accordance with law."[1] This statutory language, though far from self-defining, suggests that a reviewing court should reverse an agency action that is unreasonable in light of the underlying law and factual evidence but should accord some level of deference to the agency's decision-making process and uphold any defensible conclusion reached by the agency. Precisely what level of shoddy fact-finding or illogical reasoning rises to the level of arbitrary-or-capricious decision-making has varied over the decades since the APA's passage and depends intimately upon the facts underlying any given case, but the foremost precedent in defining this vague statutory standard is the U.S. Supreme Court's decision in *Motor Vehicle Manufacturers Ass'n v. State Farm.*

The *State Farm* Decision

The *State Farm* decision came at the end of a decades-long effort by the National Highway Traffic Safety Administration (NHTSA) to enhance automobile safety by mandating the installation of various devices designed to

1. 5 U.S.C. § 706(2)(A).

shield a vehicle's occupants in the event of a collision. The underlying statute, the National Traffic and Motor Vehicle Safety Act (NTMVSA), gave NHTSA very wide discretion, directing it to issue "practicable" rules that "meet the need for motor vehicle safety." After a rule mandating installation of seatbelts proved inadequate (as few drivers and passengers actually used the belts), NHTSA began a decade-plus process of developing a passive restraint rule. During the Carter administration, NHTSA finally settled upon a rule that required either automatic seatbelts or airbags in all new vehicles, with the manufacturer choosing which device to install. Shortly after President Reagan assumed office, his secretary of transportation abandoned the enterprise entirely and rescinded the passive restraint requirement. State Farm and other parties challenged the rescission, and the ensuing litigation worked its way up to the Supreme Court.

The Court began its opinion by clarifying that the rescission of an existing rule is subject to the same standard of review as the promulgation of a new rule. It then proceeded to parse carefully the agency's justification for its action. First, it faulted NHTSA for its failure to consider what seemed to be the obvious alternative of mandating airbags. Though NHTSA may have justifiably rejected this approach for any number of reasons (excessive cost, safety risks created when airbags deploy, etc.), it behaved arbitrarily and capriciously by overlooking that option entirely.

Second, the Court found inadequate support for NHTSA's conclusion that users would disable the automatic seatbelts. The primary study showed a marked increase in seatbelt usage in cars equipped with automatic belts. The agency attempted to distinguish this study by noting it involved automatic belts guarded by an ignition interlock system and asserting that most users would disable belts in the absence of an interlock system. The Court found the agency's rationale to be speculative and inadequate to support the agency's conclusion.

At first blush, the Court's decision appears eminently reasonable. Completely ignoring an obvious regulatory alternative and reaching one conclusion in the face of reasonably strong evidence favoring a different conclusion both seem like the type of palpably irrational decision-making that the APA's "arbitrary or capricious" standard was designed to guard against.

On the other hand, when considering the extraordinary challenges confronted by NHTSA regulators over more than a decade of designing and redesigning an automatic crash protection policy, the admittedly suboptimal decision-making process looks more defensible. It is widely accepted that the president can and should exercise political influence over the agency decision-making process[2] but that an agency must nevertheless come up with an objective and empirically sound justification for any policy that it pursues.[3] One can easily envision an agency scrambling to cobble together a justification when a new president directs it to abandon a program for which it had been carefully marshalling support over the previous years.

Indeed, then-Justice Rehnquist, joined by three other traditionally conservative members of the Court (Justices Burger, Powell, and O'Connor) dissented in part, agreeing that the agency erred in overlooking an airbag mandate but concluding that it had offered a sufficient justification for rejecting automatic seatbelts. Justice Rehnquist suggested that, absent any compelling evidence concerning whether or not automobile users would leave the automatic belts in place, the agency did not behave arbitrarily in rejecting that option and focusing instead on educating users on the importance of seatbelt usage.

Context Dependency of "Arbitrary or Capricious" Review

It is generally accepted that judges should tender greater deference to regulators when reviewing a rule that relies upon highly technical findings developed by experts in the natural sciences or other specialized disciplines, especially when they are regulating in areas in which knowledge is rapidly evolving.[4]

In one sense, the case for heightened deference in the case of rulemakings relying upon a recondite body of knowledge is virtually unassailable. Federal agencies, by design, are staffed by technical experts,[5] and their expertise is supplemented by that of outsiders who provide input on proposed rules through notice and comment.[6] By contrast, judges in a common-law

2. *See* Elana Kagan, *Presidential Administration*, 114 Harv. L. Rev. 2245, 2332–34 (2001).
3. *See, e.g.*, Midwater Trawlers Coop. v. Dep't of Com., 282 F.3d 710, 720–21 (9th Cir. 2002).
4. *See, e.g.*, Ethyl Corp. v. EPA, 541 F.2d 1, 28 (D.C. Cir. 1976).
5. *See generally* Woodrow Wilson, *The Study of Administration*, 2 Pol. Sci. Q. 197 (1887).
6. *See* 5 U.S.C. § 553(c); FCC v. Prometheus Radio Project, 592 U.S. 414 (2021).

regime are generalists who are not well positioned to second-guess expert decisions. At the same time, if merely invoking the technical nature of the regulatory process is sufficient to insulate an agency's decision from judicial scrutiny, then an important check on the bureaucratic decision-making process is removed.

Given this dynamic, many judges have not shied away from delving into arcane subject matters when reviewing agency rules, even as others prefer a more deferential posture. And judges may show an increased willingness to roll up their sleeves in certain subject matter areas more than others.

For example, over the past 35 years, courts have shown an increased willingness to delve into the economic analysis underlying agency rules.[7] In *Michigan v. EPA*,[8] the Supreme Court came quite close to holding that some form of benefit-cost analysis is implicitly required under the "arbitrary and capricious" standard, declaring that an agency's decision to ignore economic costs in deciding whether to regulate power plants "strayed far beyond [the] bounds" of reasonable statutory interpretation.[9] In dissent, despite arguing that the agency had adequately considered costs, Justice Kagan even more explicitly embraced a default benefit-cost consideration requirement, declaring that "[c]ost is almost always relevant," and suggesting that failure to consider costs would necessarily condemn an agency's rulemaking.[10]

This of course is but one illustration of the context dependency of the *State Farm* standard. As far as the technical complexity of the underlying subject matter is concerned, economic analysis likely falls somewhere between highly complex (e.g., particle physics) and very basic (e.g., traffic rules). It is therefore unsurprising that certain judges have been eager to wade into the weeds whereas others prefer to defer almost completely to the agency experts.[11] What is perhaps more interesting is the fact that the

7. *See generally* Reeve Bull & Jerry Ellig, *Judicial Review of Regulatory Impact Analysis: Why Not the Best?*, 69 ADMIN. L. REV. 725 (2017); *see also* Chamber of Com. of the United States v. SEC, 412 F.3d 133 (D.C. Cir. 2005); Am. Equity Inv. Life Ins. Co. v. SEC, 572 F.3d 923 (D.C. Cir. 2009); Bus. Roundtable v. SEC, 647 F.3d 1144 (D.C. Cir. 2011).

8. 576 U.S. 743 (2015).

9. *But see* ADRIAN VERMEULE, LAW'S ABNEGATION 177–78 (2016) (arguing that the *Michigan v. EPA* decision represents a rather routine, if arguably improper, application of *Chevron* in which the Court interpreted statutory language to mandate benefit-cost analysis).

10. *Michigan*, 576 U.S. at 769 (Kagan, J., dissenting).

11. *See generally* Reeve T. Bull & Jerry Ellig, *Statutory Rulemaking Considerations and Judicial Review of Regulatory Impact Analysis*, 70 ADMIN. L. REV. 873 (2019).

level of deference in this particular area seems to be diminishing over time, with *Michigan v. EPA* potentially ushering in a new era in which judges will be expected to scrutinize agencies' economic analyses more closely and agencies expected to furnish some such analysis even in areas in which it is not statutorily mandated (except perhaps implicitly by the APA's "arbitrary and capricious" standard).[12]

In this sense, the economic analysis case law shows how the *State Farm* standard may evolve over time, with judges constantly upgrading their technical skill set and showing less and less willingness to allow agencies to invoke "expertise" as a shield against searching judicial review. In its most recent engagement with the arbitrary-and-capricious standard, the Court may have signaled that it will subject agency explanations for rules to greater scrutiny than it has in the past.[13]

Practical Challenges

Of course, rigorous judicial review is not without its costs. As then-Justice Rehnquist's *State Farm* dissent implicitly suggested, searching review by the courts may improve the quality of agency decision-making, but it may also force the agencies to pour more and more resources into the rulemaking enterprise as they attempt to design bulletproof regulations.

In recent years, some progressives have decried the phenomenon of regulatory "ossification," in which the time it takes an agency to issue a rule has ballooned (now taking numerous years or, in some instances, even decades) and identifying the *State Farm* standard as a major culprit.[14] The political dynamics are interesting since the rigorous standard of review that the Court embraced in the *State Farm* decision was first developed over the course of

12. *But see* Vermeule, *supra* note 9, at 155–90 (contending that judicial review under the arbitrary-and-capricious standard is relatively forgiving and has become increasingly so over time).

13. *See* Ohio v. EPA, 603 U.S. 279 (2024). This 5–4 decision illustrates how judges sometimes differ on the appropriate stringency of review. Justice Gorsuch, for the majority, concluded that the Environmental Protection Agency had not adequately explained its actions; Justice Barrett, dissenting, concluded that it had.

14. *See, e.g.*, Thomas O. McGarity, *Some Thoughts on "Deossifying" the Rulemaking Process*, 41 Duke L.J. 1385, 1400–03, 1410–26 (1992); Richard J. Pierce, *Seven Ways to Deossify Agency Rulemaking*, 47 Admin. L. Rev. 59, 65–66, 79 (1995).

the 1960s and 1970s by progressive judges on the U.S. Court of Appeals for the D.C. Circuit, who articulated the so-called "hard look" standard in a series of cases that set aside agency actions deemed insufficiently protective of the public interest.[15] Regardless of the historical political dynamics, advocacy for the courts' applying a searching review of agency decision-making is now largely confined to conservatives.[16]

Whether or not ossification has increased over time is a hotly contested issue,[17] and it is unclear whether aggressive judicial review (as opposed to enhanced presidential oversight, agency mismanagement, resource limitations, etc.) is a major cause. Nevertheless, the argument that rigorous judicial review of the type embraced in *State Farm* will slow down and complicate agency decision-making certainly has a logical appeal, and the extent to which one supports either ratcheting up or watering down the *State Farm* standard will generally depend upon whether one favors robust regulation and places greater trust in agency regulators than in federal judges.

Unanswered Legal Questions

Quite apart from the fundamental political issues it raises, the *State Farm* decision also implicates some nettlesome legal questions concerning precisely where it fits into the overall process of judicial review of agency action. These issues are difficult because the courts have historically drawn arbitrary distinctions between questions of "fact," "policy," and "law" and between "procedural" review and "substantive" review, categories that tend to bleed together.

At a simplistic level, the blackletter law pertaining to judicial review of agency action is quite straightforward. The *State Farm* analysis applies to

15. *See generally* Sidney A. Shapiro & Richard W. Murphy, *Arbitrariness Review Made Reasonable: Structural and Conceptual Reform of the Hard Look*, 92 Notre Dame L. Rev. 331, 346–47 (2016).

16. *See* Sidney A. Shapiro & Rena Steinzor, *Use and Abuse of Information: Capture, Accountability, and Regulatory Metrics*, 86 Tex. L. Rev. 1741, 1749 (2008).

17. *Compare* McGarity, *supra* note 14, *with* Anne Joseph O'Connell, *Political Cycles in Rulemaking: An Empirical Portrait of the Modern Administrative State*, 94 Va. L. Rev. 889, 932 (2008); *see also* Jason Webb Yackee & Susan Webb Yackee, *Testing the Ossification Thesis: An Empirical Examination of Federal Regulatory Volume and Speed, 1950–1990*, 80 Geo. Wash. L. Rev. 1414, 1421 (2012).

factual and policy determinations made by the agency. A different set of standards applies to the agency's legal determinations.[18] Until recently, the agency's reasonable interpretation of an ambiguous statute that it administers would often command deference under the so-called *Chevron* doctrine.[19] As a result of the Court's recent decision in *Loper Bright Enterprises v. Raimondo*,[20] however, the agency's interpretation is no longer entitled to any deference, although it may be a source of guidance under the so-called *Skidmore* doctrine.[21] When the agency is interpreting its own ambiguous regulations, the courts will usually apply so-called *Auer* deference.[22]

When *Chevron* and *State Farm* coexisted, these rather neat distinctions tended to break down when applied to actual cases. First, as Professor Ronald Levin has persuasively argued, it was never entirely clear how *State Farm*'s arbitrary-or-capricious standard differed from the "reasonableness" analysis of *Chevron* step two, as both are concerned with whether the agency has offered a reasoned justification for its rule. It is inadequate to state simply that *State Farm* applied to policy questions and *Chevron* to legal questions, as the lines between the two tended to blur.[23] To illustrate, consider a hypothetical NHTSA rule issued under the NTMVSA requiring that all new passenger vehicles be self-driving, an exceedingly costly rule with dubious benefits. A court reviewing such a rule might have pointed to the shoddy underlying benefit-cost analysis and struck it down as arbitrary and capricious under *State Farm*, or it might have struck it down under *Chevron* step two, holding that the agency adopted an unreasonable

18. Section of Admin. L. & Regul. Prac., Am. Bar Ass'n, A Blackletter Statement of Federal Administrative Law pt. 3, § V (2d ed. 2013).

19. Chevron U.S.A., Inc. v. Nat. Res. Def. Council, 467 U.S. 837, 842–43 (1984). On the circumstances under which *Chevron* deference applied, see *United States v. Mead Corp.*, 533 U.S. 218 (2001). *Chevron* and *Mead* are the subjects of Chapters 16 and 18, respectively.

20. 603 U.S. 369 (2024). The case is the subject of Chapter 21.

21. Skidmore v. Swift & Co., 323 U.S. 134 (1944). The case is the subject of Chapter 15.

22. *See* Auer v. Robbins, 519 U.S. 452 (1997). In *Kisor v. Wilkie*, 588 U.S. 558 (2019), the Court narrowed the scope of *Auer* deference. *Auer* and *Kisor* are the subjects of Chapters 17 and 19, respectively.

23. *See* Ronald M. Levin, *The Anatomy of* Chevron*: Step Two Reconsidered*, 72 Chi.-Kent L. Rev. 1253, 1285–86 (1997). For the contrary argument that *Chevron* step two and *State Farm* arbitrary-and-capricious review are distinct, see Cary Coglianese, *Foreword:* Chevron*'s Interstitial Steps*, 85 Geo. Wash. L. Rev. 1339, 1374–86 (2017). *See generally* Thomas W. Merrill, The Chevron Doctrine, Its Rise and Fall, and the Future of the Administrative State 113–19 (2022) (discussing competing interpretations of *Chevron* step two).

interpretation of "practicable" under the NTMVSA by adopting such an impractical regulation. The evidence upon which the agency relied and the court's result would have been fundamentally the same in either case.

Similar difficulties have always beset the traditional distinction between "substantive" and "procedural" review. In theory, the *State Farm* standard limits itself to the latter: a judge can closely parse the rulemaking record to ensure that the agency deployed sound empirical techniques and reached justifiable conclusions based on the evidence presented, but they are not to substitute their policy preferences for those of the agency. Like the "policy"-"law" distinction, this artificial dualism tends to break down in practice. Continuing with the self-driving car hypothetical, a judge could point to deficiencies in the regulatory benefit-cost analysis as grounds for vacating the rule, but, at some point, a very rigorous procedural review (e.g., faulting the agency for failure to quantify regulatory costs) starts to bleed into substantive review (e.g., striking the rule down because the court deems the costs too high).

It is therefore better to think of the *State Farm* analysis as lying somewhere on a spectrum between purely "procedural" and purely "substantive" review.[24] Pure "procedural" review would consist of merely ensuring that the agency checked the appropriate boxes (e.g., making sure that the agency cited some evidence on regulatory costs without assessing the quality of the evidence). Pure "substantive" review would involve a court's determining whether it agrees with the agency's resolution of the evidence. The standard contemplated in *State Farm* sits somewhere between these extremes: a court can police for obvious errors in the agency's decision-making methodology, ensure that the agency grappled with relevant evidence, and even determine whether the agency reached a reasoned conclusion on the basis of the record evidence, but it must not substitute its preferred conclusion for an equally plausible conclusion reached by the agency.

In addition to such fundamental questions concerning where the *State Farm* standard has fit within the overall framework for reviewing agency decisions, there are a number of other vexing issues related to judicial review under the arbitrary-or-capricious standard. For instance, judges and scholars

24. *See* Bull & Ellig, *supra* note 7, at 808–09.

have long debated whether the arbitrary-or-capricious standard of APA section 706(2)(A)[25] differs meaningfully from the "substantial evidence" standard of section 706(2)(E).[26] Though the weight of authority seems to favor the conclusion that the stringency of the standards is identical but that the evidentiary record from which the agency may draw is narrower under the "substantial evidence" standard (which traditionally applies to adjudications or adjudication-like proceedings),[27] some judges and members of Congress have sometimes treated substantial evidence as a more rigorous standard.[28] In short, the *State Farm* decision left a number of unanswered legal questions, and both judges and lawmakers have continued to grapple with these issues over the past several decades.

Bibliography

A GUIDE TO JUDICIAL AND POLITICAL REVIEW OF FEDERAL AGENCIES (Michael E. Herz et al. eds., 2d ed. 2015).

Reeve T. Bull & Jerry Ellig, *Judicial Review of Regulatory Impact Analysis: Why Not the Best?*, 69 ADMIN. L. REV. 725 (2017).

Caroline Cecot & W. Kip Viscusi, *Judicial Review of Agency Benefit-Cost Analysis*, 22 GEO. MASON L. REV. 575 (2015).

Thomas J. Miles & Cass R. Sunstein, *The Real World of Arbitrariness Review*, 75 U. CHI. L. REV. 761 (2008).

SECTION OF ADMIN. L. & REGUL. PRAC., AM. BAR ASS'N, A BLACKLETTER STATEMENT OF FEDERAL ADMINISTRATIVE LAW pt. 3, § V (2d ed. 2013).

Cass R. Sunstein, *Deregulation and the Hard-Look Doctrine*, 1983 SUP. CT. REV. 177.

25. 5 U.S.C. § 706(2)(A).

26. *Id.* § 706(2)(E). *See generally* Lisa Schultz Bressman, *Judicial Review of Agency Discretion*, *in* A GUIDE TO JUDICIAL AND POLITICAL REVIEW OF FEDERAL AGENCIES 176, 177–95 (Michael E. Herz et al. eds., 2d ed. 2015).

27. *See, e.g.*, Ass'n of Data Processing v. Bd. of Governors, 677 F.2d 677 (D.C. Cir. 1984) (Scalia, J.); *see also* Phx. Herpetological Soc'y, Inc. v. Fish & Wildlife Serv., 998 F.3d 999, 1003 (D.C. Cir. 2021); *see generally* Bressman, *supra* note 26, at 176–78.

28. *See, e.g.*, Corrosion Proof Fittings v. EPA, 947 F.2d 1201, 1213–14 (5th Cir. 1991); *see also* Regulatory Accountability Act, S. 951, 115th Cong. §§ 4–5 (2017); Regulatory Accountability Act, H.R. 5, 115th Cong. § 108 (2017).

Adrian Vermeule, Laws Abnegation: From Laws Empire to the Administrative State (2016).

Kathryn A. Watts, *Proposing a Place for Politics in Arbitrary and Capricious Review*, 119 Yale L.J. 2 (2009).

David Zaring, *Reasonable Agencies*, 96 Va. L. Rev. 135 (2010).

PART V

Separation of Powers

Chapter 27

Myers v. United States, 272 U.S. 52 (1926)

Aditya Bamzai

The source and scope of the president's authority to supervise the executive branch has long been one of the central concerns of constitutional law, dating back to the first debate about the Constitution that occurred in Congress.[1] As a matter of constitutional law, the debate has concerned the degree to which the president has the authority to "remove" (or, in other words, to fire) subordinate "officers" within the executive branch and to "direct" those officers. The battle lines of the debate have depended primarily on inferences drawn from the constitutional grants of authority to the president and to Congress.

On the one hand, Article II of the Constitution vests the "executive Power" in the president, requires that he "take Care that the Laws be faithfully executed," and provides that he "shall appoint" "Officers of the United States" with the advice and consent of the Senate (with the exception of "inferior Officers" whose appointment Congress may vest in the "President alone, in the Courts of Law, or in the Heads of Departments").[2] On the other hand, Article I gives Congress the power "[t]o make all Laws which shall be necessary and proper for carrying into Execution . . . all [] Powers vested by this Constitution in the Government of the United States, or in any Department . . . thereof"—which presumably includes at least some

1. Saikrishna Prakash, *New Light on the Decision of 1789*, 91 Cornell L. Rev. 1021 (2006).
2. U.S. Const. art. II, §§ 1–3.

authority to organize and control the bureaucracy.[3] During the course of the 19th century, the question of how best to interpret these constitutional provisions arose during several of the nation's most prominent political disputes, including Andrew Jackson's battle to abolish the Second Bank of the United States and Congress's attempt to remove President Andrew Johnson from office during Reconstruction.[4] In the latter circumstance, Congress enacted a statute—the Tenure of Office Act—that prohibited the president from removing executive officers without the advice and consent of the Senate.[5] Johnson's subsequent impeachment and near-conviction—prompted in part by his alleged violation of this statute—provided a stark illustration of the importance of this abstract constitutional question to the concrete task of governance.

The U.S. Supreme Court, however, repeatedly avoided issuing an authoritative ruling on the question.[6] Such a ruling would wait until the 20th century, at which point the Court issued not one, but two opinions about the scope of the president's removal authority that pointed in different direc-

3. *Id.* art. I, § 8, cl. 18. To be sure, the constitutional provisions discussed in the text are not the only ones from which inferences might be drawn. Some have argued that the Constitution's system of removing "civil Officers" by impeachment in the House and conviction in the Senate establishes the exclusive method of firing such officers. *See id.* § 2, cl. 5; § 3, cl. 6; art. II, § 4. Others argue that Article II's grant of authority to the president to "require the Opinion, in writing, of the principal Officer in each of the executive Departments" cuts against inferring an unfettered presidential removal power from the more generally worded "executive power" and "take care" clauses. *Id.* art. II, § 2, cl. 1. Still others argue that Article III's creation of "good Behaviour" tenure for some "officers"—the members of the Article III judiciary—implies that executive officers cannot have life tenure. *Id.* art. III, § 1. Readers interested in further exploring the textual moves, and countermoves, should consult the articles listed in the bibliography at the end of Chapter 28.

4. For treatments of the history from a legal perspective, see STEVEN G. CALABRESI & CHRISTOPHER S. YOO, THE UNITARY EXECUTIVE: PRESIDENTIAL POWER FROM WASHINGTON TO BUSH 105–22, 179–87 (2008); Peter L. Strauss, *Overseer or "The Decider"? The President in Administrative Law*, 75 GEO. WASH. L. REV. 696, 705–07 (2007).

5. Act of Mar. 2, 1867, 14 Stat. 430.

6. The Court touched upon, but failed to address squarely, the constitutional question in a series of cases. *See Ex parte* Hennen, 38 U.S. 230 (1839); United States *ex rel.* Goodrich v. Guthrie, 58 U.S. 284 (1854); Embry v. United States, 100 U.S. 680 (1879); McElrath v. United States, 102 U.S. 426 (1880); Blake v. United States, 103 U.S. 227 (1880); United States v. Perkins, 116 U.S. 483 (1886); McAllister v. United States, 141 U.S. 174 (1891); Parsons v. United States, 167 U.S. 324, 335 (1897); Reagan v. United States, 182 U.S. 419 (1901); Shurtleff v. United States, 189 U.S. 311 (1903).

tions. These two opinions—*Myers v. United States* and *Humphrey's Executor v. United States*—remain deeply influential, although later Supreme Court opinions have clarified (and, in some respects, superseded) the Court's early 20th century analyses. The doctrine remains sufficiently unstable, however, that reference to *Myers* and *Humphrey's Executor* continues to be common.

This chapter introduces *Myers*, and the subsequent chapter addresses *Humphrey's Executor* and its aftermath.

Background on *Myers*

By the time a case addressing the authority of Congress to play a role in removing executive officers reached the Supreme Court, the Tenure of Office Act had been repealed.[7] But a comparable provision—governing the removal of postmasters of the first, second, and third classes—lingered in the U.S. Code. The statute provided that such postmasters would hold office for a four-year term unless "removed by the President by and with the advice and consent of the Senate."[8] When President Woodrow Wilson removed a postmaster of the first class whom he had previously appointed, Frank S. Myers, during Myers's four-year term and without obtaining the consent of the Senate, the stage was set for a resolution of whether the statutory provision violated the Constitution.[9]

Myers brought a lawsuit seeking his lost salary in the Court of Claims. After the Court of Claims dismissed the suit,[10] and after Myers's death, his administratrix sought an appeal to the Supreme Court. Seemingly aware of the importance of the case, the Court arranged for two oral arguments, as well as a separate amicus curiae brief filed in favor of the statute's constitutionality by Senator George Pepper (R-Pa.).

7. *See* Act of Mar. 3, 1887, 24 Stat. 500.
8. Act of July 12, 1876, § 6, 19 Stat. 78, 80–81.
9. On the factual background of *Myers*, see Saikrishna Prakash, *The Story of* Myers *and Its Wayward Successors: Going Postal on the Removal Power*, *in* PRESIDENTIAL POWER STORIES 166 (Christopher H. Schroeder & Curtis A. Bradley eds., 2009).
10. 58 Ct. Cl. 199 (1923).

The Supreme Court's Decision

In an opinion by Chief Justice Taft—himself a former president of the United States—the Court held that the law was unconstitutional. The Court concluded that the president had the exclusive power to remove executive officers of the United States appointed by and with the advice and consent of the Senate. Taft's opinion for the Court and the three separate dissents encompass 243 pages of the *U.S. Reports*—making *Myers* one of the longest opinions ever issued by the Court. It is impossible to do justice to every aspect of the Court's analysis, but its contours can be summarized as follows.

The key portion of Chief Justice Taft's opinion placed heavy weight on the "decision of 1789," a congressional debate and vote that occurred during the first session of the First Congress. This was, as Taft put it, "the Congress that launched the government" and "whose constitutional decisions have always been regarded, as they should be regarded, as of the greatest weight in the interpretation" of the Constitution. As Taft explained, during this debate, the House of Representatives struck language in the statute creating the Department of Foreign Affairs that would have made the secretary "removable by the President" in favor of statutory language that presupposed that the Constitution conferred on the president the power to remove heads of departments. Taft repeatedly cited the role played in the House debates by James Madison—who was at the time a representative from Virginia—observing that Madison had "insisted" that Article II "by vesting the executive power in the president was intended to grant to him the power of appointment and removal of executive officers except as thereafter expressly provided in that [A]rticle." Taft further observed that, because the president is "charged specifically to take care that [the laws] be faithfully executed," the "implication" was that "in the absence of any express limitation respecting removals" the "executive power" included the "power of removing those" for whom the president is responsible. After addressing the "decision of 1789," Taft went on to discuss (and in some cases to distinguish) the views of an array of legal luminaries, including Alexander Hamilton, John Marshall, Daniel Webster, James Kent, and Joseph Story, among others.

Taft acknowledged that a number of congressional enactments in the years following 1863 conflicted with the construction of Article II embraced by the First Congress. For one thing, as Taft observed, Congress in 1867 enacted the Tenure of Office Act as part of its conflict with President Andrew Johnson during Reconstruction—an action that played an important role in Johnson's impeachment by the House and near-conviction in the Senate. In Taft's words, this was a "period in the history of the government when both houses of Congress attempted to reverse" the "construction" that the First Congress had given the Constitution. He thus refused to set aside the First Congress's construction in favor of an interpretation given "during a heated political difference of opinion between the then President and the majority leaders of Congress over the reconstruction measures" after the Civil War. For another, Taft recognized that, since the Interstate Commerce Commission in 1887, Congress had created a number of "administrative boards" headed by members appointed by the president by and with the advice and consent of the Senate but removable "for specified causes." Taft dismissed these statutes as not "hav[ing] really received the acquiescence of the executive branch of the government."

Myers's Two Caveats on Presidential Removal Power

Though *Myers* is often cited as a sweeping affirmation of presidential authority, Taft acknowledged two key caveats. First, Taft observed that Congress had the power "to limit and regulate removal of [] inferior officers by heads of departments when it exercises its constitutional power to lodge the power of appointment with them." That caveat explained the Court's holding in *United States v. Perkins*,[11] and, according to the Court, also made the various civil service laws consistent with the Court's holding.[12]

Second, Taft twice carved out differential treatment for judicial functions and entities. On the first occasion, *Myers* observed that Congress may vest "duties of a *quasi*-judicial character" in "executive officers and members

11. 116 U.S. at 485. In reaching this conclusion, the *Myers* Court parsed the Appointments Clause, U.S. Const. art. II, § 2, to conclude that Congress could limit the authority to remove inferior officers appointed by the heads of departments, but could not do the same for inferior officers appointed by the president with the advice and consent of the Senate.

12. Taft contended that *Myers* would not "open the door to a reintroduction of the spoils system" because the civil service laws could constitutionally apply to such "inferior offices."

of executive tribunals whose decisions after hearing affect interests of individuals." Taft contended that, where Congress vested such "*quasi*-judicial" duties, the president could not "properly influence or control" their "discharge" "in a particular case," but could nevertheless "consider the decision after its rendition as a reason for removing the officer, on the ground that the discretion regularly entrusted to that officer by statute has not been on the whole intelligently or wisely exercised."[13] On the second occasion, Taft bracketed the question whether the Court's holding applied to "the removal of judges, whose tenure is not fixed by Article III of the Constitution, and who are not strictly United States judges under that article." *Myers* explained that issues raised by such officers "present considerations different from those which apply in the removal of executive officers, and therefore we do not decide them."[14]

Precisely whom Taft meant when he spoke of "judges, whose tenure is not fixed by Article III of the Constitution," is not crystal clear. The *Myers* opinion went on to discuss solely territorial judges. But shortly after *Myers* was decided, the Court decided *Ex parte Bakelite* and *United States v. Williams*, which held that the Court of Customs and Patent Appeals and the Court of Claims were *quasi*-judicial bodies exercising "judicial power," though not staffed by judges with the "good behavior" and undiminishable salary protections specified in Article III.[15] Perhaps inadvertently, these cases might have played a role in leading the Court to its reasoning in *Humphrey's Executor* less than a decade later.

---

13. This statement occurred in the context of a general discussion of the president's authority to "direct" subordinates in the course of their duties, contending that "[t]he ordinary duties of officers prescribed by statute come under the general administrative control of the President by virtue of the general grant to him of the executive power, and he may properly supervise and guide their construction of the statutes under which they act in order to secure [a] unitary and uniform execution of the laws."

14. Along the same lines, Taft distinguished Chief Justice Marshall's statement in *Marbury v. Madison*, 5 U.S. 137 (1803), that justices of the peace for the District of Columbia could not be removed during their five-year terms of office. *See also* Parsons v. United States, 167 U.S. 324, 335 (1897) (suggesting that *Marbury* could be explained as an exercise of Congress's exclusive jurisdiction to create offices within the District of Columbia under U.S. Const. art. I, § 8, cl. 17).

15. Williams v. United States, 289 U.S. 553 (1933); *Ex parte* Bakelite Corp., 279 U.S. 438 (1929). A plurality of the Court, as well as Congress (by statute), later disapproved of this aspect of *Williams* and *Bakelite*. *See* Glidden Co. v. Zdanok, 370 U.S. 530 (1962).

Three Justices—Holmes, Brandeis, and McReynolds—authored separate dissents. Holmes's dissent was cursory, but both Brandeis's and McReynolds's opinions were lengthy and canvassed extensive doctrinal and historical ground. In a nutshell, both argued that Congress, at the very least, had the constitutional power to fix the tenure of inferior statutorily created offices.

Bibliography

See the consolidated bibliography at the end of Chapter 28.

Chapter 28

Humphrey's Executor v. United States, 295 U.S. 602 (1935)

Aditya Bamzai

Nine years after *Myers*, the U.S. Supreme Court backtracked on some of the implications of Chief Justice Taft's reasoning in *Humphrey's Executor v. United States*.

Background on *Humphrey's Executor*

The controversy began when President Franklin Roosevelt requested the resignation of a member of the Federal Trade Commission (FTC), William E. Humphrey, before the expiration of his seven-year statutory term of office.[1] As it is today, the FTC of that era was a commission composed of five members with fixed terms, each appointed by the president with the advice and consent of the Senate.[2] And as today, the statute provided that the president may remove a commissioner for "inefficiency, neglect of duty, or malfeasance in office."[3]

After an exchange of letters—in which President Roosevelt told Humphrey that he did "not feel your mind and my mind go along together on either the policies or the administering of the Federal Trade Commission"—Humphrey

1. Humphrey, a holdover from the prior administration, had been initially appointed to the FTC in 1925 by President Calvin Coolidge and reappointed in 1931 by President Herbert Hoover. Humphrey's term of office thus expired in 1938.
2. *See* Federal Trade Commission Act § 1, 38 Stat. 717, 718 (1914) (codified as amended at 15 U.S.C. § 41).
3. *Id.*

refused to resign his office. Roosevelt responded with a letter declaring that Humphrey was "hereby removed"—a full four years before the expiration of the statutory seven-year term. In turn, Humphrey responded with a lawsuit in the Court of Claims, which (upon Humphrey's death) his executor pursued to obtain the sum of money allegedly due to him as salary from the date of Roosevelt's actions to the date of Humphrey's death.

The Supreme Court's Decision

When the case reached the Supreme Court, it had been boiled down to two questions. The first question was whether the FTC Act, in providing that "[a]ny commissioner may be removed by the President for inefficiency, neglect of duty, or malfeasance in office," restricted the president's power to remove FTC commissioners to the listed causes alone. The argument that the statute did *not* limit the president's authority was by no means frivolous and was forcefully advanced on behalf of the Roosevelt administration by Stanley Reed, then the solicitor general of the United States and later a Justice of the Supreme Court. Reed's argument rested on *Shurtleff v. United States*,[4] where the Court had held that a comparable statutory provision did not specify the sole grounds on which the president could remove members of the Board of General Appraisers. Instead, according to the *Shurtleff* Court, such a provision authorized the officer's removal on any of the three listed grounds ("inefficiency, neglect of duty, or malfeasance in office") with notice and a hearing *and* on any other ground without procedural protections.[5]

In *Humphrey's Executor*, however, the Court held that the FTC Act limited the president's authority to the specific listed causes. The Court reasoned that *Shurtleff* depended on the peculiarity that the Board of General Appraisers statute did not fix a term of office. Thus, if the Board's members could be removed only for the listed causes, they would effectively have life tenure, contrary to the "unbroken precedent against life tenure, except in the case of the judiciary." By contrast, according to the Court, the statute governing FTC commissioners was "plainly and wholly different" because

4. 189 U.S. 311 (1903).
5. *Id.* at 314.

it "fixe[d] a term of office"—namely, a term of seven years for each commissioner. In addition to this statutory argument, the Court contended that the FTC was different from the Board of General Appraisers on the basis "of the character of the commission and the legislative history" of the FTC Act. According to the Court, the FTC was "to be nonpartisan," "act with entire impartiality," and enforce "no policy except the policy of the law." The FTC's "duties," the Court claimed, were "neither political nor executive, but predominantly *quasi*-judicial and *quasi*-legislative."[6] As for the FTC Act's legislative history, the Court relied on a Senate report expressing the view that the FTC commissioner terms should "be long enough to give them an opportunity to acquire the expertness in dealing with these special questions concerning industry that comes from experience" and on snippets from debates in Congress suggesting that the FTC was "not subject to the orders of the President." All told, the Court concluded that Congress sought to "create a body of experts" that would be "independent of executive authority" and for which "certainty of tenure would vitally contribute."

The second question was whether the removal provision, as construed by the Court, unconstitutionally intruded into the president's power to remove subordinates. The Court held it did not. The Court acknowledged that, in *Myers*, "expressions occur which tend to sustain the government's contention" that the statute was unconstitutional, but it treated those expressions as dicta not subject to *stare decisis* weight.[7]

The Court distinguished the office of postmaster (at issue in *Myers*) from the office of FTC commissioner based on the two offices' nature and functions.[8] According to the Court, a postmaster is "an executive officer

6. The Court analogized the FTC to the Interstate Commerce Commission, claiming that both commissions were "called upon to exercise the trained judgment of a body of experts 'appointed by law and informed by experience.'"

7. The Court states that "the narrow point actually decided was only that the President had power to remove a postmaster of the first class, without the advice and consent of the Senate as required by act of Congress" and that other parts of *Myers* were "beyond the point involved and, therefore, do not come within the rule of *stare decisis*."

8. In his brief, counsel for Humphrey's executor also sought to distinguish *Myers* on the ground that the postmaster statute imposed a requirement to obtain the advice and consent of the Senate before removal, whereas the FTC Act only limited the grounds for presidential removal and did not require congressional involvement. *See* Brief for Samuel F. Rathbun, Executor at 26–30, Humphrey's Ex'r v. United States, 295 U.S. 602 (1935) (No. 667), 1935 WL 32964 (contending that "enactment of standards of removal is essentially different from

restricted to the performance of executive functions," who was "charged with no duty at all related to either the legislative or judicial power." As such, a postmaster was "merely one of the units in the executive department and, hence, inherently subject to the exclusive and illimitable power of removal by the Chief Executive, whose subordinate and aid he is." By contrast, the Court reasoned that FTC commissioners "occupie[d] no place in the executive department" and "exercise[d] no part of the executive power vested by the Constitution in the President." As the Court saw it, the FTC was formed "to perform [] specified duties as a legislative or as a judicial aid" "without executive leave" and "free from executive control"—"in part *quasi*-legislatively and in part *quasi*-judicially."[9] Congress could require such "*quasi*-legislative or *quasi*-judicial agencies" to act "independently of executive control" and, therefore, could "forbid their removal except for cause" during a fixed period of tenure.

The Court relied on two arguments to support the rule that it announced. The first was a "slippery slope"-style argument. The Court expressed a concern that an "illimitable power of removal" over civil officers would mean that the president had the power to remove members of the "Interstate Commerce Commission and the Court of Claims." That would mean that the "judges of the legislative Court of Claims"—which the Court described as "exercising judicial power"—held "office only at the pleasure of the President."[10]

The second was an argument based on the historical record. The Court distinguished the "decision of 1789" because, according to the Court, it

requiring the Senate's consent to removals") (capitalization altered). The *Humphrey's Executor* Court did not address this alternative argument.

9. The Court characterized the FTC's functions of "making investigations and reports thereon for the information of Congress" as "*quasi*-legislative" and its functions of acting "as a master in chancery under rules prescribed by the court" as "*quasi*-judicial." To be sure, the Court observed that a part of the FTC Act authorized "the President to direct an investigation and report by the commission" under the antitrust acts, but it characterized this provision as "so obviously collateral to the main design of the act as not to detract from the force of" the Court's general characterization of the Commission. Thus, according to the Court, if the FTC "exercise[d] any executive function, as distinguished from executive power in the constitutional sense," it did "so in the discharge and effectuation of its *quasi*-legislative or *quasi*-judicial powers, or as an agency of the legislative or judicial departments of the government." *Cf.* Buckley v. Valeo, 424 U.S. 1 (1976).

10. For the proposition that the Court of Claims "exercis[ed] judicial power," the Court cited *Williams v. United States*, 289 U.S. 553 (1933).

involved the establishment of the Department of Foreign Affairs, which was headed by a secretary who was "purely executive" and "responsible to the President . . . in a very definite sense." The Court pointed to a later proposal during the same congressional session by Madison for "a different rule in respect of executive removal" for the comptroller of the treasury[11]—an office that, as the Court put it, was "not purely of an executive nature but partook of the judiciary quality as well." And the Court pointed to *Marbury v. Madison*,[12] which the Court saw as establishing that "Chief Justice Marshall was of opinion that a justice of the peace from the District of Columbia was not removable at the will of the President."

Scholarly Commentary

Scholars have long remarked on the circumstances of the Court's *Humphrey's Executor* decision. On the same day that the Court decided *Humphrey's Executor*, it also decided *A.L.A. Schechter Poultry Corp. v. United States*, in which it declared unconstitutional a portion of the Roosevelt administration's program to intervene in the U.S. economy to counteract the Great Depression.[13] In the views of some, *Humphrey's Executor* is of a piece with other cases of the same era that sought to trim the sails of Roosevelt's policy agenda.

Be that as it may, in light of the Court's reasoning in *Humphrey's Executor*, "independent" agencies whose heads were protected from removal by the president to specified causes alone proliferated in the years following 1935. When the Court in *Wiener v. United States* relied on *Humphrey's Executor*'s "*quasi*-judicial" reasoning to find that President Eisenhower could not remove a member of the War Claims Tribunal, save for cause, the Supreme Court appeared to have woven the fundamental rationale of *Humphrey's Executor* even more tightly into the constitutional fabric.[14]

But the Court's lack of clarity in these, as well as later, cases prompted a series of questions, two of which form the focus of the Court's present-day

11. *See* 1 Annals of Cong. 611–12 (1789).
12. 5 U.S. 137, 165–66 (1803).
13. 295 U.S. 495 (1935).
14. 357 U.S. 349 (1958).

jurisprudence. First, the precise meaning of "good cause" restrictions on the president's removal authority remains unclear. A commonly used formulation—that the president may remove for "inefficiency, neglect of duty, or malfeasance in office" and no other reason—dates to the statute creating the Interstate Commerce Commission and was at issue in *Humphrey's Executor*. Statutory formulations vary, however, and so has the Supreme Court's approach to interpreting such provisions.[15]

Second, it is unclear how to distinguish "purely executive" officers from "*quasi*-judicial" and "*quasi*-legislative" officers—or even whether such a distinction remains relevant under current law. That is because, although *Humphrey's Executor* relied on this distinction, the Court in *Morrison v. Olson* did a further *volte face* by appearing to discard the "*quasi*-judicial" and "*quasi*-legislative" categories and to replace them with an approach that asked courts to determine whether statutory restrictions unduly interfere with the president's ability to supervise the executive branch.[16] The precise test for the constitutionality of restrictions on the president's removal power—and thus the precise place of *Myers* and *Humphrey's Executor* in the constitutional firmament—remains a source of dispute to this day.[17]

Bibliography

J. David Alvis et al., The Contested Removal Power, 1789–2010 (2013).

Aditya Bamzai, *Taft, Frankfurter, and the First Presidential For-Cause Removal*, 52 U. Rich. L. Rev. 691 (2018).

Marshall J. Breger & Gary J. Edles, Independent Agencies in the United States: Law, Structure, and Politics (2015).

Steven G. Calabresi & Saikrishna Prakash, *The President's Power to Execute the Laws*, 104 Yale L.J. 5431 (1994).

15. *Compare* Free Enter. Fund v. Pub. Co. Acct. Oversight Bd., 561 U.S. 477, 479, 496 (2010), *with* Bowsher v. Synar, 478 U.S. 714, 734 (1986).

16. 487 U.S. 654, 690 (1988). The case is the subject of Chapter 31.

17. For exploration of the state of the dispute as of the time of this writing, see the opinions in *PHH Corp. v. CFPB*, 881 F.3d 75 (D.C. Cir. 2018) (en banc).

Steven G. Calabresi & Christopher S. Yoo, The Unitary Executive: Presidential Power from Washington to Bush (2008).

Edward S. Corwin, *Tenure of Office and the Removal Power Under the Constitution*, 27 Colum. L. Rev. 353 (1927).

Robert E. Cushman, The Independent Regulatory Commissions (1941).

Lawrence Lessig & Cass Sunstein, *The President and the Administration*, 94 Colum. L. Rev. 1 (1994).

Jerry L. Mashaw, Creating the Administrative Constitution: The Lost One Hundred Years of American Administrative Law (2012).

Saikrishna Prakash, *The Essential Meaning of Executive Power*, 2003 U. Ill. L. Rev. 701 (2003).

Peter L. Strauss, *Overseer or "The Decider"? The President in Administrative Law*, 75 Geo. Wash. L. Rev. 696 (2007).

Peter L. Strauss, *The Place of Agencies in Government: Separation of Powers and the Fourth Branch*, 84 Colum. L. Rev. 573 (1984).

Chapter 29

Crowell v. Benson, 285 U.S. 22 (1932)

Matthew Lee Wiener

Agency adjudication continues to occupy a central place in the administrative state and, as this volume attests, in administrative law. A recurring question is what judicially enforceable limits the Constitution places on Congress's authority to assign the adjudication of matters to agencies rather than to federal courts established under Article III of the Constitution—to courts whose judges enjoy life tenure (subject to "good Behavior") and whose compensation may not be diminished. Only such courts may exercise the "judicial Power of the United States."[1]

Of the U.S. Supreme Court's decisions addressing the constitutionality of agency adjudication, *Crowell v. Benson* can still lay claim to being the most important. "*Crowell* is often seen," in Professor Laurence Tribe's words, "as signaling the birth" of agency adjudication.[2] Justice Scalia, apparently no fan of *Crowell*, called it a "landmark" decision on agency adjudicatory authority.[3]

No doubt *Crowell* is less important than it once was. What was perhaps its most notable holding quickly faded into obscurity, and the doctrinal basis it supplied for upholding much agency adjudication against constitutional challenge has been, if not abandoned, at least marginalized in modern Court

1. U.S. Const. art. III, § 1; *see* Stern v. Marshall, 564 U.S. 462, 484 (2011); *accord* Oil States Energy Serv., LLC v. Greene's Energy Grp., LLC, 584 U.S. 325, 334 (2018).
2. 1 Laurence H. Tribe, American Constitutional Law 286 (3d ed. 2000).
3. *Stern*, 564 U.S. at 504 (2010) (Scalia, J., dissenting).

decisions. Yet *Crowell* remains, if nothing else, the necessary starting point for understanding the Court's modern approach to the constitutionality of agency adjudication.

The Agency Adjudication System in *Crowell*

Crowell arose from a workers' compensation system established under the 1927 Longshoremen's and Harbor Workers' Compensation Act (LHWCA). The act required maritime employers to compensate their employees for disability or death resulting, without regard to fault, from "an injury occurring on the navigable waters of the United States."[4] Congress had passed the LHWCA in response to court decisions holding unconstitutional state workers' compensation laws that covered maritime employees. The act covered only injuries that a state could not "validly" cover under such laws.

Like state workers' compensation laws, the LHWCA assigned the adjudication of compensation claims to an administrative agency—the U.S. Employees' Compensation Commission. The act required the Commission's deputy commissioner to investigate and, upon the request of a party, hold an evidentiary hearing on any contested claim. Hearings were informal.[5]

The deputy commissioner's resulting order—an "award"—was subject to review in a federal district court. Any party to a Commission proceeding could challenge it by filing an "injunction proceeding" against the deputy commissioner. If the award was "not in accordance with law," the district court could set it aside. The act did not otherwise address the scope or standard of review. Relatively few agency awards were challenged in court.[6]

In *Crowell*, an employer (Benson) filed suit to enjoin the deputy commissioner (Crowell) from enforcing an award to a maritime worker. Benson claimed that the worker was not his employee when injured and so was not "within" the Commission's "jurisdiction."

---

4. 33 U.S.C. § 903 (1932).
5. *See* Mark Tushnet, *The Story of* Crowell: *Grounding the Administrative State*, *in* Federal Courts Stories 362 (Judith Resnick & Vicki Jackson eds., 2010).
6. *See id.*

Crowell's Appellate Model and Its Constitutional Limitations

The main question before the Court was whether the LHWCA's adjudication scheme violated the Fifth Amendment's Due Process Clause or Article III. Benson's initial pleading had also objected that the scheme violated the Seventh Amendment by depriving him of a jury trial, but the Court quickly dispatched that objection because the Seventh Amendment does not apply to cases in admiralty, only "suits at common law."

As for due process, the issue concerned only the deputy commissioner's factual conclusions. No one challenged the received understanding that all legal questions were for a reviewing court to decide *de novo*. Fifteen years later, Congress would codify that principle in the Administrative Procedure Act (APA).[7]

In an opinion by Chief Justice Hughes, the Court held that Congress had constitutionally assigned to the deputy commissioner authority to decide all questions of fact "with respect to injuries within the purview of the [LHWCA]." They included all questions "with respect to the circumstances, nature, and extent of the employee's injuries and the amount of compensation." Administrative findings on these questions bound a court if "supported by evidence." Congress also codified that basic principle in the APA.[8]

The Court emphasized that if courts did not give finality to the Commission's factual determinations, they would "defeat the obvious purpose of the legislation to furnish a prompt, continuous, expert and inexpensive method for dealing with a class of questions of fact that are peculiarly suited to examination by an administrative agency specially assigned to that task." It concluded that "the use of the [act's] administrative method"—"assuming due notice, proper opportunity to be heard, and that findings are based upon evidence"—"falls easily" within the Court's precedents "sustaining similar procedure[s]" in other administrative schemes.

With little explanation, the Court then concluded that the act's hearing procedures satisfied due process. It noted that the facts upon which the

7. *See* 5 U.S.C. § 706.
8. *See id.* § 706(2)(E) ("substantial evidence" standard of review).

deputy commissioner relied had to be put on the record "and be open to challenge and opposing evidence." Due process did not require that hearings be conducted using courtroom evidentiary rules or "technical" procedure.

The more significant objection to the act was that Congress had unconstitutionally conferred Article III "judicial power" on an agency to decide—subject only to deferential judicial review—all factual questions. Chief Justice Hughes began by drawing an important distinction that today marks the line between constitutional and unconstitutional assignment of adjudicatory authority to agencies—that between private and public rights.

A public right is one that, in the Court's still canonical but elusive phrasing, "arise[s] between the Government and persons subject to its authority in connection with the performance of constitutional functions of the executive or legislative departments." If a case concerns a public right, the Court explained, Congress is free to assign it to either a court or an agency—and, if to any agency, without providing for subsequent judicial review. The Court relied on its 19th century decision in *Murray's Lessee v. Hoboken Land & Improvement Co.* in which the Court had explained "that there are matters, involving public rights, which be presented in such form that the judicial power is capable of acting on them"—that is, they present a justiciable case or controversy under Article III—"but which Congress may or may not bring within the cognizance of the courts of the United States, as it may deem proper."[9] The *Crowell* Court gave as examples cases involving Congress's power over "interstate and foreign commerce, taxation, immigration, the public lands, public health, the facilities of the post office, and pensions and payments to veterans." The claim in *Crowell*, the Court explained, did not fall within the public-rights category. Rather, it concerned "the liability of one individual to another under the law as defined."

That *Crowell* involved private rights, however, did not preclude Congress from assigning the initial fact-finding function to an agency. "[T]here is no requirement" in even private-rights cases "that, in order to maintain the essential attributes of the judicial power, all determinations of facts" in Article III courts "shall be made by judges." The Court noted that, in "common law cases," courts relied on the "aid" of juries to decide facts; and

9. 59 U.S. (18 How.) 272, 284 (1856).

that, in equity and admiralty cases, courts historically relied on "masters and commissioners or assessors" to make factual determinations. Although the latter's were "essentially advisory," the "practice" was to accept them when they were "properly based on evidence."

In assigning a fact-finding role to the Commission, the Court held, Congress had not transgressed Article III. The Court emphasized that the act had "limited application." It covered only the relation between employer and employee, and then only with respect to "compensation awards" under "prescribed standards." And the act left all legal questions to courts. Here, as in its discussion of due process, the Court noted that an agency was "essential" to apply uniform statutory standards to a large number of similar cases and that Congress had spared the courts "a most serious burden."

But in the second half of its opinion, which pivoted in a decidedly anti-agency direction,[10] the Court recognized an important exception: The Constitution required that courts determine, *de novo*, any "jurisdictional" facts. By that the Court meant facts on whose existence Congress's constitutional power to act depended. Two facts fell into that category: first, that a worker's injury occurred on U.S. navigable waters; and second, that a worker was an employee under master-servant law. As the Court understood then-extant constitutional doctrine, Congress lacked the power to adopt a no-fault compensation scheme for maritime employees unless both "condition[s] precedent" were satisfied. The Court then interpreted the act (questionably) to allow for *de novo* judicial determination of the predicate facts.

One question remained: Whether, in determining jurisdictional facts, a court was limited to the record before the Commission or could develop its own evidentiary record. The Court concluded that the "essential independence of the exercise of the judicial power of the United States in the enforcement of constitutional rights" required that a court develop its own evidentiary record. This would not, the Court insisted, impair the "intended efficiency" of the administrative scheme since judicial review under the act was comparatively rare and review based on the absence of jurisdictional facts even more rare.

10. *See* DAVID P. CURRIE, THE CONSTITUTION IN THE SUPREME COURT: THE SECOND CENTURY, 1888–1986, at 215 (1990).

Dissenting, Justice Brandeis rejected the Court's conclusion that a party to a commission proceeding was entitled to a *de novo* trial of jurisdictional facts. The LHWCA did not allow for this conclusion—having assigned all fact-finding authority to the deputy commissioner—and the Constitution did not require it. As for Article III, Justice Brandeis insisted that it had no "bearing" on the case at all. Article III did not require that "*any*" fact be determined, "*as of the first instance*," by a federal court. Appellate review satisfied Article III.[11] Variants of this argument appeared later in the academic literature, but the Court never accepted it.[12]

Agency Adjudication After *Crowell*

Justice Brandeis was concerned that *Crowell's* "uncertain" and potentially capacious jurisdictional-fact doctrine might well undermine administrative adjudication. His critique of that doctrine's basis may have been persuasive, but his concern about its effects turned out to be misplaced. Within just a short time after the Court decided *Crowell*, its jurisdictional-fact doctrine became almost entirely irrelevant, except in cases under the LHWCA itself.[13] One reason lies with the Court's New Deal-era decisions, the first issued soon after *Crowell*, expanding Congress's powers under the Commerce Clause.[14] Seldom after those decisions would a jurisdictional fact arise in an agency case.

Shorn of its jurisdictional-fact holding, *Crowell* seemingly offered a firm constitutional basis—reflected in earlier decisions but not until *Crowell* articulated as emphatically as a holding of the Court—on agency adjudication that could not be sustained under the public-rights doctrine as it was then understood. Large claims have been made on *Crowell's* behalf in

11. *See* Richard H. Fallon, Jr., *Of Legislative Courts, Administrative Agencies, and Article III*, 101 Harv. L. Rev. 915, 933 (1988); Paul M. Bator, *The Constitution as Architecture: Legislative and Administrative Courts Under Article III*, 65 Ind. L.J. 233, 265–66 (1985).
12. *See, e.g.*, N. Pipeline Constr. Co. v. Marathon Pipeline Co., 458 U.S. 50, 86 n.39 (1981).
13. *See, e.g.*, *id.* at 82 n.33; Thomas W. Merrill, *Article III, Adjudication, and the Origins of the Appellate Model of Administrative law*, 111 Colum. L. Rev. 939, 979 (2011); *see also, e.g.*, Adrian Vermeule, Law's Abnegation 32 (2016); Tushnet, *supra* note 5, at 387; Bernard Schwartz, *Does the Ghost of* Crowell v. Benson *Still Walk?*, 98 U. Pa. L. Rev. 163 (1949).
14. *See, e.g.*, NLRB v. Jones & Laughlin Steel Corp., 301 U.S. 1 (1937).

this regard.[15] One prominent commentator has called *Crowell* "the greatest of the cases validating administrative adjudication,"[16] and another the "fountainhead for the stream of cases legitimating the role of the modern administrative agency."[17] Professor Henry Monaghan declared that *Crowell* "remov[ed] article III as a meaningful barrier to the use of administrative agencies to establish and enforce, at least initially, all the rights created by the administrative state."[18]

For nearly a century after *Crowell*, the Supreme Court affirmed the constitutionality of agency adjudicatory authority in every case in which it was presented with an Article III or related Seventh Amendment challenge. (The constitutionality of administrative adjudication was apparently so often assumed that litigants seldom bothered to question it.) The only real limitation on Congress's authority recognized in the case law was that, at least in regulatory cases implicating traditional property rights, Congress had to provide for judicial review on the model of *Crowell* and the APA.[19]

Yet *Crowell*'s role in the Court's decisions should not be overstated. Some decisions do reflect *Crowell*'s solicitude for administrative adjudication and, as the Court once put it, its "lesson" that "practical attention to substance, rather than doctrinaire reliance on formal categories, should inform application of Article III."[20] But in none of these decisions did the Court really ground its holding firmly in *Crowell*'s stated rationale for allowing agencies to adjudicate private-right cases—that, as the Court characterized it some years after *Crowell*, agencies function as fact-finding "adjuncts" to federal courts.[21]

Instead, these decisions have relied mainly on one of two—sometimes overlapping—rationales. The first is that a statutory delegation of adjudicatory authority does not, all things considered, sufficiently "intrude on the province of the judiciary"[22] to raise Article III concerns. This functional or

15. *See* 1 Tribe, *supra* note 2, at 286.
16. Bator, *supra* note 11, at 251; *accord* Tushnet, *supra* note 5, at 386.
17. Fallon, *supra* note 11, at 923.
18. Henry Paul Monaghan, Marbury *and the Administrative State*, 83 Colum. L. Rev. 1, 18 (1983).
19. *See, e.g.*, N. Pipeline Constr. Co. v. Marathon Pipeline Co., 458 U.S. 50, 70 n.24 (1982).
20. Thomas v. Union Carbide, 473 U.S. 568, 587 (1985).
21. Atlas Roofing Co., Inc. v. OSHA, 430 U.S. 442, 450 n.7 (1977); *see also, e.g.*, *N. Pipeline*, 458 U.S. at 78.
22. CFTC v. Schor, 478 U.S. 833, 851–52 (1985).

balancing approach—which is redolent of *Crowell* in some respects—is reflected especially in two 1980s decisions involving claims between private parties: (1) *Thomas v. Union Carbide Agricultural Products Corp.*,[23] where the Court upheld a statute that authorized a pesticide registrant before an agency to use an earlier registrant's data in its application, if it compensated the first registrant and submitted any compensation dispute to arbitration; and (2) *Commodity Futures Trading Commission v. Schor*, where the Court upheld an agency's authority to adjudicate a state-law counterclaim against a party that had sought reparations before an agency under the agency's own regulations. Both decisions relied on *Crowell* in concluding that the challenged adjudication schemes left much of the "essential attributes of judicial power" intact.[24] In each case, the Court emphasized, the agency's adjudicatory authority was confined to a specialized, narrow area of law; the agency's fact-finding remained subject to judicial review, albeit under a deferential standard; and a court decided all legal questions under a *de novo* standard.

The second and now-predominant rationale—recognized but held inapplicable in *Crowell*—is that an adjudication involves a public right.[25] Much of what the Court has said on the public-rights rationale—until its 2024 decision in *SEC v. Jarkesy*,[26] discussed later—it has said in three cases challenging the authority of bankruptcy courts to adjudicate state-law claims.[27] In the most recent of these cases, *Stern v. Marshall*, the Court abandoned *Schor*'s and *Thomas*'s balancing approach in concluding that Congress can assign only public-rights cases to an agency for adjudication. But the Court then defined public rights with such breadth so as to place the adjudication schemes challenged in *Thomas* and *Schor*—and nearly every other agency's—within the public-rights category. That category, the Court wrote, includes any claim that "derives from a federal regulatory scheme, or in which resolution of the claim by an expert Government agency is deemed essential to a limited regulatory objective within the agency's jurisdiction"—in short,

23. 473 U.S. 568.
24. *Schor*, 478 U.S. at 852
25. *See, e.g.*, *Atlas Roofing*, 430 U.S. at 450.
26. 603 U.S. 109 (2024).
27. *See* Stern v. Marshall, 564 U.S. 462 (2011); Granfinanciera, S.A. v. Nordberg, 492 U.S. 33 (1989); N. Pipeline Constr. Co. v. Marathon Pipeline Co., 458 U.S. 50 (1982).

any claim asserting a right that is "integrally related to particular Federal Government action."[28] The government need not even be a party.[29] Under this understanding, *Crowell* itself can be recharacterized as a public-rights case, as the Court had earlier suggested and the solicitor general noted in *Jarkesy*.[30]

In *Stern*, the Court relegated *Crowell* to a footnote, where it characterized the decision as addressing agency adjudicators with "only limited authority to make specialized, narrowly defined factual determinations regarding a particularized area of law and to issue orders that could be enforced only by action of the District Court"—that is, adjudicators who "functioned as a true 'adjunct' of the District Court."[31] This marginalization of *Crowell* drew an objection from Justice Breyer in dissent: "Were *Crowell*'s holding as narrow as the majority suggests, one could question the validity of Congress's delegation of authority to adjudicate disputes among private parties to other agencies . . . , thereby resurrecting important legal questions previously thought to have been decided."[32]

Retrenchment: *SEC v. Jarkesy*

In *Jarkesy*, the Court decided for the first time in its history that Congress had transgressed constitutional limits in assigning adjudicatory authority to an agency. *Jarkesy* raised the question whether, consistent with the Seventh Amendment, the Securities and Exchange Commission (SEC) could require private persons to defend themselves against the SEC's claims of securities fraud before the SEC itself rather than before a federal court, where it would clearly have had the right to a jury trial. There was no serious question that the SEC's claim lay within the reach of the Seventh Amendment. The dispositive question was whether the SEC was seeking to enforce

---

28. *Stern*, 564 U.S. at 490; *see also Granfinanciera*, 492 U.S. at 33 n.10.
29. *See Stern*, 564 U.S. at 490. *But see id.* at 503–08 (Scalia, J., concurring).
30. *See Granfinanciera*, 492 U.S. at 55 n.10; Brief for Petitioner at 28 n.2, SEC v. Jarkesy, 603 U.S. 109 (1994) (No. 22-859); *see also* 1 TRIBE, *supra* note 2, at 295.
31. *Stern*, 564 U.S. at 489–90 n.6; *see also id.* at 504 (Scalia, J., concurring); *cf. N. Pipeline*, 458 U.S. at 85.
32. *Stern*, 564 U.S. at 508–09 (Breyer, J., joined by Ginsburg, Sotomayor, and Kagan, JJ., dissenting).

a public right. If so, Congress "may assign the matter for decision to an agency without a jury, consistent with the Seventh Amendment"—and also consistent with Article III, though no Article III objection was presented to the Supreme Court.[33]

The Court held that the securities fraud claim, though brought by the SEC in its "sovereign capacity" under a federal regulatory statute, did not fall within the public-rights exception. Although it did not "define" the exception with any specificity, the Court made clear that it included "only historic categories of adjudication" recognized in early, mostly 19th century, cases.[34] No trace of *Stern*'s expansive characterization of public rights appears in *Jarkesy*. At most the Court allowed that claims brought by the government might fall within the exception if, unlike the fraud claim in *Jarkesy*, they have no clear common-law antecedent. It remains to be seen which agency adjudication programs *Jarkesy* will render unconstitutional.

Crowell scarcely appeared either in the Court's opinion or Justice Sotomayor's dissent.[35] Unlike Justice Breyer in *Stern*, Justice Sotomayor made no attempt to enlist *Crowell* in her defense of agency adjudication. Her concern was the Court's retrenchment of the public-rights doctrine. Only Justice Gorsuch, concurring, addressed *Crowell*—and not at all approvingly. He derided as a "fiction" *Crowell*'s conclusion that agencies, like special masters, serve as mere fact-finding "adjuncts," and he emphasized that *Crowell* was an admiralty case to which the Seventh Amendment did not apply.[36] Most of today's Justices, if pressed, would likely cabin *Crowell* in much this way. Even proponents of agency adjudication will concede that *Crowell's* characterization of adjudicating agencies as mere adjuncts does not really reflect what they actually do.

33. *Jarkesy*, 603 U.S. at 127.
34. *Id.* at 130.
35. *See also* Oil States Energy Serv., LLC v. Greene's Energy Grp., LLC, 584 U.S. 325, 334 (2017).
36. *Jarkesy*, 603 U.S. at 155–56 (Gorsuch, J., concurring); *see also* Granfinanciera, S.A. v. Nordberg, 492 U.S. 33, 55 n.10 (1989).

Conclusion

Somewhere along the way, the public-rights doctrine supplanted *Crowell*'s adjunct theory and its variants as the doctrinal basis of agency adjudication. Future debates over the constitutionality of agency adjudication will almost certainly center on the uncertain contours of that doctrine. Still, *Crowell*'s reputation as the leading decision legitimating agency adjudication will not likely recede any time soon.

Bibliography

Paul M. Bator, *The Constitution as Architecture: Legislative and Administrative Courts Under Article III*, 65 Ind. L.J. 233, 251 (1985).

William Baude, *Adjudication Outside Article III*, 133 Harv. L. Rev. 1513 (2020).

John Dickinson, Crowell v. Benson*: Judicial Review of Administrative Determinations of Questions of Constitutional Fact*, 80 U. Pa. L. Rev. 1055 (1932).

Richard H. Fallon, Jr., *Of Legislative Courts, Administrative Agencies, and Article III*, 101 Harv. L. Rev. 915, 923 (1988).

Henry M. Hart, Jr., *The Power of Congress to Limit the Jurisdiction of Federal Courts: An Exercise in Dialectic*, 66 Harv. L. Rev. 1362 (1953).

Thomas W. Merrill, *Article III, Agency Adjudication, and the Origins of the Appellate Review Model of Administrative Law*, 111 Colum. L. Rev. 939 (2011).

Henry Paul Monaghan, Marbury *and the Administrative State*, 83 Colum. L. Rev. 1 (1983).

Caleb Nelson, *Adjudication in the Political Branches*, 107 Colum. L. Rev. 559 (2007).

James F. Pfander, *Article I Tribunals, Article III Courts, and the Judicial Power of the United States*, 118 Harv. L. Rev. 643 (2004).

Bernard Schwartz, *Does the Ghost of* Crowell v. Benson *Still Walk?*, 98 U. Pa. L. Rev. 163 (1949).

Mark Tushnet, *The Story of* Crowell*: Grounding the Administrative State*, *in* FEDERAL COURTS STORIES 362 (Judith Resnick & Vicki Jackson eds., 2010).

ADRIAN VERMEULE, LAW'S ABNEGATION: FROM LAW'S EMPIRE TO THE ADMINISTRATIVE STATE ch. 1 (2016).

Chapter 30

INS v. Chadha, 462 U.S. 919 (1983)

Connor Raso

INS v. Chadha marked a major milestone in defining the separation of powers between Congress and the executive branch. The central question presented in the case is simple at first glance: Did a legislative veto of an executive branch action exercised by only one house of Congress violate the Constitution? Put another way, would such a veto be constitutional only if enacted by both houses of Congress and presented to the president for approval? The U.S. Supreme Court answered the first question in the affirmative, requiring legislative vetoes to be enacted through the same process as legislation.

The *Chadha* Case

The facts giving rise to the case were relatively straightforward. Chadha overstayed his student visa, subjecting him to deportation. Chadha applied for and the attorney general granted a suspension of deportation. Relying on a specific grant of statutory authority, the House of Representatives passed a resolution invalidating this suspension, subjecting Chadha to deportation. Chadha challenged this congressional disapproval on constitutional grounds, arguing that the suspension of deportation must be approved by the House and Senate and sent to the president. The Court agreed and held that under the Constitution the legislative veto used to invalidate Chadha's deportation suspension could be enacted only through bicameral action subject to presentment and possible presidential veto.

Chief Justice Burger grounded his decision for the Court largely on the text of the presentment and bicameralism clauses of the Constitution.[1] The critical threshold question was whether the legislative veto exercised in Chadha's case was a "legislative act" by Congress. The Court began with the presumption that the veto was a legislative act. The Court then reasoned that the veto was "essentially legislative in purpose and effect" because it was intended to have the force of law and to alter Chadha's legal rights. Moreover, the legislative veto involved a policy matter that was essentially legislative. As such, the legislative veto could only be enacted through the constitutional process of bicameral action and presentment to the president.

In reaching this conclusion, the Court noted the historical importance that the framers attached to the requirements of bicameralism and presentment. The Court also reasoned that because the Constitution explicitly lists several actions that a single house of Congress can take alone, actions not listed require bicameral action. The majority did not take a position on the policy merits of the single branch veto. Instead, it argued that the Constitution is about more than efficiency, explaining, "With all the obvious flaws of delay, untidiness, and potential for abuse, we have not yet found a better way to preserve freedom than by making the exercise of power subject to the carefully crafted restraints spelled out in the Constitution."

Although the *Chadha* holding was confined to its facts, the Court quickly affirmed challenges to one-house legislative vetoes in other contexts, such as one-house vetoes of agency rules.[2] This clarified that all one-house vetoes were unconstitutional.

Commentary

A number of commentators questioned the majority's starting presumption that the legislative veto of Chadha's stay of deportation was a legislative act. Commentary along these lines emphasizes that Congress takes other actions that alter legal rights and duties but are widely recognized as non-legislative. For instance, congressional investigations and oversight may

1. U.S. Const. art. I, § 7, cl. 2.
2. *See* Process Gas Consumers Grp. v. Consumer Energy Council, 463 U.S. 1216 (1983).

impose legal obligations on outside parties and are not legislative acts.[3] Given this range of non-legislative activity, the presumption that the legislative veto was a legislative act was misplaced.

Commentators have also argued that the legislative veto at issue in *Chadha* was not a legislative act by its very nature. The veto applied only to Chadha and was not accompanied by any generalized rationale that would change the law more generally.[4] The veto therefore did not resemble legislation but instead something more akin to oversight of an executive branch decision. In his *Chadha* dissent, Justice White followed this argument, claiming that the legislative veto did not make law, writing, "On its face, the legislative veto no more allows one House of Congress to make law than does the presidential veto confer such power upon the President." The majority's argument that the veto altered Chadha's legal rights has been attacked as circular. Professor Donald Elliott has argued that the legislative veto could just as easily be viewed as a supervisory method of congressional control included in the original delegation of authority.[5] In this view, Chadha's legal rights were always conditioned on the possibility of a legislative veto. The exercise of this veto therefore did not alter his legal rights and thus did not constitute a legislative act.

Critics have also argued that *Chadha* was decided too broadly. Justice Powell's concurrence emphasized this point, arguing that the decision should have been confined to the facts of Chadha's case. In particular, the Court should have invalidated the legislative veto solely in cases where Congress "assumed a judicial function," as it did by judging the merits of Chadha's particular deportation case and making a decision about his legal rights. In this vein, Peter Strauss has argued that the majority should have clearly restricted the *Chadha* holding to its facts.[6] The majority's broad holding unduly precluded consideration of whether the legislative veto may pass constitutional muster when used in other contexts.

3. *See* Peter L. Strauss, *Was There a Baby in the Bathwater? A Comment on the Supreme Court's Legislative Veto Decision*, 1983 Duke L.J. 789, 795.
4. *See id.* at 797–98.
5. *See* E. Donald Elliott, INS v. Chadha*: The Administrative Constitution, the Constitution, and the Legislative Veto*, 1983 Sup. Ct. Rev. 125, 134–35.
6. *See* Strauss, *supra* note 3.

Chadha has perhaps been most criticized for undermining Congress's willingness to delegate authority to administrative agencies. Congress increasingly delegated to agencies as the federal government grew in both size and complexity during the New Deal. Not coincidentally, Congress began to use the legislative veto at the time to oversee this newly delegated authority.[7] The legislative veto may have encouraged Congress to delegate more to the executive branch by enabling greater congressional oversight. Interestingly, in some cases executive branch officials actually encouraged Congress to include legislative vetoes as a "price" to get more delegated authority.[8] In this way, the legislative veto was beneficial to both Congress and the executive.

The majority's formalistic approach to the separation of powers upset these important dynamics.[9] Elliott has argued that the majority's concern in *Chadha* with the separation of powers was ironic given that the decision undermined an important check on congressional delegation to agencies.[10] Justice White's dissent also emphasized this point, arguing that Congress needs the single-house veto to monitor the vast discretion it must delegate to the executive in the modern era. One counterargument is that a single-house legislative veto may empower a relatively narrow faction within Congress to overturn an agency action. In this view, single-house legislative vetoes usually pertain to narrow issues that matter a great deal to special interest groups but not to the general public. Special interest groups are better equipped to lobby Congress on such issues. Congressional vetoes are often done with little transparency or public input, further advantaging special interests. The veto therefore favors well-organized special interests at the expense of the public. Removing the legislative veto and forcing the House, Senate, and president to jointly enact legislation requires broader support, thereby increasing democratic accountability.[11]

---

7. *See* JEFFREY S. LUBBERS, A GUIDE TO FEDERAL AGENCY RULEMAKING 15–16 (6th ed. 2018).

8. *See* Louis Fisher, *The Legislative Veto: Invalidated, It Survives*, 56 LAW & CONTEMP. PROBS. 273, 276 (1993).

9. *See* Cass R. Sunstein, *Constitutionalism After the New Deal*, 101 HARV. L. REV. 421, 494 (1987).

10. Elliott, *supra* note 5, at 147.

11. *See* Jonathan R. Macey, *Separate Powers and Positive Political Theory: The Tug of War over Administrative Agencies*, 80 GEO. L.J. 671, 694–95 (1992).

Implications of *Chadha*

Chadha reduced Congress's ability to oversee the legislative branch. Prior to *Chadha*, almost 200 statutes included a one-house veto, a partial list of which was presented in an appendix to the opinion. The *Chadha* holding therefore reduced congressional control over executive implementation of these statutes. (In some cases, the legislative vetoes remained in the laws but were never again exercised.[12]) In practice, Congress had exercised 230 legislative vetoes from 1930 to 1982. Almost half of these vetoes pertained to suspensions of alien deportation (as was the case for Chadha), and only a small portion pertained to regulatory issues.[13] Of course, the presence of veto provisions could have motivated agencies to conform to congressional preferences in many cases, making it influential even when not used.

Congress has used several alternative oversight mechanisms in place of the legislative veto.[14] Some statutes provide a process for both houses to enact a resolution disapproving of an agency decision that then goes to the president, thereby satisfying the requirements for bicameralism and presentment. For instance, the Congressional Review Act (CRA)[15] delays the effectiveness of important agency rules for 60 days while Congress considers whether to disapprove. While the act's requirements largely resemble ordinary legislation, they have at least two important advantages. First, resolutions of disapproval receive expedited consideration in the Senate, preventing a filibuster. Second, the CRA's delay of rule effective dates allows Congress to disapprove of rules before efforts at compliance have been undertaken and other reliance interests have arisen.

Legislation can also require affirmative approval of both houses of Congress for an agency action to take effect. Functionally, this structure effectively provides a one-house veto through congressional inaction.[16] Critics argue that this approach effectively cripples agencies because Congress has difficulty reaching agreement and acting. To mitigate this problem,

---

12. *See* Fisher, *supra* note 8, at 287.
13. *See* Strauss, *supra* note 3, at 790–91.
14. *See* Stephen Breyer, *The Legislative Veto After* Chadha, 72 Geo. L.J. 785, 792 (1984).
15. 5 U.S.C. §§ 801–808.
16. *See* Louis Fisher, *Judicial Misjudgments About the Lawmaking Process: The Legislative Veto Case*, 45 Pub. Admin. Rev. 705, 709 (1985).

congressional review and approval may receive fast-track legislative consideration. Shortly after *Chadha*, Congress used this procedure to evaluate proposals to reorganize the executive agencies. The Reagan administration did not ask Congress to renew the procedure after it expired because it was too burdensome.[17] The REINS Act, an unenacted bill that has been passed in the House,[18] is a more recent example of a prominent proposal along these lines. The aforementioned point regarding the influence of narrow factions on agency decision-making is relevant for this proposal as well, as it may be easier for a committed faction to block congressional approval of an agency action.

Other continued oversight mechanisms are vested in a single committee. For instance, agencies may be required to obtain approval of the House and Senate Appropriations Committees for certain actions that are typically related to expenditures of funds. Congress added more than 200 such vetoes in the ten years after *Chadha*. Although some of these provisions prompted presidents to include signing statements expressing disapproval, agencies often abided by them to preserve relationships with Congress.[19] Congressional committees may also exercise a "soft veto" of an agency action by reaching an informal agreement that an agency will consult with the committee before taking a particular action.[20] While these arrangements are not legally binding on agencies, they may be quite durable because agencies have a long-term relationship with their congressional committees and do not want to risk their ire. Many such soft vetoes arise when agencies use appropriated funds differently than originally specified.[21]

Chadha presaged subsequent decisions strictly construing the Article I, section 7 process for enacting legislation. In 1991, the Supreme Court invalidated a statute that allowed members of Congress to sit on a board that oversaw and could veto decisions of an airport authority.[22] The Court

17. Fisher, *supra* note 8, at 286.
18. *See* Jonathan R. Siegel, *The REINS Act and the Struggle to Control Agency Rulemaking*, 16 N.Y.U. J. Legis. & Pub. Pol'y 131 (2013).
19. *See* Fisher, *supra* note 8, at 288.
20. Fisher, *supra* note 16, at 708.
21. Fisher, *supra* note 8, at 290.
22. *See* Metro. Wash. Airports Auth. v. Citizens for the Abatement of Aircraft Noise, 501 U.S. 252 (1991).

reasoned in part that Congress could not exercise legislative authority and take legally effective action outside the Article I, section 7 process. In 1998, the Court invalidated the line-item veto as violating the Presentment Clause.[23] The majority reasoned that the Constitution's silence on the permissibility of the line-item veto constituted an express prohibition on it. While these decisions did not directly follow from *Chadha*, they were consistent with its broader legacy.

Bibliography

Stephen Breyer, *The Legislative Veto After* Chadha, 72 Geo. L.J. 785 (1984).

E. Donald Elliott, INS v. Chadha*: The Administrative Constitution, the Constitution, and the Legislative Veto*, 1983 Sup. Ct. Rev. 125.

Louis Fisher, *Judicial Misjudgments About the Lawmaking Process: The Legislative Veto Case*, 45 Pub. Admin. Rev. 705 (1985).

Louis Fisher, *The Legislative Veto: Invalidated, It Survives*, 56 Law & Contemp. Probs. 273 (1993).

Elliott H. Levitas & Stanley M. Brand, *Congressional Review of Executive and Agency Actions After* Chadha*: "The Son of Legislative Veto" Lives On*, 72 Geo. L.J. 801 (1984).

Jonathan R. Macey, *Separate Powers and Positive Political Theory: The Tug of War over Administrative Agencies*, 80 Geo. L.J. 671 (1992).

Peter L. Strauss, *Was There a Baby in the Bathwater? A Comment on the Supreme Court's Legislative Veto Decision*, 1983 Duke L.J. 789.

Cass R. Sunstein, *Constitutionalism After the New Deal*, 101 Harv. L. Rev. 421 (1987).

Laurence H. Tribe, *The Legislative Veto Decision: A Law by Any Other Name*, 21 Harv. J. on Legis. 1 (1984).

23. *See* Clinton v. City of New York, 524 U.S. 417 (1998).

Chapter 31

Morrison v. Olson, 487 U.S. 654 (1988)

Peter M. Shane

Morrison v. Olson upheld the independent counsel provisions of the Ethics in Government Act (EGA),[1] enacted in the wake of the Watergate affair. A 7–1 opinion by Chief Justice Rehnquist sustained Congress's authority to permit the judicial appointment of independent counsel and to limit the grounds on which an independent counsel could be dismissed. The opinion has become central to an ongoing debate about the constitutionality of independent agencies and, in general, the permissibility of limiting by statute the president's control of discretionary decision-making by executive branch officials. The U.S. Supreme Court's earlier opinion in *Humphrey's Executor v. United States*[2] had already established the constitutionality of insulating at least certain officers of the United States from at-will removal by the president. *Morrison* broke new ground in discarding the precise rationale of *Humphrey's Executor* and in extending its holding to officers who lack either adjudicative or rulemaking powers.

The case originated when the House Judiciary Committee alleged to the Department of Justice that Theodore B. Olson, then the assistant attorney general for the Office of Legal Counsel, had given false and misleading testimony during the Committee's investigation of an executive privilege dispute. The privilege fight had erupted after the Reagan administration

1. 28 U.S.C. §§ 591–599. These provisions lapsed when Congress declined to reauthorize the EGA in 1999.
2. 295 U.S. 602 (1935). The case is the subject of Chapter 28.

initially refused to turn over certain documents subpoenaed by two House committees during their inquiry into possible corruption at the Environmental Protection Agency. While the independent counsel was proceeding with her investigation, Olson challenged the authority of her office on multiple separation-of-powers grounds. Although Olson lost on the constitutional issues he raised, the independent counsel, Alexia Morrison, ultimately determined not to pursue the prosecution, concluding that Olson's testimony had been "literally true."[3]

The Structure of the EGA

The independent counsel provisions of the EGA were designed to deal with the conflicts of interest that arise when the Department of Justice is responsible for investigating possible criminal activity by the president or by certain high-level political officials in the executive branch or in a president's election or reelection campaign. While the act was in force, the attorney general was given 90 days to investigate whenever they received specific information that the president or a covered official had committed a serious federal offense. At the end of 90 days, unless the attorney general affirmatively determined that no further investigation was warranted, it would be mandatory to apply to a special division of the U.S. Court of Appeals for the D.C. Circuit for the appointment of an independent counsel. Although the counsel was subject to limited supervision by the court and was required by statute to follow generally applicable prosecutorial policies of the Justice Department, they could be fired under only very limited circumstances. Specifically, the counsel could be removed "only by the personal action of the Attorney General and only for good cause, physical or mental disability [if not prohibited by law protecting persons from discrimination on the basis of such a disability], or any other condition that substantially impairs the performance of such independent counsel's duties."[4]

3. Ronald J. Ostrow, *Independent Counsel Explains Why She Didn't Prosecute Figure in '83 EPA Probe*, L.A. Times (Mar. 21, 1989), http://articles.latimes.com/1989-03-21/news/mn-147_1_independent-counsel.
4. 28 U.S.C. § 596(a)(1) (1988).

The Appointments Issues: Defining "Inferior Officer" Status and the Scope of Interbranch Appointments

Olson had argued that Morrison's appointment was unconstitutional under the Appointments Clause of Article II.[5] He asserted that she was not constitutionally an "inferior officer" who could be appointed in any manner other than by the president with the advice and consent of the Senate. Alternatively, he argued that it was inconsistent with the separation of powers to give the judicial branch authority over the appointment and supervision of a criminal prosecutor.

The Court rejected both arguments. Declining to adopt any "exact line" distinguishing "inferior" from principal officers, the Court held that the independent counsel was an "inferior officer" because she was subject to removal by the attorney general, because she was not a policymaking official, and because of her limited jurisdiction and tenure. As for the interbranch character of the appointment, the Court noted that the Constitution imposed no textual limit on the discretion of Congress to vest the appointment of inferior officers in the courts. The Court acknowledged that some such appointments might be "incongruous" under the separation of powers but determined that the appointment of criminal prosecutors posed no such problem.

The Court likewise found that the D.C. Circuit's other statutory powers with regard to the independent counsel did not violate the separation of powers. It deemed the lower court's authorities more ministerial than supervisory and thus not posing "a sufficient threat of judicial intrusion into matters that are more properly within the Executive's authority" to warrant invalidation. Conversely, the Court concluded that the act sufficiently isolated the D.C. Circuit's judges from actively reviewing the independent counsel's work "so as to avoid any taint of the independence of the Judiciary such as would render the Act invalid under Article III."

5. U.S. Const. art. II, § 2, cl. 2.

Removability and the Reinterpretation of *Humphrey's Executor*

In addition to his arguments against the method of appointing the independent counsel, Olson also urged that the executive character of criminal prosecution required that prosecutors be fully subject to discretionary dismissal by the president. Although the Supreme Court half a century earlier had approved Congress's authority to limit the permissible grounds for dismissing a member of the Federal Trade Commission (FTC), the 1935 Court had supported its holding with the puzzling assertion that an FTC member "occupies no place in the executive department and . . . exercises no part of the executive power vested by the Constitution in the President."[6] The Court cabined that language in *Myers v. United States*,[7] suggesting that the Constitution assured that the presidential power to remove any officer of the United States at will would be applicable only to "purely executive officers."[8] Olson argued that a criminal prosecutor was just such a "purely executive officer."

The *Morrison* Court jettisoned the reasoning of *Humphrey's Executor* but not its holding. The majority stated its "considered view . . . that the determination of whether the Constitution allows Congress to impose a 'good cause'-type restriction on the President's power to remove an official cannot be made to turn on whether or not that official is classified as 'purely executive.'" It offered instead a new test for the permissibility of such restrictions, namely, whether they "are of such a nature that they impede the President's ability to perform his constitutional duty."

Olson had argued, of course, that the restrictions on independent counsel removability did "impede the President's ability to perform his constitutional duty" in two respects. The asserted duties were his responsibility to "take Care that the Laws be faithfully executed"[9] and the responsibility, supposedly rooted in the executive power Vesting Clause of Article II,[10] for criminal prosecutions. The Court held that the act respected the president's

6. *Humphrey's Executor*, 295 U.S. at 628. The case is the subject of Chapter 28.
7. 272 U.S. 52 (1926). The case is the subject of Chapter 27.
8. *Humphrey's Executor*, 295 U.S. at 628.
9. U.S. Const. art. II, § 3.
10. *Id.* § 1.

faithful-execution duty because the attorney general was authorized to discharge an independent counsel for good cause. Presumably because of the attorney general's own accountability to the president, this discharge authority would preserve the president's capacity to fulfill his Article II mandate.

The Court was less clear about the president's constitutional role vis-à-vis criminal prosecution. The opinion implicitly distinguished between functions that "are 'executive' in the sense that they are . . . functions that typically have been undertaken by officials within the Executive Branch" and functions that constitutionally must be committed to the president's plenary control. The Court again took note of the factors supporting its determination that Morrison was an "inferior officer" and added, without further elaboration, that "we simply do not see how the President's need to control the exercise of that discretion is so central to the functioning of the Executive Branch as to require as a matter of constitutional law that the counsel be terminable at will by the President."

The Court's reference to the independent counsel's inferior officer status might be taken to imply a distinction between the president's entitlement to fire at-will principal versus inferior officers. *Humphrey's Executor*, however, upheld the limited removability of FTC commissioners, who are principal officers, and *Morrison* reaffirmed the holding of *Humphrey's Executor*. The *Morrison* Court therefore necessarily rejected a removability test based categorically on principal or inferior officer status.

The Court's reference to whether the independent counsel's discretion was "central to the functioning of the Executive Branch" might suggest that the Court envisioned a kind of balancing test for the permissibility of good-cause removability. Measuring "centrality," however, would seem an awkward judicial task. It is perhaps more helpful to read the *Morrison* test as turning on the extent to which an officer is performing functions that the executive branch implements exclusively under statutory authority and not with regard to any power vested in the president by Article II. Good-cause removability of such an officer would not impede the president in discharging his Article II functions precisely because the president would have no such functions in connection with that officer other than helping to ensure faithful execution. For such a statutory officer, the scope of presidential removal authority would be a matter for Congress to decide. Congress need only provide an adequate means for the president to remove, directly or indirectly, an officer who is not faithful to whatever law that the officer is involved in executing.

The Scalia Dissent

Morrison drew a much-noted solo dissent from Justice Scalia—Justice Kennedy did not participate in the case—that castigated the majority for failing in the categorical protection of executive power as Justice Scalia saw it. Once criminal prosecution is recognized as an exercise of executive power, Justice Scalia argued, the president is constitutionally guaranteed exclusive control of that power. On that basis, he would have upheld Olson's argument against the limits on independent counsel removal. Justice Scalia also argued that the Court was wrong to take a balancing approach in distinguishing principal from inferior officers. In his view, an officer could be deemed inferior only if truly subordinate to a superior officer. Because not even the attorney general had complete control over the independent counsel's exercise of her discretionary powers, she was not, in Scalia's judgment, actually subordinate to anyone.

Arguably the most rhetorically powerful portion of the Scalia dissent, however, was his insistence that, even under a balancing approach, the Court was significantly understating the independent counsel's power and potential impact on the functioning of the executive branch. Justice Scalia wrote: "Only someone who has worked in the field of law enforcement can fully appreciate the vast power and the immense discretion that are placed in the hands of a prosecutor with respect to the objects of his investigation." In his view, vesting such power and discretion in an officer not accountable to the president ran the risk of seriously weakening presidents who might find themselves pursued with a zeal both fueled by partisanship and undisciplined by an independent counsel's accountability for any task other than investigating their designated target.

Implications for Independent Agencies Generally

There seems little doubt that, in analyzing the issues before it, the *Morrison* Court understood that the stakes of its ruling went beyond even the critical issue of whether Congress could create independent prosecutors. The articulation of a new rationale for *Humphrey's Executor* coupled with an unquestioning acceptance of its holding suggests that the Court intended its new test on the permissibility of removal restrictions to apply to independent agencies across the board. In other words, whether restrictions on an officer's removability would "impede the President's ability to perform his constitutional duty" is a test that could and should be applied not only to independent counsel, but also to FTC commissioners, National Labor Relations Board members, the administrator of the Environmental Protection Agency, and presumably any other principal or inferior officer in the executive branch.

What makes the reach of the doctrine apparent is the Court's eschewal of any of the readily available narrower rationales that it could have deployed to sustain the EGA. For example, the Court might have accepted *arguendo* the position that criminal prosecution is an inherently executive function but treated the EGA as the kind of carefully tailored surgical intrusion into presidential discretion that would be justified by Congress's compelling interest in preserving public confidence in criminal investigations involving high political officials. After all, not only was the act limited in scope by the range of persons and offenses covered, but key attorney general decisions under the act—namely, whether information was sufficiently specific to trigger a preliminary investigation and whether grounds existed to seek independent counsel—were not made judicially reviewable.[11]

Alternatively, the Court could have followed the lead of then-Judge Bader Ginsburg, who, in her dissent in the panel decision, relied in part on the history of criminal prosecution to determine it was not a power "at the 'core' of the executive branch's constitutionally-assigned functions, in the sense that the job must be kept, in any and all cases, under the President's wing

11. *Cf.* Nixon v. Adm'r of Gen. Servs., 433 U.S. 425, 443 (1977) ("In determining whether [the Presidential Recordings and Materials Preservation Act] disrupts the proper balance between the coordinate branches, the proper inquiry focuses on the extent to which it prevents the Executive Branch from accomplishing its constitutionally assigned functions. Only where the potential for disruption is present must we then determine whether that impact is justified by an overriding need to promote objectives within the constitutional authority of Congress.") (citation omitted).

and cover."[12] However, had the Court followed this line of reasoning or the sort of balancing test employed in *Nixon v. Administrator of General Services*[13] to uphold the Presidential Recordings and Materials Preservation Act, *Morrison* would have gone no further than ratifying the permissibility of independent criminal prosecutors or at least an independent criminal prosecutor in carefully limited circumstances. The Court's apparent decision not to follow either mode of analysis strongly suggests an intent to send a broader message.[14]

Has a More Pro-Executive Court Limited *Morrison*?

An intriguing feature of *Morrison* was the involvement in the case of three lawyers accustomed to the vigorous defense of executive authority during their respective stints as assistant attorneys general in charge of the Office of Legal Counsel: the respondent, Olson; the dissenter, Justice Scalia; and the author of the majority opinion, Chief Justice Rehnquist. Since 1988, however, four Justices in the *Morrison* majority, including Chief Justice Rehnquist, have been succeeded by jurists more receptive to Justice Scalia's view of executive power. As a result, one can see in subsequent cases some retreat from *Morrison*, or at least a potential curbing of its fullest implications.

"Inferior Officer" Status. The clearest example is *Edmond v. United States*,[15] which allowed the secretary of transportation to appoint civilian members of the Coast Guard Court of Appeals. The case gave Justice Scalia, writing for a new majority, an opportunity to apply his preferred test for whether an officer is "inferior," writing, "[I]n the context of a clause designed to preserve political accountability . . . we think it evident that 'inferior officers' are officers whose work is directed and supervised at some level by others who were appointed by Presidential nomination with the

12. *In re* Sealed Case, 838 F.2d 476, 526 (D.C. Cir. 1988) (Ginsburg, J., dissenting), *rev'd sub nom.* Morrison v. Olson, 487 U.S. 654 (1988).
13. 433 U.S. 425 (1977).
14. *Cf.* Adrian Vermeule, *Conventions of Agency Independence*, 113 COLUM. L. REV. 1163, 1172 (2013) (observing that "*Morrison* gives Congress broad, albeit ill-defined, authority to make agencies independent of the President").
15. 520 U.S. 651 (1997).

advice and consent of the Senate."[16] The case did not formally overrule the balancing approach of *Morrison*, which arguably would have produced the same result. Nonetheless, Justice Scalia's seemingly bright-line rule is now carried forth in a precedential case more recent than *Morrison*.

A Return to Removal Power Formalism. A case yet more consequentially in tension with Morrison is *Seila Law LLC v. CFPB*.[17] The Court's 5–4 decision held that the statutory for-cause restriction on the removability of the director of the single-headed Consumer Financial Protection Bureau was an unconstitutional infringement on the president's plenary Article II removal power. *Morrison* had read *Humphrey's Executor* as upholding the general scope of Congress's power to create independent administrators and deemed *Myers* but a discrete exception for "purely executive" officers. *Seila Law* flipped the script. The *Seila Law* majority treated *Myers* as establishing a categorical presidential power to remove subordinate officers, which the Roberts Court saw as confirming both what the text of Article II requires and what the First Congress settled.[18] Seen against this baseline, the *Seila Law* majority recast *Morrison* as one of just "two exceptions to the President's unrestricted removal power."[19] One exception, exemplified by *Humphrey's Executor*, comprises "expert agencies led by a group of principal officers removable by the President only for good cause."[20] The other allows Congress to protect "certain inferior officers with narrowly defined duties," such as the independent counsel upheld in *Morrison*.[21] Read narrowly, *Seila Law* might be deemed to cover only single-headed independent agencies that wield "significant executive power."[22] The Court's decision a year later in *Collins v. Yellen*,[23] however, applied *Seila Law* to cover the head of the Federal Housing Finance Agency. The majority opinion applied no test of "significance" with regard to the executive power at issue: "Courts are not well-suited to weigh the relative importance of the regulatory and enforcement authority of disparate agencies, and we do not think that the

16. *Id.* at 663.
17. 591 U.S. 197 (2020). The case is the subject of Chapter 34.
18. *Id.* at 204.
19. *Id.*
20. *Id.*
21. *Id.*
22. *Id.*
23. 594 U.S. 220 (2021).

constitutionality of removal restrictions hinges on such an inquiry."[24] And although the Court was explicit that it was not at the moment reconsidering *Morrison* or *Humphrey's Executor*, neither of these "exceptions" is easily reconciled in principle with the Court's reasoning in *Seila Law*.

Unitary Executive Theory and the Future of *Morrison*

Morrison and *Humphrey's Executor* stand as the Supreme Court precedents most directly in conflict with so-called "unitary executive theory," an interpretation of Article II that vests in the president plenary control over the discretionary decision-making of all executive branch officers, including discretion conferred entirely by statute. There is little doubt that the Roberts Court embraces that view more than did its recent predecessors or that the ascent to the federal bench of yet more judges sympathetic to Justice Scalia's interpretive methods will intensify interest in curbing or even overruling those cases.

Yet the historical premise of Justice Scalia's dissent remains contested, and, perhaps just as importantly, the Court cannot help but confront the existence of independent establishments exercising administrative power at least since the 1887 founding of the Interstate Commerce Commission and arguably since the 1791 chartering of the First Bank of the United States. For more than two centuries, the Supreme Court has repeatedly adverted to Chief Justice Marshall's caution:

> [A] doubtful question, one on which human reason may pause, and the human judgment be suspended, in the decision of which the great principles of liberty are not concerned, but the respective powers of those who are equally the representatives of the people, are to be adjusted; if not put at rest by the practice of the government, ought to receive a considerable impression from that practice.[25]

To a significant degree, our institutional history, as well as *stare decisis*, may carry weight in protecting both precedents.

24. *Id.* at 253.
25. McCulloch v. Maryland, 17 U.S. 316, 401 (1819).

Bibliography

Jack M. Beermann, *An Inductive Understanding of Separation of Powers*, 63 Admin. L. Rev. 467 (2011).

Patricia L. Bellia, PCAOB *and the Persistence of the Removal Puzzle*, 80 Geo. Wash. L. Rev. 1371 (2012).

Aziz Z. Huq, *Removal as a Political Question*, 65 Stan. L. Rev. 1 (2013).

Lawrence Lessig & Cass R. Sunstein, *The President and the Administration*, 94 Colum. L. Rev. 1 (1994).

Saikrishna Prakash, *The Chief Prosecutor*, 73 Geo. Wash. L. Rev. 521 (2005).

Benjamin J. Priester et al., *The Independent Counsel Statute: A Legal History*, 62 Law & Contemp. Probs. 5 (1999).

Peter M. Shane, *The Originalist Myth of the Unitary Executive*, 19 U. Pa. J. Const. L. 323 (2016).

Peter M. Shane, *Prosecutors at the Periphery*, 94 Chi.-Kent L. Rev. 241 (2019).

Peter L. Strauss, *On the Difficulties of Generalization*—PCAOB *in the Footsteps of* Myers, Humphrey's Executor, Morrison, *and* Freytag, 32 Cardozo L. Rev. 2255 (2011).

Chapter 32

Whitman v. American Trucking Associations, Inc., 531 U.S. 457 (2001)

Craig N. Oren

Federal administrative agencies derive their authority from laws passed by Congress. The delegation doctrine limits the amount of policymaking power that such laws may assign to an agency. U.S. Supreme Court decisions require that Congress articulate an "intelligible principle" for the agency to follow in exercising its delegated authority.[1] *Whitman v. American Trucking* is the most significant of the Court's modern engagements with the delegation doctrine (also referred to as the nondelegation doctrine).

The Delegation Doctrine Before *American Trucking*

Delegations by Congress go back to the First Congress, which gave the president the authority to estimate tariffs and to make rules governing the award of pensions to Revolutionary War veterans.[2] Delegations of power

1. *See, e.g.*, J.W. Hampton, Jr. & Co. v. United States, 276 U.S. 394, 409 (1928). As noted *infra* note 25, it is arguably a misnomer to say that Congress can "delegate." But the term "delegation" has become a familiar one in expressing the thought of Congress conferring power on an agency, and so the term is used here.
2. *See* 1 Kristin E. Hickman & Richard J. Pierce, Jr., Administrative Law Treatise § 1.4 (7th ed. 2024). Recent scholarship has explored the original understanding of congressional delegations. Little consensus has emerged. *Compare, e.g.*, Julian Davis Mortenson & Nicholas Bagley, *Delegation at the Founding*, 121 Colum. L. Rev. 277 (2021), *with, e.g.*, Ilan Wurman, *Nondelegation at the Founding*, 130 Yale L. Rev. 1490 (2021).

to regulate the private sector go back at least as far as steamboat regulation in the 1830s.[3] The federal courts have been very accepting of delegations. Only twice—in the 1935 decisions of *Panama Refining Co. v. Ryan*[4] and *A.L.A. Schechter Poultry Corp. v. United States*[5]—has the Supreme Court invalidated delegations as excessive. Both cases concerned delegations under the National Industrial Recovery Act, a 1933 statute intended to help the United States recover from the Great Depression.

These cases, particularly *Schechter*, can be explained on several grounds. First, the agency involved, the National Recovery Administration, came close to being both omnicompetent (with jurisdiction over the entire American economy) and omnipotent (possessed of all possible ways of acting).[6] Moreover, in *Schechter*, responsibility for exercising the agency's power fell almost entirely to an association of private industry with little governmental oversight.[7] The power involved—to make codes of competition—was questionable under the Supreme Court's then-prevailing interpretation of the Commerce Clause; indeed, the Court's alternate ground of decision was that Congress had gone beyond its Commerce Clause authority.[8] In addition, the statute did not require any explanation from the agency of its decisions.[9] Finally, today's *Federal Register* and *Code of Federal Regulations* did not exist, so there was little opportunity for the public to know of an administrative action. Indeed, it turned out that the code involved had been inadvertently repealed without anyone noticing.[10]

The Supreme Court has never again used the delegation doctrine to overturn a statute, although Congress has engaged in some very broad

3. *See* Jerry L. Mashaw, Creating the Administrative Constitution 192 (2012); *see also* Harold J. Krent, *Delegation and Its Discontents*, 94 Colum. L. Rev 710, 738–39 (1994).
4. 293 U.S. 388 (1935).
5. 295 U.S. 495 (1935).
6. *See* Todd D. Rakoff, *The Shape of Law in the American Administrative State*, 11 Tel Aviv U. Stud. L. 9, 22 (1992).
7. *Cf.* Carter v. Carter Coal Co., 298 U.S. 238 (1936) (striking down a delegation that authorized coal producers and their employees to establish maximum hours and minimum wages for the entire industry).
8. *Schechter*, 295 U.S. at 542–51.
9. *Cf.* Yakus v. United States, 321 U.S. 414, 426 (1944) (upholding a World War II price-control statute partly on the ground that the agency was required to release a "statement of considerations" explaining its decision).
10. *See* Louis L. Jaffe, Judicial Review of Administrative Action 61–62 (1965).

delegations. Consider, for instance, the Supreme Court's approval of a delegation by Congress to the Wage and Price Administration of the authority to set prices during the Second World War on the basis of what the agency considered "generally fair and equitable" and in accord with the purposes of the statute.[11]

The doctrine was, however, invoked in the so-called *Benzene* case in 1980.[12] There the Court divided in its rationale for overturning a standard by the Occupational Safety and Health Administration (OSHA) that limited concentrations of benzene in workplace air. Only one Justice, then-Justice Rehnquist, thought that the statute, which authorized OSHA to regulate benzene to the extent feasible, lacked an intelligible principle and therefore was unconstitutional. But the plurality of the Court, speaking through Justice Stevens, instead considered the statute constitutional but decided that OSHA's action had gone beyond its statutory authority. Justice Stevens used the delegation doctrine not as a constitutional doctrine, but rather as a rule of statutory construction that should lead a court to adopt a narrow interpretation of a statute when a broader one might raise a constitutional question about whether the delegation has been excessive.[13] While the delegation doctrine has not since been used to invalidate a federal statute, the Court has at times used something like Justice Stevens's approach to construe a doubtful statute narrowly.[14] In this way, the delegation doctrine has been significant even though only twice used to strike down a statutory provision.

Still, the *Benzene* case suggested that the Court might make the delegation doctrine more exacting. In *American Trucking*, the Court made clear that it did not wish to do so.

---

11. *Yakus*, 321 U.S. at 420.

12. Indus. Union Dep't, AFL-CIO v. Am. Petroleum Inst., 448 U.S. 607 (1980). *See generally* Cass R. Sunstein, *It All Started with Benzene*, 76 ADMIN. L. REV. 673 (2024).

13. *See generally* John F. Manning, *The Nondelegation Doctrine as a Canon of Avoidance*, 2000 SUP. CT. REV. 223, 240; Cass R. Sunstein, *Nondelegation Canons*, 67 U. CHI. L. REV. 315 (2000).

14. *See* Nat'l Cable Television Ass'n, Inc. v. United States, 415 U.S. 336 (1974); Kent v. Dulles, 357 U.S. 116 (1958).

Congress's Delegation in *American Trucking*

American Trucking involved the authority of the Environmental Protection Agency (EPA) to establish ambient air quality standards under the Clean Air Act (CAA). These standards specify the maximum permissible concentrations of air pollutants in the outdoor air to which the general public has access (e.g., that the concentration of ozone in that air should not exceed 70 parts per million). The stringency of the air quality standards determines the rigor of control requirements for stationary sources (e.g., factories and electricity-generating plants) and mobile sources (motor vehicles such as automobiles) of air pollution. In this way, the ambient air quality standards are the cornerstones of the CAA; much of the rest of the act is devoted to establishing mechanisms to ensure that these standards are attained and maintained.[15]

In the 1990s, under the Clinton administration, EPA began to consider tightening the standards for ozone (smog) and fine particles (soot).[16] Setting these standards was, and remains, difficult. So far as science can determine, there are no completely safe concentrations of these pollutants. As a result, standard setting requires EPA to decide what effects constitute health effects against which the standards should protect and at what point the evidence of health effects becomes sufficiently uncertain that regulation is not appropriate. EPA's standard-setting decisions therefore involve reaching not only scientific conclusions but also policy judgments about how uncertainties in science should be handled and how safe is safe enough.

The levels of the ambient air quality standards for these two pollutants affect the many sources that emit volatile organic compounds, nitrogen oxides, fine particles, and sulfur oxides. Not surprisingly, there was a great deal of controversy when EPA proposed to make the standards stricter. One congressman called what happened "the mother of environmental fights."[17] Industry argued that there was too much uncertainty about the health effects of low levels of ozone and fine particles to justify tighter

---

15. *See* Richard E. Ayres et al., *Setting National Ambient Air Quality Standards*, *in* The Clean Air Act Handbook 15 (Julie R. Domike & Alec C. Zacaroli eds., 4th ed. 2016).
16. *See* Craig N. Oren, Whitman v. American Trucking Ass'ns—*The Ghost of Delegation Revived . . . and Exorcised*, *in* Administrative Law Stories 7, 12–16 (Peter L. Strauss ed., 2006).
17. *Id.* at 20.

standards. In addition, industry urged that the economic effects of stricter standards would be devastating. Environmentalists defended the proposed standards as necessary to protect public health. Both sides sought to sway public opinion, EPA, and Congress. The controversy was so great that the issue of whether to tighten the standards was finally decided by the White House; EPA's view prevailed, with opponents of the new standards then trying and failing to get Congress to overturn them.[18]

American Trucking Before the D.C. Circuit

Suits challenging the tightened standards were then brought before the U.S. Court of Appeals for the D.C. Circuit by industry and some states. Oral argument centered on whether EPA had violated statutory requirements in setting the standards; on whether EPA had an obligation to consider cost in setting the standards; and on whether EPA had explained its choice of standard reasonably or had been arbitrary and capricious. The delegation doctrine was barely briefed and came up at oral argument only because the panel seemed interested in it.[19]

Nevertheless, a divided panel of the D.C. Circuit relied on the delegation doctrine to vacate EPA's choice of standards.[20] According to the panel opinion written by Judge Williams, the CAA did not give EPA sufficient guidance in deciding what effects are health effects against which the standards should protect, or in deciding how much uncertainty would justify a decision not to protect against a given health effect. In the court's words, it was though the statute told EPA to regulate "big guys" without any guidance as to how tall or how heavy a "big guy" was. At the same time, the court agreed with EPA that the agency could not consider costs in setting the standards. The court's solution was to vacate and remand the standards for EPA to develop an intelligible principle for deciding the levels of the standards. Judge Tatel dissented, arguing that there was no substance for the court's delegation objection.

18. *See id.* at 18–26.
19. *See id.* at 29–30.
20. Am. Trucking Ass'ns v. EPA, 175 F.3d 1027 (D.C. Cir. 1999).

A closely divided D.C. Circuit declined to grant rehearing en banc.[21] Both the government and industry then petitioned the Supreme Court for certiorari, and both petitions were granted.

The Supreme Court's Decision

The government argued that the CAA did contain a satisfactory intelligible principle; industry contended that EPA had to use costs in determining how stringently to set the standards. In industry's view, these two arguments dovetailed; if EPA did not need to consider cost, then the statute would be unconstitutional as an excessive delegation. In other words, industry sought to use Justice Stevens's approach in *Benzene* rather than to try to defend the D.C. Circuit's rationale.

At oral argument, it became clear that the Court did not agree with the lower court's or industry's reasoning. Justice Scalia pointed out that the consideration of costs would give EPA more, not less, discretion in setting the standards.[22] The government had a much easier time.[23]

Less than four months after oral argument—a sign that the Court did not consider the case close—the Court vacated the D.C. Circuit's judgment and held that the CAA indeed contained a satisfactory intelligible principle. Justice Scalia, writing for the Court, first addressed whether the CAA directed EPA to use costs in setting the ambient air quality standards. Remarking that "Congress does not hide elephants in mouse holes," Justice Scalia looked for a definite statement in the CAA compelling EPA to consider costs in setting the air quality standards; finding none, he concluded that the agency was not so required.

The Court then had to decide whether the statute, as thus construed, violated the delegation doctrine. Justice Scalia's opinion for the Court held that it did not. He began by dismissing the D.C. Circuit's view that a delegation problem could be remedied by having the agency devise an intelligible principle. Rather, according to Justice Scalia, a statute that lacks an

21. Am. Trucking Ass'ns v. EPA, 195 F.3d 4 (D.C. Cir. 1999).
22. *See* Transcript of Oral Argument at *5, Whitman v. Am. Trucking Ass'ns, 531 U.S. 457 (2001), 2000 WL 1674207.
23. *See* Oren, *supra* note 16, at 38.

intelligible principle must be invalidated; Congress, not the agency, must supply the intelligible principle. This is consistent with one of the leading arguments to limit delegations: that they allow Congress to evade its responsibility to legislate and instead leave fundamental policy decisions to unelected administrators.[24]

Justice Scalia then turned to whether the delegation was unconstitutionally excessive. He saw the question as being whether Congress had given EPA the power to legislate as opposed to only the responsibility to execute the law; if the former, the statute was invalid. The answer depended, he wrote, on whether Congress had given EPA an intelligible principle.

In a concurring opinion, Justice Stevens, joined by Justice Souter, expressed doubt over Justice Scalia's statement of the issue. Justice Stevens argued that the Constitution does give Congress the power to delegate legislative authority to administrative agencies so long as Congress has provided an intelligible principle. Academics and students can debate which approach is right; it is necessary for our purposes to note only that under both views the question is the same: Did Congress provide an intelligible principle?[25]

Justice Scalia's opinion for the Court found that Congress had provided such a principle. He accepted the government's view that the CAA's requirement that the standards be set at the level "requisite" to protect public health meant that EPA's standards had to be sufficient, but no more than necessary, to do so. This standard, Justice Scalia wrote, was "well within the outer limits of our nondelegation precedents."[26]

---

24. *See* Indus. Union Dep't, AFL-CIO v. Am. Petroleum Inst., 448 U.S. 607, 671–76 (1980) (Rehnquist, J., concurring). For an argument that an approach like the D.C. Circuit's has merit, see Lisa Schultz Bressman, *Disciplining Delegation After* Whitman v. American Trucking Ass'ns, 87 Cornell L. Rev. 452 (2002).

25. Justice Kagan used Justice Scalia's formulation in her plurality opinion in *Gundy v. United States*, 588 U.S. 128, 135 (2019), and her opinion for the Court in *FCC v. Consumers' Research*, 606 U.S. 656 (2025). Under Justice Scalia's and Justice Kagan's view, it is a misnomer to say that Congress can "delegate" because Congress may not give an agency any of Congress's legislative power; hence it cannot "delegate" but may only confer on the agency authority to carry out the legislation Congress has enacted. But, as explained *supra* note 1, the term "delegate" is a familiar one and so it is used here.

26. Justice Scalia therefore did not adopt the earlier view of Professor Scalia that the "delegation doctrine is worth hewing from the ice." Antonin Scalia, *A Note on the Benzene Case*, Regulation, July/Aug. 1980, at 28. Justice Scalia had already departed from the latter view in *Mistretta v. United States*, 488 U.S. 361, 415–16 (1989) (Scalia, J., dissenting).

Only Justice Thomas uttered a discordant note, suggesting in his concurrence that the "intelligible principle" requirement is not always sufficient to prevent unconstitutional delegation. He has since reiterated this position, expressing doubt about whether the Constitution allows obligations to be imposed on citizens except by congressionally enacted laws.[27] This view is in accord with Professor Phillip Hamburger's suggestion that modern administrative law is "unlawful."[28] As we will see, Justice Thomas's view of the "intelligible principle" requirement has since attracted support from other Justices although not to the point where *American Trucking* is in danger.

The Supreme Court remanded the case to the D.C. Circuit to consider whether the standards were arbitrary and capricious; the D.C. Circuit panel—the same that had heard the case originally—ruled that they were not.[29] Thus, EPA continues to have considerable discretion in deciding issues in which both science and policy play an important part.[30]

Scholarly Commentary

The Court's approval of broad delegations displeases some commentators. Several have argued that allowing broad delegation permits Congress to avoid difficult policy choices that should be made by elected officials,[31] or that it encourages the passage of legislation that makes it possible for private actors to seek "rents" (that is, financial advantages created by governmental action).[32]

But others have contended that there are strong reasons not to invoke the delegation doctrine. Doing so involves drawing fine lines about when

27. *See* Dep't of Transp. v. Ass'ns of Am. R.R.s, 575 U.S. 43, 86–87 (2015) (Thomas, J., concurring).
28. Phillip Hamburger, Is Administrative Law Unlawful? (2014).
29. Am. Trucking Ass'ns v. EPA, 283 F.3d 355 (D.C. Cir. 2002).
30. In March 2025, the EPA announced that it was going to again reconsider the particulate matter standard. *See* Press Release, EPA, Trump EPA Announces Path Forward on National Air Quality Standards for Particulate Matter ($PM_{2.5}$) to Aid Manufacturing, Small Businesses (Mar. 12, 2025), https://www.epa.gov/newsreleases/trump-epa-announces-path-forward-national-air-quality-standards-particulate-matter.
31. *See* David Schoenbrod, Power Without Responsibility (1993); John Hart Ely, Democracy and Distrust: A Theory of Judicial Review 131–34, 177 (1980).
32. *See* Peter H. Aranson et al., *Theory of Legislative Delegation*, 68 Cornell L. Rev. 1 (1982).

Congress has gone too far, a task arguably beyond judicial capability.[33] Restricting Congress's ability to delegate would also bog down Congress in detail, making it difficult for Congress to deal with important and technical social problems. It has also been suggested that voters can hold agencies accountable by deciding who should be president because agencies are responsible to the president in greater or lesser degree.[34] Finally, Congress itself can limit delegation. Congress often legislates in detail even in controversial areas; examples include many environmental statutes (such as the CAA itself), health care legislation, and tax laws. Congress has an incentive to be detailed because its preferences often diverge from the president's, and Congress wants to be sure its own policy predilections are followed. This is especially true in an era in which Congress and the presidency have often been controlled by different political parties.

There are many restraints on agencies even when delegations are broad. The willingness of courts to accept broad delegations is partly due to the availability of judicial review.[35] Courts can enforce the procedural requirements of the Administrative Procedure Act and set aside agency action that exceeds the authority given to the agency by Congress[36] or that is arbitrary and capricious.[37] Congress and the presidency also act as checks, both formally and informally; in Congress's case, for example, through "oversight" hearings and the appropriations process, and in the president's by, for instance, review of proposed rulemakings by the Office of Management and Budget or even overt White House pressure.[38]

---

33. *See* Richard B. Stewart, *The Reformation of American Administrative Law*, 88 Harv. L. Rev. 1667, 1695–97 (1975).

34. *See* Jerry L. Mashaw, Greed, Chaos, and Governance 152–53 (1997).

35. *See* Ethyl Corp. v. EPA, 541 F.2d 1, 69 (D.C. Cir. 1976) (Leventhal, J., concurring statement).

36. *See* Chevron, U.S.A., Inc. v. Nat. Res. Def. Council, Inc., 467 U.S. 837 (1984); Section of Admin. L. & Regul. Prac., Am. Bar Ass'n, A Blackletter Statement of Federal Administrative Law 34–35 (2d ed. 2013).

37. *See* Motor Vehicle Mfrs. Ass'n v. State Farm Mut. Auto. Ins. Co., 463 U.S. 29 (1983). The case is the subject of Chapter 26.

38. *See, e.g.*, Sierra Club v. Costle, 657 F.2d 298, 407–08 (D.C. Cir. 1981). The case is the subject of Chapter 9. The Congressional Review Act, 5 U.S.C. § 801 *et seq.* (2020), has proven useful as a means for a new presidential administration and Congress to set aside rules made at the end of the previous administration.

Where Is the Court Headed?

The Court has since upheld broad delegations in *Gundy v. United States*[39] and *FCC v. Consumers' Research*.[40] The Court's division in the former case suggested that the Court might drastically revise its approach to delegations to administrative agencies. But the latter decision shows that *American Trucking* is alive and well.

Gundy concerned a statute that compels sex offenders to register with state governments. The statute requires the attorney general to "specify the applicability" of the statute's registration requirement to offenders convicted before the statute's effective date and to "prescribe rules" for their registration.[41]

Writing for a plurality, Justice Kagan, like Justice Scalia in *American Trucking*, began by construing the statute at issue. She interpreted the statute to require the attorney general to apply the registration requirements to all pre-act sex offenders as soon as feasible. As thus construed, the statute, in Justice Kagan's view, easily "passe[d] constitutional muster" under the intelligible principle standard. Justice Kagan stressed that the Court had "over and over upheld even very broad delegations" under the "not demanding" intelligible principle standard. If the delegation at issue was unconstitutional, she emphasized, "then most of government is unconstitutional—dependent as Congress is on the need to give discretion to executive officials to implement the programs."[42]

Dissenting, Justice Gorsuch, joined by Chief Justice Roberts and Justice Thomas, interpreted the statute to delegate untrammeled discretion to the attorney general to decide whether (and not just how) to regulate pre-act offenders. In itself, this represented only a disagreement between Justice Kagan and Justice Gorsuch about whether the statute contained an intelligible principle, since Justice Kagan agreed that the statute, if construed to give the attorney general unchecked discretion, would pose a delegation issue.

---

39. 588 U.S. 128 (2019).
40. 606 US. 656 (2025).
41. For a further defense by Justice Kagan of allowing broad delegations, see *West Virginia v. EPA*, 597 U.S. 697, 779–84 (2022) (Kagan, J., dissenting). The case is the subject of Chapter 20.
42. *Gundy*, 588 U.S. at 141 (plurality).

But Justice Gorsuch went on to challenge the intelligible principle standard, arguing that delegations should be tested under "traditional" separation-of-powers principles, and that the intelligible principle standard rested on an improper understanding of precedent and had "taken on a life of its own." According to Justice Gorsuch, Congress can delegate power only to allow the executive branch to (1) "fill up details" in a statutory scheme; (2) find the facts upon which application of a statutory provision depends; or (3) exercise powers that the Constitution assigns to the executive branch (e.g., foreign affairs). Justice Gorsuch did not specify which post-*Schechter* cases satisfied those standards, saying only that "some of the results the Court had reached under the banner of the abused 'intelligible principle' doctrine may be consistent with more traditional teachings."[43]

As noted earlier, some defenders of allowing broad delegation point to the difficulty of drawing the line between what would and what would not be permissible under a stricter approach to congressional delegations. Justice Gorsuch's approach can be criticized on these grounds.[44] It is far from clear what constitutes "filling up the details"; there is an element of policy choice in any agency decision. Policy can also be involved in finding facts. For instance, the finding that a substance presents an "imminent hazard" (an example cited by Justice Gorsuch, although he did not say whether a delegation to an agency to make such a finding would be permissible) involves, as did EPA's establishment of the ambient air quality standards, value judgments about how to handle scientific uncertainty and about what is an acceptable level of risk.[45] Justice Gorsuch's proposed standard is therefore too vague to give Congress guidance in crafting legislation.

The breakdown of the Justices in *Gundy* suggested that the Court might substitute Justice Gorsuch's approach for *American Trucking*. As we saw, Justice Gorsuch's approach was supported in *Gundy* by the Chief Justice and Justice Thomas. Justice Alito joined neither Justice Kagan's plurality opinion nor Justice Gorsuch's dissent in *Gundy* but instead concurred in

43. *Id.* at 149 (Gorsuch, J., joined by Roberts, C.J., and Thomas, J., dissenting).
44. *See* Ronald M. Levin, *Law & Leviathan: The Best Defense?*, YALE J. ON REGUL.: NOTICE & COMMENT (Apr. 12, 2021), https://www.yalejreg.com/nc/law-leviathan-redeeming-the-administrative-state-part-0.
45. *See* Touby v. United States, 500 U.S. 160 (1991).

the judgment upholding the delegation. He noted that the delegation passed muster under the Court's post-1935 (that is, post-*Schechter*) precedents but said he would support reconsidering existing doctrine if a majority would do so.[46] Thus there appeared to be four likely votes for Justice Gorsuch's overhaul of the doctrine if there were a fifth vote.

The question then became whether Justice Kavanaugh, who did not participate in *Gundy* because he joined the Court after oral argument, or Justice Barrett, who joined the Court after *Gundy*, would be a fifth vote for Justice Gorsuch's approach. *Consumers' Research* indicates that neither will be.

In *Consumers' Research*, the Court rejected a delegation doctrine challenge to Congress's mandate that the Federal Communications Commission (FCC) establish a universal service charge on telecommunications bills and use the proceeds to ensure adequate telecommunications services for those (e.g., low-income or rural consumers) whom the private market might not serve. Speaking for a six-Justice majority, Justice Kagan used the intelligible principle test articulated in *American Trucking* to uphold the delegation. She implicitly endorsed *American Trucking* by analogizing the statutory language commanding the FCC to set a fee "sufficient" to support universal service programs to the requirement in *American Trucking* that air quality standards be set at a level "requisite" to protect public health; both provisions, in her view, established both a floor and a ceiling for the agency's decision.

As in *Gundy*, Justice Gorsuch dissented. But he barely mentioned his attack in his *Gundy* dissent on the intelligible principle test. Rather, he urged that the test should apply with special rigor to what he regarded as a congressional authorization to an agency to impose a tax and argued the majority was incorrect in reading the statute to provide an intelligible principle. Even so, he was able to attract only Justices Thomas and Alito, thus showing that the Court is not prepared to significantly revise its delegation doctrine.

Justice Kavanaugh, though joining Justice Kagan's majority opinion, wrote separately. He argued that the Court's recently developed "major questions" doctrine and its repudiation in 2024 of the *Chevron*[47] doctrine in

46. *Gundy*, 588 U.S. at 148–49 (Alito, J., concurring).
47. Chevron, U.S.A., Inc. v. Nat. Res. Def. Council, Inc., 467 U.S. 837 (1984). The case is the subject of Chapter 16.

Loper Bright[48] do much of the work of the delegation doctrine by insisting that Congress state clearly its intention to give an agency broad authority. The "major questions" and *Loper Bright* doctrines have the advantage of limiting agencies while avoiding the confrontation inherent in declaring a statute unconstitutional as the delegation doctrine can do.

On the other hand, Justice Kavanaugh argued that the intelligible principle test is not adequate to control independent agencies—those whose heads are protected from presidential dismissal during their terms except for cause.[49] Such agencies, he contended, pose special concerns because they are not supervised by the president or any other democratically elected official and therefore are not clearly accountable to the public. Justice Kavanaugh therefore suggested that delegations to independent agencies be subject to special requirements assuming that the Court continues to allow them rather than overturn *Humphrey's Executor*,[50] the foundational case allowing such agencies.

In sum, *American Trucking* is a leading case allowing Congress to delegate policymaking authority to an agency so long as Congress furnishes an intelligible principle. The case signals that the intelligible principle test is not a strong restraint on delegations.

Bibliography

Larry Alexander & Saikrishna Prakash, *Reports of the Nondelegation Doctrine's Death Are Greatly Exaggerated*, 70 U. Chi. L. Rev. 1297 (2003).

Peter H. Aranson et al., *Theory of Legislative Delegation*, 68 Cornell L. Rev. 1 (1982).

Lisa Schultz Bressman, *Disciplining Delegation After* Whitman v. American Trucking Ass'ns, 87 Cornell L. Rev. 452 (2002).

48. Loper Bright Enters. v. Raimondo, 603 U.S. 369 (2024). The case is the subject of Chapter 21.

49. The FCC, while often spoken of as an independent agency, does not fit Justice Kavanaugh's definition because its commissioners can be dismissed without cause. *See* FCC v. Consumers' Rsch., 606 U.S. 656, 708–09 (2025) (Kavanaugh, J., concurring).

50. Humphrey's Executor v. United States, 295 U.S. 602 (1935). The case is the subject of Chapter 28.

Ronald A. Cass, *Delegation Reconsidered: A Delegation Doctrine for the Modern Administrative State*, 40 Harv. J. L. Pub. Pol'y 147 (2017).

Cary Coglianese, *Dimensions of Delegation: Constitutional Limits on the Administrative State*, 167 U. Pa. L. Rev. 1849 (2019).

Kenneth Culp Davis, *A New Approach to Delegation*, 36 U. Chi. L. Rev. 713 (1969).

William K. Kelley, *Justice Scalia, the Nondelegation Doctrine, and Constitutional Argument*, 92 Notre Dame L. Rev. 2107 (2017).

Gary Lawson, *Discretion as Delegation: The "Proper" Understanding of the Nondelegation Doctrine*, 73 Geo. Wash. L. Rev. 235 (2005).

Gary Lawson, *Non-Delegation and Original Meaning*, 88 Va. L. Rev. 327 (2002).

Jerry L. Mashaw, Creating the Administrative Constitution (2012).

Thomas W. Merrill, *Rethinking Article I, Section 1: From Nondelegation to Exclusive Delegation*, 104 Colum. L. Rev. 2097 (2004).

Craig N. Oren, Whitman v. American Trucking Ass'ns—*The Ghost of Delegation Revived . . . and Exorcised*, *in* Administrative Law Stories 7 (Peter L. Strauss ed., 2006).

Eric A. Posner & Adrian Vermeule, *Interring the Nondelegation Doctrine*, 69 U. Chi. L. Rev. 1721 (2002).

David Schoenbrod, *The Delegation Doctrine: Could the Court Give It Substance?*, 83 Mich. L. Rev. 1223 (1985).

David Schoenbrod, Power Without Responsibility: How Congress Abuses the People Through Delegation (1993).

Cass R. Sunstein, *The American Nondelegation Doctrine*, 86 Geo. Wash. L. Rev. 1181 (2018).

Keith E. Whittington & Jason Iuliano, *The Myth of the Nondelegation Doctrine*, 165 U. Pa. L. Rev. 379 (2017).

Chapter 33

Free Enterprise Fund v. Public Co. Accounting Oversight Board, 561 U.S. 477 (2010)

Peter Strauss

In the wake of the accounting scandal associated with the collapse and eventual bankruptcy of the Enron Corporation in 2001, Congress created the Public Company Accounting Oversight Board (PCAOB) as a subsidiary element of the Securities and Exchange Commission (SEC). Although built to a degree on the model of established private self-regulatory organizations overseen by the Commission, such as the New York Stock Exchange and the Financial Industry Regulatory Authority (FINRA), Congress gave the SEC more comprehensive control over the PCAOB; it could appoint its members, more intensively oversee its activities, and remove its members—but only "for cause." This degree of integration and this limitation on SEC control over members' tenure in office gave rise to separation-of-powers concerns that Chief Justice Roberts, in his opinion for five Justices, captured in the opinion's opening paragraphs:

> May the President be restricted in his ability to remove a principal officer, who is in turn restricted in his ability to remove an inferior officer, even though that inferior officer determines the policy and enforces the laws of the United States?
>
> We hold that such multilevel protection from removal is contrary to Article II's vesting of the executive power in the President. The President cannot "take Care that the Laws be faithfully executed" if

> he cannot oversee the faithfulness of the officers who execute them. Here the President cannot remove an officer who enjoys more than one level of good-cause protection, even if the President determines that the officer is neglecting his duties or discharging them improperly. That judgment is instead committed to another officer, who may or may not agree with the President's determination, and whom the President cannot remove simply because that officer disagrees with him. This contravenes the President's "constitutional obligation to ensure the faithful execution of the laws."

Restrictions on the authority of the president to remove principal or inferior officers of the United States, an issue on which our Constitution is silent, had been before the U.S. Supreme Court before, and readers of this chapter may wish to consult the chapters on *Myers v. United States*,[1] *Humphrey's Executor v. United States*,[2] and *Morrison v. Olson*.[3] Chief Justice Roberts's opinion remarked that "[t]he parties do not ask us to reexamine any of these precedents, and we do not do so." The opinion, in fact, echoes the "new test for the permissibility of . . . restrictions" on presidential oversight authority to be found in *Morrison* as Professor Peter Shane presents it in this book—whether they "are of such a nature that they impede the President's ability to perform his constitutional duty."[4] Neomi Rao, President Trump's first administrator of the Office of Management and Budget's Office of Information and Regulatory Affairs and subsequently a judge of the U.S. Court of Appeals for the D.C. Circuit, had questioned while a law professor whether *Humphrey's* "for cause" constraint on presidential removal of Federal Trade Commission (FTC) commissioners (principal officers) might in fact be undercut by the decision.[5] Yet the reasoning of the opinion fully accepts the possibility of a single for-cause limitation on removal authority—restraining either the president in the case of principal officers such

1. 272 U.S. 52 (1925). The case is the subject of Chapter 27. Note that the only necessary holding of *Myers* was that the Senate could not constitutionally claim participation in the removal decision; *Humphrey's Executor*, then, is a case about the permissibility of restrictions on the president's removal authority quite independent of the *Myers* holding.
2. 295 U.S. 602 (1935). The case is the subject of Chapter 28.
3. 487 U.S. 654 (1988). The case is the subject of Chapter 31.
4. *Id.*
5. *See* Neomi Rao, *A Modest Proposal: Abolishing Agency Independence in* Free Enterprise Fund v. PCAOB, 79 FORDHAM L. REV. 2541, 2559–60 (2011).

as SEC commissioners,[6] or principal officers who serve at the president's pleasure in the case of inferior officers. The case was decided 5–4, over a forceful dissent by Justice Breyer questioning the majority opinion's implications, to be discussed later. Upon both concluding that the members of the PCAOB were inferior, not principal, officers of the United States and assuming that SEC commissioners could be removed only for cause, the majority held that the constitutional problem identified in the quoted paragraph could be cured by severing from the statute, as unconstitutional, the members' "for cause" protection. That done, it found to be constitutional every other element of the statute creating the PCAOB, including the SEC's power to appoint its members:

> Concluding that the removal restrictions are invalid leaves the Board removable by the Commission at will, and leaves the President separated from Board members by only a single level of good-cause tenure. The Commission is then fully responsible for the Board's actions, which are no less subject than the Commission's own functions to Presidential oversight.

The holding, then, fully accepts—indeed, depends upon—the constitutionality of a one-level, "for cause" restriction. If SEC commissioners must, as principal officers, serve at the president's pleasure, the "for cause" protection of PCAOB members, as inferior officers, would have presented no constitutional difficulty. Their tenure would then have been identical to that of all those members of the civil service who, as members of the Senior Executive Service (SES) now and ordinary high-level civil servants

---

6. In Chapter 31, Professor Shane persuasively remarks about *Morrison*:

> It is perhaps more helpful to read the *Morrison* test as turning on the extent to which an officer is performing functions that the executive branch implements exclusively under statutory authority and not with regard to any power vested in the president by Article II. Good-cause removability of such an officer would not impede the president in discharging his Article II functions precisely because the president would have no such functions in connection with that officer other than helping to ensure faithful execution. For such a statutory officer, the scope of presidential removal authority would be a matter for Congress to decide.

Congress would lack that power only for the secretary of state and other principal officers who are, under the Constitution, in Chief Justice Marshall's words, "the political or confidential agents of the executive, merely to execute the will of the President." Marbury v. Madison, 5 U.S. 137, 166 (1803).

previously, exercise, under supervision, substantial levels of governmental authority. Indeed, it was striking, albeit consistent with assumptions long held, that the majority acted on the understanding that SEC commissioners' tenure is protected by "for cause" restraints when no statute so provides.[7] Congress created the SEC after the decision in *Myers* and before the decision in *Humphrey's Executor*, and, as Justice Breyer pointed out forcefully in his dissent, its failure to provide "for cause" protection to SEC commissioners appears to have been deliberate—an effort to avoid what was then seen as an unconstitutional governmental structure.

The narrowness of the Court's holding, maximizing its acceptance of Congress's judgments, reflects a frequent characteristic of Chief Justice Roberts's opinions[8] and votes.[9] And elements of the opinion having some doctrinal significance appear to have been unanimously accepted. The Court found the case to have been properly brought in district court as an action for declaratory judgment, with no need to await SEC action, given the nature of the issues raised—and this element is frequently mentioned in lower court cases citing the opinion.[10] Since the SEC had the authority to appoint the PCAOB's members, they were properly regarded as inferior officers of the United States—in this respect unlike the officials of FINRA; yet, since they were subject in their actions to SEC control, they were "inferior" and not "principal" officers. The SEC is properly to be regarded as a constitutional "Department" located in the executive branch, and thus necessarily subject to presidential oversight; its members, collectively, may be regarded as its "head" for constitutional purposes. The sole issue arming Justice Breyer's extensive and forceful dissent was the proposition that "the Act before us imposes a new type of restriction—two levels of protection from removal for those who nonetheless exercise significant executive power. Congress cannot limit the President's authority in this way."

7. *See* Peter L. Strauss, *On the Difficulties of Generalization*—PCAOB *in the Footsteps of* Myers, Humphrey's Executor, Morrison, *and* Freytag, 32 CARDOZO L. REV. 2255, 2270, 2277–78 (2011).

8. *See, e.g.*, King v. Burwell, 576 U.S. 473 (2015).

9. *See, e.g.*, Yates v. United States, 574 U.S. 528 (2015).

10. In *Axon Enterprises, Inc. v. FTC*, 598 U.S. 175 (2022), the Court relied on *PCAOB* in holding that suits challenging FTC adjudications on structural constitutional grounds—among them that the multiple layers of for-cause protection enjoyed by the Commission's administrative law judges violated the separation of powers—could proceed in court without awaiting an agency decision.

The Complications of *Freytag v. Commissioner*

Understanding this dispute and its implications not merely for the removals about which the Constitution is silent, but also for the appointments about which it has a good deal to say, requires brief consideration of the Court's enigmatic decision in *Freytag v. Commissioner*.[11] There, Congress had authorized the chief judge of the U.S. Tax Court to appoint special judges whose authority, all the Justices agreed, was extensive enough to render them "inferior officers" in constitutional terms. After unmistakably requiring that principal officers of the United States be appointed with senatorial advice and consent, the Constitution, in terms, permits Congress "by Law [to] vest the Appointment of such inferior Officers, as they think proper, in the President alone, in the Courts of Law, or in the Heads of Departments."[12] Justice Blackmun, for five Justices, penned an impeccable originalist opinion concluding that "the heads of departments" must be construed narrowly, since the understanding animating this "exceptions clause" was the preservation of political responsibility for appointments. "This Court for more than a century has held that the term 'Departmen[t]' refers only to 'a part or division of the executive government, as the Department of State, or of the Treasury,' expressly 'creat[ed]' and 'giv[en] . . . the name of a department' by Congress."[13] Because the Tax Court did not have the dignity of cabinet status, which Justice Blackmun's reasoning in the text of his opinion found the exceptions clause to require, it could not be considered a department. The majority was able to rescue the chief judge's appointment power only by finding the Tax Court to be one of the "courts of law."[14]

In a footnote in striking tension with the opinion's reasoning and text, the majority seemed to recognize the complications it might have introduced:

> We do not address here any question involving an appointment of an inferior officer by the head of one of the principal agencies, such as the Federal Trade Commission, the Securities and Exchange Commission, the Federal Energy Regulatory Commission, the Central Intelligence Agency, and the Federal Reserve Bank of St. Louis.[15]

11. 501 U.S. 868 (1991).
12. U.S. CONST. art. I, § 2, cl. 2.
13. *Freytag*, 501 U.S. at 886.
14. *Id.* at 891.
15. *Id.* at 887 n.4.

It might have mentioned, as well, appointments of inferior officers made by the heads of major agencies embedded within departments, such as the Food and Drug Administration (FDA), or appointments associated with the SES of high-ranking and powerful civil servants. A clause written in contemplation of a few thousand government employees applies today to a government of several million.

Reflecting the willingness to build on precedent and practice that often moderated his bent to formalism and originalism, Justice Scalia wrote a concurrence for four Justices in *Freytag* accepting the Tax Court as a "department" for the exceptions clause's purposes. He disagreed that an Article I court, embedded in the executive branch, could be regarded as a "court[] of law." Rather, he reasoned, the size of contemporary government required understanding the exceptions clause as reaching any governmental body headed by a senatorially confirmed nominee.[16]

The *PCAOB* Court, unanimously finding the SEC to be a "department" within the executive branch for exceptions clause purposes, and its several members, collectively, to be its "head," in effect converted this element, prompting Justice Scalia's concurrence, into the *Freytag* holding. Its opinion, however, created tensions of its own.

Resulting Tensions in *PCAOB*

The less important of these tensions appears in a majority footnote: "We express no view on whether the Commission is thus an 'executive Departmen[t]' under the Opinions Clause, Art. II, § 2, cl. 1." That clause empowers the president "to require the Opinion, in writing, of the principal Officer in each of the executive Departments, upon any subject relating to the Duties of their respective Offices." The clause states the *only* power our Constitution affirmatively grants the president in relation to the workings of domestic government once an appointment to office has been made. The Constitution is, recall, silent on the issue of removal: the president's constitutional responsibility to "take care that the laws be faithfully executed," although often invoked in support of presidential authority, does not, in

16. *See id.* at 916–22 (Scalia, J., concurring).

terms, define presidential authority; it imposes a presidential duty and does so in a passive voice, suggesting that actual execution was expected to be in the hands of those Congress would authorize to administer federal laws. The text of *PCAOB* is appropriately emphatic that the performance of that presidential duty requires a capacity to oversee effectively the SEC and its subordinate parts. The president enjoys this capacity in relation to a PCAOB stripped of for-cause protection, the majority reasoned, despite SEC commissioners' (assumed) protected tenure. But then what are the president's oversight powers, other than their potential to effect cause-restricted removals of SEC commissioners? How can the Opinions Clause not apply? Perhaps the footnote was written only to ease congressional fears that the "independence" Congress had sought to create in these agencies was being unacceptably compromised. But once "independent regulatory commissions" are seen—as indeed they must be—as "departments" in the executive branch, it must follow that the president enjoys the only power the Constitution affirmatively provides him over the actions of departments, the power contained in the Opinions Clause.

The more important tension lies in the difference between regarding the *PCAOB* opinion as one limiting Congress's *institutional* choices and regarding it as expressing a limitation on Congress's capacity to create somewhat protected tenure in office for individual government employees holding significant decisional authority. If all that has been said is that Congress cannot create one "independent regulatory commission" within another "independent regulatory commission," then the opinion stands for very little. And there are some suggestions that this is all it decided. The opinion frequently refers to the PCAOB as a body with which the president has insufficient relations to ensure his ability to take care that the laws be faithfully executed. If Congress can create one "independent" institution within an institution, why not five layers, like Russian nesting dolls? But the opinion also speaks to the oversight of individuals protected from removal and thus has been dominantly seen, as by Justice Breyer's dissent, to stand for the proposition that Congress cannot constitutionally create two layers of *individual* for-cause protection from removal by the president (or a Senate-confirmed appointee).

Can it be, then, that neither an "independent regulatory commission," nor any individual who might properly be afforded "for cause" protection from removal from office, can have as a subordinate any individual who is similarly protected, yet powerful enough to be denominated an "inferior officer" of the United States, not merely an employee? An appendix to Justice Breyer's dissenting opinion documents just how many such individuals there are in federal service, from independent agency administrative law judges (ALJs) to bureau chiefs in the SES. SES tenure can be ended only with the agreement of the Merit Systems Protection Board (MSPB)—itself an independent body whose members are for-cause protected.

The Supreme Court's subsequent decision in *Lucia v. SEC*[17] held that (at least the SEC's) ALJs were "inferior officers" whose appointment therefore, if made without Senate confirmation, constitutionally must be authorized by statute and made by the president alone, the judiciary, or the head of a department (i.e., in this case, the SEC itself).[18] Writing for all but Justice Breyer in this respect, Justice Kagan's opinion for the Court used *Freytag* as a comparison point to establish that ALJs' *quasi*-judicial powers qualified them as "inferior officers." This approach permitted the *Lucia* Court to avoid addressing the situation of other officials for whom the "inferior officer" question might arise, such as SES members (a class embracing powerful officials like those Herbert Kaufman once identified as federal bureau chiefs—civil servants with important executive and decisional authority).[19] Even so, as a presidential executive order soon made clear,[20] *Lucia*'s holding converts the appointments process for the government's most important *quasi*-judicial officials from civil-service-constrained to permissibly political.

Lurking still is the issue of removal, about which the Constitution is notoriously silent, but which drove the *PCAOB* decision. Perhaps surprisingly, the government attempted to make that an issue in *Lucia*, but Justice Kagan's steadfastly minimalist opinion declined any discussion of that issue. Suppose a future Court having to decide this question does not, as suggested, choose

17. 585 U.S. 237 (2018).

18. Justice Breyer concurred that the appointment must have been made by the SEC itself, but on statutory grounds. The Administrative Procedure Act provides for ALJ appointments to be made by "[e]ach agency." 5 U.S.C. § 3105. No SEC-specific statute provides otherwise; nor had the SEC purported to delegate its authority in this regard (assuming it could) to a subordinate bureau or employee. *See Lucia*, 585 U.S. at 256–58 (Breyer, J., concurring in the judgment in part and dissenting in part).

19. *See* Herbert Kaufman, Administrative Behavior of Federal Bureau Chiefs (1981).

20. Exec. Order No. 13843, 83 Fed. Reg. 32,755, 32,755–56 (July 13, 2018).

to explain *PCAOB* as a decision about Congress's choice of institutional structures rather than individual tenure protection as such. To say that ALJs must be removable at will by their appointing agency, rather than, as the Administrative Procedure Act (APA) provides,[21] in proceedings before the independent MSPB, would create considerable tension with *Wiener v. United States*.[22] There, Justice Frankfurter, for a unanimous Court, held improper the president's attempted removal of a member of the *quasi*-judicial War Claims Commission. "The most reliable factor for drawing an inference regarding the President's power of removal," he reasoned, "is the nature of the function that Congress confided to the . . . Commission."[23] Permitting removal for political reasons, or because a politician disapproved of a *quasi*-judicial decision reached, was unacceptable and should remain so. Indeed, for ALJs the removal concern can readily be defused by reference to those passages in *Myers* that make clear the opinion is not speaking to adjudicatory officials.

For inferior officers who are *not quasi*-judicial officials and for whom removal is the prerogative of "for cause" protected supervisors, such as SES members, *Myers* and *PCAOB* may present a greater threat to their protected tenure. Here, too, precedent suggests a means for avoiding that conclusion. The earlier decision in *United States v. Perkins*,[24] sustaining "for cause" protection for a naval officer, has been understood to protect the civil service as well, and it was favorably mentioned in relation to that service in *Myers*. At the time of *Myers*, and indeed until the creation of the SES during the Carter administration, bureau chiefs like the head of the Forest Service were civil servants, fully protected in their tenure by civil service laws. The oversight flexibility added by creation of the SES lessens, not increases, any concerns one might have about oversight controls over their behavior.

21. 5 U.S.C. § 7521(a).

22. 357 U.S. 349 (1958). In *PCAOB*, Chief Justice Roberts noted in a footnote that the Court's decision did not address the constitutionality of the statutory removal protection for ALJs. In *SEC v. Jarkesy*, 603 U.S. 109 (2024), the Court granted certiorari to resolve this issue, but it declined to do so in its decision, instead resolving the case on other constitutional grounds.

23. *Wiener*, 357 U.S. at 353.

24. 116 U.S. 483 (1886).

And what of senatorially confirmed subordinate officials in cabinet departments—the head of the Food and Drug Administration or Federal Aviation Administration, say—whom Congress has authorized to appoint "inferior officials" working in their agencies? Or others to whom a cabinet secretary or other "head" may have purported to delegate the appointment authority that formally is theirs? *Freytag*'s reasoning, *not* repudiated in this respect by *PCAOB* and in significant respects strengthened by *Lucia*, also casts a dark shadow there. Justice Scalia's concurrence in *Freytag*, understanding the exceptions clause as reaching any governmental body headed by a senatorially confirmed nominee, may again point the way.

One other issue about appointments perhaps warrants mention, although, to the author's knowledge, it has not yet surfaced in litigation. Article II is explicit that "[the president] . . . shall Commission all the Officers of the United States."[25] One may doubt that any "inferior officer" of an independent regulatory body holds a presidential commission. All commissions in the Nuclear Regulatory Commission when I was its general counsel, including mine, were signed by the commissioners; probably the same is true of "inferior officers" appointed by the "Heads of Departments" throughout the government. Perhaps here the word "officers" refers only to military officers—although, again, the rationale of the exceptions clause, as explained in *Freytag*, points the other way. Other recent occasions that have thrown the Court up against Appointments Clause language designed for a government of a few thousand, at a time when it numbers millions, have created their own puzzles and controversies.[26] Here, the "living Constitution" arguments find a true home.

Bibliography

Patricia L. Bellia, PCAOB *and the Persistence of the Removal Puzzle*, 80 GEO. WASH. L. REV. 1371 (2012).

Michael J. Gerhardt, *On Candor,* Free Enterprise Fund, *and the Theory of the Unitary Executive*, 22 WM. & MARY BILL RTS. J. 337 (2013).

25. U.S. CONST. art. II, § 3.
26. *See* NLRB v. Noel Canning, 573 U.S. 513 (2014).

Aziz Z. Huq, *Removal as a Political Question*, 65 Stan. L. Rev. 1 (2013).

Neomi Rao, *A Modest Proposal: Abolishing Agency Independence in* Free Enterprise Fund v. PCAOB, 79 Fordham L. Rev. 2541 (2011).

Peter M. Shane, *The Originalist Myth of the Unitary Executive*, 19 U. Pa. J. Const. L. 323 (2016).

Peter L. Strauss, *On the Difficulties of Generalization*—PCAOB *in the Footsteps of* Myers, Humphrey's Executor, Morrison, *and* Freytag, 32 Cardozo L. Rev. 2255 (2011).

Chapter 34

Seila Law LLC v. CFPB, 591 U.S. 197 (2020)

Aaron Nielson

How much control does the Constitution give the president over the executive branch? That question has been at the core of many of the nation's most important separation-of-powers cases—including *Myers v. United States*,[1] *Humphrey's Executor v. United States*,[2] and *Free Enterprise Fund v. Public Co. Accounting Oversight Board* (*PCAOB*),[3] each covered elsewhere in this book.

In the wake of *PCAOB*'s holding that two levels of removal restrictions from the president is one level too many, commentators began wondering just how far the U.S. Supreme Court was willing to take the idea that unless the president can freely remove executive branch officers, "the buck would stop somewhere else."[4] Would the Court limit that potentially far-reaching principle to narrow, relatively insignificant contexts, or would the Court apply it broadly—even if doing so could call into question key pillars of agency independence?[5]

In *Seila Law*, the Court took a large step towards embracing the broader view. The Court rejected the structure of the Consumer Financial

1. 272 U.S. 52 (1926). The case is the subject of Chapter 27.
2. 295 U.S. 602 (1935). The case is the subject of Chapter 28.
3. 561 U.S. 477 (2012). The case is the subject of Chapter 33.
4. *Id.* at 514.
5. *See, e.g.*, Neomi Rao, *A Modest Proposal: Abolishing Agency Independence in* Free Enterprise Fund v. PCAOB, 79 FORDHAM L. REV. 2541 (2011).

Protection Bureau (CFPB) because it was headed by a single person whom the president could not freely remove. By itself, that holding is significant—especially for the CFPB and other agencies headed by a single person. But *Seila Law* may prove to be even more significant because of how it reached that conclusion, and in particular the Court's narrow reading of *Humphrey's Executor*. Indeed, after *Seila Law*, if Congress wants a measure of agency independence, it may need to rely on political tools rather than statutory removal restrictions.

Setting the Stage for *Seila Law*

Following the Great Recession of 2008, Congress created the CFPB as "an independent regulatory agency tasked with ensuring that consumer debt products are safe and transparent." The CFPB, by design, is a powerful agency. Not only did Congress assign the CFPB authority to enforce nearly 20 statutes—including major ones such as the Truth in Lending Act, the Fair Debt Collection Practices Act, and the Fair Credit Reporting Act—Congress also empowered the CFPB with rulemaking authority to prohibit "any unfair, deceptive, or abusive act or practice" within the consumer finance industry. Congress also gave the CFPB robust enforcement and adjudicative authority.

Congress further gave the CFPB an unusual structure. Most independent agencies are headed by multimember bodies; by contrast, most agencies statutorily subject to the president's plenary control are single-headed. Congress, however, determined that the CFPB should be an independent agency headed by a single person. By statute, the CFPB director—who is nominated by the president and confirmed by the Senate—"serves for a term of five years, during which the President may remove the director from office only for 'inefficiency, neglect of duty, or malfeasance in office.'" The only other agencies existing today with similar structures are the Office of the Special Counsel, the Social Security Administration (SSA), and the Federal Housing Finance Agency (FHFA). Historically, Congress also protected the comptroller of the currency from plenary presidential removal for one year during the Civil War; Congress, however, amended the statute in 1864 to allow the president to freely remove the comptroller so long as the president communicates the reason for removal to the Senate.[6]

The CFPB's unusual structure, coupled with the agency's significant authority, prompted sharp constitutional challenges.[7] In *PHH Corp. v. CFPB*, a panel of the U.S. Court of Appeals for the D.C. Circuit initially ruled against the agency's structure in an opinion written by then-Judge Kavanaugh.[8] The D.C. Circuit en banc, however, rejected the panel's analysis and concluded, based on its reading of *Humphrey's Executor* and *Morrison v. Olson*,[9] that the CFPB's structure did not offend Article II.[10] The court also read *PCAOB* narrowly, describing it as applying to "extreme" removal restrictions rather than more "ordinary" ones. Kavanaugh dissented, arguing that the court overread *Humphrey's Executor* and *Morrison* while underreading *PCAOB*. He also emphasized both the lack of historical precedent for the CFPB's structure and the threat to liberty it posed. Indeed, he warned that "other than the President, the [CFPB] director enjoys more unilateral authority than any other official in any of the three branches of the U.S. Government."

In 2017, the CFPB sent a civil investigative demand to Seila Law LLC, a law firm that specializes in debt matters, demanding information and documents regarding the firm's business practices. Rather than complying, Seila Law challenged the CFPB's constitutionality. The dispute eventually ended up before the U.S. Court of Appeals for the Ninth Circuit, which followed the en banc D.C. Circuit's analysis from *PHH Corp*. Seila Law then petitioned for certiorari. The Supreme Court, with Justice Kavanaugh as a member, granted the petition.

---

6. *See* Aditya Bamzai, *Tenure of Office and the Treasury: The Constitution and Control over National Financial Policy, 1787 to 1867*, 87 GEO. WASH. L. REV. 1299, 1370–79 (2019).

7. *See* Ganesh Sitaraman, *The Political Economy of the Removal Power*, 134 HARV. L. REV. 352 (2020).

8. *See* 839 F.3d 1, 38–39 (D.C. Cir. 2016), *rev'd en banc*, 881 F.3d 75 (D.C. Cir. 2018).

9. 487 U.S. 654 (1988) (upholding constitutionality of independent counsel statute). *Morrison* is the subject of Chapter 31.

10. *See* PHH Corp. v. CFPB, 881 F.3d 75 (D.C. Cir. 2018) (en banc).

The *Seila Law* Decision

With Chief Justice Roberts wielding the pen, the Court held that the CFPB's structure violates the separation of powers. The Court began its analysis with first principles, explaining that Article II vests "the 'executive Power'—all of it" in the president and that "lesser officers must remain accountable to the President, whose authority they wield." This indicated to the Court that the president must be able to remove such officers. The Court also leaned heavily on precedents such as *Myers* and *PCAOB*, as well as history, concluding that congressional debate during the First Congress (known as the Decision of 1789) broadly supports presidential removal. The Court thus announced that "the President's removal power is the rule, not the exception."

But what about *Humphrey's Executor* and *Morrison*? The Court did not overrule those decisions, but it "decline[d] to elevate [them] into a freestanding invitation for Congress to impose additional restrictions on the President's removal authority." The Court stated, for example, that "*Humphrey's Executor* permitted Congress to give for-cause removal protections to a multimember body of experts, balanced along partisan lines, that performed legislative and judicial functions and was said not to exercise any executive power." It is doubtful that *any* agency, the Federal Trade Commission (FTC) included, fits within that narrow reading of *Humphrey's Executor*. In fact, the Court observed that *Humphrey's Executor*'s "conclusion that the FTC did not exercise executive power has not withstood the test of time." The Court also stated that *Morrison* stands for the idea that Congress can provide removal protection to "inferior officers with limited duties and no policymaking or administrative authority."

After reading *Humphrey's Executor* and *Morrison* so narrowly, the Court unsurprisingly concluded that neither of those decisions supports the CFPB's structure. The Court explained, for example, that "the Director's enforcement authority includes the power to seek daunting monetary penalties against private parties on behalf of the United States in federal court—a quintessentially executive power not considered in *Humphrey's Executor*." And unlike the independent counsel at issue in *Morrison*, whom the Court characterized as a mere inferior officer with limited duties, "the CFPB Director has the authority to bring the coercive power of the state to bear on millions of private citizens and businesses, imposing even billion-dollar penalties through administrative adjudications and civil actions."

The Court thus declined "to extend" *Humphrey's Executor* and *Morrison* to "an independent agency led by a single Director and vested with significant executive power." The Court explained that this type of "agency has no basis in history and no place in our constitutional structure." As to history, the Court explained that there have only been a handful of agencies headed by single officials whom Congress has protected from removal, none of which "involve regulatory or enforcement authority remotely comparable to that exercised by the CFPB." And as to structure, the Court reasoned that the Constitution safeguards the use of executive power by making "the President the most democratic and politically accountable official in Government." Under this scheme, the president must be fully accountable to the public for how executive power is used.

Justice Kagan dissented, joined by three other Justices, and argued at length that constitutional text, history, and precedent all support Congress's authority "to create zones of administrative independence by limiting the President's power to remove agency heads." She also emphasized that the Court's focus on the CFPB's single-headed structure "does not respond to the constitutional values at stake" because "the President has at least as much control over an individual as over a commission—and possibly more." More broadly, she warned that the majority opinion "commits the Nation to a static version of governance, incapable of responding to new conditions and challenges."

The Future of Agency Independence

Seila Law would be an important case even if its consequences were limited to single-headed agencies. After all, not only is the character of the CFPB different now that presidents feel free to fire the CFPB director for any reason, but the entire category of single-headed agencies with removal restrictions is on thin ice. One year after *Seila Law*, for example, the Court decided *Collins v. Yellen*, which concerned the FHFA.[11] The FHFA is also headed by a single person who by statute cannot be removed at will. Whereas the CFPB regulates millions of private individuals, however, the FHFA only

11. 594 U.S. 220 (2021). *Disclosure*: I was appointed by the Court to serve as amicus curiae to argue in defense of the FHFA's structure after the U.S. Department of Justice refused to defend it.

regulates a handful of *quasi*-governmental entities, primarily the Federal National Mortgage Association and the Federal Home Loan Mortgage Corporation—better known as Fannie Mae and Freddie Mac. One of the FHFA's main functions, moreover, is to serve as a conservator rather than a regulator. And whereas the CFPB director, by statute, can only be removed for "inefficiency, neglect of duty, or malfeasance in office," the president can fire the FHFA director whenever there is "cause" to do so—a term that arguably permits a broader range of reasons. Despite those differences, however, *Collins* held that the FHFA's structure also violated the separation of powers, concluding that "our decision last Term in *Seila Law* is all but dispositive." In the wake of *Collins*, President Biden removed the head of the SSA despite a statutory removal restriction.[12]

Seila Law, however, may have consequences far beyond single-headed agencies. The Court's discussion of *Humphrey's Executor* merits close attention. Not once does the Court suggest that *Humphrey's Executor* may have been correctly decided; instead, the Court read that case so narrowly that few if any agencies seemingly fall within it. Notably, Justice Thomas wrote separately to observe that "with today's decision, the Court has repudiated almost every aspect of *Humphrey's Executor*" and to urge the Court to overrule it outright. And as Justice Sotomayor observed in her dissenting opinion in *Collins*, the Court has already retreated from its suggestion in *Seila Law* that its analysis only applies to agencies that exercise "significant executive power."[13] Instead, any amount of executive power triggers unrestricted presidential removal for single-headed agencies. But if any amount of executive power unilaterally exercised by a single person is sufficient to trigger presidential removal, why would that principle not extend to multimember agencies like the Federal Reserve with chairs who have their own fixed terms and statutory duties? Or to administrative law judges who exercise some executive power but are protected from at-will removal? Perhaps such situations can be distinguished, but doing so is not straightforward.

After *Seila Law*, Congress therefore may need to change its strategy if it wishes to preserve a measure of policy independence for agencies. Rather

---

12. *See, e.g.*, Constitutionality of the Comm'r of Soc. Sec.'s Tenure Prot., 45 Op. O.L.C. 1 (2021) (providing legal justification for termination).
13. *Collins*, 594 U.S. at 283–94 (Sotomayor, J., dissenting).

than relying on statutory removal restrictions, Congress could make greater use of political tools to limit removal, such as through the confirmation and appropriations processes.[14] *Seila Law* also hints that Congress may require the president to provide reasons for removal, which may create some political reluctance on the White House's part to remove officials in certain lower profile positions without a good reason—though the Court may be skeptical of such reason-giving requirements if they have formal legal effects rather than just political significance. These political tools, however, will likely not be as potent as statutory removal restrictions. *Seila Law* thus may well have sweeping implications for the future of agency independence itself.

Bibliography

Christine Kexel Chabot, *Is the Federal Reserve Constitutional? An Originalist Argument for Independent Agencies*, 96 Notre Dame L. Rev. 1 (2020).

Jane Manners & Lev Menand, *The Three Permissions: Presidential Removal and the Statutory Limits of Agency Independence*, 121 Colum. L. Rev. 1 (2021).

Richard W. Murphy, *The DIY Unitary Executive*, 63 Ariz. L. Rev. 439 (2021).

Aaron L. Nielson & Christopher J. Walker, *Congress's Anti-Removal Power*, 76 Vand. L. Rev. 1 (2023).

Jed Handelsman Shugerman, *Vesting*, 74 Stan. L. Rev. 1479 (2022).

Ganesh Sitaraman, *The Political Economy of the Removal Power*, 134 Harv. L. Rev. 352 (2020).

Cass R. Sunstein & Adrian Vermeule, *The Unitary Executive: Past, Present, Future*, 2020 Sup. Ct. Rev. 83.

Ilan Wurman, *The Removal Power: A Critical Guide*, 2020 Cato Sup. Ct. Rev. 157 (2019/2020).

14. *See* Aaron L. Nielson & Christopher J. Walker, *Congress's Anti-Removal Power*, 76 Vand. L. Rev. 1 (2023).

Chapter 35

United States v. Arthrex, Inc., 594 U.S. 1 (2021)

Nina Mendelson and Rebecca Eisenberg

United States v. Arthrex addressed a seemingly straightforward Appointments Clause[1] challenge to the secretarially appointed administrative patent judges (APJs) who serve on the Patent Trial and Appeal Board (PTAB). The challengers successfully argued that APJs exercised too much authority with too little supervision to qualify as "inferior" officers. Importantly, in *Arthrex* the U.S. Supreme Court also extended a recent string of invalidations of legislative structures that had been aimed at enhancing agency independence. The *Arthrex* Court asserted the need for political control over agency adjudication decisions and did so, moreover, in an old department with a long administrative adjudication history. The Court's reasoning and remedy may signal a new judicial appetite to constitutionalize political control over agency adjudication. *Arthrex* also should raise concerns about a cookie-cutter judicial approach to agency adjudication structures and should prompt commentators, legislators, and judges to consider the reasons for the wide variation in federal adjudication structures, to recognize the pitfalls as well as the promise of political control over adjudication decisions, and to uphold the role of the political branches in legislating the design of institutions.

1. U.S. Const. art. II, § 2, cl. 2.

The Lead-Up to *Arthrex*

In a series of cases in the years before *Arthrex*, the Supreme Court found Article II Vesting Clause violations in for-cause removal restrictions on heads of independent agencies.[2] The Court reasoned that these arrangements left the president with too little control over the agency heads to ensure electoral accountability for agencies that wielded rulemaking, executive, and adjudicative powers, making federal policy in the process. But in resolving these recent cases, the Court had not expressed concern about agency adjudication regimes in particular.[3] Adjudication structures are often designed to enhance the separation of adjudication functions from enforcement, as well as to insulate adjudicators to some extent from political control. In the mid-1880s, the Court declined to imply cabinet secretary review authority over patent adjudication, given its *quasi*-judicial nature and the statutory judicial review structure that vested final agency decision authority in the commissioner of patents.[4] In a mid-20th century case, the Court unanimously upheld the constitutionality of a for-cause restriction on the president's removal power over an adjudication official, rejecting Vesting Clause arguments,[5] and in 1997, it unanimously upheld secretarially appointed Coast Guard Court of Criminal Appeals judges against an Appointments Clause challenge, finding them adequately supervised despite the lack of within-agency decisional review.[6] *Arthrex* may have changed all that.

In *Arthrex*, the Court considered an Appointments Clause challenge to the secretarially appointed APJs who, as members of PTAB, adjudicated patent validity challenges in *inter partes* review proceedings brought under the Leahy-Smith America Invents Act of 2011. That act made no change in statutory provisions that, for more than 90 years, had allowed parties to appeal decisions of PTAB and its predecessors directly to an Article III court, but provided no opportunity for further within-agency review.

2. *See* Collins v. Yellen, 594 U.S. 220 (2020); Seila L., LLC v. CFPB, 591 U.S. 197, 213 (2020); Free Enter. Fund v. Pub. Co. Acct. Oversight Bd. (*PCAOB*), 561 U.S. 477 (2010). *Seila* and *PCAOB* are addressed in Chapters 34 and 33, respectively.
3. *See, e.g.*, *PCAOB*, 561 U.S. at 507 n.10 (distinguishing administrative law judges in Vesting Clause analysis); *see also* Myers v. United States, 272 U.S. 52, 135 (1926) (distinguishing "*quasi*-judicial" agency duties in Vesting Clause analysis). *Myers* is the subject of Chapter 27.
4. *See* Butterworth v. United States *ex rel.* Hoe, 112 U.S. 50, 53 (1884).
5. *See* Wiener v. United States, 357 U.S. 349 (1958).
6. *See* Edmond v. United States, 520 U.S. 651 (1997).

A PTAB panel of three APJs held invalid Arthrex's patent on a device used in orthopedic surgery. On appeal to the U.S. Court of Appeals for the Federal Circuit, Arthrex challenged the PTAB's structure under the Appointments Clause, pointing to a statutory for-cause restriction on removal of APJs together with the restriction on within-agency review of final PTAB decisions. The Federal Circuit agreed that the APJs were improperly appointed principal officers and sought to remedy the Appointments Clause violation by modifying the for-cause removal restriction so that APJs could be removed at will, reasoning that this would render them inferior officers who properly could be secretarially appointed.[7]

The *Arthrex* Decision in the Supreme Court

Chief Justice Roberts's *Arthrex* majority opinion on the merits of the Appointments Clause challenge echoed—and relied upon—Article II Vesting Clause decisions in which the Court invalidated the for-cause removal restrictions governing the Consumer Financial Protection Bureau director and the members of the Public Company Accounting Oversight Board.[8] Although the Appointments Clause *constrains* presidential autonomy by requiring Senate confirmation for principal officers and authorizing Congress to vest inferior officer appointments elsewhere, the five-member *Arthrex* majority nonetheless saw it as requiring presidential control over APJs, emphasizing the importance of a "'clear and effective chain of command'" in the executive branch with the president at the top to supply "legitimacy and accountability" for the actions of executive officers. The presidentially appointed, Senate-confirmed Patent and Trademark Office (PTO) director did possess administrative oversight powers with respect to the APJs, including the ability to designate PTAB decisions as precedential, to institute *inter partes* review proceedings, and to select APJs for panels. But the majority found this executive supervision insufficient for the APJs to qualify as inferior officers who could be secretarially appointed. The Court focused on the "unreviewable authority wielded by APJs," commenting that higher level agency reconsideration was the standard, almost-universal way

7. *See* Arthrex, Inc. v. Smith & Nephew, 941 F.3d 1320, 1335 (Fed. Cir. 2019).
8. *See* Seila L., LLC v. CFPB, 591 U.S. 197, 204 (2020); *PCAOB*, 561 U.S. at 496–97.

to maintain political accountability and effective oversight for adjudication. The Court expressed particular concern that the director could use administrative powers to affect PTAB decision-making while still blurring the lines of political accountability between the decision and the president.

A different majority modified the statutory scheme to provide for review of PTAB decisions by the PTO director. Chief Justice Roberts, now writing only for a four-member plurality of the Court, reasoned that the appropriate remedy was to refuse enforcement of the statutory section that restricted directorial review of the APJs' final decisions, thereby enabling unfettered agency-head review. The director was thus authorized to "issue decisions himself on behalf of the Board." Despite dissenting from the majority's finding of an Appointments Clause violation, Justice Breyer, writing for himself and two other Justices, nonetheless concurred in this aspect of the judgment as appropriately tailored.

Political Review of Adjudication Across the Administrative State

The *Arthrex* decision concerns only one statutory regime, but it could have reverberations across the administrative state. In declining to enforce the 94-year-old limit on agency-head review of patent adjudication decisions, the *Arthrex* decision suggested that agency-head review of adjudication decisions is "standard," thus making it a straightforward choice to remedy the Appointments Clause violation. Such an assertion could also ground an argument that the restricted agency-head review of many agency adjudications is out of step or even "novel." In other settings, these arguments have increased the vulnerability of administrative structures to constitutional challenge.

But, in fact, federal adjudication regimes utilize an extraordinary array of procedures for both hearing and post-hearing review. Adjudication subject areas also range widely, including, for example, patent validity determinations, immigration issues, government contract disputes, and all sorts of benefits determinations. The multimember independent commissions, such as the National Labor Relations Board and Securities and Exchange Commission, typically do have the final word on those agencies' adjudications, and some executive branch adjudication programs give similar authority to agency heads. But in the Social Security and veterans' benefits adjudication programs, the federal government's largest by far, agency appellate tribunals have the last word. While unhappy litigants may seek judicial review, agency heads have no further authority to review those decisions. The authority of the Board of Veterans' Appeals is defined by statute. For Social Security, binding regulations in place since the 1940s also do not provide for review by the agency head, now the commissioner, of decisions of the agency's Appeals Council. The Final Report of the Attorney General's Committee on Administrative Procedure, widely seen as the intellectual foundation of the 1946 Administrative Procedure Act, specifically referenced the limits on the Social Security agency head's review authority. The report explained that, consistent with its administrative procedure recommendations, within-agency appellate review of formal adjudication decisions could be conducted either by an agency head or by the agency's highest adjudicatory body.[9]

In other legislation, Congress has also restricted agency-head review (while still enabling judicial review) of decisions of the Labor Department's Benefits Review Board, which reviews black lung benefits and longshoremen workers' compensation decisions. Legislation similarly restricts agency review of decisions of the four Boards of Contract Appeals, which decide government contract appeals.

In finding an Appointments Clause violation in the appointment and authority of APJs, the *Arthrex* majority's key concern was political control as a form of accountability. It invoked this concern with respect to executive officers whose sole function is adjudication. But the Court's one-size-fits-all insistence on control by a political official is a particularly poor fit for our diverse federal adjudication regimes.

Agency-head review advocates focus on an agency's ability to make policy through adjudication and argue that agency-head review supplies valuable political accountability for these choices. Individual adjudications can, of course, address unresolved policy matters, perhaps by interpreting statutes or regulations.

9. Off. of Att'y Gen., U.S. Dep't of Just., Final Report of the Attorney General's Committee on Administrative Procedure 51 & n.20 (1941).

But in context, the value of such oversight may be more apparent than real. Policy issues generally dominate rulemaking more than adjudication, a difference partly reflected in the systematic White House review of significant executive branch rulemaking (but not adjudication) since the Reagan administration. Agency heads also have other tools to make policy and to constrain adjudicators besides reviewing individual adjudication decisions, including rulemaking, the declaration of authoritative interpretations, and the selection of "precedential" opinions.

Agency-head review of adjudication decisions seems most likely to supply political accountability when the decision is transparent and the policy issues are at least somewhat salient to voters, as with Federal Communications Commission decisions imposing liability on television stations broadcasting spoken expletives. But for many adjudication decisions—take patent validity, and especially the basis for such a decision—both the issue and the decision are likely opaque to voters. Even with the guidance of interest groups, such a decision may be unlikely to make it onto a voter's list of concerns at the ballot box.

Meanwhile, when adjudicated issues are mainly technical or factual, agency-head control of individual adjudication decisions may add little in the way of error correction or consistency. Review by a busy agency head may be haphazard at best, and the head may lack the relevant technical expertise; an expert appellate panel without other duties may do better in reviewing individual decisions.

Moreover, agency-head control of individual decisions can compromise other long-valued adjudication features. The prospect of such review may increase the temptation of adjudicators to side with agency enforcement officials when the agency is a party to the dispute. More broadly, political control over individual decisions may make some adjudications vulnerable to inappropriate political influence, especially low-visibility, high-value controversies such as patent challenges, medical device approvals, or government contract disputes. The White House's general practice of refraining from contacting agencies either about particular enforcement actions or specific agency adjudications implicitly recognizes the potential for pernicious political influence. Agency-head review advocates have stopped short of arguing for presidential supervision of adjudication that parallels the supervision of rulemaking, but review of individual decisions by agency heads close to the White House could pose many of the same risks. Finally, regularizing agency-head review of adjudication might tempt agencies to choose to make policy through adjudication rather than through procedures such as rulemaking that enable broader public input and provide greater accountability.

In short, no single model of internal agency review is likely to be appropriate in all adjudication settings; the political branches may have sound reasons for legislation that either provides for or restricts agency-head review of particular individual adjudications. Designing the appropriate review model calls for weighing complex, nuanced concerns that vary by subject area and by affected institutions and individuals. This function is better suited to the legislative process, with its capacity for information-gathering and deliberation, than to judicial decision-making.

In fact, the political branches have a long history of designing and reevaluating agency adjudication structures through the legislative process, as they learn from experience, assess tradeoffs, and revise institutions to address public needs. Patent adjudication in particular has been repeatedly modified in legislation. After an inauspicious beginning with 1790 legislation that allocated final patent decisions to a board of three cabinet secretaries (a rapidly abandoned design choice, given the secretaries' other pressing duties), Congress repeatedly revised systems for deciding initial patent claims and resolving disputes between "interfering applications" from multiple inventors for the same invention. For a time beginning in 1861, legislation allocated final agency review of patent adjudication decisions to the Senate-confirmed commissioner of patents. But in 1927, Congress eliminated agency-head review of individual decisions in favor of final review within the agency by appellate boards, subject only to judicial review. That legislative choice was informed by political branch investigation and deliberation, after consulting the recommendations of experienced former commissioners and weighing the need for uniformity, the cost of delays, and the superior overall technical expertise of an expert board of appeals. Agency appellate panels had the final word in agency adjudications until the 2021 *Arthrex* decision.

Congress similarly learned from experience and assessed tradeoffs when it considered how much administrative law judges should be separated from agency officials engaged in investigative or prosecutorial functions. Congress chose one level of separation in the Administrative Procedure Act but, following further investigation, required more separation for the National Labor Relations Board and, ultimately, less for the Federal Communications Commission to enable full use of its technical staff.

As history suggests, the political branches may have particular advantages over the courts in broadly gathering information from the agencies and affected entities, learning from experience, and revising adjudicating institutions in response. When the Court redesigns agency structures without deference to the judgments expressed in legislation, as it did in *Arthrex*, it risks unnecessarily and unhelpfully intruding on responsibilities traditionally and more appropriately exercised by the political branches.

Future Directions After *Arthrex*

The split decision and unusual circumstances of *Arthrex* may leave the Court some wiggle room in future cases involving agency adjudication. Senate confirmation of adjudicating officials serving on an agency's appellate tribunal could immunize an adjudication scheme from Appointments Clause challenges, for example. Furthermore, a future Court hearing a Vesting Clause challenge to an adjudication regime could align itself with earlier decisions that mainly deferred to legislative judgments on how to structure the adjudication process, including legislative concerns for independence and insulation from enforcement staff and political control. Finally, courts might distinguish between statutory and agency-imposed limitations on agency-head review, deeming only the former (as in *Arthrex*) to be unconstitutional.[10]

On the other hand, the future could also bring a less nuanced approach. The Court could extend *Arthrex* by finding that agency-head review of adjudication is not only sufficient to resolve an Appointments Clause violation involving adjudicators but is required by Article II's Vesting Clause. Future decisions will have to resolve the tension between invoking the Constitution to ensure political accountability for adjudication and preserving appropriate deference to legislative judgments as to when, where, and why individual adjudication decisions should be reviewed.

---

10. *See, e.g.*, *In re* Palo Alto Networks, Inc., 44 F.4th 1369 (Fed. Cir. 2022).

Bibliography

Michael Asimow, Admin. Conf. of the U.S., Evidentiary Hearings Outside the Administrative Procedure Act (2016).

Kent Barnett, *Against Administrative Judges*, 49 U.C. Davis L. Rev. 1643 (2016).

Kent Barnett et al., Admin. Conf. of the U.S., Non-ALJ Adjudicators in Federal Agencies (2018).

Emily Bremer, *The Exceptionalism Norm in Administrative Adjudication*, 2019 Wis. L. Rev. 1351.

Ronald A. Cass, Admin. Conf. of the U.S., Agency Review of Administrative Law Judges' Decisions (1983).

Kenneth Culp Davis, Administrative Law Treatise (1958 & 1970 Supp.).

Rebecca S. Eisenberg & Nina A. Mendelson, *The Not-So-Standard Model: Reconsidering Agency-Head Review of Administrative Adjudication Decisions*, 75 Admin. L. Rev. 1 (2023).

Matthew A. Gluth et al., Admin. Conf. of the U.S., Participation of Senate-Confirmed Officials in Administrative Adjudication (2024).

Jennifer Mascott & John F. Duffy, *Executive Decisions After* Arthrex, 2021 Sup. Ct. Rev. 225.

Section of Admin. L. & Regul. Prac., Am. Bar Ass'n, A Blackletter Statement of Federal Administrative Law pt. 1, § IV (2d ed. 2013).

Christopher J. Walker & Melissa F. Wasserman, *The New World of Agency Adjudication*, 107 Calif. L. Rev. 141 (2017).

Christopher J. Walker & Matthew L. Wiener, Admin. Conf. of the U.S., Agency Appellate Systems (2020).

Table of Cases

Index